Performance Analysis of Transaction Processing Systems

Performance Analysis of Transaction Processing Systems

Wilbur H. Highleyman

 Prentice Hall, Englewood Cliffs, New Jersey 07632

Library of Congress Cataloging-in-Publication Data

Highleyman, Wilbur H.
  Performance analysis of transaction systems / Wilbur H. Highleyman.
  Includes index.
  ISBN 0-13-657008-9
  1. Computers—Evaluation.   2. Electronic data processing—
Evaluation.   I. Title.
  QA76.9.E94H54 1989
  004.2′4—dc19   88-14842
                                                            CIP

Editorial/production supervision: *Karen Winget*
Cover design: *Karen Stephens*
Manufacturing buyer: *Marianne Gloriande*

© 1989 by Prentice-Hall, Inc.
A Division of Simon & Schuster
Englewood Cliffs, New Jersey 07632

Printed in the United States of America
10 9 8 7 6 5 4 3 2 1

ISBN 0-13-657008-9

Prentice-Hall International (UK) Limited, *London*
Prentice-Hall of Australia Pty. Limited, *Sydney*
Prentice-Hall Canada Inc., *Toronto*
Prentice-Hall Hispanoamericana, S.A., *Mexico*
Prentice-Hall of India Private Limited, *New Delhi*
Prentice-Hall of Japan, Inc., *Tokyo*
Simon & Schuster Asia Pte. Ltd., *Singapore*
Editora Prentice-Hall do Brasil, Ltda., *Rio de Janeiro*

To my parents—
Peach and Bud

Contents

Preface

This book provides the tools necessary for predicting and improving the performance of real-time computing systems, with special attention given to the rapidly growing field of on-line transaction-processing (OLTP) systems. It is aimed at two audiences:

1. The *system analyst* who thoroughly understands the concepts of modern operating systems and application structures but who feels lacking in the mathematical tools necessary for performance evaluation.
2. The *mathematician* who has a good grasp of probability and queuing theory but who would like to gain a better understanding of the technology behind today's computing systems so that these tools might be effectively applied.

OLTP systems are rapidly becoming a part of our everyday life. Merchants pass our credit cards through slot readers so that remote systems can check our credit. Every commercial airplane ride and hotel stay is planned and tracked by these systems. When we are critically ill, OLTP systems monitor our critical signs. They control our factories and power plants. We obtain cash from ATMs, play the horses and lotteries, and invest in stocks and bonds thanks to OLTP systems.

No wonder their performance is becoming a growing concern. A poorly performing system may simply frustrate us while we wait for its response. Even worse, it can be life-threatening to a business—or even to our loved ones.

We define the performance of an OLTP system as the time required to receive a response from it once we have sent it a transaction. Our transaction must wait its turn over and over again as it passes from one service point to another in the OLTP system, since it is just one of many transactions that the system is trying to process simultaneously. These service points may be processors, disks, critical programs, communication lines—any common resource shared among the transactions.

As the system gets busier, the delays at each service point get longer; and the system may bog down. The study of the behavior of these delays as a function of transaction volume is the subject of the rapidly expanding field of queuing theory.

A performance analyst is one who has an intimate knowledge of the structure of these systems and who can apply the practical tools available from queuing theory and other mathematical disciplines to make reasonable statements about the expected performance of a system. The system may be one still being conceived, an existing system in trouble, or a system undergoing enhancement.

This book is intended to train performance analysts. For the system analyst who may be a bit intimidated by higher mathematics, it presents mathematical tools that have practical use. Moreover, the derivations of these tools are for the most part explored, perhaps not always rigorously, but in a manner designed to give a full understanding of the meaning of the equations that represent the tool. For the most part, only a knowledge of simple algebra is required.

For the practicing mathematician, there is an in-depth description of each OLTP system component that may have a performance impact. These components include communication lines, processors, memories, buses, operating systems, file systems, and software application architectures. System extensions for fault tolerance, an important attribute of OLTP systems, are also covered.

This book is organized so that the reader may skip easily over material that is already familiar and focus instead on material of direct interest. The book does not present a "cookbook" approach to performance analysis. Rather, it stresses the understanding of the use of basic tools to solve a variety of problems. To this end, many examples are given during the discussion of each topic to hone the reader's ability to use the appropriate tools.

As of the date of this writing, the title "performance analyst" has not been accepted as a usual job description. This is certainly not due to a perception that performance analysis is unnecessary but perhaps instead to the perception that meaningful performance analysis is somewhat that of a mythical art. If this book can advance the acceptance of the practicing performance analyst, it will have achieved its goal.

ACKNOWLEDGMENTS

A work of this magnitude is the result of the efforts of many. I would like to take this opportunity to thank:

- All my anonymous reviewers, whose in-depth criticisms played a major role in the organization of the book.

- My partner, Burt Liebowitz, who often challenged my fuzzy thinking to enforce a clarity and accuracy of presentation.
- My daughter Leslie for the typing and seemingly endless retyping of the manuscript as it progressed through its various stages.
- My wife, Janice, a professional writer in her own right, for turning my writing into real English.
- Charles Reeder, who prepared the illustrations for this book, often with "real-time" responses.
- My many customers, who have provided the real-life testing ground for the methodology presented in the book, and especially to Concurrent Computers Corp. and Syntrex Inc., for their kind permission to use the studies presented in chapters 6 and 11, respectively.
- Last, but not least, my editors, Paul Becker and Karen Winget, for their encouragement and guidance in the mechanics and business issues of bringing a new book to press.

ABOUT THE AUTHOR

Dr. Highleyman has over 30 years' experience in the development of real-time on-line data processing systems, with particular emphasis on high performance multiprocessor fault-tolerant systems and large communications-oriented systems. Other application areas include intelligent terminals, editorial systems, process control, and business applications. Major accomplishments include the first computerized totalizator system for racetrack wagering installed for the New York Racing Association, the first automation of floor trading for the Chicago Board of Trade, the international telex switching systems utilized by ITT World Communications, the fault-tolerant data-base management system used by the *New York Daily News,* a 6000-terminal lottery system for state lotteries, an electronic billing data collection system for the telephone operating companies, and message switching systems for international cablegram and private network services.

Dr. Highleyman is founder and Chairman of The Sombers Group, a company which has provided turnkey software packages for such systems since 1968. He is also founder and chairman of MiniData Services, a company using minicomputer technology to bring data processing services to small businesses. Prior to these activities, he was founder and vice-president of Data Trends, Inc., a turnkey developer of real-time systems since 1962. Before that, he was employed by Bell Telephone Laboratories, where he was responsible for the development of the 103 and 202 data sets, and by Lincoln Laboratories, where he worked on the first transistorized computer.

In addition to his management activities at The Sombers Group, Dr. Highleyman is currently active in:

- performance modeling of multiprocessor systems.
- fault-tolerant considerations of multiprocessor systems.

- architectural design of hardware and software for real-time and multiprocessor systems.
- functional specifications for data processing systems.

He has performed analytical performance modeling on many systems for several clients including:

A. C. Nielson	ITT World Communications
Autotote	MACOM DCC
Bunker Ramo	PYA/Monarch
Concurrent Computer	Smith Kline
Digital Equipment Corp.	Stratus
First National Bank of Chicago	Syntrex
FTC Communications	Systeme
G.E. Credit Corp.	Tandem
Harris	Telesciences
Hewlitt Packard	*Time*

Dr. Highleyman received the D.E.E. degree from Brooklyn Polytechnic Institute in 1961, the S.M.E.E. degree from Massachusetts Institute of Technology in 1957, and the B.E.E. degree from Rensselaer Polytechnic Institute in 1955. He holds four U.S. patents and has published extensively in the fields of data communications, pattern recognition, computer applications, and fault-tolerant systems.

He also sits or has sat on several boards, including:

- The Sombers Group (Chairman)
- Science Dynamics, Inc.
- MiniData Services, Inc. (Chairman)
- International Tandem User's Group (Past President)
- Vertex Industries

1

Introduction

Ubiquitous, mysterious, wonderful—and sometimes aggravating—computers. They truly are becoming more and more involved in what we do today. What they do often affects our quality of life, from the success of our businesses to the enjoyment of our free time to our comforts and conveniences.

Businesses enter transactions as they occur and obtain up-to-the-minute status information for decision-making. Banks are extending on-line financial services to their corporate customers for interactive money transfers and account status, giving corporate money managers the ultimate in cash-flow management.

Call your telephone company or credit card company about a bill, and your charge and payment history appears on the screen for immediate action. See your travel agent for airline tickets, and the computer presents all options, makes your reservations, and issues your tickets.

Time for fun? Buy tickets through your local ticket outlet from the inventory kept on computer. Play the horses or the state lottery—if you're a lucky winner, the computer will calculate your payoff.

Not feeling well? Computers will arrange your hospital stay, will order your tests, and, of course, will prepare your bills. Other computers will monitor your specimens as they flow through the clinical laboratory, thus ensuring the quality and accuracy of the test results.

Need to communicate? Computers will carry your voice, your data, and your written words rapidly to their destinations.

And quietly in the background, computers monitor the material fabric of our daily lives, from power and energy distribution to traffic control and sewage disposal.

All of the preceding examples are types of transaction-processing systems. *These systems accept a transaction, process it using a base of data, and return a response.* A transaction may be an inquiry, an order, a message, a status. The data base may contain customer information, inventory, orders, or system status. A response may be a status display, a ticket, a message, or a command.

For instance, in a wagering system, the wager information is a transaction that is stored in the data base, and the reply is a ticket. Subsequently, the ticket becomes the transaction as the system compares it to the data base to see if it is a winner. The reply is the payoff amount.

In the control system for an electrical power network, the transactions are status changes such as power loading, transformer temperatures, and circuit failures. The data base is the current network configuration and status. The new status change updates the data base, and a command to alter the configuration may be issued as a response (e.g., reduce the voltage to prevent a power overload, thereby avoiding a brownout).

In a message-switching system, the transaction is an incoming message (text, data, facsimile, or even voice). The data base is the set of messages awaiting delivery and the routing procedures. The response is the receipt and delivery acknowledgments returned to the sender and the message routed to the destination.

In an airline or ticket reservation system, the transaction is first an inquiry. Schedule status is returned from the data base, which also holds an inventory of available seats. A subsequent transaction is the order, which will update the inventory. A ticket will be issued in response.

No wonder we become affected—even aggravated—by the performance of these systems. Have you ever waited several minutes on the telephone for the clerk on the other end to get your billing status? Have you ever watched the anxiety and the anger of a racehorse player trying to get the bet in before the bell goes off, only to be frustrated by an ever-slowing line at the window? Have you ever watched a merchant get impatient waiting for a credit card validation, give up, and make the sale without authorization, thus risking a possible loss? Have you ever...? The list goes on.

And that is what this book is all about: the prediction and control of the performance[1] of these transaction-processing systems, which are weaving their way into our lives.

PERFORMANCE MODELING

We all know that as a computer system becomes loaded, it "bogs down." Response times to user requests get longer and longer, leading to increased frustration and aggravation of

---

[1]Of course, system availability is an equally important concern. Have you ever been told that you can't get a ticket at this time because "the computer is down"? The reliability analysis of these systems is not a topic for this book. However, performance degradation due to actions taken by the systems to ensure reliable operation is a concern and is covered.

Techniques for the reliability analysis of transaction-processing systems may be found in Liebowitz [17].

the user population. A measure of the capacity of the system is the greatest load (in transactions per hour, for instance) at which the response time remains marginally acceptable.

Deterioration of response time is caused by bottlenecks within a system. These bottlenecks are common system resources that are required to process many simultaneous transactions; therefore, transactions must wait in line in order to get access to these resources. As the system load increases, these lines, or queues, become longer, processing delays increase, and responsiveness suffers. Examples of such common system resources are the processor itself, disks, communication lines, and even certain programs within the system.

One can represent the flow of each major transaction through a system by a model that identifies each processing step and highlights the queuing points at which the processing of a transaction may be delayed. This model can then be used to create a mathematical expression for the time that it takes to process each type of transaction, as well as an average time for all transactions, as a function of the load imposed on the system.

This processing time is, of course, the *response time* that a user will see. The load at which response times become unacceptable is the *capacity* of the system. Performance modeling concerns itself with the prediction of the response time for a system as a function of load and, consequently, of its capacity.

A simple example serves to illustrate these points. Figure 1-1a shows the standard symbol used throughout this book for a resource and the attendant queue of transactions awaiting servicing by that resource. The ''service time'' for the resource is often shown near it (T_s in this case). The service time is the average time it takes the resource to process a transaction queued to it.

Figure 1-1b is a simple view of a transaction-processing computer system. Transactions arrive from a variety of incoming communication lines and are queued to a program (1) that processes these inbound requests. This program requires an average of 80 milliseconds (msec.) to process a transaction, which is then sent to the disk server (2) to read or write data to a disk. The disk server serves these and other requests and requires an average of 50 msec. per request. Once it has completed all disk work, it forwards a response to an output program (3), which returns these and other responses to the communication lines. The output program requires 20 msec. on the average to process each response.

Since the programs and the disk system are serving multiple sources, queues of transactions awaiting service may build in front of each of these servers. As the servers get busier, the queues will get longer, the time a transaction spends in the system will get longer, and the system's response time will get slower.

One implied queue not shown in Figure 1-1b is the processor queue. We assume in this system that many programs are running—many more than are shown. But there is only one processor. Therefore, when a program has work to do, it must wait in line with other programs before it can be given access to the processor and actually run.

Let us now do a little performance analysis using Figure 1-1b (which, by the way, will later be called a ''traffic model''). If the system is idle, no queues will build; and an average transaction will work its way through the system in $80 + 50 + 20 = 150$ msec.

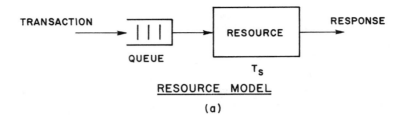

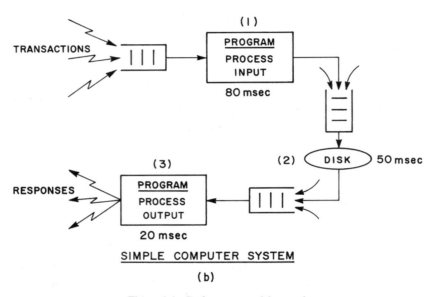

Figure 1-1   Performance model example.

(the sum of the individual service times for each server in its path). Not a bad response time.

Now let us look at the response time in a more normally loaded system in which the queue lengths for all servers, including the processor, average 2. That is, on the average, any request for service will find 2 requests in front of it—one being serviced and one waiting for service. The newly entered request will be the second request in line, not counting the request being serviced at the time. (As will be shown later, resource loads of $\frac{2}{3}$ will often result in queue lengths of 2. That is, if a server is busy 67 percent of the time on the average, its average queue length will be 2.)

With these queue lengths, each transaction must wait 2 service times before being serviced, and then each transaction must be serviced. Sounds like the response time should triple from 150 msec. to 450 msec., right? Wrong. The response time degradation is even worse since each program must wait in a queue for the processor. Let us assume that the average time the processor spends running a program is 50 msec. Let us also assume that the disk server is an intelligent device that does not use the processor and so is not slowed by having to wait in the processor queue. Remember that the processor is 67 percent loaded, so its queue length is 2.

When the input program wants to run, it must wait in the processor queue for $2 \times 50 = 100$ msec. and then must spend 80 msec. serving the incoming transaction. So far as the incoming transaction is concerned, the service time of this program is 180 msec., not 80 msec. Likewise, the effective service time of the output program in the loaded processor is $2 \times 50 + 20 = 120$ msec. rather than 20 msec. The disk server time remains at 50 msec. since it doesn't rely on the processor.

An average queue length of 2 in front of each server now causes the response time to triple relative to the effective service times. Thus, at a load of ⅔, system response time degrades from 150 msec. to $3(180 + 50 + 120) = 1050$ msec!

Note that we could plot a curve of response time versus load if we just knew how to relate queue size to load. Then, given the maximum acceptable response time, we could determine that load representing the capacity of the system, as shown in Figure 1-2.

This is what performance modeling is all about.

USES OF PERFORMANCE MODELS

Ideally, a performance model should be validated and tuned. Its results should be compared to measured results. If they are significantly different, the reasons should be understood and the model corrected. Usually, this results in the inclusion of certain processing steps initially deemed trivial or in the determination of more accurate parameter values.

A performance model, no matter how detailed it may be, is nevertheless a simplification of a very complex process. As such, it is subject to the inaccuracies of simplification. However, experience has shown these models to be surprisingly accurate. Moreover, the trends predicted are even more accurate and can be used as very effective decision tools in a variety of cases, such as

1. *Performance Prediction.* The performance of a planned system can be predicted before it is built. This is an extremely valuable tool during the design phase, as bottlenecks can be identified and corrected before implementation (often requiring significant architectural changes), and performance goals can be verified.
2. *Performance Tuning.* Once a system is built, it may not perform as expected. The performance model can be used along with actual performance measurements to ''look inside'' the system and to help locate the problems by comparing actual processing and delay times to those that are expected.
3. *Cost/Benefit of Enhancements.* When it is planned to modify or enhance the system, the performance model can be used to estimate the performance impact of the proposed change. This information is invaluable to the evaluation of the proposed change. If the change is being made strictly for performance purposes, then the cost/benefit of the change can be accurately determined.

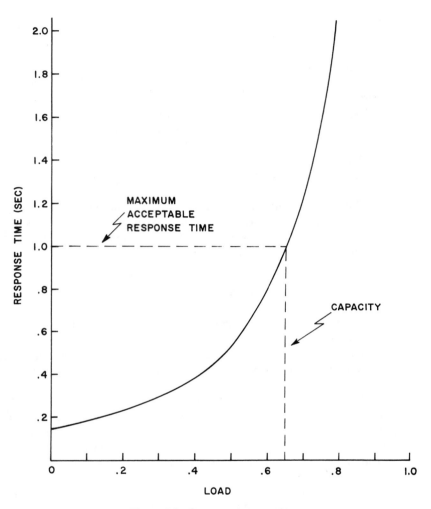

Figure 1-2 Response time/capacity.

4. *System Configuration.* As a product is introduced to the marketplace, it often has several options that can be used to tailor the system's performance to the user's needs—for example, the number of disks, the power of the processor, or communication line speeds. The performance model can be packaged as a sales tool to help configure new systems and to give the customer some confidence in the system's capacity and performance.

THE SOURCE OF PERFORMANCE PROBLEMS

It is interesting to speculate about the main cause of the poor performance that we see in practice. Is it the hardware—the processors, memories, disks, and communication systems of which these systems are built? Is it the software—the operating systems and applications that give these systems their intelligence? Is it the users of the systems, through inexperienced or hostile actions? The data base organization? The system managers?

Actually, it is none of these. The second most common cause of poor performance is that the designers of the system did not understand performance issues sufficiently to ensure adequate performance. The first most common cause is that they did not understand that they did not understand.

If this book does nothing more than focus attention on those issues that are important to performance so that designers may seek help when they need it, the book will have achieved a major part of its goal. If it allows the designers to make design decisions that lead to an adequately performing system, it will have achieved its entire goal.

THE PERFORMANCE ANALYST

The effective prediction of performance has been a little-used art—and for a very good reason. It requires the joining of two disciplines that are inherently contradictory.

One is that of the mathematical disciplines—from probability and statistical theory to the Laplace-Stieltjes transforms, generating functions, and birth-death processes of queuing theory. The other discipline is that of the system analyst—data-base design, communication protocols, process structure, and software architecture.

Qualified system analysts are certainly adept at algebra. They most likely are a little rusty at elementary calculus, probability theory, and statistics. Do they know how to solve differential-difference equations, apply Bessel functions, or understand the attributes of ergodicity? Probably not. They don't need to know, and they probably don't want to know.

Practicing applied mathematicians, for the most part, have not been exposed to the inner workings of contemporary data processing systems. Third-normal form, pipelining, and SNA may be not much more than words to them. And when they do understand a system's performance problem, it is difficult for them to make pronouncements on it because the assumptions required for reasonable calculations often diverge so far from the real world that the mathematicians' old college professors—and certainly the great body of contemporary colleagues—would never approve.

Performance analysts are in an awkward position. They must be reasonably accomplished in system analysis to understand the nature of the system they are analyzing, yet they must be practical enough to make those assumptions and approximations necessary to solve the problem. Likewise, they must understand the application of some fairly straightforward mathematical principles to the solution of the problem without being so embarrassed by the accompanying assumptions as to render themselves ineffective. In short, performance analysts must be devout imperfectionists. The only caveat is that they must set forth clearly and succinctly the imperfections as part of the analysis.

A performance model is a very simple mathematical characterization of a very complex physical process. At best, it is only an approximate statement of the real world (though actual results have been surprisingly useful and accurate). But isn't it better to be able to make some statement about anticipated system performance than none? Isn't it better to be able to say that response time should be about 2 seconds (and have some confidence that you are probably within 20% of the actual time) than to design a system for a 1-second response time and achieve 5? Based on actual experience, the most honest statement that can be made without a performance analysis is of the form ''The system will probably have a capacity of 30 transactions per second, but I doubt it.'' The purpose of this book is to eliminate the phrase ''but I doubt it.''

THE STRUCTURE OF THIS BOOK

To that end, this book takes on both system analysis and mathematics. It is designed to give applied mathematicians the background they need to understand the structure of contemporary transaction-processing systems so they can bring their expertise to bear on the analysis of their performance. It is also designed to give system designers the mathematical tools required to predict performance. In either case, we have created performance analysts.

It is the author's strong contention that a tool is most useful if the users are so familiar with it that they can make it themselves. This applies to the various relationships and equations which are used in this book. Most will be derived, at least heuristically if not rigorously; in this way, the assumptions that go into the use of the particular tool are made clear. Most derivations are simple, requiring only basic algebra, a little calculus perhaps, and an elementary knowledge of probability and statistics. The derivations are included in the main body of the text. More complex derivations are left for the appendixes. Just occasionally a derivation is so complex that only a reference is given.

The book is structured to support the system analyst seeking better mathematical tools, the mathematician seeking a better system understanding, and either one seeking anything in between. This structure is shown in Figure 1-3.

Chapter 2 is a major review of the contemporary technology involved in transaction-processing systems. It will be most useful to those seeking a better understanding of the architecture of these systems, but this chapter could be skimmed or bypassed by system analysts knowledgeable in transaction processing.

Chapter 3 gives a simple but in-depth example of performance modeling based on chapter 2 material extended by some elementary mathematics introduced as the modeling progresses. This chapter represents a preview of the rest of the book. A thorough understanding of chapters 2 and 3 will equip the reader with the tools necessary to perform elementary performance analyses. The rest of the book then hones the tools developed in these two chapters.

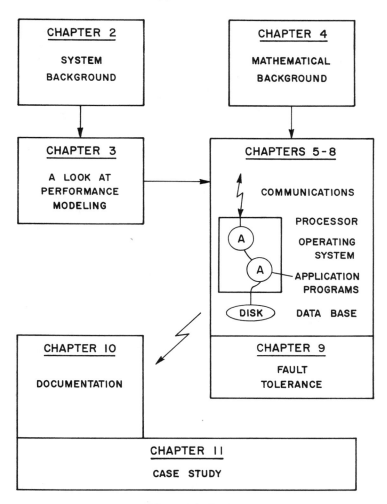

Figure 1-3 Book structure.

Chapter 4 presents a variety of mathematical tools that are useful in certain situations. While the bulk of the chapter is a review of queuing theory, which allows us to relate queue lengths to resource loads, many other useful tools are summarized, including basic concepts in probability and statistics and expansion of useful series.

Chapters 5 through 8 expand concepts relative to the major building blocks of a transaction-processing system. These building blocks include the communication network (chapter 5), the processor and operating system (chapter 6), the data base (chapter 7), and the application programs (chapter 8). Chapter 9 extends these concepts to fault-tolerant systems. These chapters contain insight for both the analyst and the mathematician. System concepts are explored in more depth, and the application of the mathematical tools to these areas is illustrated.

Chapters 10 and 11 are summary chapters. Chapter 10 discusses the organization and components of the formal performance model so that it will be useful and maintainable as the system grows and is enhanced. Chapter 11 includes a complete example of a performance model.

References are given following chapter 11 and are organized alphabetically.

Appendix 1 summarizes the notation used, and Appendix 2 summarizes the major queuing relationships. Further appendixes give certain derivations that will be of interest to the more serious student.

The book is not intended to be exhaustive; the rapidly progressing technology in TP systems prevents this anyway. Nor is it intended to provide a cookbook approach to performance modeling. The subject is far too complex for that. Rather, it is intended to provide the tools required to attack the performance problems posed by new system architectures and concepts.

The book is also not intended to be a programming guide for performance model implementation. Though the complexity and interactive nature of many models will require them to be programmed in order to obtain results, it is assumed that the performance analyst is either a qualified programmer or has access to qualified staff. No programming examples are given; however, useful or critical algorithms are occasionally presented.

The author highly recommends that the serious student read references [19] and [24]. James Martin and Thomas Saaty both present highly readable and in-depth presentations of many of the concepts necessary in performance analysis. Also, Lazowska [16] provides an interesting approach by which many performance problems can be attacked using fairly simple and straightforward techniques.

SYMBOLOGY

One final note on symbology before embarking on this subject. The choice of parameter symbols, I find, is one of the most frustrating and mundane parts of performance analysis. Often, symbols for several hundred parameters must be invented; there are just not enough characters to go around without enormous subscripting. Therefore, the choice of symbols is often not reflective of what they represent. This is a problem we live with.

The symbols used in the body of this book are summarized in Appendix 1 for easy reference. Notwithstanding the problems of naming conventions mentioned above, the author does impose certain restrictions:

1. All symbols are at most one character plus subscripts. Thus, TS is never used for service time; but T_s may be. This prevents products of symbols from being ambiguous. The only exception is var(x), used to represent the variance of x.
2. Only characters from the Arabic alphabet are used (uppercase and lowercase A through Z, numerals 0 through 9). There are two reasons for doing this:

a. Most of the typewriters, word processors, and programming languages I use provide little if any support for the Greek alphabet.
b. More important, performance models are most useful if understood and used by middle and upper technical management. I usually find this level of user to be immediately and terminally intimidated by strings of Greek letters.

This convention can be particularly disturbing to the applied mathematician who is used to ρ, λ, and μ as representing occupancy, arrival rates, and service rates, respectively. Instead, in this text he or she will find L, R, and T as representing load, arrival rate, and service time. Rather than $\rho = \lambda/\mu$, he will find $L = RT$. However, the first time he or she tries to program a model in Greek, he or she will quickly learn to translate.

The only exception to this is delta. Δ is used to indicate a small increment, and δ is used to represent the delta (impulse) function in certain derivations. They never appear in resulting expressions.

One other convention used is the floor ($\lfloor$) and ceiling ($\rceil$) operators. The symbol $x\rfloor$ means truncate x (i.e., round down to the next lower integer if x is not already an integer). The symbol $x\rceil$ implies rounding up to the next highest integer if it is not already an integer.

Finally, multiplication is taken as having precedence over division. Thus, $A = B/CD$ is interpreted as $A = B/(CD)$.

2

Transaction-Processing Systems

This chapter explores the basic architecture of transaction-processing systems. Special attention is given to process structure and management, a thorough knowledge of which is mandatory for an appreciation of performance issues. Strategies for fault tolerance are also presented.

The term *transaction-processing system* is a rather general term whose definition in this book has importance only in terms of the applicability of the material presented in the following chapters. It can be defined as readily by what it is as it can be by what it is not.

A TP system is an on-line real-time multiuser system that accepts requests and returns responses to those requests. The act of generating a response usually implies accessing a base of data maintained by the TP system. This data base is often a complex set of interrelated information maintained on disk files by a sophisticated data-base manager. In some TP applications, simple memory-resident tables may be sufficient.

On-line means that the user has a direct connection to the system. A user who calls a billing clerk is not on-line, though the billing clerk with a terminal is. A system in which requests are entered via punched cards is not on-line. Systems in which users interact with the system via terminals connected by private or dialed communication lines are on-line, as are systems in which remote sensors communicate status over communication lines and receive commands in response to status changes.

Martin [19] defines *real time* as follows:

> A real-time computer system may be defined as one which controls an environment by receiving data, processing them, and taking action or returning results *sufficiently quickly to affect the functioning of the environment* at that time. (Emphasis added.)

"Sufficiently quickly" is a matter of the application. In a TP system, this is satisfied if responses are received in a time that appears short to the user, i.e., the system appears responsive to the user. For a human user, this usually means one or two seconds. For a real-time control application, acceptable response times might be much shorter or perhaps even much longer.

A single word that means "on-line real time" is *interactive*. If the user can communicate directly with a system, and the system responds quickly, then the user is in a position to interact with the system. He or she can ask questions and get responses without having to preplan his session with the system. His next request can be a function of the system's previous response.

All TP systems are interactive. If the system's response slows to the point that interaction is not feasible or is overly frustrating, the TP system loses its value. Thus, the importance of performance analysis.

Conversely, a TP system is not a batch system in which data is accumulated over a long period of time and then processed as one long contiguous file (say once per day). However, there is an important connection between batch and TP systems. Most TP systems have a batch component. There are certain functions that are simply more efficient in batch mode than if done interactively. A prime example is data-base updating. An interactive update involves finding one or more individual records in a large file, updating them, returning them, and modifying any key files used to locate them. The system may also have to update audit files required to recover the data base in the event of a system failure during the update. If, instead, updates are batched, sorted periodically, and passed against the file in an ordered manner, the total system time required for these updates can be significantly less. Chapter 7 explores this in more detail.

Therefore, many TP systems will do interactively those updates which are required to support interactive requests and will batch updates and reports that can be delayed. Often, batch processing will run in background mode while the system is supporting interactive traffic. Thus, the contention for resources (primarily processor, memory, and disk) between simultaneously operating batch and TP systems must be understood and accounted for.

Also, a TP system is not a scientific number-crunching application, such as a weather-prediction system (or a performance model, for that matter). These systems are characterized by very long processing times (minutes to hours) before results are available. A TP system is not an intelligent terminal, a circuit switch, or a packet switch which massages data and passes it on. Finally, for purposes of this book, a TP system is not a single-user system, such as a personal computer, since performance degradation due to loading does not occur. A network of personal computers accessing a common data base, though, is very much a TP system.

Though the performance concepts discussed in this book do have some relation to non-TP systems, they are primarily pertinent to interactive data-base systems.

COMPONENT SUBSYSTEMS

TP systems have the following subsystem components, as shown in Figure 2-1:

- Communication network
- Processors
- Memory
- Application programs
- Data base
- Other peripherals

The functions of each of these subsystems are described below.

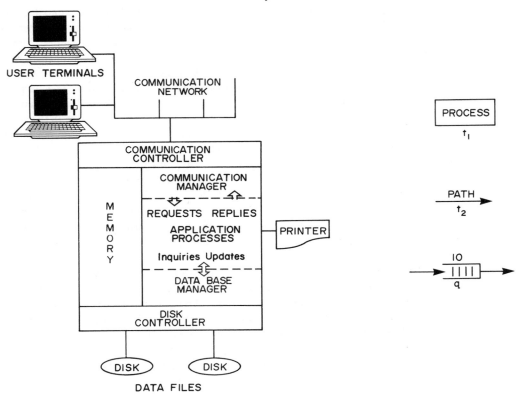

Figure 2-1 Components of a TP system.

Communication Network

A communication network interconnects the users with the system. This network could include point-to-point and multidrop lines, dialed lines, packet networks, local area networks, and satellite links. These links could utilize a variety of protocols, both half duplex and full duplex.

The communication subsystem also includes the communication hardware that interfaces the communications network with the processor and the software that manages the communication network (noted as the communication manager in Figure 2-1).

The communication subsystem is responsible for doing everything necessary to get a request to the application programs and to return a reply to the user. However, it has no knowledge, nor need it have any, of the content of a request or reply message.

Processors

One or more processors provide the processing power required for the communication manager, application programs, and data-base manager. If multiple processors are provided, there must be some means to coordinate their activities and to share work between them.

For purposes of performance analysis, the concept of a processor is extended beyond the hardware to encompass the operating system. That is to say, the processor provides the environment in which the application programs, communication manager, and data-base manager operate. This includes memory management (swapping pages or overlays), task dispatching, priority management, and interprogram messaging. For systems comprising multiple processors, this also includes the mechanisms for load sharing, interprocessor communication, and fault recovery (if any).

Memory

A memory system supports the functions of the processor. For a single processor system, the memory is intimately associated with the processor and is considered to be one and the same with the processor for performance analysis purposes. The union of a processor with its input/output ports and dedicated memory is called a computer. (Note: in general, a computer has a processor, memory, bulk storage, and peripheral devices, including printers and communication lines. However, a processor with I/O ports and memory is sufficient to perform useful functions and represents a computer in many applications.)

A system with many processors, each with its own memory, is called a multicomputer system. Memory as a separate subsystem loses its identity in this case.

However, in a system with several processors sharing the same memory, the memory is a common resource for which the various processors compete and must be viewed as a separate subsystem. Such systems are called multiprocessor systems and are distinct from multicomputer systems. Such systems, by the way, often have small high-speed *cache memories* associated with each processor. These cache memories are used to retain the most recently used data and instructions (i.e., those likely to be reaccessed in the near future) in an effort to unload common memory.

Of course, a multicomputer system may also have associated with it a common memory to which all computers in the system have access. This case, though, is no different from any other external data device, such as disk units, and is treated in the same way.

Multiprocessor and multicomputer systems are described in some greater detail later in this chapter.

Application Processes

Application programs process requests and issue replies. To be more accurate, let us define more precisely a *program*. A program is something created by a programmer, who has written it by specifying some data structures and some processing procedures in some programming language. (This is called the *source code*.) The programmer has then compiled that source code by using a language compiler (another program), which translates the source code into *object code* that is executable by the processor. That object code is bundled with common system library routines into an object module and sits as a file on a disk unit somewhere in the system. It is this object module that is the physical embodiment of the program. It contains all data structures and computation procedures but is not actually executing.

In order to execute, the object module must be loaded into the memory accessible by a processor and then executed by that processor. Most contemporary systems provide a multiuser environment. This means that the same program may be loaded many times into the same computer to service different users simultaneously. (In practice, usually only one copy of the procedures is loaded, as it can be shared by all users; a copy of the data structures is individually loaded for each user.) To keep these different instantiations of the same program identified, they are given independent names. A *program* running in a *computer* with a system-unique *name* is called a *process*.

Thus, to be more accurate, the application subsystem comprises one or more processes that accept requests from the communication manager (as shown in Figure 2-1), make requests for data or updates to the data-base manager, formulate replies, and return these replies to the user via the communication manager.

Note also that the communication manager and data-base manager usually run as processes in the TP system. Though the operating system may be implemented as a set of concurrently executing processes, it is often desirable from a performance viewpoint to not treat it as such. Rather, the operating system, in conjunction with the hardware, provides the environment within which the processes execute.

Data Base

The data base contains the data upon which transaction replies are based. This data is usually stored on disk in contemporary systems but may be stored in other bulk storage devices, such as large RAMs (random access semiconductor memories), bubble memories, or drums.

The data-base subsystem includes the following:

- One or more physical storage media and associated controllers, such as multiple disks and their controllers.
- The computer I/O channels used to transfer data between the storage system and the computer's memory. This data transfer is usually made directly to or from computer memory (DMA, or direct memory access), with the processor being notified (via an interrupt) upon completion of the transfer.
- The data-base manager, which runs as a process or a set of cooperating processes in the computer. Its job is to execute (read/write/update) requests and other data management commands (open/close file, lock/unlock record, etc.) received from the application subsystem. It knows everything about the details for storing and retrieving information but knows nothing about the content of that information.

Other Peripherals

Other peripherals may be needed in the TP application. Most other peripherals that one might find on a computer system, such as tapes, printers, and card readers, are not used for interactive processing. One exception might be a printer used to log status changes and to request corrective action by the operator. However, in contemporary systems, status logs are usually written to disk; the operator interfaces to the system via a CRT terminal, with the operator's actions also logged to disk.

SYSTEM ARCHITECTURES

A common characteristic of TP applications is that they grow. Growth occurs as a result of two factors. One is simply the growth in transaction volume. As a system is successfully used and finds acceptance among the user community, more and more users are found for the system. Transaction volume grows—and grows—sometimes with no apparent limit in sight.

Home banking is an excellent example of this. What is the size of the potential user population for a home banking system? And what load will it impose on the system? No one knows in advance (at least, not at the time of this writing). So how big a system should a bank purchase to provide home banking? A little one in case the service doesn't catch hold? A big one in case it does? How big is *big?*

The second factor that causes growth is increased functionality. A racetrack, for instance, buys a totalizator system to handle wagering. This system is designed to accept bets, maintain and display pools, calculate payoffs, and cash winning tickets. But once the system is successfully installed and running, management sees new and expanded uses for it. Exotic new wagers such as the Reinvested Quadrifecta (whatever that is). Telephone account betting. Off-track betting. The racing secretary's selection procedures and calendar. State audit reports. Maybe even payroll and general ledger.

Many of these enhancements must operate during active wagering and therefore impose additional load on the primary TP functions. Clearly, the system needs more power than that called for by the initial specifications. Just as clearly, the "tote" system, having been procured under competitive bidding procedures, is configured very tightly. It has no excess capacity. What to do?

Expandability

The answer is to design the initial TP system with expandability in mind. Not with a hierarchy of "boxes" such that the user "trades in" (that is, tries to sell on the used market) a current box for a bigger box, with all the attendant conversion effort required to get full advantage of the enhanced features of the bigger box. Rather, expandability is obtained today by choosing a multiprocessor or multicomputer architecture that allows expansions to system capacity to be made by simply adding processors or computers, disks, and communication lines as volume warrants. And in today's art, such expansion can be achieved with no software changes whatsoever—a paramount consideration.

Distributed Systems

This is not to say that there are not a lot of TP systems in use based on single-computer technology. There are. But understanding the performance of multiprocessor and multicomputer systems (*distributed systems,* as we will call them) allows one to easily model a single-computer system since it is simply a degenerate example of either.

The basic structure of expandable systems is shown in Figures 2-2 and 2-3. A multicomputer system (Figure 2-2) comprises two or more computer systems interconnected by a high-speed bus (typically with a capacity of 2 to 30 megabytes/second). The bus is used primarily to pass messages between processes. This architecture is called *loosely coupled* because the coupling between components is only at the message level (i.e., processes being run by different processors communicate with each other by exchanging messages).

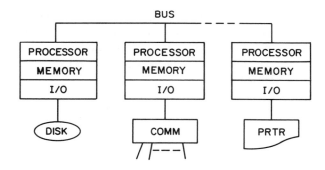

Figure 2-2 Multicomputer architecture.

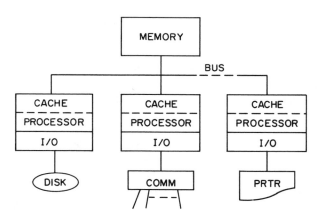

Figure 2-3   Multiprocessor architecture.

A multiprocessor system (Figure 2-3) comprises two or more processors connected via a high-speed bus to a common memory. Each processor may have its own small local memory (called a *cache memory*) to try to minimize main memory accessing. In this case, the bus speed is typically 10 to 80 megabytes/second because of its higher utilization in a higher speed environment. Such systems are termed *tightly coupled* because coupling is at the data level (i.e., processes being run by different processors communicate with each other by sharing common data in memory).

In either case, input/output devices are distributed across the processors or computers to divide up the I/O load appropriately.

The multicomputer and the multiprocessor architectures have advantages and disadvantages relative to each other. A multicomputer system requires more memory than the multiprocessor system since the operating system and common process code must be replicated in each processor instead of being shared in a common memory.

Interprocess communication is also slower in a multicomputer system since such communication is based on messages being passed through a messaging system (typically, a few milliseconds is required to send a message to another process). With the availability of common accessible memory, a multiprocessor system can pass messages between processes in times measured in microseconds.

Finally, once again from a performance viewpoint, a multiprocessor system has inherent load balancing properties, since all processors can operate off a single task queue maintained in common memory. For example, a process may be ready to run and will be processed by processor 3 until a disk call is made. It is then paused and, upon completion of the data transfer, is requeued to the task queue. When it works its way to the head of the queue, processor 6 is the next processor that becomes available, and it processes the next step in that process. Thus, a process will be passed at each step to another processor, and all processors will be kept 100% busy as long as there is work to do. No such provision exists for the processors in a multicomputer system. Each is preassigned a fixed set of tasks and typically keeps busy 50 percent to 90 percent of the time. If a processor gets very busy, there is no way for a less busy processor to share its load.

On the other hand, the multiprocessor architecture can suffer from a severe potential fault mechanism. A sick processor (one with one of a set of specific hardware malfunctions, especially in its memory interface circuits) or a sick process may run amok and contaminate critical parts of memory. The system has then crashed. A process in a multicomputer system, on the other hand, may protect itself from the faults of others by ensuring that all messages received from other processes at least appear to be sane and will not crash that process.

Thus, a multicomputer system trades reliability for performance relative to a multiprocessor system. The common memory that gives the multiprocessor system its superior performance advantages is its Achilles heel when system reliability is considered.

An interesting modification to the above architecture is the hybrid approach shown in Figure 2-4. In this architecture, a series of *processing modules* are interconnected via a high-speed bus. This is a loosely coupled architecture, since each processing module is a full computer, and processing modules communicate via messages. A processing module, however, comprises a tightly coupled architecture of several processors executing tasks off a common queue in common memory. Hybrid architectures have the potential of achieving the benefits of both loosely and tightly coupled architectures while giving up little in terms of either performance or reliability.

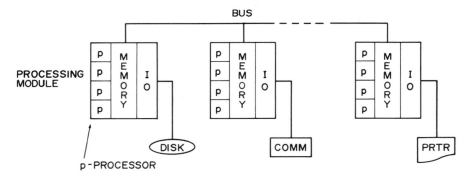

Figure 2-4   Hybrid architecture.

Fault Tolerance

These expandable architectures have one additional very important capability. With a little added enhancement (at least conceptually), they may be made to be *survivable*. That is, they will continue to maintain full functionality in the presence of any single (and often multiple) hardware fault. A common architecture applicable to loosely coupled, tightly coupled, and hybrid architectures is shown in Figure 2-5.

Basically, only two hardware enhancements need be made:

1. The bus connecting the processors or computers is replicated so that communication between processes can continue in the event of a bus failure. If both buses

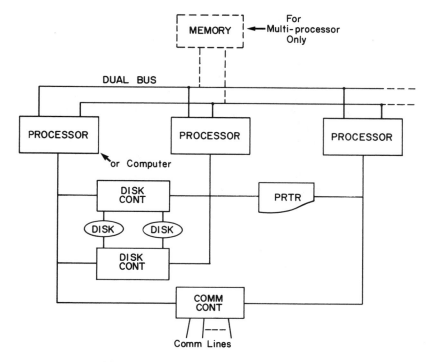

Figure 2-5   Fault-tolerant distributed architecture.

are operational, they share the communication load. If one fails, the other assumes the full load.

2. All I/O controllers are dual-ported and connect to two processors. Thus, there is a path to every peripheral device even in the case of a processor or computer failure. In addition, physical disks may be dually ported to dual controllers so that full access to files is guaranteed even in the event of a disk controller failure.

Note that memory in a closely coupled system is generally not replicated. It would be to no avail, since a sick processor or process would contaminate both memories anyway. However, memory in these systems is partitioned so that if a memory partition fails, it can be configured out of the system and the remaining memory used to run the system. (Sequoia Systems is an exception in that it provides a system with replicated memory protected by fault-tolerant processors.)

In addition to the hardware configuration shown in Figure 2-5, significant operating system enhancements must be made to support fault tolerance and recovery. These are described in later sections in this chapter.

Summary

In terms of contemporary offerings, fault-tolerant loosely coupled systems have been offered by such vendors as Tandem Computers, Tolerant Systems, Digital Equipment Corp., and Concurrent Computer. Tightly coupled fault-tolerant systems are offered by Sequoia Systems and Concurrent Computer. Fault-tolerant hybrid systems are offered by Stratus and Parallel Computers. Other distributed-system vendors include Arete, Enmasse, IBM, Nixdorf, and NCR, among others.

Another architecture not described is that of a dually redundant data-base system supporting multiple intelligent work-stations. Such systems are offered by No Halt Computers of Farmingdale, Long Island, and Syntrex of Eatontown, N.J. (Syntrex's offering is basically a word-processing system.)

Note that a fundamental property of distributed systems, as these architectures are collectively called, is that of *transparency*. Since a process can be run in any processor in the system, it must be able to communicate with any other process or peripheral device, no matter where that component currently resides. Thus, the configuration of the system must be logically transparent to the process. It cares not where the other processes and I/O devices are. It simply wants to be able to communicate with them. In the following sections, the concept of a process, its management, the management of memory in which it resides, and its role in transparency and survivability will be discussed further.

Excellent in-depth coverage of distributed systems is given by Liebowitz and Carson [17].

TRANSPARENCY

In order for a distributed system to be completely general-purpose, the first and foremost requirement is that the user must not be required to be aware that it is a distributed system. When preparing programs, the user should not be concerned with the processor to be used or to which processors the various peripherals to be used are connected.

The operating system must provide all the features required for any program running on one processor to communicate with any peripheral device or any other program running on any other processor. This characteristic is called *transparency*. It hides the intricacies and complexities of the distributed environment from the user, who thus can treat the system as if it were a single computer.

The Process

The concept of transparency is illustrated in Figure 2-6. Let us consider a simple data-base inquiry program. To the user, this is a program that accepts an inquiry from the user terminal, accesses a data base stored on disk, and returns a response as shown in Figure 2-6a. In a single-processor system, Figure 2-6a might be a good representation of the physical paths involved in the application.

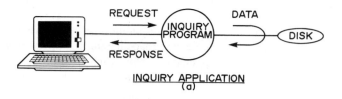

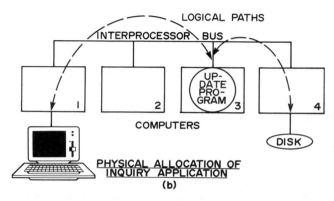

Figure 2-6   Distributed system transparency.

In a distributed system, Figure 2-6a represents how we would want to view the application logically. However, the physical representation might be quite different, as shown in Figure 2-6b. Here the application is running in a four-computer system. The operator's terminal is physically connected to computer 1, the inquiry process is physically running in computer 3, and the disk is physically connected to computer 4. Via the interprocessor bus, however, the terminal is logically connected to the inquiry process, which is logically connected to the disk. It is the logical connections that are apparent to the user (Figure 2-6a); the physical connections (Figure 2-6b) are transparent in that the user doesn't necessarily know which computers are involved in a specific application.

Thus, the operating system provides transparency if the application program requires no advance knowledge of the system configuration. The identical inquiry program shown in Figure 2-6b would support a terminal connected to computer 2 communicating with a disk on computer 1 while it itself ran as a process in computer 4, and so on.

Since the physical computers are immaterial in the design of an application for a truly transparent system, let us restructure our thinking a little by redefining the following terms:

- A *computer* (or CPU) is a physical piece of hardware comprising logic, memory, and I/O.

- A *program* is a physical set of object code, probably residing on a disk connected to some computer.

- A *process* is a program running in a processor. (There is nothing to restrict multiple copies of a program from running in one or more computers, thus creating several like processes, each perhaps handling a different terminal but otherwise providing the same application as its companion processes.)
- *Physical* means the way things really are.
- *Logical* means the way things appear to the user.

Thus, a process is the logical result of a physical program running in a physical computer. The user sees the application provided by the process but is not aware of which physical computer is being used nor of where the physical program resides.

A process, then, is the basic logical unit within a distributed system. Each logical task is handled by a process. To the user, there are two types of tasks to be performed and therefore two types of processes: application processes written by the user and device-handling, or I/O, processes provided by the operating system.

I/O Processes

We have already talked about application processes. *Device-handling processes,* or I/O processes, are typically considered part of the operating system but are in fact identical in structure to application processes. Their job is that of the classical device handler: they handle transfers to and from their respective devices (writes and reads), as well as other control functions, in response to requests from application processes. They differ from application processes only with regard to certain restrictions:

- An I/O process must reside in the same computer to which its corresponding device controller is attached.
- An I/O process cannot originate communication to another process (except to its backup, as described later); it can only respond to requests from other processes.
- An I/O process can execute I/O instructions, whereas an application process cannot.

Thus, the inquiry application of Figure 2-6 does not involve just the application process. It also involves a terminal I/O process and a disk I/O process. The logical structure of the application is therefore better represented by Figure 2-7. Here, the physical inter*processor* bus has been replaced with a logical inter*process* bus. Application processes are shown above the bus and I/O processes below the bus.

Figure 2-7b shows a more extended application in which orders are entered from several terminals. The order entry processes (one per terminal) access various files on disk to verify and build the order on disk. Once an order is complete, the common invoice process is informed so that it can print an invoice on the printer. It reads the disk-resident invoice file and prints the requested invoices. (Note: An application process can be designed to handle a single terminal, as above, or multiple terminals.)

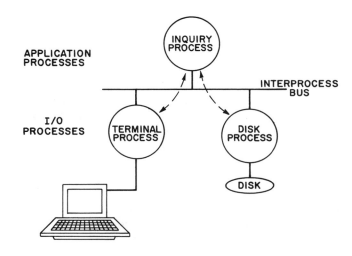

INQUIRY APPLICATION
(a)

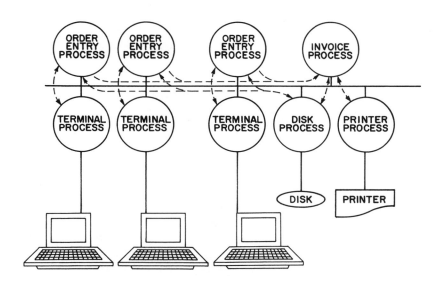

ORDER ENTRY APPLICATION
(b)

Figure 2-7   Applications as sets of processes.

The example of Figure 2-7b shows that application processes not only communicate with I/O processes but also with other application processes. (An I/O process will never communicate directly with another I/O process since an I/O process cannot initiate a communication; it can only respond to one.) In fact, *except for its internal processing, the only thing an application process in a multicomputer environment can do is to communicate with another process.* As we shall see, it is the simplicity of this statement of the role of a process that leads to the elegance of the multicomputer structure and forms the basis of the transparency and survivability functions.

A process in a multiprocessor environment is not similarly restrained but still forms the basis for transparency.

This description of processes is exemplary of contemporary systems today. No hard-and-fast rules are followed, and the properties of processes in different systems may be somewhat different from those described here. However, the principles described are sound and will form a satisfactory basis for understanding the nature of a process and its management for performance analysis purposes.

Interprocess Communications

Let us now look in more detail at interprocess communications. One process communicates with another by sending it an interprocess message. To do so, it merely provides to the operating system the name of the process, the content and length of the message, and whether a response is required.

Note that this leads to three types of interprocess messages, which we will designate as follows:

- *Write*. A message is sent to another process with no response required (except for completion status, i.e., success or error condition).
- *Read*. A null message (i.e., no data, length of zero) is sent to another process with a response expected.
- *Writeread*. A message is sent to another process, and a response is expected.

In the example of Figure 2-7b, an order entry process might return information to its terminal and wait for the next operator entry. This is a WRITEREAD interprocess message. When it receives data from the operator, it may verify or expand certain information, such as part number, by sending READ messages to the disk process, which will read requested data from the disk and return it to the order entry process.

The order entry process may then write invoice data to disk by sending WRITE messages to the disk process and will then inform the invoice process that the invoice is ready by sending it a WRITE message. The invoice process will READ the invoice from the disk process and will print it by sending WRITE messages to the printer process. Note again that I/O processes never send interprocess messages; they can only respond to them.

In order to support interprocess messages, the system must provide three facilities:

- a hardware path interconnecting all computers, with supporting software.
- a provision to assign a unique name to each process.
- an operating system capability to know in which computer each process is currently operating.

The hardware path can be implemented in any one of a number of ways, as shown in Figure 2-8. Each has its own advantages and disadvantages:

- The bus is simple but must resolve contention and carry the entire multicomputer load.
- The ring can use different paths simultaneously but places a load on computers not involved in the message.
- A star can use different paths simultaneously but requires additional hardware: the switch. The switch must carry the entire multicomputer load.
- A fully connected system provides maximum capacity but requires N−1 bus connections at each computer for an N−computer system.
- A partially connected system is application-dependent.

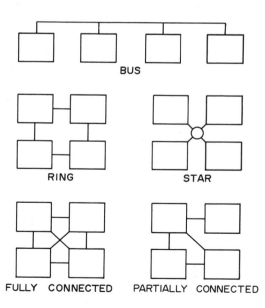

Figure 2-8   Interprocessor communication networks.

No matter which network is chosen, the important fact is that it is transparent to the user. We do not care how an interprocess message physically gets from one process to another as long as it logically gets there.

In most contemporary cases, the bus network is used. However, DEC's VAXcluster is a star network; and Stratus uses a modified star/ring network.

Process Names

The next facility required is that of process names. A process is named when it is *created*. A process is created at the request of an operator command or at the request of another process. Creating a process causes the operating system, in the CPU in which the process is to run, to schedule that program (i.e., object code on disk) to be rolled into memory and run as the named process. A typical command to run a process might be RUN ORDER / NAME ORDER1, CPU 3, PRI 150 /.

This command would cause the program with the physical object file name ORDER (on disk) to be run on physical computer 3 as a logical process named ORDER1 at priority 150. (If the CPU were not specified, the process would run on the same CPU as the creating terminal or process. If the name were not specified, an arbitrary unique name would be assigned. But no process other than the creator would know this name; therefore, no process other than the creator could communicate with it. If the priority were not specified, a default priority would be used.)

Finally, the operating system must know in which computer each process is operating. Whenever a process is created, all computers are informed of this event (via the bus). Each computer maintains a process directory that contains the name of each process and the CPU in which it is currently running. I/O processes are created at system generation time and are permanent entries in the process directory.

An exception to this is disk files. A disk I/O process controls one physical disk controller. This controller may be connected to several physical disk units. Many named disk files are on these disks and are therefore accessible through a common disk process. However, the application program will want to reference a file by its name; it doesn't need to know the name of the disk process with which it must communicate in order to reach the physical disk containing that file. Disk files are typically organized into volumes, each volume being handled by a specific disk process. The name assigned to a disk process is, in fact, the name of the volume it is handling. When a request is made to read or write a disk file in a given volume, the process directory is searched to determine the process and CPU handling that disk volume.

Thus, when a process wants to send an interprocess message to another process, its local operating system looks up the process name in its process directory, finds the CPU in which that process is running, and, if it is in another computer, sends the message over the interprocessor bus to the receiving process. If a response is expected, it will return that response to the transmitting process when it is received.

Note that the process itself need have no knowledge whatsoever of where other processes reside nor how to get a message to other processes. These functions have been totally handled by the operating system, thus providing the transparency we desire.

Process Mobility

The fact that a process may be mobile (i.e., move from one computer to another) leads to two important characteristics of multicomputer systems:

- *Load sharing*. The creator of a process can request the status of all computers and can then create the process in the least-loaded computer. It is common practice among programmers to display the status of all computers before deciding in which computer to run a compile, edit, or other utility.
- *Survivability*. Process mobility allows us to re-create a process (or switch to a backup process) if another computer that was running that process has failed. This subject will be dealt with later in depth.

Of course, in multiprocessor systems, no such mobility is required, as the system is automatically load balancing; a failed processor simply does not execute any tasks off the common queue.

A final point should be made about system transparency. As we have said, in a truly transparent system, the user is unaware of where the various peripherals and processes are in a distributed system because he or she is unaware of the mechanism involved in routing a message from one process to another. This mechanism involves the high-speed inter-processor bus.

Though the high speed of the bus is necessary to achieve good system throughput, that is the primary reason for its speed. There is no logical reason why part of the bus could not be a slower communication line, allowing geographical separation of groups of computers. The system of Figure 2-6b might be distributed as shown in Figure 2-9. This provides a geographical distribution for a large system, which can offer many advantages:

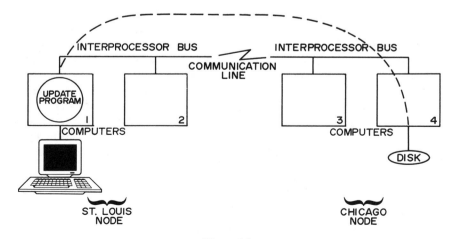

Figure 2-9

- The use of a common corporate data base without excessive line costs.
- Load balancing in a large, geographically distributed system by running large jobs at the least-loaded node.
- Printing of reports at the user's site even if the data base is remote.
- Message delivery among all users of the distributed network.
- Local control over local processing capability while having access to the network for load sharing and data-base access.

This distributed system requires no substantial effort on the part of the user, for the same transparency concepts of interprocess communication hold as described previously. It is only necessary for the operating system to be able to know the geographical node, as well as the computer in which a process is running via the process directory.

Summary

We have seen that distributed system transparency has been achieved by considering an application as a communications network. The nodes of the network are the processes which communicate with each other via interprocess messages over an interprocess bus.

As in any communications system, node or path failures may cause loss or duplication of messages. This is one of the major considerations when we discuss survivability. Also, communication path delays and queuing at the nodes impose a limit on the capacity of the system. This will become the basis of our throughput analysis.

PROCESS STRUCTURE

We have described the *process* as the fundamental logical unit of a distributed system from the applications viewpoint. A process is simply a program running in a computer. There are two types of processes: application processes, which perform a portion or all of the application-oriented logic, and I/O processes, each of which is a device handler for a specific device or device group. An application is implemented by a set of appropriate processes that communicate among themselves via interprocess messages.

In order to understand the techniques used to achieve survivability and to be able to analyze and enhance the throughput of a distributed system, we must understand a process in more detail. In this section, we will describe a typical structure for a process and then explore how it is managed by the operating system.

Process Functions

Since a process is a program—in the classical sense—running in a computer, it has some of the characteristics we naturally associate with programs. That is, it comprises a set of instructions, or code, that operates on data. However, several restrictions are placed on the code and data at this point that make a process a subset of what we generally think of as a program. In fact, a process is allowed to do only two things:

- Perform its assigned logical duty by operating on its own local data (this includes communicating with and controlling its device in the case of an I/O process).
- Exchange interprocess messages with other processes. These messages are used to pass data and control functions from one process to another.

A process is specifically not allowed, for instance, to modify its own code, to access or manipulate the data of another process, or to directly interface with a device not under its control as an I/O process.

The structure of a process is shown in Figure 2-10. We will characterize it as comprising three parts:

- A process control block (PCB), which is used by the operating system to schedule and control the process.
- The code that implements the functions of the process.
- The data local to the process, upon which the code interacts.

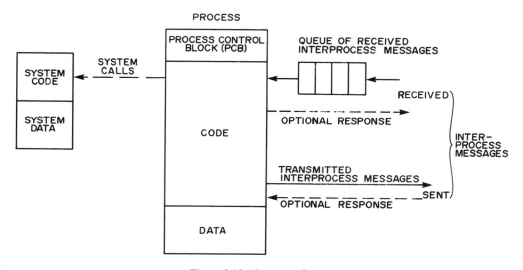

Figure 2-10   Structure of a process.

Interprocess Messages

As shown in Figure 2-10, the process is allowed to do only two things in addition to processing its own local data. It may exchange messages with other processes and may make certain calls to routines (not processes) contained within the operating system (these calls are considered part of its assigned logical duty).

Only three types of interprocess messages may be sent by a process:

- A message to another application process, perhaps with a response. These messages are used to pass control functions and data between application processes.
- Read, write, and control requests to I/O processes for peripheral device activity. These messages are similar in all respects to messages sent to other application processes.
- Data to its backup process, if any, to inform the backup process of the current status of the data in case a failure should cause the backup to have to take over processing. These "checkpointing" messages will be described later.

The first two message types may be sent by application processes only. As we have said before, they cannot be originated by I/O processes. However, any process—application or I/O—may send a checkpoint message to its backup process. This forms the basis of one of the survivability strategies, which will be described later.

In addition to these interprocess messages, a process (application or I/O) may receive messages that appear to be interprocess messages but are in fact generated by the operating system. These messages are generally status messages concerning situations, such as processor down or up events or the stopping or aborting of a process that was created by this process.

As shown in Figure 2-10, messages sent to a process need not necessarily be processed immediately. Rather, they are queued to the process (via links in the PCB) until the process is ready to read and process them.

This queuing facility will become important in our discussions of survivability, since there may be no way for the backup process to know about messages queued but not read by its primary process, nor may there be any way for the operating system to know that a message has been read and processed but not answered. Lost and duplicate messages in the event of a takeover are as important in multicomputer survivability considerations as they are in any communications network.

The system calls that a process can make to the operating system generally fall into two classes:

- Calls to routines that are simply common routines supplied by the operating system but which in reality are logically part of the process's code. For the most part, these routines implement the transmission and reception of the various types of interprocess messages. They are formally part of the operating system because they use system-level tables and common buffer pools that must be "hidden" from the application programmer.
- Scheduling requests for itself and other processes. A process can request that it be suspended until any one of a set of events occurs (discussed later), or it can request that another process be created or stopped.

Addressing Range

The rather formal structure of a process, as described above, has important implications with respect to addressing within the process. In the process structure defined above, there is not a requirement that any memory location in the system be available from any memory location within a process. Conversely:

- The code cannot modify itself. Therefore, a data instruction can access only the data area, and a jump, branch, or routine call instruction can refer only to the code area. Thus, code and data spaces are mutually exclusive. In physical memory, the code and data areas are separate and identifiable.
- A process can access only its own local data area. No addressing range is necessary or allowed to access the data within the local range of another process.

Note that one process does not have direct access to the data of another process. This is not an arbitrary restriction but is necessary to the fundamental requirement of survivability. It is of paramount importance that the data area of a process not be corrupted by another process that is ''sick'' because of faulty hardware or software.

If a faulty process had access to the data areas of other processes, it could indeed corrupt those areas and cause a system failure. However, processes have access to the data of other processes only through the mechanism of interprocess messages. This gives a process the ability to edit and reject improper accesses to its data area, thus ensuring to any arbitrary extent the integrity of its own data. This may not be true of multiprocessor systems that share a common memory.

Process Code Area

For purposes of some of the following discussions, particularly with regard to survivability, it is important to understand in more detail the structure of the code and data areas in a process. The code area comprises a collection of procedures. A procedure is a routine that has an entrance and an exit (or perhaps multiple entrances and exits). One procedure is designated the main procedure. It is given control when the process is first run and has no exit except to stop the process. It ''calls'' other procedures, which may in turn call other procedures, and so on.

When a procedure exits, it returns control to the procedure that called it at the point in the code following the call. There is no other way for a procedure to exit (short of terminating the process). Figure 2-11 shows a typical code area and its associated data area as processing progresses through several stages.

Process Data Area

The data area is separated into two distinctly different areas, global data and the process local data, the latter often implemented via a stack, as will be described. The global data

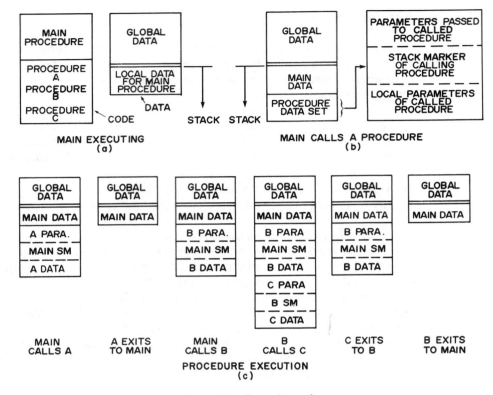

Figure 2-11 Processing cycle.

is available to all procedures within the process. The stack is used to hold the data that is local to the procedures currently invoked and to control the nesting of those procedures.

There is some similarity between processes and procedures. Just as a process has exclusive access to its data area, a procedure has local data to which only it has access. Moreover, just as a process can pass data to another process via an interprocess message, so can a procedure pass data to another procedure when it calls it.

Therefore, a procedure has access to only three types of data:

- The global data of the process, which is accessible by all procedures within that process.
- Its own local data.
- Data passed to it by the procedure that called it.

The Stack

A *stack* allows data items to be *pushed* onto it and then *popped* from it in inverse order (last-in, first-out).

The last two types of data listed above are created in the stack area and are then deleted as procedures are entered and exited. Therefore, this data requires addressable memory space only when it is meaningful, i.e., when the procedure is invoked. The data simply does not exist when the procedure is not being used.

The use of a stack for procedure data thus brings a degree of efficiency to memory utilization. Figure 2-11 shows an example of stack usage as a process executes. When the process is first created, it is given a data area containing its global data and the local data for the main procedure (since the main procedure always exists, so does its local data). The code and data areas at process creation time are shown in Figure 2-11a.

As the main procedure executes in-line code, the data area remains in this configuration. However, when the main procedure decides to call another procedure, it does so by pushing a *procedure data set* onto the stack. The procedure data set comprises all of the data needed by the called procedure and, in fact, is the only data available to that procedure (except, of course, that the global data is available to all procedures). The procedure data set comprises three types of data, as shown in Figure 2-11b.

- The parameters being passed to the called procedure by the calling procedure. These parameters can include pointers to data in the global area or pointers to local data of the calling procedure.

- A *stack marker* defining how the procedure is to exit. The stack marker contains the address in the calling procedure to which the called procedure is to return (the address following the procedure call) and the machine environment that is to be restored following the called procedure's return.

- The local data for the called procedure.

The called procedure then executes, operating on the parameters passed to it and the global data pertinent to it. When it has completed, it deletes its data set from the stack and returns to the calling procedure according to the stack marker.

Of course, a procedure can call another procedure, which can call another, and so on. In this case, the stack grows, with the nesting of procedures being defined by the sequence of stack markers.

Figure 2-11c shows the stack configuration as the main procedure executes. The main procedure first calls procedure A, which executes and returns. The main procedure then calls procedure B, which in turn calls procedure C. At this point, the stack contains two procedure data sets, one for B and one for C. Procedure C then completes, returning to B, which itself completes, returning to the main procedure with a clean stack.

A vital point that will form one of the foundations of our survivability discussion is that the data area with its stack completely defines the state of the process at any instant in its processing cycle. If we were to interrupt a process and then could somehow move its data area as it then stood and its code area to another processor and restart execution at the interrupted instruction, the process would continue to run as if nothing had happened (having, of course, copied the machine environment in terms of memory maps, condition codes and so forth). More about this later.

Summary

In summary, a process is the basic logical entity at the applications level in a distributed system. It can do only two things: perform its own assigned processing functions (including process scheduling) and exchange interprocess messages with other processes. An application process can send interprocess messages to other application processes, to I/O processes, and to its own backup. An I/O process can respond to messages received from application processes and can send messages to its own backup. A process comprises a data area and unmodifiable code that implements a series of procedures. The data area contains global data, which is available to all procedures, and a stack. The stack holds all local data pertinent to the procedures currently invoked and controls their nesting. The data area and the current machine environment totally define the current state of the process.

PROCESS MANAGEMENT

Having described the process as the basic logical element in a distributed system, and having explored its structure and the way in which it interacts with other processes to implement an application, we must now turn our attention to how the process shares its environment cooperatively with other processes competing for the same resources.

Obviously, in a large distributed system, many things go on simultaneously. Many users perform their various tasks while sitting at many terminals while operatorless background tasks may be at work updating data bases, maintaining statistics, and doing sundry other tasks. Many processes are active simultaneously.

Shared Resources

Processes in one computer generally run independently of processes in other computers. However, that group of processes assigned to a given computer (all processes in a multiprocessor system) must share its resources in such a way that all processes may complete their tasks in a timely manner. There are two dominant computer resources to be considered: time and space.

The time resource is processor time. Though it appears to the user that multiple processes are running concurrently in a processor, we know, in fact, that at any instant only one process is actually running. It will run until it decides to relinquish control of the processor, at which time another process will be given the processor. Therefore, there must be a way to know which processes are awaiting the processor and to transfer control of the processor from one process to another in an orderly and efficient manner. This is called *process scheduling*. A necessary efficiency in process scheduling is that processes carry priorities and that, in fact, the highest-priority process desiring the processor has it.

The space resource is memory. The sum total of the memory requirements of all the processes that are to run in a given computer could well exceed that computer's memory size. This is particularly true with mobile processes in a multicomputer system, for we do not necessarily know in advance which processes are going to run where. Therefore, we must have a way to allocate the available memory to those processes currently requiring memory. This is called *memory management*.

The functions of process scheduling and memory management in a distributed system do not differ significantly from the way in which they are handled in any one of many modern-day single processor operating systems; the reader who is familiar with these operating systems will already understand the concepts to be discussed. However, they are important for our following discussions of survivability and performance and will therefore be described so that we will all be talking the same language.

Process Scheduling

Let us first discuss process scheduling. We assume that several processes have been created in a computer and are currently taking turns running in that computer. A process can be in one of three states:

- *Waiting*. The process is currently idle but is waiting for one or more events to occur. Until one of these events occurs, there is nothing the process can do; therefore, it is not a candidate for scheduling. These events may typically be one of three types: (1) the receipt of an interprocess message; (2) a device interrupt signifying an action has been completed and requires process action (for I/O processes only); (3) a time interval specified by the process has elapsed.
- *Ready*. An event has occurred, one that must be handled by the process. The process is ready to make use of the computer when it is given the chance.
- *Active*. The process is currently the process running in the computer.

(Note that there is no such thing as a dormant process. Once a process is created, it is waiting, ready or active. If it decides to stop itself, it no longer exists. The physical program that was used to create it still exists, but the logical process has disappeared from the system.)

The active process will continue to run and to consume all processor time (except for interrupt and cycle-stealing activities, which are transparent to it) until one of the following situations occurs:

- It decides it must wait for an event (interprocess message or response, interrupt, and/or time interval).

- It decides to stop itself. (The process is of no further interest to us, since it is no longer a candidate for scheduling.)
- A higher-priority process becomes ready (it will preempt the active process).

In the first case (waiting for an event), the process goes into the waiting state. In the second case (termination), the process disappears. In the third case (higher priority process), the process returns to the ready state. In any event, the highest priority ready process, if any, is given control of the processor. This switching of processes proceeds indefinitely and is the basis of process scheduling within a computer.

Mechanisms for Scheduling

Processor scheduling is handled via two fairly straightforward mechanisms that we will call the *ready list* and the *timer list*. The ready list is a list of all processes in the ready state, in order of priority (within the same priority, the processes are ordered on a first-come basis). The timer list is a list of all processes awaiting time-outs, in order of their time-out interval. A process may be on the timer list, on the ready list, or on neither. Processes are maintained in a list via links in their PCBs.

Figure 2-12 shows a typical process scheduling sequence. In Figure 2-12a, 10 created processes, named A through J, are running in a computer. Process A is currently the active process; it is the one that is actually running in the computer. Processes B, C, D, and E are all ready to run but are lower priority than process A (priority 1 is the highest, to simplify this example). Therefore, they are linked in the ready list via their PCBs, with process B being at the head of the list, since it is the highest-priority ready process.

Processes F, G, H, I, and J are waiting for some event to occur, and processes F, G, and H are furthermore being controlled by time-outs. For example, if an event does not occur within six seconds, process G will become ready anyway. (A process can also wait simply for the purpose of timing and not for any other event but its own time-out). Processes F, G, and H are linked via their PCBs into the timer list, with process F being at the head of the list, since it has the shortest time-out. Time-out values in the PCBs for this example are incremental values to be added to those ahead of them on the list. Thus, processes F, G, and H are waiting 1, 6 and 16 seconds, respectively.

In Figure 2-12b, process Z has been created and has been added by the operating system to the ready list. Since it has higher priority than any other process in the ready list, it is placed at the head of that list.

In Figure 2-12c, process A has completed and has suspended itself until it receives another event. It is not timing on that event. Process Z, being the highest-priority ready process, is removed from the ready list and made the active process.

In Figure 2-12d, process Z has suspended itself to await an event and has requested an eight-second time-out. It is therefore placed in the waiting state and added to the timer list between processes G and H, which have smaller and greater time-outs, respectively (process H's time-out is adjusted by Z's increment). Note that process F timed out and has been added to the ready list. Also note that process J has received an event and has

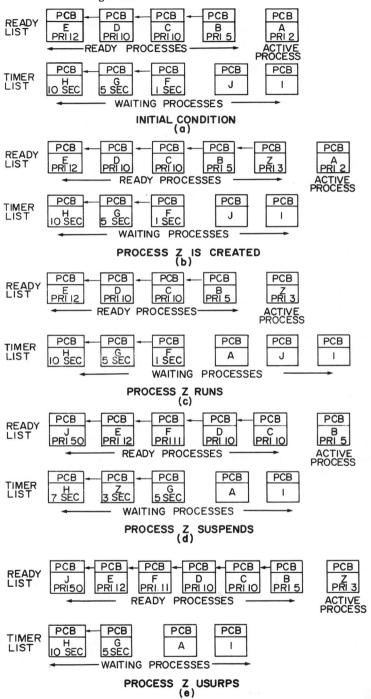

Figure 2-12 Process scheduling.

therefore been scheduled by being added to the ready list. Since process Z is now suspended, process B is removed from the head of the ready list and is made active.

In Figure 2-12e, process Z has received an event prior to its time-out. It is removed from the timer list, and process H's time-out is readjusted to include what had been Z's time-out interval. Process Z has a higher priority than the currently active process. Therefore, it is not placed on the ready list. Instead, the currently active process B is returned to the head of the ready list, and process Z is made active, thus usurping control of the processor from process B. This is called *preemptive scheduling*.

The foregoing example shows that processes share the processor by simply moving from active to waiting to ready and back to the active state again. Via the timer and ready lists and via appropriate actions in response to events by the operating system, the current state of each process is known and controlled. Process scheduling gives a computer a multitasking capability because, in effect, several different tasks may be running concurrently.

Memory Management

Turning now to memory management, the problem is how to stuff five pounds of potatoes into a two-pound bag. Since in a distributed system we generally do not know in advance what processes will be running, much less in which computer, we must be prepared to support a set of processes that have memory requirements exceeding the memory availability of the computer in which they are running, perhaps by a wide margin. The requirements of a single process might even be bigger than the memory on its computer.

Paging

The first step in memory management is to realize that all processes often cannot fit into memory simultaneously, but somehow the contents of their data areas must be maintained. Therefore, an image of the process's data area is created on disk when the process itself is created. (Code areas never change, and their images are already available on disk.) This disk image represents the current contents of all memory locations in the data area that are not currently in the physical memory of the computer.

It is the responsibility of memory management to ensure that if a section of a process's data area is to lose its place in memory to another process, its disk image must first be updated. Since the disk image of a process (code and data) is merely a representation of the true process, which exists only when it is actually in memory, it is called *virtual memory*. By proper management of virtual memory, the computer can be made to *appear* to have a memory as big as is needed to hold all processes.

Virtual memory may be managed via a mechanism known as *page faulting*. Physical memory is organized into "pages," typically 0.5K to 4K bytes in size. When a process addresses a word in its memory (either in its data area or in its code area), the processor (by hardware) ensures that the page containing that word is, in fact, in memory; if not, obviously, it cannot be accessed.

If the processor finds that the page currently being referenced is not in memory, it generates a page-fault indication. This means that the processor must bring this page into memory from its disk image before the current process can continue. In order to do that, the processor must select a memory page that it is willing to overwrite with the new process page (note that every memory page contains valid code or data from some process or another).

The algorithm used to select a memory page for destruction varies from system to system but is generally based on two considerations:

- *Age.* When was this page last referenced? If the contents of a page have not been used for awhile, the page is considered dormant and a candidate for overwriting.
- *Modification.* "Dirty" pages are data pages (never code pages) that have been modified since they were last read from their disk images. If a dirty page is to be overwritten, it must first be written out to update its disk image, whereas a clean page does not need to be written out. Clean pages, therefore, have priority over dirty pages as candidates for overwriting, since less system resources will be used.

Once the processor has selected a page for overwriting, it will write it to its disk image if it is dirty (has been modified) and will then read in to that same physical page in memory the process page being accessed. At this point, the process may continue.

Some systems use overlay areas to swap process portions between memory and disk. However, the basic concepts of page faulting and overlays are similar, except that overlays are of variable size and usually larger and may be controlled by the process itself.

Though virtual memory significantly expands the capabilities of a computer, it must be emphasized that page faulting is an extremely hazardous event with respect to system performance. It can virtually stall a processor if allowed to get out of hand. When a page fault occurs, not much else can go on in the system. Certainly, another page fault cannot be honored until the first has been processed. Otherwise, one could find so many page faults in progress that when one page fault completed, that page would already have been reseized by a later request (an extreme but possible scenario). Therefore, during page faulting, the processor becomes very limited in what it does and may stall, thus drastically reducing its throughput.

To alleviate this, one may be able to "fix" part or all of the code or data of critical processes into physical memory. These pages are never subject to paging. They will always be in memory when needed but will reduce the amount of memory available for paging.

One of the obvious characteristics of virtual memory as described above is that one never knows what physical page in memory currently contains a particular logical page of a process. In fact, a logical process page migrates randomly through physical memory as page faulting occurs. Sometimes it is there, and sometimes it isn't. And whenever it disappears, it pops up somewhere else.

Keeping track of which logical page is currently in which physical page is called *memory mapping*. Like page faulting, it is largely a hardware-supported function since it must be performed on-the-fly with instruction execution.

To accomplish this, the processor typically has a set of hardware memory maps. One may be used, for instance, to map the code area and one to map the data area. These maps can be loaded by software and then used by the hardware as a process executes. The contents of a memory map are illustrated in Figure 2-13.

LOGICAL PROCESS PAGE ADDRESS	PHYSICAL MEMORY PAGE ADDRESS
O	113
I	27
2	–(97)
3	–
4	72
•	•
•	•
•	•

CODE MAP

LOGICAL PROCESS PAGE ADDRESS	PHYSICAL MEMORY PAGE ADDRESS
O	16
I	17
2	79
3	–
4	13
•	•
•	•
•	•

DATA MAP

Figure 2-13   Memory mapping.

Likewise, each process has a code map and a data map associated with it. When it is running, its maps are loaded into the processor's hardware maps.

Let us say that the example of Figure 2-13 shows the maps for the currently running process and that the process is currently executing code in its first logical page (page 0). This code is found in physical page 113 by the processor, and the processor is thus executing code located in physical page 113.

If the process's code execution falls through to page 1 or branches to page 4, execution proceeds normally since these pages are in physical memory. However, if it should attempt to execute an instruction in its logical page 2, the processor will not find that page to be currently in physical memory. It will page fault, find an old page to overwrite (say physical page 97) and will read the current process's logical page 2 into physical page 97. Any maps referencing the old contents of physical page 97 must be modified to show that logical page to be no longer in physical memory. The process may now proceed to execute code in its logical page 2 (physical page 97).

A similar scenario holds for data-page accesses. In the example of Figure 2-13, data accesses to logical pages 0, 1, 2, or 4 will be executed normally. A data access to page 3 will cause a page fault.

Note that under memory mapping, the code or data area of a process is not necessarily (and probably is not) mapped into contiguous physical memory. Though memory space appears logically to be contiguous to the user, it is in fact spread quite randomly throughout physical memory.

We have described separate memory maps for code and data areas, for these areas are totally exclusive and may each range over the entire address space.

Managing Multiple Users

One additional fallout from these types of operating systems should be noted. As we have said, a process is a program running in a computer and comprises a code area and a data area. The code area is never modified. There is no reason that in that same computer, another process could not be created, using the same program but simply carrying another name. In fact, since its code area would be identical to that of the first process, the code area would not have to be duplicated; both processes would map into the same code area in physical memory, as shown in Figure 2-14.

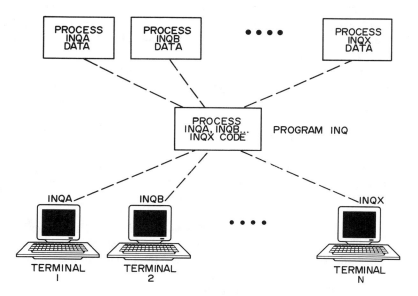

Figure 2-14   Multiuser operation.

Let us introduce one more concept, that of the *home terminal*. When a process is created by an operator, it is created by that operator typing in a command at a terminal. The process then knows that terminal as its home terminal and may refer to it as such.

Consider a program written to perform a task (maybe an inquiry task) to support one and only one terminal, which is its home terminal. The program file is stored as an object file on disk and is named INQ.

One operator could walk up to terminal 1 (in Figure 2-14) and type

RUN INQ/NAME INQA/

and the process INQA would be created. A copy of the code corresponding to program INQ would be made available to process INQA, and a data area image for process INQA would be created on disk. The operator can now use process INQA for inquiry purposes. As the process executes, pages required by it will be paged in and mapped as previously described.

A second operator can walk up to terminal 2 and enter a similar command:

RUN INQ/NAME INQB/

and process INQB will be created as was INQA, except that a second copy of INQ's code does not need to be paged into physical memory if INQB is running in the same computer as INQA (that is, the terminals are on the same computer, or the CPU is specified in the RUN command). Process INQB will use the same code area as INQA. Of course, a separate data area is created for process INQB.

This can continue virtually without limit, allowing more and more simultaneous users of the same single-user program by creating more and more uniquely named processes using the same program. All such processes running in a common computer will use a common memory-resident copy of the code, but each will have its own data area. In fact, the sum total of memory used by many single-user processes is about the same as the memory used by one large multiuser process since the separate data areas are required anyway. The duplication of common data areas and the additional multiprocess overhead (e.g., PCBs) are perhaps offset by the simpler code required.

Additional Considerations

The creation of a large number of processes does not come without problems, and there are some instances in which it is desirable to design a process to handle a number of users. Among these considerations are the following:

- Each process requires a PCB and other system structures, such as file control blocks, that are allocated from very valuable common buffer space in the system data area. This imposes a practical limit on the number of processes that can exist in one computer at any one time. Typical contemporary systems can support from 100 to a few hundred concurrent processes.

- If large buffers are required for each user, n users will require n buffers if each process is single-user. This could result in excessive page faulting. A multiuser process could get by with a smaller buffer pool, which it dynamically allocates to users as needed, so page faulting would be reduced or eliminated.

- Interprocess messages are time-consuming in multicomputer systems. Typical interprocess message times range from 1 msec. to 50 msec. In some applications, it is possible to batch transactions in one process before sending them to another process, thus saving many interprocess messages. In this case, it may be desirable to have a process control many users so it can accumulate a batch in a relatively short period of time. Otherwise, data-base updating and other functions dependent on these transactions might drag.

- The act of process switching adds operating system overhead. Typical overheads run from 0.5 msec. to 10 msec. When processes are switched, the old active process must be switched to waiting and perhaps added to the timer list, the new active process must be removed from the ready list, and maps must be switched.

A single-user process must be switched after every transaction. A multiuser process must be switched only when it has processed all transactions pending from all its users.

Summary

This description of processes and process management highlights another important feature of contemporary distributed systems: simple software development. Let us look at what this type of operating system allows us to do.

A programmer can write a program designed to support a single user and, with virtually no additional effort, find that the program has the following attributes:

- It is a multiuser program, one that can be used by many users simultaneously.
- It is a program that will run in a multitasking environment (i.e., many other tasks may be running concurrently).
- It is a program that will run on a computer regardless of the amount of memory it requires or the amount of memory available to that computer.
- It is a program that will run in a distributed environment in which the programmer can be unaware of the particular computer that will be used or to which computers the programmer's various peripheral devices are connected.

Thus, the problem of writing multiuser, multitasking, distributed programs has been reduced to the writing of a single-thread, single-user program—the simplest possible solution.

Unfortunately, this has not come without penalty. The penalty is in system capacity because of the high overhead of this do-all operating system. But this is the trade-off we will be willing to make as hardware costs go down and as software costs go up—more hardware for less software. The critical subject of system capacity and responsiveness thus becomes even more important and creates a stronger focus on the need for performance analysis.

SURVIVABILITY

The simple expedient of formally defining the process as the basic logical unit in a system, bounding its capabilities, and then building an operating system that effectively manages such processes leads us to a powerful programming environment. We can now write multiuser applications that run in a multitasking, distributed environment while concerning ourselves only with the problems of a single-user, single-thread application.

The distributed aspect allows us a further extension of these capabilities. Since the system now has at least two processors, and since we have the option of adding two of anything else that might be critical, we have the opportunity to make the system highly fault-tolerant. We can create a system that will survive any single failure (and many cases of multiple failures) in that it will continue to perform functionally in the same way in the face of these failures. The user may notice a loss of capacity or responsiveness but will not lose any of the system's capabilities. We will see that the structure and management of processes play a big role in achieving this goal.

Hardware Duality

The first step in achieving survivability is hardware duality. If a critical hardware component fails, there must be at least one other identical component that can be used immediately. Equally important are the paths to all components. If one path fails, there must be an alternate path to that component. For instance, if the processor to which a user's terminal is connected fails, and there is no means to connect the terminal to another processor, then so far as the user is concerned, the system has failed.

   This leads to the concept of dual-ported devices, in which each device controller has two ports, each of which can be connected to a separate computer. At any one time, one of the ports is being actively used, and the other is dormant, playing a backup role. The computer connected to the active port is said to "own" the device.

   As an example, Figure 2-15 shows a dual-ported printer. The printer (a normal, everyday, single-ported printer) is connected to a controller that can be driven either by processor A or processor B via two independent ports. Each of these processors runs an I/O process, which controls the printer via its connected port (remember that an I/O process must reside in the same computer to which the device is connected). Processor A currently owns the printer, and the operating system knows this. Therefore, interprocess messages containing data to be printed on the printer are routed to the printer I/O process in processor A.

   There are several failures that could cause this path to the printer to fail. Specifically, processor A could fail, or logic in the printer controller port connected to processor A could fail. In the former case, the operating system would realize the failure of pro-

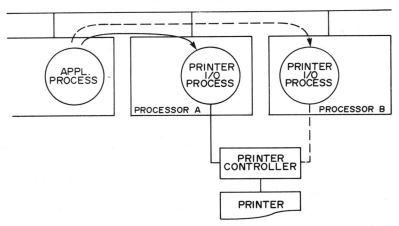

Figure 2-15   Dual porting.

cessor A and would transfer ownership of the printer to processor B. In the latter case, the printer I/O process would detect the fault in the controller and would transfer ownership to processor B.

In either event, subsequent interprocess printer messages are sent to the printer I/O process in processor B. Therefore, the failure of a processor or a device port is indeed transparent to the user insofar as the user's access to that device is concerned (providing the application process is written to reissue an I/O message in the event of an error).

Unfortunately, in all devices there are simplex points of failure that will totally remove that device from service. For instance, the failure of a printer motor or even common logic, such as a line driver in the printer controller, will disable the printer. This can be overcome only by totally duplicating the device and its controller and by making provision in the system for rerouting work away from the failed device to an alternate device. In the case of a printer, for instance, a sophisticated spooler queues work for all printers on the system. If a printer fails, it simply becomes unavailable to the spooler, which continues to despool all work to the remaining printers. In many cases, the duplication of a device is not economically justifiable; and work for a failed device is simply held until the device once again becomes available.

There are two cases in which the continued operation of the device is every bit as important as the processors themselves. One case involves the interprocessor bus; without it, all paths but local paths within a processor are lost. Therefore, this bus must be duplexed. The other case is that of disk files containing critical data bases and system files (program and process images).

Data-Base Integrity

If a disk containing a critical file goes down, and there is no alternate, the system goes down. Totally. Furthermore, just having a backup disk is not satisfactory. It must contain completely updated files, i.e., it must be a mirror image of its partner. As data comes in that updates one disk of a "mirrored pair," it must also update the other disk.

Figure 2-16 shows the configuration for a mirrored disk pair. Three levels of mirroring may be used:

- One controller and two disks (Figure 2-16a). However, if controller logic common to both disks fails, then access to both disks is lost.
- One controller per disk (Figure 2-16b). No single failure will prevent access to the data.
- Dual-ported disk devices connected to dual-ported controllers (Figure 2-16c). This adds an additional level of redundancy to the mirrored pair.

There is an important utility that must be available to support mirrored files if they are to be truly effective: an on-line disk copy utility to be used when a disk that is part of a mirrored pair is to be returned to service. When a disk unit fails, the files are handled by the remaining simplex disk. When the disk is repaired or replaced with a spare and is to be

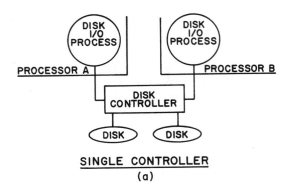

SINGLE CONTROLLER
(a)

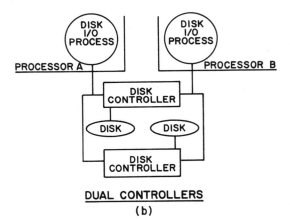

DUAL CONTROLLERS
(b)

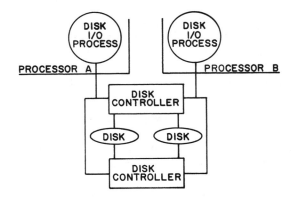

DUAL-PORTED DISKS
(c)

Figure 2-16 Mirrored disks.

put back in the system, it must be brought back to its mirrored condition (i.e., containing an exact copy of the other disk) even while further modifications are received for that data. That is the job of the on-line disk copy utility: to copy one disk to another while at the same time ensuring that file updates are kept current.

To summarize hardware duality, Figure 2-5, which was previously discussed, shows a simple system with communication lines, printer, and mirrored disk pair. That figure shows how these peripherals might be configured physically. Figure 2-17 shows the logical I/O process configuration as it would interact with an application process. Primary paths are indicated as solid lines, backup paths as dashed.

One final point should be made about hardware duality in a survivable system. Duality is fruitless if a failed device cannot be repaired and returned to service while the system is running (this led to the need of an on-line disk copy utility for mirrored files). Therefore, any piece of hardware—including processors, buses, device controllers, power supplies, even fans—must be capable of being removed, repaired, or replaced and plugged back in while power is still on the system and without inducing "glitches" in the system operation.

Software Redundancy

There are several approaches to software redundancy in contemporary distributed systems. These approaches can be classified according to the following general methods, which are discussed in the following paragraphs.

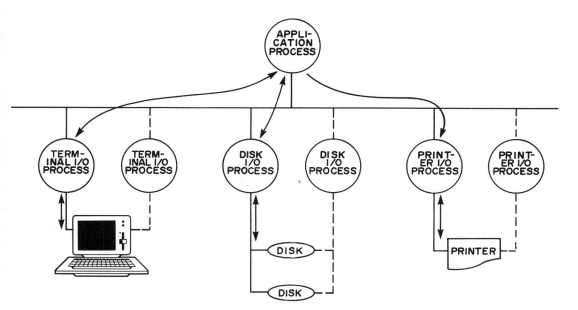

Figure 2-17   Logical dual porting.

- Transaction protection
- Synchronization
- Message queuing
- Checkpointing

Software redundancy presents different problems, depending upon whether a multiprocessor or multicomputer (including hybrid) architecture is used.

Transaction Protection

Using transaction protection, no attempt is made to keep a backup process updated. Rather, each transaction is logged to disk in a set of audit files in such a way that transactions that were in progress at the time of failure can be backed out of the system. The user is then requested to reenter that transaction. In this case, the failure is not transparent to the user, though its impact is minimal and usually acceptable. However, recovery may take several minutes as the audit files are played back and the data files corrected.

Transaction protection is used extensively by multiprocessor systems, as it must be assumed that a fault has contaminated memory and that no other recovery mechanism is available. It is also used in certain multicomputer system offerings and in many single computer systems for which it is the only means of recovery.

Note that backup processes are unnecessary if transaction protection is used as the fault-recovery strategy since they need not be kept up-to-date anyway. Should a fault occur in a processor, the system will reconstruct its data base via the audit files and then recreate the failed processes in a surviving processor before restarting the system. In fact, in a true load-sharing multiprocessor system, the concept of a backup process is meaningless, since the process is represented by control structures (the Process Control Block, for instance), a code area, and a data area in common memory. It survives even if a processor fails and needs to be recreated only if a memory partition failure destroys some control information pertinent to that process.

The transaction-protection procedure developed by the former Synapse Corporation of Milpitas, California, for their multiprocessor system is a very good example of this technique. Basically, all changes to files are logged in separate audit files as transactions are processed. In the event of failure, the system is paused, and all files are returned to a previously established "consistency point," which ensures the integrity of the data base. Transactions that have been completed following the consistency point are "rolled forward" from the log, or recompleted. Transactions that have not been completed are "rolled backward," or deleted. The system is then restarted, and uncompleted transactions must be reentered.

Figure 2-18 shows the auditing activities that Synapse used in order to reconstruct its data base following a system fault. All changed data are written to two logs: the history log and the temporary log. The history log contains all before and after record images of changed data. These records must be physically written to the history log before a trans-

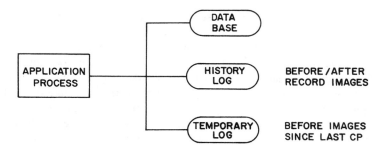

LOGGING

- HISTORY LOG

     BEFORE/AFTER RECORD IMAGES

     PHYSICAL DISC WRITE GUARANTEED AT COMMIT TIME

          BEFORE PROCESS CAN PROCEED

- TEMPORARY LOG

     BEFORE IMAGES OF CHANGED DATA

     NO DATA CAN BE PHYSICALLY WRITTEN UNTIL

          TEMPORARY LOG IS WRITTEN

- CONSISTENCY POINT (CP)

     EVERY FEW (2) MINUTES-USER SPECIFIED

     HISTORY LOG WRITTEN TO DISC

     TEMPORARY LOG DATA DELETED

     ALL CHANGED DATA WRITTEN TO DISC

Figure 2-18   Logging.

action is considered to be complete (i.e., is "committed"). Therefore, at transaction commit time, the user is briefly paused until all of the changed data is written to the history log.

The temporary log contains only before images of changed data. No data can be written to a data-base file until the before image has been physically written to the temporary log.

Periodically (typically every two minutes), the entire system pauses to establish a consistency point (CP). At this point, all pending data are written to the history log, the contents of the temporary log are deleted, and all changed data are written to the appropriate data-base files. At the consistency point, the entire set of application processes are correctly represented on disk. All that is required in the event of a failure is to restore the system to this consistency point, redo transactions since completed, and restart the users. This recovery process is done via the history and temporary logs.

Since the temporary log was cleared at CP time and contains only the before images of any data-base changes since that time, the data base is rolled back to its CP state via the temporary log. The history log is then used to replay transaction activity, as shown in Figure 2-19. There are seven possible transaction scenarios, as shown. Transactions that started before the consistency point but never completed before the time of failure or that were aborted (rolled back) per an operator request following the consistency point are rolled back (types 1 and 2). A transaction that started before the consistency point and successfully completed before the failure is reconstructed by rolling forward from the history log (type 3). Transactions that started after the consistency point and either didn't complete (type 4) or were rolled back at the request of the user (type 5) are ignored. Transactions that started after the consistency point and that completed prior to the failure are reconstructed by rolling forward from the history log (type 6). No action is required for any transaction that completed before the consistency point (type 7).

RECOVERY

– REESTABLISH SYSTEM AT CP VIA TEMPORARY LOG

– RECONSTRUCT SUBSEQUENT ACTIVITY VIA HISTORY LOG
     INCLUDING ROLLBACKS

– ROLLBACK INCOMPLETED TRANSACTIONS VIA HISTORY LOG

– RESULT
     ROLLBACK TYPES 1,2
     ROLLFORWARD TYPES 3,6
     IGNORE TYPES 4,5,7

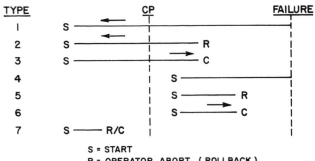

S = START
R = OPERATOR ABORT (ROLLBACK)
C = COMPLETED TRANSACTION

Figure 2-19 Recovery

This procedure recovers, via software, activity on a transaction basis. If a failure should occur, the user may see a delay measured as a few minutes and may be asked to reenter information that already had been entered. Beyond this, the procedure ensures full data integrity of the data base and continued operation of the system.

Synchronization

In a synchronizing system, every process is replicated in a different processor. All processes execute, i.e., they all process the transaction and periodically compare results. This synchronizing point is usually an operating system function and may typically occur at I/O request points or completion points. Figure 2-20a shows a dually-redundant synchronizing system. When one process is ready to synchronize, it will wait for the other process to catch up and itself be ready for synchronization. Certain interprocess checks are made, and if everything compares, the processes proceed. If there is an error, diagnostic procedures are invoked to determine the faulty process, after which the surviving process continues with the transaction (after, perhaps, creating another backup process to maintain survivability).

One way to provide diagnostic checking to determine the identity of the failed processor is to have more than two processors (say, three or four) involved in the transaction. If there is then a failure, a simple vote of all processors will determine the culprit (assuming only single-point failures). Such voting systems (Figure 2-20b) are used for ultrahigh-reliability requirements such as the space program. August Systems (Salem, Oregon) offers a triplexed voting system for process control applications (such as nuclear power plants), in which the concept of voting is even applied to the digital and analog inputs and outputs of the system (for analog signals, the median signal is taken).

An important example of a synchronizing system is the product introduced by Stratus (Marlboro, Massachusetts). This system is a quadraplexed voting system in which synchronizing is done by hardware at the system clock frequency (typically several times per microsecond). The four processors are grouped as pairs of dual processors (Figure 2-20c), with all four executing in "lock step," i.e., all doing exactly the same operation at each system clock time. If one processor fails, it will not agree with its companion, and both are taken out of service. The other pair continues unaffected. This is the only method to date that requires no software support whatsoever (except, of course, to diagnose the problem).

A modified approach that is somewhat similar to that developed by Stratus is taken by ATT in its 3B20D product (Figure 2-20d). This is a dual computer system in which one operates while the other provides a hot standby. As data areas in memory are modified in the primary system, a hardware link updates those areas in the memory of the standby system. Should the primary fail, the standby uses the process control blocks (which, of course, are part of the memory-resident data that was kept updated) to load the active processes and to continue execution. One might also consider this system as a class of checkpointing systems, described later.

Note that all synchronizing systems require at least two processors to do the job of one. However, recovery is virtually instantaneous.

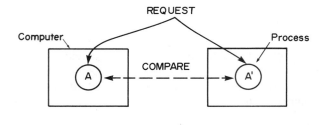

DUAL SYNCHRONIZATION
(a)

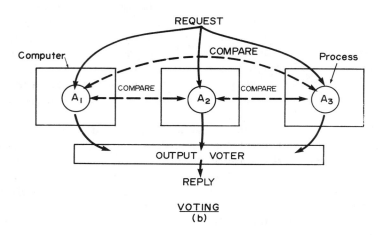

VOTING
(b)

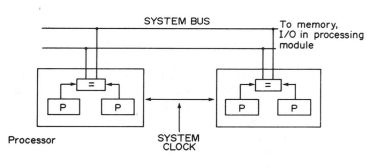

LOCK STEP
(c)

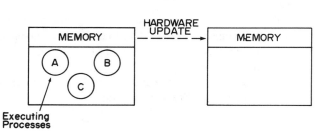

MEMORY UPDATE
(d)

Figure 2-20 Synchronizing systems.

Backup Processes

Transaction recovery, as described above, requires no backup process. If there is a failure, failed processes are recreated in a surviving computer, incomplete transactions are backed out, and the user reenters the last request if it had not been completed. This procedure could take several minutes.

Synchronizing systems require two or more fully active processors executing in parallel but give nearly instantaneous recovery. Thus, these two approaches represent the extremes of the cost-performance tradeoff: minimal hardware and long recovery times (transaction recovery) versus maximum hardware and almost instantaneous recovery times (synchronization).

The software redundancy techniques to be discussed next—message queuing and checkpointing—are aimed at getting near-instantaneous (i.e., seconds) recovery while using little additional processing power to keep the backup process (which is dormant) updated.

Before describing these methods, we must first discuss the mechanism for creating and managing the backup process.

Just as each hardware unit must have a backup, so must each software unit, or process. Should the computer in which a process is running fail, then that process will cease to exist (and the capabilities it provides will be lost to the user) unless a spare process can be ''switched in.''

This requires two capabilities of the process:

- It must be able to create a backup copy of itself in another computer whenever it is created or has taken over from a failed process.
- It must be able to keep its backup informed of what it is currently doing (for instance, what transaction it is currently working on) so that the backup can continue its work uninterrupted should the primary process fail.

Let us first consider the creation and management of the backup process. Assume that process A has been created. One of the first things process A does is to request the operating system to create a backup copy of itself in another computer. We will call this backup process A'. It has the same name as process A but is created by and runs in a different computer. A' detects that it is the backup (because it can sense that its companion already exists) and immediately calls a monitor procedure that is responsible for monitoring the primary process and taking over in the event of primary failure. The monitor procedure is provided by the operating system.

Just as the operating system must know of process A so that it can route interprocess messages to it, so must it know about process A'. As we discussed earlier, it knows about process A and all other processes in the system via the process directory, a copy of which is maintained in each physical processor. Let us now extend the concept of the process directory to what we will call the *process pair directory* (PPD). The PPD contains the name of each process, the computer in which the primary is running, and the computer in which the backup, if any, is running. Figure 2-21 shows a part of a typical PPD.

PROCESS NAME	PRIMARY PROCESSOR	BACKUP PROCESSOR
INQUIRE	3	2
MAINT	2	
REPORTA	4	I
•		
•		
•		

Figure 2-21   Process pair directory.

As process A is performing its duties, the operating system routes all interprocess messages destined for process A to it. However, should process A fail (most likely because of a processor failure but possibly because of a software fault that causes the operating system to abort process A), the operating system will look in the PPD and find that process A, in fact, has a backup. It will send process A' what appears to be an interprocess message indicating that process A has failed and the reason for its failure (processor failure, abort, or whatever). This causes the operating system in the process A' computer to schedule process A' (i.e., put it on the ready list). Further interprocess messages for process A are now routed to process A' for processing, and the system survives. At this point, process A' may create its own backup to protect itself from further failure.

Figure 2-22 shows a typical life of a process in the presence of a computer failure. A three-computer system is shown in which process A is created in computer 1. It creates its backup, A', in computer 2. Later, computer 1 fails; and process A' takes over, creating its backup, A'', in computer 3. Subsequently, computer 1 is repaired. The system could be left as is. However, in this case, it is desired to reestablish load balancing. Therefore, process A' stops its backup, A'', and recreates a backup A in computer 1. It then switches control to process A, resetting the system to its initial configuration.

As can be seen, a variety of strategies can be employed to ensure system survival in a degrading system. Load sharing should be an important consideration in the strategy. The illustration has shown how a process can move itself from one computer to another by creating a backup in the new computer and then switching primary/backup roles. This capability can be used to dynamically balance the load in a multicomputer system, either under operator control or under the influence of some monitoring process.

Message Queuing

Having a backup process to switch to in case the primary process fails is essential to surviving. However, if the system is to perform fuctionally in the same way it would have

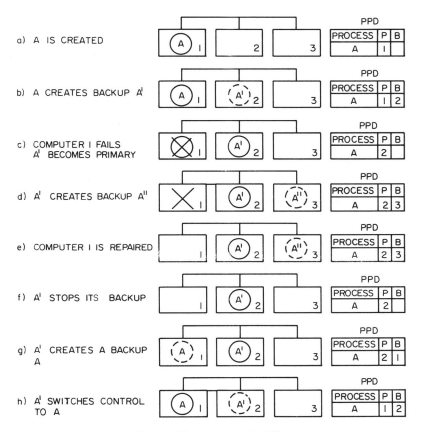

Figure 2-22   Process survivability.

had no failure occurred, the backup process must take over where the primary left off. This means it must know what the primary is doing.

One way to accomplish this is to queue all interprocess messages received by the primary process to its dormant backup so that the backup process may "catch up" if it has to take over (see Figure 2-23). Message queuing was first introduced in a distributed system by Auragen (Fort Lee, New Jersey).

The basic concept as implemented by Auragen is for a process to send each interprocess message to three destinations:

1. The primary process that is the intended destination.
2. The backup process for the intended destination process.
3. The backup process for the sending process.

Separate actions are taken by each of these receiving processes:

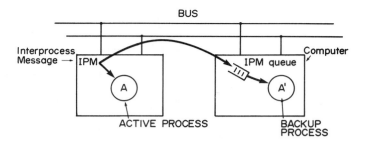

Figure 2-23   Message queuing.

- The primary destination process processes the message as is appropriate, with no consideration given to the other receiving processes.
- The backup process for the intended destination process does nothing. It simply keeps the message in its input message queue.
- The backup of the sending process notes that a message has been sent by incrementing a counter and then discards that message.

Thus, each backup process has a queue of all messages that have been received by its active counterpart and knows how many messages its active half has sent.

Should a failure terminate an active process, its backup will take over and begin doing what is natural: process its message queue. Thus, it will redo all processing that the former active process had done, resulting in a data space identical to that of the previous active process at the time of its failure. Furthermore, by using the count of messages transmitted by its other half, it will prevent the sending of duplicate messages, such as disk updates, terminal displays, etc. (This, of course, implies that the operating system guarantees that the order of messages in the backup's receive queue is precisely identical to the order of message execution by the primary process.)

One flaw in this strategy as presented so far is that the backup process's input queue will become arbitrarily long with time, thus consuming an arbitrarily large amount of storage space and requiring an arbitrarily long recovery time. This problem is solved by periodically "synchronizing" the backup process with its primary. Synchronizing in this sense is accomplished simply by forcing all dirty data pages of the primary process to disk; i.e., invoking the page fault mechanism of the processor on behalf of this process to write all modified data pages in memory to disk.

At this point, if the backup took over, it would page-in up-to-date memory. Thus, its receive queue can be deleted, and its count of messages sent can be cleared to zero.

Synchronization points are generally based on queue length or time. They typically occur every minute or so with active processes, and recovery should take a few (5 to 10) seconds. The time between synchronizing points is clearly a compromise. By making the time shorter, the page faulting load on the system increases. By making the time longer, the recovery time increases.

Though message queuing systems require software support to provide recovery from failure, this support is applications-independent and can be made a function of the operating system. Thus, as with a lock-step, synchronized system, the application programmer can be totally unconcerned with the problems of survivability.

Checkpointing

Checkpointing in the sense used here was first introduced by Tandem Computers (Cupertino, California) for use in its Non-Stop™ series of fault-tolerant systems. This type of checkpointing takes advantage of the fact that it only is necessary for the data area of the backup process to be identical with that of the primary process at certain critical points in the process's execution.

Going back to our discussion of process structure, checkpointing is done quite simply as the result of one of the characteristics of the structure of a process. A process contains a code area and a data area. The data area comprises global data and a stack that is used to nest procedures, to pass parameters between procedures, and to hold temporary data needed locally by a procedure. The state of a process is determined by the state of its data area, i.e., give two like processes (two processes with the same code area) the same data area and environment, and they will perform identical functions. Therefore, if we could somehow maintain the data area of the backup process so that it was identical to the data area of the primary process, it would behave exactly the same as if it were the primary process at the time of a primary process failure.

Unfortunately, the system load that would be imposed by constantly updating the backup's data area precludes such an approach. However, it only is necessary that the data areas be identical at certain critical points in the process's execution. For instance, if the data areas were made identical immediately following the receipt of a transaction to process, then if the primary failed after partially processing the transaction, the backup would start at the point at which the transaction was received and would reprocess it. In many applications, this would be acceptable.

The backup's data area is updated via a mechanism called *checkpointing*. This is simply an interprocess message sent by the primary process to its backup, the contents of which are the current contents of the data area. Like other interprocess messages, the receipt of this checkpoint message by the backup process causes it to be scheduled to run. As described previously, the backup process executes the monitor procedure. This procedure will receive the checkpoint message and will store it in its data area, thus updating the data area as desired. Updating the data area includes updating the stack.

Should the primary process subsequently fail, the receipt of a system-generated message describing that failure (as described previously) will cause the monitor procedure to return to the main flow of the process at the last received checkpoint. That is to say, the backup process takes over and starts executing according to the last checkpoint.

But how does the monitor know specifically which instruction it is to start executing? The program counter is not part of the data area and is therefore not sent over as part of the checkpoint message. This is handled via the last stack marker in the data area's stack. Each stack marker indicates the place at which the current procedure was called and causes the current procedure to return to the instruction following its call when it has completed. Upon the procedure's return, the stack marker also contains the processor environment to restore.

When a primary process wants to send a checkpoint message, it does so by calling an operating system procedure that takes care of actually issuing the interprocess message. Therefore, the last stack marker on the checkpointed stack was placed there as a result of the call to the checkpoint procedure by the primary process; it points to the instruction in the application program following the checkpoint call. When the monitor procedure wants to turn on the backup process, it simply executes a procedure return according to the last stack marker, i.e., the backup process will turn on at the instruction following the checkpoint call as if it were the primary process exiting the checkpoint procedure. This is illustrated in Figure 2-24.

The checkpoint procedure also returns with a status condition. This status condition normally indicates success when the primary process is running. However, if the backup process is turned on, the monitor procedure forces an error status that indicates that the primary failed and why. This allows the backup process to perform special takeover logic, should any be required.

In actual practice, it is usually unnecessary to checkpoint the entire data area. The global data often contains a large data base, whereas the stack is typically small. Since

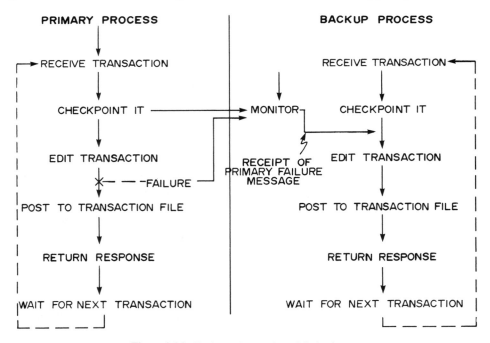

Figure 2-24 Backup takeover from failed primary.

large (multi-Kword) checkpoint messages would represent a large bus and processor load, it is advantageous to send over just that part of the data area that has changed since the last checkpoint. This often is simply certain elements of the global data plus the stack.

In some cases, it may not even be necessary to checkpoint the stack. If certain messages simply update internal parameters, it only is necessary to process the message, update those parameters, and then checkpoint the changed data. In this case, the stack is not checkpointed, so backup processing will resume at the last point at which the stack was checkpointed rather than at noncritical checkpoints.

The basic concepts of checkpointing are quite straightforward: create backup processes and keep them informed at critical processing points via checkpoint messages. Checkpointing does represent a significant system load and should not be used casually. Each checkpoint is, in effect, an interprocess message requiring several milliseconds, as discussed earlier. Checkpointing is an important consideration in performance analysis. Checkpointing strategies should be carefully thought out in terms of minimizing the number of checkpoint messages and checkpoint lengths while achieving the degree of fault transparency desired in the system.

More important, these strategies must be established as part of the design of the process. It is insufficient to implement simplex processes initially without giving thought to survivability and then worry later about where to put the checkpoints. This can lead to a process organization in which the checkpointing task burden is so large it cannot realistically be carried.

Let us explore various levels of checkpointing. As we have said, the level of checkpointing should be commensurate with the level of fault transparency desired. Consider an inquiry application in which the operator enters an inquiry, a file is searched, and data is returned to the operator. In many situations, it may be quite reasonable to ask the operator to reenter the inquiry in the rare occurrence of a system fault that has interrupted the inquiry process. No checkpointing need be done at all. Should the backup process find it has taken over, it might simply send a repeat request to all operators, not knowing which ones had active inquiries.

An even better situation than the above is one in which the terminals buffer the inquiry and pass it to the system in response to a poll. In this case, the new primary process need only poll all terminals; those with unanswered inquiries will retransmit those inquiries for reprocessing. Full fault transparency has been achieved without checkpointing.

However, if it is undesirable to request again the transaction from the operator once it has been received, the process can checkpoint it as soon as it receives it and then process the inquiry. In this case, if the process fails, the backup has the transaction and will reprocess it without having to request it again. The operator will receive a response without ever knowing there was a fault.

In this case, if a failure occurs after the system had responded to the last inquiry and before it has obtained the next one, the response to the last inquiry will be retransmitted to the operator since the transaction is being totally reprocessed. If this is undesirable, a second checkpoint is required following the return of the inquiry response.

Unfortunately, applications usually aren't this simple. Typically, a transaction is used to update a file. The simplest case of this is when the transaction is simply logged to a transaction file for later processing. In this case, all of the aforementioned strategies hold. If the operator or terminal can be requested to resubmit the transaction, no checkpointing is required. Otherwise, the transaction should be checkpointed when it is received.

In this example, a failure could cause the transaction to be logged twice. Often, the processing programs can handle the case of duplicate transactions (transactions may carry serial numbers, for instance). If this is intolerable, then (as above) the process should checkpoint following the logging of the transaction to cause the backup to pick up at this point.

Often, however, the transaction is used to perform an on-line update of a file. In this case, a record must be read, modified according to the transaction, and then rewritten. Whether or not the transaction was checkpointed when it was received, it is imperative that it and the record be checkpointed when the read of the record has been completed. Otherwise, a double update could occur (unless this is allowed).

Consider a transaction that contains a count that is to be added to a field in a record. If the transaction is simply reprocessed following a failure, it would be added again to the field if the first transaction had completed. However, by checkpointing the read record and by assuming a failure after the transaction had been completed, the backup process would continue from the point at which the read had completed. It would add the transaction count to the original field and would return the record, overwriting identical data left behind by the primary process.

So far as transaction processing is concerned, this is the case of most general interest and is shown in Figure 2-25. The first checkpoint is needed only if the transaction cannot be requested again from the user. The middle checkpoint is needed only if a double update is not allowed. This same checkpoint can be used to protect multiple updates, provided all data is read, the checkpoint is sent, and then files are updated. The last checkpoint is needed only if a repeat response cannot be tolerated.

Most processes, whether they deal with transaction processing, external event control, communication switching, or whatever, can be framed as subsets of Figure 2-25. Therefore, we can see that the usual worst case for a transaction is three checkpoints.

It is important to minimize the number of checkpoints because they create system overhead. Sometimes no checkpoints are required. It is frequently possible to design the system so that no more than one checkpoint per transaction is required. However, considerations to allow this often range throughout the system, from operating procedures (reentering a transaction) to terminals (block transmit, ignoring unexpected responses) to processing functions (detecting and ignoring duplicate transactions). Therefore, the determination of checkpoint strategies belongs in the very early stages of design and is not a candidate for afterthought.

The above discussion has concerned itself with a software mechanism for checkpointing. The ATT 3B20D, discussed earlier and shown in Figure 2-20d, can be considered a system in which checkpointing is accomplished via hardware.

As memory in the primary system is modified, a hardware checkpointing mechanism updates corresponding memory in the standby system. As opposed to the check-

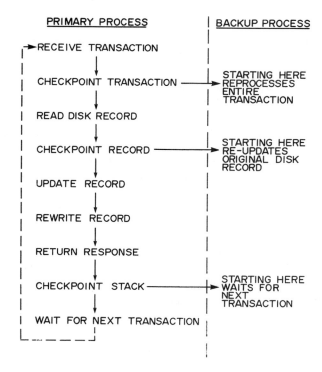

PRIMARY PROCESS | BACKUP PROCESS

RECEIVE TRANSACTION

CHECKPOINT TRANSACTION ——→ STARTING HERE REPROCESSES ENTIRE TRANSACTION

READ DISK RECORD

CHECKPOINT RECORD ——→ STARTING HERE RE-UPDATES ORIGINAL DISK RECORD

UPDATE RECORD

REWRITE RECORD

RETURN RESPONSE

CHECKPOINT STACK ——→ STARTING HERE WAITS FOR NEXT TRANSACTION

WAIT FOR NEXT TRANSACTION

Figure 2-25   General transaction checkpointing.

pointing technique described above, however, this hardware approach requires that the memory contents of both the primary and standby systems be identical. Therefore, both systems must be dedicated to the same tasks; in this sense, the ATT system is more akin to a synchronizing system.

SOFTWARE ARCHITECTURE

The performance of a TP system is only partly determined by its hardware configuration. The impact of the software is usually even more crucial. This impact ranges from the efficiency with which programs are written to language considerations, operating system characteristics, and application software architecture.

Bottlenecks

In almost every TP system, there is a software bottleneck somewhere that may limit ultimate system capacity no matter how much hardware is added.

The most common bottleneck is the data-base manager. Since it must coordinate the activity of many application processes that wish to access the data base simultaneously, all data-base requests must be funneled through it. This is largely because of the problem of simultaneous updates to a record. Let us say that process A and process B both want to read a record and perhaps update it. For both to read the record is no problem. But now let us assume that both modify the record and want to rewrite it. If process A is the first to rewrite its record, then the updated record submitted by process B will overwrite process A's changes, which are now lost.

By funnelling all requests through a common data-base manager, mechanisms can be established to prevent such conflicts. Typically, a process that wishes to update a record will request that record (or file, or field within a record, depending upon the system) be locked and thus be made unavailable to any other process desiring to modify that record until it has been updated by the requesting process (it is, however, usually available for reading by other processes). If another process makes a request to lock this record while it is locked by another record, the new request is either rejected or the requesting process is placed in a queue for that record.

In some systems, multiple data-base manager paths are provided to minimize the data-base bottleneck effect. This can be done sometimes by segregating unrelated files or, alternatively, by segregating unrelated operations (open/closes versus read/writes, for instance).

Another bottleneck that can exist is a common log. If, for instance, all system actions must be logged to a common log file or printer, that log becomes a bottleneck. The audit files required for transaction recovery, described earlier, are a good example of such a potential bottleneck.

Requestor-Server

One common software architecture that is found in many TP systems is the requestor-server model, shown in Figure 2-26. In this model architecture, requestor processes each service one or more user terminals. When a requestor receives a request from a user, it evaluates the request and passes it to an appropriate server process that is designed to handle that request type. Figure 2-26, being very simplistic, shows two types of servers: one for handling inquiries and one for handling updates.

A server will do whatever it has to do to satisfy the request. This usually involves interacting with the data-base manager to gain access to—or update—data in the data base. It then formulates a reply and returns it to the user via its requestor process.

Dynamic Servers

Requestor processes are permanently created and assigned to support a fixed set of user terminals. However, server processes are often dynamically allocated according to the load on the system. For instance, let us assume that the volume of updates becomes very high in the afternoon. Seeing that queues of waiting update requests are beginning to form, thus slowing down response time (i.e., the system is beginning to appear sluggish to the user), the system will spawn additional update server processes and will spread the waiting transactions over them to achieve a degree of parallel processing.

If this is a distributed system, new servers can be created in the least-heavily loaded computers. If the system has multiple disk spindles, system performance might be nearly

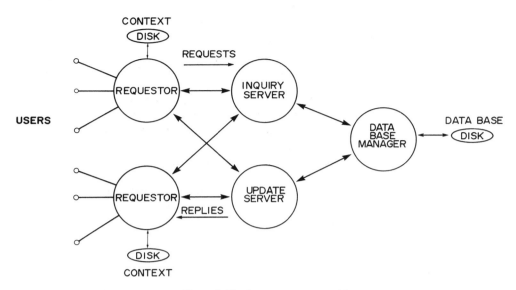

Figure 2-26   Requestor-server model.

proportional to the number of servers up to the point, at least, that all servers are being kept busy. Of course, the disk system will ultimately be a bottleneck, limiting system performance.

As the load on a particular server class diminishes, servers are killed off until only one remains. A common queue may be maintained for all servers in a class, with the next server that becomes free getting the next request; or each server may have its own queue, with requests being distributed to the servers according to some algorithm (round robin, or to the shortest queue, for instance).

Note that an important characteristic of the requestor-server model has a significant design impact. Since there can be multiple servers in a class, there is no guarantee that a request will be routed to a particular server. Many transactions comprise a sequence of request/reply interactions with the operator, with the next request depending upon information from the previous reply. This information is termed the *context* of the request, i.e., it is the context in which the request is to be interpreted. This context is not logically required to be carried in the request; in principal, at least, it is known to the system.

For instance, let us assume that the user has asked to see billing information for a particular customer and that, as part of that request, has supplied a customer number. However, there is more reply information than can fit on the screen, so a partial reply is returned. To see the next "page" of this information, the user should be able simply to send a "next" message, as the system knows which function (billing inquiry, in this case) is being exercised on which customer and which of many pages is currently being viewed. This continuing information—the function, the customer, and the page—is the context of the user's next request.

But where can this context be kept? Not in the server, because it is not known in advance which server within a class will get the next request. It can be maintained in the requestor; but perhaps the requestor services many terminals. Moreover, if the context data size is large for the worst-case request, large amounts of memory may be required for a requestor to store context. So much, in fact, that it may have to keep context areas on disk (as shown in Figure 2-26). And these extra disk accesses are going to have an impact on system performance.

Therefore, an element of good TP design is to minimize request context. One excellent way in today's art is through the use of intelligent terminals, which can store the context at the user's site. Then the context can simply be added to each request as that request is sent to the TP system.

Of course, this compounds another in the ongoing saga of performance issues: communication-line loading. So we see that achieving optimum performance is an unending search for best compromises. How could we ever do that effectively without performance modeling? The answer is simple—we don't!

In the next chapter, we introduce the basic concepts of performance modeling. This will set the stage for the more detailed discussions to follow.

3

Performance Modeling

The degradation of performance as a TP system gets busier is caused by two related factors: queues and bottlenecks. Queues of transactions awaiting service will form in a busy TP system for each shared resource. As the system becomes busier, these queues will get longer, causing processing delays and performance degradation. The system resource with the lowest capacity will limit the ultimate throughput of the system and is the system's bottleneck.

The primary role of a *performance model* is simply to identify the queues and bottlenecks in a system and to evaluate their impact on system performance. The system designers will then know what to expect from the system and which areas within the system provide the most fertile opportunities for performance enhancement.

In this chapter, we explore the characteristics of queues and bottlenecks, with a simple yet realistic and complete performance analysis. As noted in the Introduction, a thorough understanding of the contents of this chapter provides the system analyst not otherwise interested in becoming a performance "specialist" with the tools necessary for elementary performance analysis.

BOTTLENECKS

A bottleneck is nothing more than a common system resource that can run out of capacity before other common system resources do. Any common resource within the TP system is a candidate for a bottleneck. The disk is the most common bottleneck in TP systems; but given enough disk spindles to provide multiple access paths in order to spread data uniformly (in terms of access requirements) over the disks, this bottleneck can be broken. The processor (or processors) might run out of capacity before the disks and thus become the bottleneck.

Or memory could be the bottleneck if there is not enough to provide common data structures (such as I/O buffers) or if there is not enough to accommodate the bulk of process memory requirements. This leads to excessive overlay swapping or page faulting.

The bus that connects multiple processors or computers in a distributed system can be a bottleneck, as can communication lines when many user terminals share a common line (multidropped lines or local area networks).

Finally, processes themselves can become the bottleneck. This is often true of the data-base manager, since data-base consistency requirements often preclude multiple instantiations of the data-base manager. Log servers and other nondynamic server processes are other examples of a potential process bottleneck, as discussed in the previous chapter.

Sometimes, a bottleneck is built into the system unintentionally. More than one designer has brought a system to its knees by deciding to log unsuccessful transactions on the console printer for operator action. If the printer is a 30-character-per-second printer, and if the failed transaction requires 300 characters to describe it, it will take 10 seconds to print. Let us say that the TP system was designed to handle 50 transactions per second— or 500 in 10 seconds. If only 0.2% of all transactions are unsuccessful, the console printer becomes the bottleneck!

QUEUES

Queues are much more exciting than bottlenecks. However, we wouldn't have queues if we didn't have bottlenecks, for a queue is simply a line of requests for service by a common system resource that, of course, is a candidate for a bottleneck. In fact, the closer it is to being a system bottleneck, the longer in general will be the queue waiting for it.

Some system resources don't provide a queuing capability. Our infamous console printer could be an example of that if each process wanting to print a message has to seize it, print its message, and then release it. If the console printer has already been seized, then the process must back off and try again later. In this case, transactions back up in the queues of the requesting processes, providing they support queues of awaiting transactions, or back up to previous queues, or eventually even to the user.

Of course, the console printer syndrome can be cured by providing a console process that drives the printer. Other processes will send their messages to the queue of the console process, which will then leisurely print them without holding up the other processes.

A more critical situation is characteristic of common memory. If the common memory subsystem of a multiprocessor system does not provide queuing, there is no way for software to provide it because of the very high-speed nature of this subsystem. In fact, by definition, memory speed must be comparable to the instruction execution speed of the processors that it supports, since it is one of the limiting factors in execution speeds. Therefore, some processors contending for common memory will have to back off and wait while the current processor is being serviced.

Some common memory systems do provide a queue implemented via hardware buffers. Sophisticated processors with look-ahead capability can anticipate their data and instruction needs and can therefore queue memory requests while they continue processing. Of course, being a very high-speed and expensive buffer, the common memory queue is usually very short. Once filled, processors will have to wait as if there were no queue.

We have now seen three simple classes of queues: none, limited size, and infinite (at least practically so). Queues are explored in great depth in the next chapter, where it is seen that maximum queue length is only one of several attributes characterizing the behavior of a queue.

The time required for processing by a common resource is the sum of two component times: the time spent waiting in the queue and the time spent actually being serviced. These are called the *wait time* and the *service time,* respectively. The sum of these two times is called the *delay time,* i.e., the time that the transaction is delayed due to a service requirement by that resource:

$$\text{Delay Time} = \text{Wait Time} + \text{Service Time}.$$

For a large class of queuing situations (randomly distributed arrivals and service times in a steady-state system), the delay time is given by (see chapter 4):

$$\text{Delay} = \frac{T}{1 - L}. \tag{3-1}$$

Here T is the average service time of the resource (or the *server* as it is called in queuing theory, not to be confused with the use of *server* in the requestor-server model, which is also a server in the queuing sense. Oh, well!). L is the load imposed on the resource (the proportion of time that it is busy). L is also called the occupancy of the server. The term $\frac{1}{1-L}$ can be thought of as a "stretching factor." It stretches out the service time of the resource as the load on that resource increases to account for the queue waiting time. In fact, the service time is stretched without bound, i.e., the queue grows arbitrarily large as the load approaches 100% ($L=1$).

THE RELATIONSHIP OF QUEUES TO BOTTLENECKS

We can illustrate the relationship between bottlenecks and queues with a simple example. Assume that a request requires six process dispatches to service: once for the requestor process to receive the request, once for the server process to receive it, once for the data-base manager to receive it and to initiate a disk request, and once for each of the above processes to receive and return the reply. Notice that this request also requires one disk access. Further assume that there are several requestor and server processes handling a volume of like transactions, each vying with the others for access to the data-base manager and each competing with the other and with the data-base manager for the use of the processor.

Using equation 3–1, we can predict the performance of this system. Let t_p be the average processing time required for a process dispatch, t_d be the average disk access time, and R be the total system transaction rate. Then the load on the processor is $6Rt_p$, and the load on the disk is Rt_d. Since the total response time that the operator will see is the sum of the processor and disk delays (since each step must be performed in series, one after the other), we can use equation 3–1 to write

$$\text{Response time} = \frac{6t_p}{1 - 6Rt_p} + \frac{t_d}{1 - Rt_d}. \tag{3-2}$$

This expression shows the process waiting in line and being serviced six times by the processor and being serviced once by the disk.[1]

Let's put some numbers into this equation and plot the results. We will consider two cases. For case 1, let the average processing time required for each process dispatch, t_p, be five milliseconds (msec); and let the disk access time, t_d, be 50 msec. Response time as a function of system load, R, is plotted in Figure 3–1a for this case, along with the component delay times for the processor and disk. Note that the disk capacity is 20 transactions per second (1/.05 seconds) and that the processor capacity is 33.3 transactions per minute (1/(6 × .005) seconds). Thus, the disk is the bottleneck; and the response-time curve reflects this.

Now let us double the processing time to 10 msec. The resulting response-time curves are shown in Figure 3–1b. The processor now becomes the bottleneck, with a capacity of 16.7 transactions per second, as compared to 20 for the disk.

As the system load approaches the bottleneck capacity, the response time grows quite large. In fact, note that at around 60% of system capacity (12 and 10 transactions per second, respectively), the response time increases dramatically with small increases in volume. This is the point at which users may really become frustrated and which emphasizes a basic rule in the design of real-time systems: never load a component to more than 60% to 70% of its capacity. Unfortunately, the use of this rule is often the sole attempt at performance analysis.

PERFORMANCE MEASURES

Before we can get seriously into performance modeling, we must first come to agreement on what we are measuring. Since TP systems are interactive, and since the most common user complaint is system sluggishness, it seems reasonable that response time be our

---

[1]In this example, queues building at the data-base manager and the processes are ignored to simplify the calculations. The resulting concepts at this point are more important than is the proper modeling technique, which will be refined shortly.

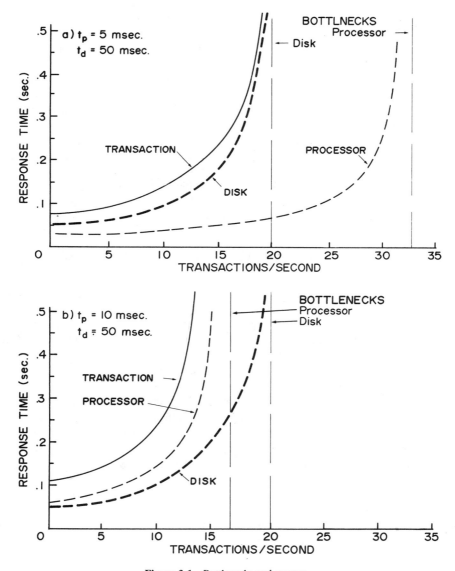

Figure 3-1 Bottlenecks and queues.

primary candidate. We have already explored the concept of response time in some detail in the previous section.

However, response time comes in many varieties. What we have described so far is the *average,* or mean, response time. In Figure 3–1a, for a load of 10 transactions per second, the average response time is .143 seconds.

In many cases, the system operator's concern is not with the average customer but with the irate customer. Therefore, the operator wants to specify a maximum response time—let's say of two seconds—that ensures a level of performance that may keep everybody happy.

Unfortunately, the specification of an absolute cap on response time is quite unreasonable, because the worst-case response time will occur only for the very unlikely (in fact, nearly impossible) case of simultaneous receipt of transactions from all users. For instance, assume for the case of Figure 3–1a that there are 600 customers using the system. If, on the average, each generated a transaction once a minute during peak activity, the average transaction load on the system would be 10 transactions per second, giving an average response time of 143 msec. A pretty swift system.

Nevertheless, the worst case would indeed occur if all transactions arrived simultaneously. Then, since the disk would be the bottleneck and would process only 20 transactions per second, the last transaction would be completed in 30 seconds. Pretty horrible. And also very unrealistic. Taken to its conclusion, only 40 users could be supported and still guarantee a maximum response time of two seconds.

A more realistic statement would be to say "99.99% of all transactons will finish in less than two seconds," or some equivalent statement. This still would leave an occasional irate customer, but the level of hassling could certainly be controlled (1 out of 10,000 may not be too bad).

To achieve the level of performance described in that statement, not only do we need to know the average value of response time, but we also need to know its distribution. We must be able to state that with probability p, all responses will be received in less than t seconds, whatever p and t are specified to be. This, then, is the second performance measure (average response time being the first).

Analyzing the distribution of response time is a much more difficult problem than estimating its mean and is solved for only a few cases. Fortunately, for the general case, there is an elegant and simple approximate solution that we will often use. For many of the queues we will analyze, one can make the statement that 95% of all response times will be less than three times the average response time, 99% will be less than five times the average, 99.9% will be less than seven times the average, and 99.99% of all responses will be less than nine times the average. (These statements are based on the Gamma function, which is explored further in chapter 4).

Thus, to achieve a level of performance such that 99.99% of all response times will be less than two seconds requires an average response time of no more than $\frac{2}{9}$ = .22 seconds. From Figure 3–1a, this allows a transaction rate of 15 transactions per second. The difference between 99.99% and 100% satisfaction is the difference between 40 users and 900 users! Lesson: Turn a deaf ear to absolute maxima.

We have, incidentally, just introduced the third performance measure: *capacity*. As we have seen, the capacity of a TP system is the sustained transaction rate that produces the maximum acceptable response time, whether that response time is stated as a mean response time or as the probability that a response time will not exceed a certain limit.

In summary, the performance measures with which we will be concerned are the following:

- *Mean response time*. The average response time to a transaction seen by a user, taken as a function of system load.
- *Maximum response time*. That time such that a specified proportion of all responses will occur in less time, also taken as a function of system load.
- *Capacity*. Measured in terms of system load, that which results in the minimum acceptable performance as specified by a response-time requirement.

THE ANALYSIS

A proper performance analysis comprises many parts:

1. A *system description* of the TP system to be modeled.
2. A *scenario model* that describes the characteristics of the transaction load being placed on the TP system.
3. A *traffic model* that describes the flow of data through the system.
4. A *performance model document* recording for posterity the above three items.
5. A *performance model program* that implements the equations of the model if they are too complex for manual calculation.
6. *Result memoranda* that give results of the model's predictions as "what if" games are played with it.

Items 1, 4, and 6 (system description, performance model document, and result memoranda) are discussed in the summary chapters 10 and 11. Item 5, the program, is not a topic for this book; the need for it is mentioned only in passing, though it is briefly considered in chapter 10.

However, items 2 and 3, the scenario model and the traffic model, represent the bulk of the performance analyst's work and will be introduced here. First, the scenario model.

Scenario Model

The scenario model deals with characterizing the transaction load being placed on the system by the users. There is nothing very complicated about it—it is really just a case of bean counting—but it can be a very large (and admittedly dull) task at times.

The scenario model identifies every transaction that will be offered to the system and characterizes the transaction's use of resources: communication message lengths, disk accesses, processing requirements, and other special requirements. It also establishes the probability of each transaction occurring.

Using these probabilities, the load on each resource imposed by an "average transaction" can then be calculated by summing the products of each probability and the use of that resource.

Sometimes we cheat and don't take all transactions into consideration. It may be that 3 transaction types account for 95% of the load and 30 transaction types account for 5% of the load. In this case, it is perfectly reasonable to consider only the 3 types and add 5% to their imposed load to make up the difference. At other times, we're not so lucky and must account for many, many transaction types.

As an example, let's play lucky. Let us assume that there are only two types of transactions: an inquiry and an update. Each has its own unique request- and reply-message formats and undergoes similar processing in a requestor-server environment, except that inquiries are processed by the inquiry server and updates by the update server. Inquiries require a single disk read, and updates require a read to fetch the record to be updated and a write to return the updated record. Thirty-five percent of all transactions are inquiries, and 65% are updates.

Our scenario model can then be summarized in the following table, with values added for processing times and for communication line message lengths:

TABLE 3-1. SCENARIO MODEL

Transaction	Probability	Message size (bytes)		Disk accesses	Server time (msec)
		Request	Reply		
Inquiry	.35	20	400	1	10
Update	.65	200	15	2	15

In many cases, the values in this table will be expressions. For instance, the number of disk accesses required for a cashing transaction in a wagering system may be a function of the number of bets on a ticket. The size of a communication request message for an insert transaction in a word-processing system may be a function of the size of the insert, and so forth. In the example performance model report presented in chapter 11, the scenario table is quite complex. The above example is, of course, quite simple.

Traffic Model

The traffic model is the fun of performance modeling. It is the characterization of the flow of requests and replies (the system traffic) through the system. Every step that may have an impact on performance should be included, as we do not want to judge *a priori* what is important and what is not. Let the results of the model tell us that.

It is often helpful to draw a traffic diagram. This diagram is only a tool; it is not intended to be rigorous. Only three symbols are needed, but feel free to invent additional ones if they will help you organize your thoughts. The three symbols are

1. A processing step, typically representing a process or a disk access. The step is described in the box, and a service-time expression is provided.

2. A message path, such as a communication line or an interprocess message. As with a processing step, the path is identified, and a service-time expression is given.

3. A queue. If the queue has a maximum size, it is shown. A queue-length expression is also shown.

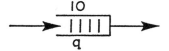

The traffic diagram is structured to show in the processing of a transaction each step that is significant relative to performance. It is often helpful to number the steps so that the diagram may be easily described (part of good documentation that will be stressed in chapter 10). For some systems, multiple traffic diagrams may be required to characterize different classes of transactions if their processing sequences are significantly different.

The average response time can then be expressed as the sum of the response times of the component processing and message paths plus the time spent in the various queues.

As an example of a traffic model, let us consider a variation on the requestor-server system described in chapter 2 and as illustrated in Figure 3-2. Requests are received by a request handler process and routed to one of two servers: an inquiry server dedicated to handling inquiries and an update server dedicated to handling updates. Each issues its own data-base directives to the data-base manager, as described in the scenario of the

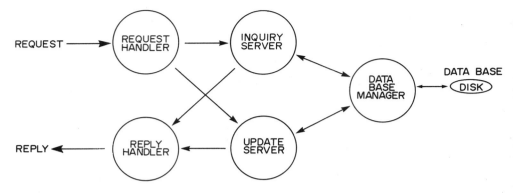

Figure 3-2 A TP system.

previous section, i.e., the inquiry server will request the read of a record; the update server will request a read followed by a write of the updated record. Servers are single-threaded. Each processes only one transaction at a time.

Each server formulates a reply to the user when it has finished processing the transaction and returns that reply via the reply handler. Replies to inquiries contain the requested data; replies to updates contain a completion status.

Communication-line message sizes, server processing times, and the distribution of transaction types are given in Table 3-1 (the scenario model developed in the previous section).

User terminals are connected to the system via point-to-point 9600-baud (960 bytes per second) asynchronous communication lines (one terminal per line). All I/O is done by the request/reply handlers for communications and by the data-base manager for disk; there are no separate I/O processes. All processes run at the same priority, and interrupt processing can be ignored.

A traffic model for this system is shown in Figure 3-3. Referring to the numbered steps in parentheses on that diagram, we find a request being transmitted from the user terminal over the communication line (1), requiring a time, t_{ci}. This request is received by the request handler process (2), which requires a processing time of t_{ri} before passing the request via an interprocess message (3) to the queue of the appropriate server (4). Interprocess messages require a time, t_{ipm}, and the servers (5) require t_{si} time to totally process an inquiry request and send back its reply and t_{su} time to provide similar service for an update request. Average queue lengths for the inquiry server and update server are q_i and q_u, respectively. (Note the symbology difficulty in the use of the subscript i to mean *input* as in t_{ci} and t_{ri} and *inquiry* as in q_i and t_{si}. This problem is compounded in larger models but is a hazard of the profession. Clear and unambiguous definition is the only solution.)

The server must make an average of n_d disk calls to process a transaction. For the inquiry server, $n_d = 1$ (one read) and $n_d = 2$ for the update server (a read followed by a write in order to update the record). Each requires an interprocess message (6) to send a request to the data-base manager's queue (7), which averages q_b items in length. The

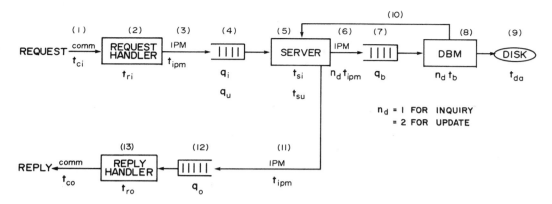

Figure 3-3 Traffic model.

data-base manager (8) requires a processing time of t_b to service each request plus a disk access time (9) of t_{da}. Note that there is no queue for the disk, as its only user is the data-base manager, which itself provides a queue for its users.

The return of the disk data (for a read) or status (for a write) (10) to the inquiry server or update server is time-free, as it is the READ portion of the original WRITEREAD interprocess message which sent the request to the data-base manager and is therefore included in the original message time. Disk responses do not queue for the server, since each server is single-threaded and is waiting for the response.

When the server has finished processing the request and has formulated a reply, it sends that reply via an interprocess message (11) to the reply handler queue (12), which averages q_o replies in length. The reply handler then returns the reply to the user (13), requiring a processing time of t_{ro} and a communication time of t_{co}.

What is your intuitive feel for the capacity of this system? What is the predominant bottleneck? Let's see how good your guess is.

Performance Model

We can now express response time as a function of load, using no more mathematics than that of equation 3-1 and no more system knowledge than that given in chapter 2. The only subtlety is the effective service time of the processes, since they all compete for a common processor. This is dealt with below.

To lend a bit of organization to the development of the model, we modularize it into bite-size components and work topdown (not unlike good structured programs). The modules are defined as follows:

T_c = communications line component of response time (seconds).

T_i = request handler component of response time (seconds).

T_s = server component of response time, including the data-base manager time (seconds).

T_o = reply handler component of response time (seconds).

Then,

$$T = T_c + T_i + T_s + T_o \qquad (3\text{-}3)$$

is the system response time, where

$$T = \text{system response time (seconds).}$$

Communications.   Since there is no sharing of communication lines (they are point-to-point lines), there are no line queues. Communication time is fixed.
Let

s = communication line speed (bytes per second),

m_{ii} = inquiry request message size (bytes),

m_{io} = inquiry reply message size (bytes),

m_{ui} = update request message size (bytes),

m_{uo} = update reply message size (bytes),

p_i = probability of an inquiry transaction,

p_u = probability of an update transaction.

Of course, $p_i + p_u = 1$.

Then the total communication traffic for an inquiry is $(m_{ii} + m_{io})$ bytes and for an update is $(m_{ui} + m_{uo})$ bytes. The average message length is the sum of these weighted by their probability of occurrence. Thus, the average transaction time contributed by the communication line, T_c, is

$$T_c = [p_i(m_{ii} + m_{io}) + p_u(m_{ui} + m_{uo})]/s \qquad (3\text{-}4)$$

Request handler.   The component of response time introduced by the request handler comprises the following items:

1. The service time for servicing the request.
2. An interprocess message time for sending the request to the server queue. (Where we put this is arbitrary. For this model, we will load interprocess message times onto the sender.)

The request handler service time must include the process dispatch time, since when the requestor is ready to service an item, it must first get in line with the other processes to wait for the processor. Once it has the processor, it completes its service before relinquishing it.
Let

$$t_d = \text{average process dispatch time (seconds).}$$

Then

$$T_i = t_{ri} + t_d + t_{ipm} \tag{3-5}$$

t_d will be evaluated later.

Server.   The server response-time component comprises the following steps:

1. A wait in the server queue.
2. The service time for processing the request and formulating the reply.
3. Interprocess message times to send data-base requests to the data-base manager queue (n_d requests per transaction).
4. The data-base manager service time for each disk request.
5. An interprocess message time to send the reply to the outgoing requestor.

Let us define the following terms:

t_{qi} = delay time for inquiry service (queue plus service time in seconds).

t_{qu} = delay time for update service in seconds.

Since the probability of these two types of transactions is p_i and p_u, respectively, the server response time component, T_s, is

$$T_s = p_i t_{qi} + p_u t_{qu} \tag{3-6}$$

By further defining

T_b = data-base manager delay time (seconds),

L_{si} = load on the inquiry server,

L_{su} = load on the update server,

we can express the response-time component for an inquiry transaction, t_{qi}, as

$$t_{qi} = \frac{t_{si} + 2t_d + T_b + 2t_{ipm}}{1 - L_{si}} \tag{3-7}$$

and for an update transaction, t_{qu}, as

$$t_{qu} = \frac{t_{su} + 3t_d + 2T_b + 3t_{ipm}}{1 - L_{su}} \tag{3-8}$$

Remember that an inquiry requires one disk access and that an update requires two disk accesses. The server process must be dispatched once upon the receipt of the request and once upon the receipt of each disk response.

The server loads are, respectively,

$$L_{si} = p_i R(t_{si} + 2t_d + T_b + 2t_{ipm}) \tag{3-9}$$

$$L_{su} = p_u R(t_{su} + 3t_d + 2T_b + 3t_{ipm}) \tag{3-10}$$

where

$$R = \text{transaction rate (transaction per second).}$$

Data-base manager.   Note that the data-base manager time, T_b, becomes a part of the server service time because it is in a closed loop with the server; that is, the server must wait for each disk request to be completed before it can go on. Thus, this time becomes part of its service time. Since the data-base manager has its own queue, the server delay time is a solution to a compound queue problem but in a straightforward and obvious way.

Letting

$$L_b = \text{data-base manager load, then the data-base manager}$$

delay time, T_b, is

$$T_b = \frac{t_b + t_d + t_{da}}{1 - L_b} \tag{3-11}$$

where

$$L_b = R(p_i + 2p_u)(t_b + t_d + t_{da}) \tag{3-12}$$

Reply handler.   Once a reply has been issued by a server, it suffers the following further delays:

1. A wait in the reply handler queue.
2. The service time for processing the reply.

Letting

$$L_o = \text{reply handler load}$$

the reply handler service time component, T_o, is

$$T_o = \frac{t_{ro} + t_d}{1 - L_o} \tag{3-13}$$

where

$$L_o = R(t_{ro} + t_d) \tag{3-14}$$

Dispatch time.   We now have expressions for all parameters based on known inputs, except for the dispatch time, t_d. This is the average time that a process must wait in the processor queue (the ready list, as described in chapter 2) before gaining access to the processor.

For each transaction, the following dispatches take place:

Process	Number of dispatches	Service time
Requestor		
Requests	1	$t_{ri} + t_{ipm}$
Replies	1	t_{ro}
Server		
Inquiries	$2p_i$	$t_{si} + 2t_{ipm}$
Updates	$3p_u$	$t_{su} + 3t_{ipm}$
Data-base manager	$p_i + 2p_u$	t_b
Total dispatches	$2 + 3p_i + 5p_u$	

From this list, one can state that the dispatch rate, r_d, is

$$r_d = R(2 + 3p_i + 5p_u) \qquad (3\text{-}15)$$

The average process time per dispatch, t_p, is calculated by summing the various process service times weighted by their probabilities of occurrence for a transaction. This probability of occurrence is the ratio of their frequencies of occurrence in a transaction to the total number of dispatches per transaction. Thus, average process time, t_p, may be expressed as

$$t_p = [t_{ri} + t_{ro} + p_i t_{si} + p_u t_{su} + (1 + p_u)t_b + (3 + p_u)t_{ipm}]/(2 + 3p_i + 5p_u). \qquad (3\text{-}16)$$

The processor load, L_p, is

$$L_p = r_d t_p \qquad (3\text{-}17)$$

Thus, average dispatch time, t_d, (the time spent waiting in the processor queue but excluding the service time) is from equation 3-1:[1]

$$t_d = \frac{t_p}{1 - L_p} - t_p = \frac{L_p}{1 - L_p}t_p \qquad (3\text{-}18)$$

Model summary.   This model is summarized in Tables 3-2 and 3-3. Table 3-2 lists all model parameters, separated into four categories:

- *Result parameter*. Those calculated parameters that are of most probable interest as a result (only T in this case).
- *Input variables*. Those parameters which are most likely to be varied to play "what if" games (only R in this case).

---

[1]A more accurate approach would calculate different dispatch times for each process by excluding the processor load of the process being evaluated. See Appendix 6 and a comparable example in Chapter 8.

TABLE 3-2. PERFORMANCE MODEL PARAMETERS

1. *Result Parameters*
   T Average transaction response time (seconds)
2. *Input Variables*
   R Average system transaction rate (transactions per second)
3. *Input Parameters*
   m_{ii} Average inquiry request message length (bytes)
   m_{io} Average inquiry reply message length (bytes)
   m_{ui} Average update request message length (bytes)
   m_{uo} Average update reply message length (bytes)
   p_i Probability of an inquiry transaction
   p_u Probability of an update transaction
   s Communication line speed (bytes per second)
   t_b Average data-base manager processing time per disk request (seconds)
   t_{da} Average disk access time (seconds)
   t_{ipm} Interprocess message time (seconds)
   t_{ri} Average request handler processing time for a request (seconds)
   t_{ro} Average reply handler processing time for a reply (seconds)
   t_{si} Average inquiry server processing time for an inquiry (seconds)
   t_{su} Average update server processing time for an update (seconds)
4. *Intermediate Parameters*
   L_b Data-base manager load
   L_o Reply handler load
   L_p Processor load
   L_{si} Inquiry server load
   L_{su} Update server load
   r_d Process dispatch rate (processes per second)
   t_d Average dispatch time (waiting time for the processor in seconds)
   t_p Average process time per dispatch (seconds)
   t_{qi} Average inquiry server delay time (seconds)
   t_{qu} Average update server delay time (seconds)
   T_b Average data-base manager delay time required to process a disk request (seconds)
   T_c Communication-line response time component (seconds)
   T_i Request handler response time component (seconds)
   T_o Reply handler response time component (seconds)
   T_s Server response time component (seconds)

- *Input parameters*. Those parameters which characterize the system and for which values are assumed for purposes of the model.
- *Intermediate parameters*. All calculated parameters except for result parameters.

Table 3-3 summarizes the equations, with equation numbers to reference back to the text. Note the top-down presentation of all parameter expressions in Table 3-3. The expression for an intermediate parameter is not presented until it appears in a previous expression. This is an invaluable aid in organizing a model and in organizing your own thought process.

Model Results

The average response time, T, as a function of the transaction load, R, is shown in Figure 3-4, using the values of input parameters largely suggested in previous sections and summarized in Table 3-4. Note the rather precipitous break in the curve—much sharper than we would expect from a $T/(1-L)$ relationship. This is usually caused by a "sleeper" in the system: a bottleneck that contributes little delay at low loads but becomes the system bottleneck at high loads. In fact, with this response-time characteristic, the system will "break" very suddenly as load is increased, and it is well to stay away from the knee of the curve.

If the system capacity is taken as four transactions per second (67% of full capacity), we are fairly safe, with an average response time of about 0.6 seconds. Note that if we

TABLE 3-3. PERFORMANCE MODEL SUMMARY

1. *Response time*

$$T = T_c + T_i + T_s + T_o \tag{3-3}$$

2. *Communications*

$$T_c = \frac{[p_i(m_{ii} + m_{io}) + p_u(m_{ui} + m_{uo})]}{s} \tag{3-4}$$

3. *Request handler*

$$T_i = t_{ri} + t_d + t_{ipm} \tag{3-5}$$

4. *Servers*

$$T_s = p_i t_{qi} + p_u t_{qu} \tag{3-6}$$

$$t_{qi} = \frac{t_{si} + 2t_d + T_b + 2t_{ipm}}{1 - L_{si}} \tag{3-7}$$

$$t_{qu} = \frac{t_{su} + 3t_d + 2T_b + 3t_{ipm}}{1 - L_{su}} \tag{3-8}$$

$$L_{si} = p_i R(t_{si} + 2t_d + T_b + 2t_{ipm}) \tag{3-9}$$

$$L_{su} = p_u R(t_{su} + 3t_d + 2T_b + 3t_{ipm}) \tag{3-10}$$

5. *Data-base manager*

$$T_b = \frac{t_b + t_d + t_{da}}{1 - L_b} \tag{3-11}$$

$$L_b = R(p_i + 2p_u)(t_b + t_d + t_{da}) \tag{3-12}$$

6. *Reply handler*

$$T_o = \frac{t_{ro} + t_d}{1 - L_o} \tag{3-13}$$

$$L_o = R(t_{ro} + t_d) \tag{3-14}$$

7. *Dispatch time*

$$t_d = \frac{L_p}{1 - L_p} t_p \tag{3-18}$$

$$L_p = r_d t_p \tag{3-17}$$

$$t_p = \frac{[t_{ri} + t_{ro} + p_i t_{si} + p_u t_{su} + (1 + p_u)t_b + (3 + p_u)t_{ipm}]}{(2 + 3p_i + 5p_u)} \tag{3-16}$$

$$r_d = R(2 + 3p_i + 5p_u) \tag{3-15}$$

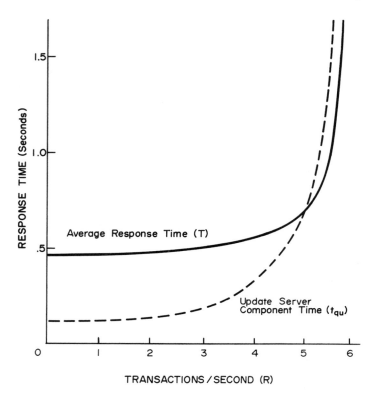

Figure 3-4   System response time.

TABLE 3-4.   INPUT PARAMETER VALUES

Parameter	Meaning	Value
m_{ii}	Inquiry request length (bytes)	20
m_{io}	Inquiry reply length (bytes)	400
m_{ui}	Update request length (bytes)	200
m_{uo}	Update reply length (bytes)	15
p_i	Probability of an inquiry	0.35
p_u	Probability of an update	0.65
s	Communication line speed (bytes per second)	960
t_b	Data-base manager processing time (seconds)	.010
t_{da}	Disk access time (seconds)	.035
t_{ipm}	Interprocess message time (seconds)	.005
t_{ri}	Request handler processing time (seconds)	.005
t_{ro}	Reply handler processing time (seconds)	.005
t_{si}	Inquiry server processing time (seconds)	.010
t_{su}	Update server processing time (seconds)	.015

should push the capacity up by 25% to 5 transactions per second, we only get a 15% increase in response time (to 0.7 seconds). However, at this point, a mere 10% increase in load gives almost a 50% increase in response time!

This fairly low capacity—four transactions per second—is not an uncommon characteristic of TP systems as a per processor measure. One to ten transactions per second per processor is the common range for contemporary systems. This emphasizes the great importance of performance analysis and its companion, performance planning.

Note that we can use the model to "peek" into the system to analyze its performance more deeply. Not only can we plot the component response times—T_c, T_i, T_s, T_o, t_{qi}, and t_{qu}—but we also can evaluate component loading—L_{si}, L_{su}, L_b, L_o, and L_p. This capability is our tool to determine where the system can best be modified to enhance its performance.

Let us apply this tool to our example system. Peeking inside will identify our "sleeper," the update server. Its response time component, t_{qu}, is also shown in Figure 3-4. It is initially hidden by the communications component, which is independent of load because of the point-to-point lines. However, it becomes the bottleneck at six transactions per second.

What can we do to enhance the system? Simply add another update server, and we have doubled the capacity of the system. No extra hardware needed. In fact, the model will show the following component loads for the single server case at a load of six transactions per second:

Inquiry server (L_{si})	0.27
Update server (L_{su})	0.94
Data-base manager (L_b)	0.49
Reply handler (L_o)	0.06
Processor (L_p)	0.35

By adding a second update server, its load is reduced from a very high load (0.94) to a reasonable load (0.47) at six transactions per second.

Since the hardware components of the system—the disk and processor—are only carrying a 35% to 50% load, significant capacity enhancement could be achieved by moving into a multiserver environment without purchasing any new hardware. The model could be changed to reflect this and could be used to predict the optimum number of servers required to balance the software with the hardware. Of course, dynamic servers, as described in chapter 2, would be self-adjusting. The performance analysis would then be directed to predict the performance of that system.

Analysis Summary

The above discussion has presented, to some extent, the content of a proper performance analysis. The system description has spanned chapter 2 and this chapter, though this description would normally be contained in a more formal and localized section of the performance analysis.

A scenario model is developed along with a traffic model; significant explanatory text accompanies these developments. The model is summarized, and results are presented (no program was necessary to allow calculation of this simple model), as well as recommendations for system performance improvement at no additional hardware cost.

In short, not only has an analysis been undertaken, but it also has been thoroughly documented. Not only have we completed a real performance model, but we also have completed our first performance analysis! This analysis was completed using only a simple queuing equation, a knowledge of TP systems as presented in chapter 2, and a little native ingenuity. This is all it takes to be a performance analyst. Why, then, are there so few of us?

The remaining chapters add some tricks to our tool kit, give us a better understanding of our tools, and stress the importance of documenting our model and analysis.

4

Basic Performance Concepts

The mathematical foundation required for performance modeling is very much a function of the depth to which the analyst is interested in diving—from skimming the surface to over one's head. As we saw in chapter 3, a great deal of performance modeling can be achieved with one queuing equation (equation 3-1), a lot of simple algebra, and some system sense.

However, there are many unusual and complex TP system architectures that can be more accurately analyzed with some better tools. This chapter can be considered the "tool kit" for the book.

Three of the six sections of this chapter provide the basic foundation of queuing theory for the remaining chapters. Below is a brief overview of these three sections.

1. *Queues—An Introduction* gives a simple, intuitive derivation of perhaps the most important relationship for the performance analyst: the Khintchine-Pollaczek equation, which characterizes a broad range of queue types. Equation 3-1 is a subset of this equation. Nonmathematicians should find the intuitive derivation understandable and illuminating in terms of understanding the behavior of queues. Those knowledgeable in queuing theory will find definitions of terms and nomenclature used throughout the rest of the book.

2. *Characterizing Queuing Systems* summarizes the Kendall classification system for queues. This classification system is used throughout the book.

3. *Comparison of Queue Types* summarizes the queuing concepts presented in this chapter by discussing the comparative behavior of queuing systems as a function of service time distribution, number of servers, and population size.

The other three sections of the chapter deal with a broad range of mathematical tools, including probability concepts, useful series, and queuing theory. Those less inclined to mathematics will be pleased to know that the rest of the book is completely understandable without a detailed knowledge of these tools.

QUEUES—AN INTRODUCTION

As we have seen in the simple performance examples in chapter 3, queues are all-important to the study of system performance. In the simplest of terms, a *queue* is a line of items awaiting service by a commonly shared resource (which we hereinafter will call a *server*). Let us first, therefore, take an intuitive look at the phenomenon of queuing. Through just common sense and a little algebra, we can come close to deriving the Khintchine-Pollaczek equation, which is one of the most important tools available for performance analysis. Its formal derivation is presented in Appendix 3, but it is not much more difficult than that presented here.

Let us consider a queue with very simple characteristics. Interestingly enough, these characteristics are applicable as a good approximation to most queues that we will find in real-life systems.

These characteristics are

1. There is only a single server.
2. No limit is imposed on the length to which the queue might grow.
3. Items to be serviced arrive on a random basis.
4. Service order is first-in, first-out.
5. The queue is in a steady-state condition, i.e., its average length measured over a long enough period is constant.

In Figure 4-1, a server is serving a line of waiting transactions. On the average, it takes the server T seconds to service a transaction. Some transactions take more, some take less, but the average is T. T is called the *service time* of the server. The average number of transactions in the system, which we will call *queue length,* is Q transactions. This comprises W transactions waiting in line plus the transaction (if any) currently being serviced. Finally, transactions are arriving at a rate of R transactions per second.

The server is busy, or occupied, RT of the time. (If transactions are arriving at a rate of $R = 1$ per second, and if the server requires $T = 0.5$ seconds to service a transaction, then it is busy 50% of the time.) This is called the *occupancy* of the server or the *load* (L) on the server:

$$L = RT \qquad\qquad (4\text{-}1)$$

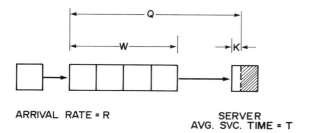

ARRIVAL RATE = R   SERVER
                                    AVG. SVC. TIME = T

T_q = QUEUE TIME (TIME WAITING IN LINE)

T_d = DELAY TIME (TIME IN LINE PLUS SERVICE TIME)   **Figure 4-1** Queuing delay.

L also represents the probability that an arriving transaction will find the server busy. (Obviously, if the server is not busy, there is no waiting line.)

When a transaction arrives to be serviced, it will find in front of it, on the average, W transactions waiting for service. With probability L, it will also find a transaction in the process of being serviced. The servicing of the current transaction, if any, will have been partially completed. Let us say that only kT time is left to finish its servicing.

The newly arrived transaction will have to wait in line long enough for the current transaction to be completed (kT seconds L of the time) and then for each transaction in front of it to be serviced (WT seconds). Therefore, it must wait in line a time T_q (the queue time):

$$T_q = WT + LkT \qquad (4\text{-}2)$$

From the time that it arrived in line to the time that its servicing begins, an average of W other transactions must have arrived to maintain the average line length. Since transactions are arriving at R transactions per second, then

$$W = T_q R$$

or

$$T_q = W/R \qquad (4\text{-}3)$$

Equating 4-2 and 4-3 and solving for the waiting line length gives (using 4-1)

$$W = \frac{kL^2}{1-L} \qquad (4\text{-}4)$$

The total length of the queue as seen by an arriving transaction is the waiting line, W, plus a transaction being serviced L of the time:

$$Q = W + L \qquad (4\text{-}5)$$

or

$$Q = \frac{L}{1 - L} [1 - (1 - k)L] \qquad (4\text{-}6)$$

The delay time, T_d, is determined in a similar manner. It is the total amount of time the transaction must wait in order to be serviced—its waiting time in line plus its service time. During the time that the transaction is in the system (T_d), Q transactions must arrive to maintain the steady state:

$$Q = T_d R = T_d L/T \tag{4-7}$$

Setting this equal to equation 4-6 and solving for the response time, T_d, gives

$$T_d = \frac{1}{1 - L} [1 - (1 - k)L]T \tag{4-8}$$

From 4-2 and 4-4,

$$T_q = \frac{kL}{1 - L} T \tag{4-9}$$

Equations 4-4, 4-6, 4-8, and 4-9 are the basic queuing equations for a single server. As stated previously, the primary assumptions inherent in these expressions are that transactions arrive completely independently of each other and are serviced in order of arrival. The equations are, therefore, very general expressions of the queuing phenomenon. They are quite accurate when the transactions are being generated by a number of independent sources, as long as the number of sources is significantly greater than the average queue lengths. A common limiting case of accuracy occurs when there is a small number of sources, each of which can have only one outstanding transaction at a time (a common case in computer systems). In this case, the queue length cannot exceed the number of sources; and the arrival rate becomes a function of server load. (Arrivals will slow down as queues build, since sources must await servicing before generating a new transaction.) However, in this case, the above expressions will be conservative, since they will in general predict queue lengths somewhat greater than those that actually will be experienced. (Obviously, the limiting case of only one source will never experience a queue, although equation 4-6 will predict a queue.)

The parameter k in these equations is a function of the service-time distribution. It is the average amount of service time that is left to be expended on the current transaction being serviced when a new transaction arrives. Let us look at these expressions for certain important cases of service-time distributions.

Exponential Service Times

For exponential service times, the probability that the remaining service time will be greater than a given amount t is exponential (e^{-at}). We discuss this and other probability concepts later in this chapter. An exponential distribution has the characteristic that the remaining service time after any arbitrary delay, assuming that the servicing is still in progress, is still exponential, i.e., it has no memory. Thus, one has the following interesting situation: If the average service time of the server is T, and if the server is currently busy (for no matter how long), one is going to have to wait an average time of T for the service to complete. Since k is the proportion of servicing remaining when a new transaction enters the queue, then $k = 1$ for exponential service times. Thus, equations 4-6, 4-8, and 4-9 become

$$Q = \frac{L}{1 - L} \tag{4-10}$$

$$T_d = \frac{T}{1 - L} \tag{4-11}$$

and

$$T_q = \frac{L}{1 - L} T \tag{4-12}$$

These are the forms of the queuing expressions often seen in the literature and represent a typical worst case for service-time distributions (though it is possible to construct unusual distributions that are worse than exponential). Equation 4-11 is the form that was used in chapter 3 as equation 3-1.

Constant Service Times

If the service time is a constant, then on the average, half of the service time will remain when a new transaction enters the queue. Therefore $k = \frac{1}{2}$, and

$$Q = \frac{L}{1 - L} \left(1 - \frac{L}{2} \right) \tag{4-13}$$

$$T_d = \frac{1}{1 - L} \left(1 - \frac{L}{2} \right) T \tag{4-14}$$

and

$$T_q = \frac{L/2}{1 - L} T \tag{4-15}$$

These expressions show queues and delays that are somewhat less than those predicted for exponential service times. Constant service times generally represent the best case.

General Distributions

Khintchine and Pollaczek have shown in general that

$$k = \frac{1}{2} \left[1 + \frac{\text{var}(T)}{[E(T)]^2} \right] = \frac{1}{2} \frac{E(T^2)}{T^2} \tag{4-16}$$

where

$E(T)$ = the mean of the service-time distribution (simply represented as T herein),

$\text{var}(T)$ = the variance of the service-time distribution,

and

$E(T^2)$ = the second moment of the service-time distribution.

This result is derived in Appendix 3. We will hereafter refer to k as the *distribution coefficient* of the service time for the server.

For exponentially distributed service times, as we will see later, the standard deviation equals the mean. Since the variance is the square of the standard deviation, then $k = 1$, consistent with our argument above.

For constant service times, the variance is zero, and $k = \frac{1}{2}$, as also just shown.

Uniform Service Times

A service time that can range from zero to s seconds with equal probability is uniformly distributed. It has a mean of $s/2$ and a second moment of

$$E(T^2) = \frac{1}{s}\int_0^s t^2 dt = s^2/3$$

Therefore,

$$k = \frac{1}{2} \frac{s^2/3}{(s/2)^2} = 2/3 \tag{4-17}$$

This is between the cases of constant and random service time, as would be expected.

Discrete Service Times

Often times, the service time will be one of a set of constant times, each with a duration of T_i and a probability of p_i. In this case,

$$k = \frac{1}{2} \frac{\Sigma p_i T_i^2}{(\Sigma p_i T_i)^2} \tag{4-18}$$

Summary

The above equations are the very important queuing equations derived by Khintchine and Pollaczek (actually, equation 4-9 for the queue time, T_q, is formally known as the Khintchine-Pollaczek equation, or the Pollaczek-Khintchine equation, depending upon to whom you wish to give primary credit). These are so important to performance analysis that we summarize them here:

$$W = \frac{kL^2}{1-L} \tag{4-4}$$

$$Q = \frac{L}{1-L}[1 - (1 - k)L] \tag{4-6}$$

$$T_d = \frac{1}{1-L}\,[1 - (1 - k)L]T \tag{4-8}$$

$$T_q = \frac{kL}{1-L}\,T \tag{4-9}$$

and

$$k = \frac{1}{2}\,\frac{E(T^2)}{T^2} \tag{4-16}$$

where

W = average number of items waiting to be serviced,

Q = average length of the queue, including the item currently being serviced, if any,

T_d = average delay time for a transaction, including waiting plus service time,

T_q = average time that a transaction waits in line before being serviced,

k = distribution coefficient of the service time,

T = average service time of the server,

L = load on (occupancy of) the server.

Equation 4-8 for the delay time is the one which will be most often used in this book. The queue length, W or Q (equation 4-4 or 4-6), is often necessary when we are concerned with overflowing finite queues. The queue time, T_q (equation 4-9), is useful when the queue contains items from diverse sources, each with a different mean service time. In this case, the queue time is calculated using the weighted mix of all transaction service times. The average delay time is calculated for an item by adding the average queue time, calculated for the mix of all items in the queue, to the average service time for that item. Thus,

$$T_d = T_q + T \tag{4-19}$$

as is supported by equations 4-8 and 4-9.

Other useful relations between these parameters that can be deduced from the above equations and that have already been presented, are

$$Q = W + L \tag{4-20}$$

$$T_q = \frac{WT}{L} \tag{4-21}$$

and

$$T_d = \frac{QT}{L} = T_q + T \tag{4-22}$$

Note that L is the average load on the server. As we shall see later, in a multiserver system with c servers, the total load on the system is cL. Equations 4-20 through 4-22 still hold after substituting cL for L.

Equation 4-7, derived earlier, provides another important insight into queuing systems:

$$Q = RT_d \qquad\qquad (4\text{-}7)$$

This is known as Little's Law (Little [18], Lazowska [16]) and states that the number of items in a system is equal to the product of the throughput, R, and the residence time of an item in the system, T_d.

These relationships are surprisingly valid across many more queue disciplines than the simple first-in, first-out discipline discussed here. This point is explored further in Appendix 3, where it is shown that the order of servicing is not important so long as an item is not selected for service based on its characteristics. For instance, these relationships would apply to a round-robin (or polling) service algorithm but not to a service procedure that gave priority to short messages over long messages.

CONCEPTS IN PROBABILITY, AND OTHER TOOLS

Performance analysis can at times require some innovative ingenuity. This typically does not require any knowledge of higher mathematics. However, a basic knowledge of probability concepts and other helpful hints can often be useful. The material presented in this section is intended to simply touch on those concepts that have proven useful to the author over the course of several performance analyses.

We will launch into some detail, however, concerning randomness as it relates to the Poisson and exponential probability distributions. Not that we need these so much in our analysis efforts but because an in-depth knowledge of them is imperative in order to clearly understand many of the simplifying assumptions that we will often have to make in order to obtain even approximate solutions to some problems.

Excellent coverage of these topics for the practicing analyst may be found in Martin [19] and Gorney [7].

Random Variables

Probability theory concerns itself with the description and manipulation of *random variables*. These variables describe real-life situations and may be classified into discrete and continuous random variables.

Discrete Random Variables

A *discrete variable* is one which can take only certain discrete values (even though there may be an infinite set of these values, known as a *countably infinite set*). The length of a queue is a *discrete random variable;* it may have no items, one item, two items, and so on without limit. The length of a queue with a fixed maximum length is an example of a discrete variable with a finite number of values.

If we periodically sampled a queue in a real-life process, we would find that at each sample point it would contain some specific number of items, ranging from zero items to the maximum number of items, if any. If we sampled enough times and kept counts relative to the total number of samples (and assumed that the queue is in steady state), we would find that the proportion of time that there were exactly n items in the queue would converge to some number. This would be true for all allowable values of n. For instance, if we made 100,000 samples and found that for 10,000 times there was nothing in the queue, for 20,000 times there was 1 item in the queue, and for 1,000 times there were 10 items in the queue, we would be fairly certain that the queue would normally be idle 10% of the time, have a length of 1 for 20% of the time, and have a length of 10 for 1% of the time.

These values, expressed as proportions rather than as percentages, are, of course, the probabilities of their corresponding events. That is, the probability in this case of a queue length of zero is .1, etc. We will note the probability of a discrete event as p_n, where n in some way describes the event. For instance, in the case of a queue, p_n is the probability of there being n items in the queue. If we were drawing balls of different colors from an urn, we might choose p_1 to be the probability of drawing a red ball and p_2 that probability for a green ball. Thus,

$$p_n = \text{Probability of the occurrence of event } n.$$

The set of p_n that describes a random variable, n, is called the probability density function of n.

There are several important properties of discrete variables, but the most obvious are

1. Each probability must be no greater than 1, since we can never be more certain than certain:

$$0 \le p_n \le 1 \tag{4-23}$$

2. The probability density function must sum to 1, since 1 and only 1 event on each observation is certain:

$$\sum_n p_n = 1 \tag{4-24}$$

where the summation is over all allowed values of n.

3. Assuming that events are independent, the probability of a specific combination of events is the product of their probabilities. Thus, if we were to draw a ball from an urn containing balls of several different colors, put it back, and draw another ball, and if p_1 were the probability of drawing a red ball and p_2 the probability of drawing a green ball, then the probability of drawing a red ball and a green ball is $p_1 p_2$. (Note that we have to put the first ball back in order to avoid changing the probabilities; otherwise, the two events would not be independent.)

Probability of occurrence
of a set of independent events $= \pi_n p_n$ (4-25)

where the product, π_n, is over the specified events.

Thus, "and" implies product (the probability of event 1 *and* event 2 is $p_1 p_2$).

4. Assuming that events are independent, the probability that an event will be one of several is the sum of those probabilities. In the above example, the probability of drawing either a red ball or a green ball on a single draw is $p_1 + p_2$.

Probability of occurrence
of one of a set of independent events $= \sum_n p_n$ (4-26)

where the summation is over the desired events. Thus, "or" implies "sum" (the probability of event 1 or event 2 is $p_1 + p_2$).

5. The probability of a sequence of dependent events depends upon the conditional probabilities of those events. If we did not return the ball to the urn, then the probabilities would change for the second draw. The probability of a red and then green draw would be the probability of a red draw times the probability of a green ball *given* that a red ball has been drawn. Thus, the probability of red, then green $= p_1 p_2(1)$, where $p_n(m)$ is the probability of event n occurring (a green ball in this case) given that event m has occurred. In general, letting $p(n, m)$ be the probability of the sequence of events n and m,

$$p(n, m) = p_n p_m(n)$$ (4-27)

6. The average value (or mean) of a random variable that has numeric meaning is the sum of each value of the variable weighted by its probability. Let $\bar{n}$ be the mean of the variable with values n and probabilities p_n. Then

$$\bar{n} = \sum_n n p_n$$ (4-28)

where the sum is taken over all allowed values of n.

7. It is often important to have a feel for the "dispersion" of the random variable. If its mean is p, will all obervations yield a value close to p (low dispersion), or will they vary widely (high dispersion)? A common measure of dispersion is to calculate the average mean square of all observations relative to the mean. This is called the variance of the random variable, denoted var (n):

$$\text{var}(n) = \sum_n (n - \bar{n})^2 p_n$$ (4-29)

where the sum is taken over all allowed values of n.

The square root of the variance is called its standard deviation and, of course, has the same dimension as the variable (i.e., items, seconds, transactions, etc.).

8. The moments of the variable are also sometimes used. The mth moment of a variable, n, is represented as $\overline{n^m}$ and is

$$\overline{n^m} = \sum_n n^m p_n \tag{4-30}$$

where the summation is over all allowable n. Note that the mean is the first moment ($m = 1$). There is also an important relation between the variance and the second moment:

$$\mathrm{var}(n) = \sum_n (n-\overline{n})^2 p_n$$

$$= \sum_n n^2 p_n - \sum 2n\overline{n}p_n + \sum \overline{n}^2 p_n$$

From equations 4-24 and 4-28,

$$\mathrm{var}(n) = \overline{n^2} - \overline{n}^2 \tag{4-31}$$

That is, the variance of a random variable is the difference between its second moment and the square of its mean. (See equation 4-16 for a use of this relationship.)

9. If x is a random variable that is the sum of other random variables, then the mean of x is the sum of the means of its component variables, and the variance of x is the sum of the variances of its component variables. Thus, if

$$x = a + b + c + \ldots$$

then

$$\overline{x} = \overline{a} + \overline{b} + \overline{c} + \ldots \tag{4-32}$$

and

$$\mathrm{var}(x) = \mathrm{var}(a) + \mathrm{var}(b) + \mathrm{var}(c) + \ldots \tag{4-33}$$

10. If x is a choice of one of a possible set of variables, then its mean is the weighted average of those variables, and its second moment is the weighted average of the second moments of those variables. Thus, if a, b, c, $\ldots$ are each random variables, and if x may be a with probability p_a, b with probability p_b, etc., then

$$\overline{x} = \overline{a}p_a + \overline{b}p_b + \overline{c}p_c + \ldots \tag{4-34}$$

and

$$\overline{x^2} = \overline{a^2}p_a + \overline{b^2}p_b + \overline{c^2}p_c + \ldots \tag{4-35}$$

Note that weighted second moments are added when x is a choice, whereas variances are added when x is a combination.

11. The set of probabilities p_n that describe a random variable may be summed up to, or beyond, some limit. This sum is called the cumulative distribution func-

tion of n. If the sum is up to but does not include the limit, then the cumulative distribution function gives the probability that n will be less than the limit. This is denoted by $P(n < m)$, where m is the limit:

$$P(n < m) = \sum_{n<m} p_n \qquad (4\text{-}36)$$

where the summation is over all n less than m. Note as m grows large, $P(n < m)$ tends toward unity.

If the sum is beyond the limit $(n > m)$, then $P(n > m)$ is the probability that n will exceed the limit:

$$P(n > m) = \sum_{n>m} p_n \qquad (4\text{-}37)$$

where the sum is over all n greater than m. As m grows large, $P(n > m)$ tends to zero.

A simple example will illustrate many of these points. Figure 4-2a gives a probability density function for the size of a message that may be transmitted for a terminal. Its size in bytes is distributed as follows:

Message size (n)	Probability (p_n)
20	.1
21	.2
22	.3
23	.2
24	.2

Note that the probability of all messages is 1:

$$\sum_{n=20}^{24} p_n = 1$$

The mean message size is

$$\bar{n} = \sum_{n=20}^{24} n p_n = 22.2$$

The variance of the message size is

$$\text{var}(n) = \sum_{n=20}^{24} (n-\bar{n})^2 p_n = 1.56$$

Its standard deviation is 1.25.
The second moment is

$$\overline{n^2} = \sum_{n=20}^{24} n^2 p_n = 494.4$$

Note the relationship between variance and second moment:

$$\text{var}(n) = \overline{n^2} - \overline{n}^2 = 494.4 - 22.2^2 = 1.56$$

This illustrates one potential computational pitfall. The variance calculated in this manner can be a small difference between two relatively large numbers. For that reason, the calculation should be made with sufficient accuracy.

The cumulative distribution functions for this variable are shown in Figure 4-2b. As with the density function, these functions have meaning only at the discrete values of the variable. Thus, the probability that the message length will be greater than 22 is .4 (i.e., $p_{23} + p_{24} = .4$) and that it will be less than 22 is .3 (i.e., $p_{20} + p_{21} = .3$).

Now, let us assume that we have a second message type with a mean of 35 bytes and a variance of 3. Denote as m_1 the first message described by the distribution of Figure 4-2, and denote as m_2 the new message just defined. Consider the following two cases:

Case 1. m_1 is a request message, and m_2 is the response. What is the average communication line usage (in characters) and its variance for a complete transaction?

In this case, the communication line usage is the sum of the message usages. The mean and variance of this total usage are the sum of the means and variances for the individual messages. Let the total line usage per transaction be m. Then

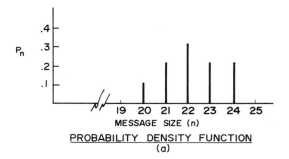

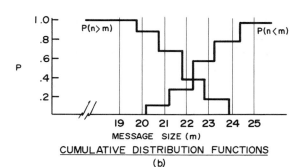

Figure 4-2 Discrete probability functions.

$$m = m_1 + m_2$$

$$\overline{m} = \overline{m}_1 + \overline{m}_2 = 22.2 + 35 = 57.2$$

$$\text{var}(m) = \text{var}(m_1) + \text{var}(m_2) = 1.56 + 3 = 4.56$$

Thus, average communication traffic per transaction will be 57.2 bytes with a variance of 4.56 or a standard deviation of 2.14 bytes.

Case 2.   Both m_1 and m_2 are request messages. m will be m_1 30 percent of the time and m_2 70 percent of the time. What are the mean and variance of m?

m is now a choice between messages. Its mean is

$$\overline{m} = .3 \times 22.2 + .7 \times 35 = 31.16$$

The second moment of m is found by adding the weighted second moments of m_1 and m_2. The second moment of m_2 is the sum of its variance and the square of its mean:

$$\overline{m_2^2} = \text{var}(m_2) + \overline{m}_2^2 = 3 + 35^2 = 1228$$

Then

$$\overline{m^2} = .3 \times 494.4 + .7 \times 1228 = 1007.92$$

The variance of m, then, is

$$\text{var}(m) = \overline{m^2} - \overline{m}^2 = 1007.92 - 31.16^2 = 36.97$$

Thus, the request messages will average 31.16 bytes in length, with a variance of 36.97 or a standard deviation of 6.08 bytes.

Continuous Random Variables

The previous section described discrete random variables—those that take on only certain discrete (often integer) values, such as the number of items in a queue or the number of bytes in a message.

But what about the number of seconds in a service? If a process requires somewhere between 2 and 17 msec to process a transaction, it can vary continuously between these limits. We can say that the probability is .15 that the service time for this process is between 10 and 11 seconds, but this probability includes service times of 10, 10.2, and 10.25679 seconds. The service time variable is not discrete in this case. It can assume an infinite number of values and is therefore called a *continuous random variable*.

All of the rules we have established for discrete variables have a corollary for continuous variables, often with the summation sign simply replaced with an integral sign.

The characteristics and rules with which we will be concerned in performance analyses are as follows:

1. The probability density function is continuous. If x is a random value, $f(x)$ is the probability that x will fall within the infinitesimal range $f(x)dx$. More specifically, the probability that x will be between a and b is

$$P(a \leq x \leq b) = \int_a^b f(x)dx \leq 1 \qquad (4\text{-}38)$$

The probability density function of x is $f(x)$. Notice that there is no requirement that $f(x) < 1$ for all values of x, only that equation 4–38 results in a value no greater than 1 over any range. For instance, if x has equal probability of ranging from 0 to .1, $f(x) = 10$ for $0 \leq x \leq .1$.

2. Since x must have some value, the integral of the probability density function must be one:

$$\int_x f(x)dx = 1 \qquad (4\text{-}39)$$

where integration is over the allowed range of x.

3. The average, or mean, value of x is its integral weighted by its probability over its range:

$$\bar{x} = \int_x xf(x)dx \qquad (4\text{-}40)$$

where the integration is over the allowed range of x.

4. The variance of x is the square of the deviation of x from its mean weighted by its probability and integrated over its range:

$$\text{var}(x) = \int_x (x - \bar{x})^2 f(x)dx \qquad (4\text{-}41)$$

where the integration is over the allowable range of x.

5. The mth moment of x is x^m, weighted by its probability and integrated over the range of x:

$$\overline{x^m} = \int_x x^m f(x)dx \qquad (4\text{-}42)$$

where the integration is over the allowed range of x. Note that the variance given in equation 4–41 can be expanded to

$$\text{var}(x) = \int_x x^2 f(x)dx - \int_x 2x\bar{x}f(x)dx + \int_x \bar{x}^2 f(x)dx$$

Using equation 4–39, 4–40, and 4–42,

$$\text{var}(x) = \overline{x^2} - \bar{x}^2 \qquad (4\text{-}43)$$

just as with discrete variables.

6. The properties of calculating means and variances for sums of variables or choices of variables are the same as for discrete probabilities. That is,

   a. If x is a sum of continuous random variables $x_1, x_2, x_3, \ldots$, then its mean is the sum of the means, and its variance is the sum of the variances of x_1, x_2, x_3
    . . . .

b. If x is a choice between continuous random variables $x_1, x_2, x_3, \ldots$ with probabilities $p_1, p_2, p_3, \ldots$, then its mean is the weighted sum of the means, and its second moment is the weighted sum of the second moments of $x_1, x_2, x_3, \ldots$, where the weighting factors are the probabilities $p_1, p_2, p_3, \ldots$.

7. The cumulative distribution functions for x are

$$P(x<a) = \int_{x<a} f(x)\mathrm{d}x \qquad (4\text{-}44a)$$

and

$$P(x>a) = \int_{x>a} f(x)\mathrm{d}x \qquad (4\text{-}44b)$$

Equation 4–44a is the probability that x is less than the limit a, where the integration is over all allowed values of x less than a. Equation 4–44b is the probability that $f(x)$ is greater than a, where the integration is over all allowed values of x greater than a.

Figure 4–3 shows an example of a continuous probability density function and its cumulative distributions.

It is not often in performance analysis that we are forced into the calculus of continuous distribution functions. However, there are two prominent examples. One is the calculation of the distribution coefficient in the Khintchine-Pollaczek equation for a continuous variable. Such an example was given earlier in this chapter (equation 4–17).

Another is the following. Consider a medium whose length is b. From one random position, x_1, what is the mean distance to any other random position, x_2? There are several physical processes corresponding to this case:

- The average seek distance of a disk moving from its current track to a new track,

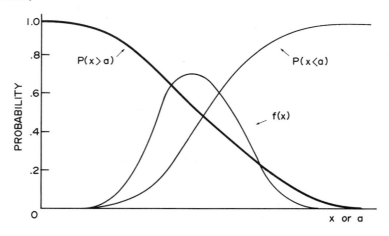

Figure 4-3   Continuous probability functions.

- The distance between two terminals on the bus of a local area network,
- The amount of tape that must be passed in a tape search starting at one random point and moving to another.

The solution to this problem is presented here as an example tying many of the above concepts together.

The probability density function that x will be at any given point on b, $f(x)$, is

$$f(x) = 1/b,\ 0 \le x \le b$$

Otherwise,

$$f(x) = 0$$

Thus,

$$\int_0^b f(x)\mathrm{d}x = \int_0^b \frac{1}{b}\mathrm{d}x = \left[\frac{x}{b}\right]_0^b = 1$$

The average distance between one random point, x_1, and another, x_2, is the average distance $x_1 - x_2$ given a point, x_1, then averaged over all possible values of x_1.

If x_2 is greater than x_1, then its value can range between x_1 and b. Therefore, its probability density function is

$$f(x_2) = \frac{1}{b - x_1},\ x_2 > x_1$$

and its average distance from x_1 is

$$\overline{x_2 - x_1} = \int_{x_1}^b (x_2 - x_1) f(x_2) dx_2 = \frac{1}{b - x_1} \int_{x_1}^b (x_2 - x_1) dx_2 = \frac{(b - x_1)}{2},\ x_2 > x_1$$

If x_2 is less than x_1, then its value can range from 0 to x_1. Therefore, its probability density function for this case is

$$f(x_2) = \frac{1}{x_1},\ x_2 < x_1$$

and its average distance from x_1 is

$$\overline{x_1 - x_2} = \int_0^{x_1} (x_1 - x_2) f(x_2) dx_2 = \frac{1}{x_1} \int_0^{x_1} (x_1 - x_2) dx_2 = \frac{x_1}{2},\ x_2 < x_1$$

The probability that x_2 will be greater than x_1 is $(b - x_1)/b$, and the probability that it will be less is x_1/b. Thus, the average distance between x_1 and x_2 for a given value of x_1 is

$$\frac{(b - x_1)}{b}\frac{(b - x_1)}{2} + \frac{x_1}{b}\frac{x_1}{2} = \frac{b^2 - 2bx_1 + 2x_1^2}{2b}$$

Since x_1 can range from 0 to b, its probability density function is

$$f(x_1) = \frac{1}{b}$$

The average distance that x_2 is from x_1 when x_1 is varied over its range will be called $\bar{x}$ and is

$$\bar{x} = \int_0^b \frac{b^2 - 2bx_1 + 2x_1^2}{2b} f(x_1)dx$$

$$\bar{x} = \frac{1}{2b^2} \left[b^2x_1 - \frac{2bx_1^2}{2} + \frac{2x_1^3}{3} \right]_0^b$$

$$\bar{x} = b/3.$$

Thus, the average distance between x_1 and x_2 is $1/3\, b$. This means that the average seek distance on a disk is 1/3 of all tracks. The average distance between two terminals on a local area network is 1/3 of the bus length. The average random seek distance for a tape is 1/3 of its length.

Permutations and Combinations

It is sometimes useful to be able to calculate the number of ways in which we can select n objects from a group of m objects. Sometimes the order in which we select them is important, and sometimes it is not.

If order is important, we are talking about *permutations*. Let there be m distinct objects in a group, and we desire to choose n of them. How many different ways can we choose these n objects?

On the first choice, we will choose one of m objects. Given n choices, the total number of different ways we can choose n objects is

$$m(m - 1)(m - 2) \ldots (m - n + 1)$$

This can be written as

$$P_n^m = \frac{m!}{(m-n)!} \tag{4-45a}$$

where P_n^m is the number of permutations of m objects taken n at a time.

However, if order is not important, we have counted too many possibilities in the above analysis. We have counted all of the permutations for each set of choices but are only interested in counting that particular combination of choices once. For instance, if one set of choices was ABC, we have counted it as

ABC   BAC   CAB

ACB   BCA   CBA

or six times, whereas we are only interested in counting it once. We are interested in the number of *combinations* of objects, not in all of their permutations.

The first item chosen could have occurred during any of the n choices. Given that, the second item could have occurred during any one of the remaining $(n - 1)$ choices and so on. The same combination has been counted $n(n - 1)(n - 2) \ldots (1)$ times for a total of $n!$ times. Thus, the total number of combinations is the number of permutations divided by $n!$:

$$C_n^m = \frac{m!}{n!(m-n)!} \tag{4-45b}$$

where C_n^m is the number of combinations of m objects taken n at a time.

Series

In many of the cases with which we will work, we will find ourselves with a summation over an infinite (or at least a very large) number of items. Often, these infinite *series* can be reduced to a very manageable expression. Some of the more useful ones are summarized here.

a. $1 + x + x^2 + x^3 + \ldots, 0 \le x \le 1$
   This can be written in the form

$$\sum_{i=0}^{\infty} x^i = \frac{1}{1-x} \tag{4-46}$$

The similar series, which is truncated on the left, directly follows and is

$$x^a + x^{a+1} + x^{a+2} + \ldots, 0 \le x \le 1$$

This may be written as

$$\sum_{i=a}^{\infty} x^i = x^a \sum_{i=0}^{\infty} x^i = \frac{x^a}{1-x} \tag{4-47}$$

Likewise, this series truncated to the right is

$$1 + x + x^2 + \ldots + x^{b-1}, 0 \le x \le 1$$

which may be written as

$$\sum_{i=0}^{b-1} x^i = \sum_{i=0}^{\infty} x^i - \sum_{i=b}^{\infty} x^i = (1-x^b) \sum_{i=0}^{\infty} x^i = \frac{1-x^b}{1-x} \tag{4-48}$$

The doubly truncated series is

$$x^a + x^{a+1} + \ldots + x^{b-1}, 0 \le x \le 1$$

This may be written as

$$\sum_{i=a}^{b-1} x^i = x^a \sum_{i=0}^{b-a-1} x^i = x^a \frac{1-x^{b-a}}{1-x} = \frac{x^a-x^b}{1-x} \tag{4-49}$$

b. $x + 2x^2 + 3x^3 + \ldots, 0 \le x \le 1$

This can be expressed as

$$\sum_{i=1}^{\infty} ix^i = \frac{x}{(1-x)^2} \tag{4-50}$$

c. $1 + x + \frac{x^2}{2!} + \frac{x^3}{3!} + \ldots, 0 \le x \le 1$

This can be expressed as

$$\sum_{i=0}^{\infty} \frac{x^i}{i!} = e^x \tag{4-51}$$

Conversely,

$$1 - x + \frac{x^2}{2!} - \frac{x^3}{3!} + \ldots, 0 \le x \le 1$$

may be expressed as

$$\sum_{i=0}^{\infty} (-1)^i \frac{x^i}{i!} = e^{-x} \tag{4-52}$$

The Poisson Distribution

We now discuss the Poisson and exponential distributions in some detail. Not because we will use them in our calculations so often (though simulation studies certainly do) but because they represent much of the statistics of queuing theory and form an important underpinning to our understanding of the use of the tools we will bring to bear on the analysis of performance problems.

The Poisson distribution provides the probabilities that exactly n events may happen in a time interval, t, provided that the occurrence of these events is independent. That the independence of events is the only assumption made is the reason that this distribution is so important.

Event independence simply says that events occur completely randomly. They do not occur in batches. The occurrence of one event is not at all dependent on what has occurred in the past, nor has it any influence on what will occur in the future. The process has no memory; it is memoryless. We will call a process that creates such random events a *random process*.

In queuing theory, there are two important cases of a random process:

1. The arrival of an item at a queue is a random event and is independent of the arrival of any other item. Therefore, arrivals to a queue are random.

2. The instant at which the servicing of an item by a server completes is a random event. It is independent of the item being serviced and of any of its past service cycles. Therefore, service completions by a server are random.

Note that randomness has to do with events: the event of an arrival to a queue, the event of a service time completion.

Let us determine the probability that exactly n random events will occur in time t. We will represent this probability by $p_n(t)$:

$p_n(t)$ = the probability that n random events will occur in time t

(Remember that n is a discrete random variable. Its values are the result of a random process. These two uses of *random* are unrelated. Random variables also are the result of nonrandom processes.)

Note that $p_n(t)$ is a probability function that depends on an additional parameter, t. As t becomes larger, the probability that n events will occur changes. This is unlike our simple probability functions described earlier. Such a process is called a *stochastic* process.

The average rate of the occurrence of events is a known parameter and is the only one we need to know. We will denote it by r:

r = average event occurrence rate (events per second)

Thus, on the average, rt events will occur in time t.

Since events are completely random, we know that we can pick a time interval, t, sufficiently small that the probability of two or more events occurring in that time interval can be ignored. We will note this arbitrarily small time interval as Δt and will assume that the only things that can happen in Δt are that no events will occur or that one event will occur.

Let us now observe a process for a time t. At the end of this observation time, we find that n events have occurred. We then observe it for Δt more time. The probability that one further event will occur in Δt is $r\Delta t$. The probability that no further events will occur in Δt is $(1 - r\Delta t)$.

Thus, the probability of observing n events in the time $(t + \Delta t)$ is

$$p_n(t + \Delta t) = p_n(t)(1 - r\Delta t) + p_{n-1}(t)r\Delta t \qquad (4\text{--}53)$$

This equation notes that n events may occur in the interval $(t + \Delta t)$ in one of two ways. Either n events have occurred in the interval t *and* no events have occurred in the subsequent interval, Δt, or $n - 1$ events have occurred in the interval t *and* one more event has occurred in the subsequent interval, Δt. (Note that since the arrival of an event is independent of previous arrivals, all of these probabilities are independent and may be combined as shown, according to rules 3 and 4 in the earlier section entitled "Discrete Random Variables.")

If no events occurred in the interval $t + \Delta t$, this relationship is written

$$p_o(t + \Delta t) = p_o(t)(1 - r\Delta t) \qquad (4\text{--}54)$$

since p_{n-1} does not exist. That is, the probability of no events occurring is the probability that no events occurred in the interval t and that no events occurred in the interval Δt.

Equations 4–53 and 4–54 can be rearranged as

$$\frac{p_n(t + \Delta t) - p_n(t)}{\Delta t} = -rp_n(t) + rp_{n-1}(t) \tag{4-55}$$

and

$$\frac{p_o(t + \Delta t) - p_o(t)}{\Delta t} = -rp_o(t) \tag{4-56}$$

As we let Δt become smaller and smaller, this becomes the classical definition of the derivative of $p_n(t)$ with respect to t, $dp_n(t)/dt$. Denote the time derivative of $p_n(t)$ by $p_n'(t)$:

$$p_n'(t) = \frac{dp_n(t)}{dt}$$

We can express equations 4–55 and 4–56 as

$$p_o'(t) = -rp_o(t) \tag{4-57}$$

and

$$p_n'(t) = -rp_n(t) + rp_{n-1}(t) \tag{4-58}$$

This is a set of differential-difference equations; their solution is shown in Appendix 4 to be

$$p_n(t) = \frac{(rt)^n e^{-rt}}{n!} \tag{4-59}$$

This is the *Poisson distribution*. It gives the probability that exactly n events will occur in a time interval t, given *only* that their arrivals are random with an average rate r. Though the serious student is encouraged to review the solution to these equations in Appendix 4, the main lesson to be learned is the simple and underlying fact that the Poisson distribution depends only on the randomness of event occurrence.

All this is summarized by saying that the distribution of the number of random events that will occur in a time interval t is given by the Poisson distribution. In queuing theory, the random events of concern are arrivals to queues and completions of service.

Let us look at some properties of the Poisson distribution. First, the sum of the probabilities over all values of n is

$$\sum_{n=0}^{\infty} \frac{(rt)^n e^{-rt}}{n!} = e^{-rt} \sum_{n=0}^{\infty} \frac{(rt)^n}{n!} = e^{-rt} e^{rt} = 1$$

as would be expected (the infinite series given by equation 4–51 is used).

We now derive the mean value of n for the distribution:

$$\bar{n} = \sum_{n=0}^{\infty} n \frac{(rt)^n e^{-rt}}{n!} = rt \sum_{n=1}^{\infty} \frac{(rt)^{n-1}}{(n-1)!} e^{-rt}$$

and

$$\bar{n} = rte^{-rt}\sum_{i=0}^{\infty}\frac{(rt)^i}{i!} = rte^{-rt}e^{rt} = rt$$

where i has been substituted for $n-1$ in the summation. Thus, the mean number of events that will occur in a time interval t is rt, as we would expect:

$$\bar{n} = rt \tag{4-60}$$

The second moment of n for the Poisson distribution is derived in a similar manner:

$$\overline{n^2} = \sum_{n=0}^{\infty}n^2\frac{(rt)^n e^{-rt}}{n!}$$

and

$$\overline{n^2} = rte^{-rt}\sum_{n=1}^{\infty}\frac{n(rt)^{n-1}}{(n-1)!}$$

Letting $i = n-1$,

$$\overline{n^2} = rte^{-rt}\sum_{i=0}^{\infty}(i+1)\frac{(rt)^i}{i!}$$

$$\overline{n^2} = rte^{-rt}\left[rt\sum_{i=1}^{\infty}\frac{(rt)^{i-1}}{(i-1)!} + \sum_{i=0}^{\infty}\frac{(rt)^i}{i!}\right]$$

$$\overline{n^2} = rte^{-rt}(rte^{rt} + e^{rt})$$

and

$$\overline{n^2} = (rt)^2 + rt \tag{4-61}$$

From equation 4–31, the variance of n is

$$\text{var}(n) = \overline{n^2} - \bar{n}^2$$

Since the mean n is rt, then

$$\text{var}(n) = rt \tag{4-62}$$

Thus, both the mean and the variance of n is rt for a Poisson distribution.

Note the memoryless feature of the Poisson distribution. The probability that any number of events will happen in the time interval t is a function only of the arrival rate, r, the number of events, n, and the time interval, t. It is completely independent of what happened in the previous time intervals. Even if no event has occurred over the past several time intervals, there is no increased assurance that one will occur during the next time interval.

The Exponential Distribution

The *exponential distribution* is very much related to the Poisson distribution and can be derived from it, as will soon be shown. It deals with the probability distribution of the time between events. Note that the Poisson distribution deals with a discrete variable: the number of events occurring in a time interval t. The exponential distribution deals with a continuous variable: the time between event occurrences.

To derive the distribution of interevent times, we assume that events are arriving randomly at a rate of r events per second. Let us consider the probability that, given that an event has just occurred, one or more events will occur in the following time interval, t. This is the probability that the time between events is less than t. If T is the time to the next event, we can denote this probability as $P(T < t)$ and can express it as

$$P(T < t) = \sum_{n=1}^{\infty} \frac{(rt)^n e^{-rt}}{n!} \tag{4-63}$$

That is, the probability that the next event will occur in a time interval less than t is the probability that one event will occur in time t plus the probability that two events will occur in time t, and so on.

Manipulating equation 4–63, we have

$$P(T < t) = e^{-rt}\left[\sum_{n=0}^{\infty} \frac{(rt)^n}{n!} - 1 \right]$$

and

$$P(T < t) = 1 - e^{-rt} \tag{4-64}$$

This is a cumulative distribution for the interevent time t. Its density function, $p(t)$, is the derivative of its cumulative distribution function. That is, from equation 4–44a,

$$P(T < t) = \int_0^T p(t)\mathrm{d}t$$

Differentiating both sides with respect to t gives

$$p(t) = C\frac{d}{dt} P(T < t) = C\frac{d}{dt}(1 - e^{-rt})$$

where C must be chosen such that the integral of the density function is unity (see equation 4–39). Thus,

$$p(t) = Cre^{-rt}$$

Since

$$Cr\int_0^{\infty} e^{-rt} = 1$$

then

$$Cr\left[-\frac{1}{r} e^{-rt} \right]_0^{\infty} = 1$$

$$Cr \frac{1}{r} = 1$$

and

$$C = 1$$

Thus, the probability density function for the interevent time, t, is

$$p(t) = re^{-rt} \qquad (4\text{--}65)$$

We can also express the alternate cumulative distribution giving the probability that T is greater than t. From equation 4–44b, we have

$$P(T > t) = \int_t^\infty re^{-rT} dT$$

$$= r\left[-\frac{1}{r} e^{-rt} \right]_t^\infty$$

and

$$P(T > t) = e^{-rt}, \qquad (4\text{-}66)$$

as would be expected from equation 4–64, since $P(T < t) + P(T > t) = 1$. Since t is a continuous variable, $P(T = t)$ is zero, and can be ignored.

The mean, variance, and second moment of the exponential distribution can be shown to be

$$\bar{t} = 1/r \qquad (4\text{-}67)$$

$$\text{var}(t) = 1/r^2 \qquad (4\text{-}68)$$

and

$$\overline{t^2} = 2/r^2 \qquad (4\text{-}69)$$

Note once again the memoryless feature of the exponential distribution. No matter when we start waiting for an event (even if one has not occurred for awhile), the expected time to the next event is still $1/r$.

Also note that t has been redefined here relative to the way it is used in the Poisson distribution. In the Poisson distribution, t is a fixed interval over which the probability of occurrence of n events is expressed. In the exponential distribution, t is the random variable expressing the time between events.

Random Processes Summarized

To summarize the above, we make three statements about a random process with an average event rate of r events per second.

1. A *random* process is one in which events are generated randomly and independently. The probability that an event will occur in an arbitrarily small time interval Δt is $r\Delta t$, independent of the event history of the process.

2. The probability $p_n(t)$ that n events will occur in a time interval t is given by the Poisson distribution:

$$p_n(t) = \frac{(rt)^n e^{-rt}}{n!}$$

with

$$\bar{n} = rt$$

$$\text{var}(n) = rt$$

and

$$\overline{n^2} = (rt)^2 + rt$$

3. The probability density function $p(t)$ for the interevent time t is the exponential function

$$p(t) = re^{-rt}$$

with

$$\bar{t} = 1/r$$

$$\text{var}(t) = 1/r^2$$

and

$$\overline{t^2} = 2/r^2$$

Thus, random, Poisson, and exponential distributions all imply the same thing: a random process. This is a process in which events occur randomly, the distribution of their occurrences in a given time interval is Poisson-distributed, and the distribution of times between events is exponentially distributed.

In queuing theory, there are two random processes with which we frequently deal. One is *arrivals to a queue*. An arrival of an item to a queue is a random event. Arrivals are said to be Poisson-distributed, and the interarrival rate is exponentially distributed. The statements *random arrivals* and *Poisson arrivals* are equivalent.

The other process is the *service time of a server*. Assuming the server is busy servicing items in its queue, the completion of a service is a random event. The distribution of service completions is Poisson-distributed (though we don't normally express this), and service times (which are the times between completion events in this case) are exponentially distributed. The statements *random service times* and exponential service times are equivalent. Due to the memoryless nature of random processes, if we begin the observation of a random server with average service time t_s, as it is in the middle of processing an item, the average time required to complete this service is still t_s, no matter how long the item had been in service prior to our observation. This property was used as an argument concerning the evaluation of the service time distribution coefficient for exponential service times in the derivation of equations 4–10 through 4–12.

CHARACTERIZING QUEUING SYSTEMS

Kendall [13] has defined a classification scheme for queuing systems that lends order to the various characteristics these can have. A queuing system is categorized as

$$A/B/c/K/m/Z$$

where

A = the arrival distribution of items into the queue,

B = the service time distribution of the servers,

c = the number of servers,

K = the maximum queue length,

m = the size of the population which may enter the queue, and

Z = the type of queue discipline (order of service of the items in the queue).

Several representations for the arrival and service time distributions (A and B) have been suggested, but for our purpose we will deal with four. A or B may be

M for a random (memoryless) distribution,

D for a constant distribution (such as a fixed service time),

G for a general distribution, and

U for a uniform distribution (this, admittedly, is added to the list by this author).

Thus, M/D/3/10/40/FIFO represents a queuing system in which arrivals are random, service time is constant, and there are 3 servers serving a queue which can be no longer than 10 items, serving a population of 40 on a first-come, first-serve basis.

If the maximum queue length is unlimited ($K = \infty$), if the population is infinite ($m = \infty$), and if the queue discipline is FIFO, then the last three terms are dropped. Then, for instance, an M/M/1 system is a system in which random arrivals are served by a single server with random service times. This is the simplest of all queuing systems. An M/G/1 system is one in which random arrivals are serviced by a single server with general service times. This is the case solved by Khintchine and Pollaczek.

INFINITE POPULATIONS

One of the parameters in Kendall's classification scheme is the size of the population m using the queue. This is a particularly important parameter for the following reason. If the size of the population is infinite, then the rate of arrival of users to the queue is independent of queue length and therefore of the load on the system. That is to say, no matter how long the queue, there is still an infinite population of users from which the next entry to the queue will emerge.

However, if the user population is finite, then those waiting in the queue are no longer candidates for entering the queue. As the queue grows, the available population dwindles, and the arrival rate falls off. As the load on the system grows, the imposed load decreases. Thus, the load on the system is an inverse function of itself (this is sometimes referred to as the graceful degradation of a system).

The analysis of queues formed from infinite populations is quite different from that of queues formed from finite populations. We will first consider infinite populations, about which a great deal can be said.

Some Properties of Infinite Populations

Regarding infinite populations, there are some general properties that can be useful. These include

1. *Queue input from several sources.* If several random sources each feed a common queue, each with different average arrival rates, r_i, then the total arrival distribution to the queue is a Poisson distribution with an arrival rate r equal to the sum of the component arrival rates, r_i (Martin [20], 393). (See Figure 4-4a.)

2. *Output distribution of M/M/c queues.* If one or more identical servers with exponential service times service a common queue with Poisson-type arrivals, then the outputs from that queue are Poisson-distributed, with the departure rate equal to the arrival rate, i.e., the departures have the same distribution as the arrivals (Saaty [24], 12-3). (See Figure 4-4b.)

3. *Transaction stream is split.* If a randomly distributed transaction stream is split into multiple paths, the transactions in each path are random streams with proportionate arrival rates (IBM [11], 49). (See Figure 4-4c.)

4. *Tandem queues.* From 2, a randomly distributed transaction stream passing through tandem compound queues will emerge as a randomly distributed stream with the same average rate as when it entered the system (IBM [11], 50). (See Figure 4-4d.)

5. *Order of service impact on response time.* The mean queue time and mean queue length as predicted by the Khintchine-Pollaczek equation is independent of the order in which the queue is serviced, so long as that order is not dependent upon the service time. This would not be true, for instance, if items requiring less service were serviced in advance of other items (Martin [19], 423). (See Figure 4-4e.)

Dispersion of Response Time

We have already discussed the need to be able to make a statement relative to the dispersion of the response time, something in the form "the probability that response time will be less than two seconds is 99.9%." We will discuss three approaches to this problem.

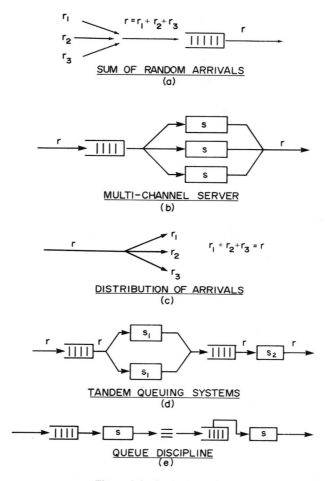

Figure 4-4   Queue properties.

Gamma distribution.   Without going into great detail, the Gamma function is the key to this statement. It is a more general form of a probability function of which the exponential distribution is a special case (see Martin [19], 437–439). It has the property that the sum of a set of variables follows a Gamma function if each of the variables follows a Gamma function.

In TP systems, a transaction usually passes through a series of servers, as we have seen. The response time of the system is the sum of the component delay times of each server. These are often servers with exponentially distributed service times (at least approximately). Though the sums of these delay times may not be exponential, they will be Gamma-distributed, and this distribution can be used to determine the probability that the system response time will be greater than a multiple of its mean.

To use this technique, we need to know the mean system response time and the variance of the system response time. The mean system response time is, of course, the primary focus of the performance model. The variance of this response time is more difficult and often impossible to calculate.

However, a reasonable limiting assumption to make is that the response time is random, i.e., it is exponentially distributed. In this case, the variance is the square of the mean. Real systems will usually have a smaller variance than this, i.e., the response time will not be completely random.

The Gamma distribution is used for these purposes as follows. First calculate the Gamma distribution parameter, R, where

$$R = \frac{\overline{T}^2}{\text{var}(T)} \tag{4-70}$$

T is the response time, and $\overline{T}$ is its mean. Then use the Gamma cumulative distribution function with parameter R to determine the probability that the response time will not exceed a multiple of the mean time.

Note that $R=1$ for a randomly distributed response time. Real-life response time variations will probably be less random and thus have a greater value of R. Certain values of these probabilities are listed in the following table for values of R from 1 to 10 (the range in which we would normally be interested).

TABLE 4-1.   TABLE OF $k = T/\overline{T}$

$R = \overline{T}^2/\text{var}(T)$		1	2	3	5	10
Probability of	.95	3.0	2.4	2.1	1.9	1.6
response time T	.99	4.7	3.4	2.8	2.4	1.9
not exceeding	.999	6.9	4.6	3.8	3.0	2.3
$k\overline{T}$	.9999	8.9	5.7	4.5	3.5	2.6

To take the conservative case of $R=1$, we can say that 95 percent of all services will finish in less than three mean service times, 99 percent in less than five mean service times, 99.9 percent in less than seven mean service times, and 99.99 percent in less than nine mean service times. This is often sufficient to conservatively validate the performance of a system. (These are the values that were used in the example in chapter 3.)

Central Limit Theorem.   According to the Central Limit Theorem, "the distribution of the sum of several random variables approaches the normal distribution for a wide class of variables as the number of random variables in the sum becomes large."

The precise test of how closely a system will approach a normal distribution is quite complex. However, the theorem has been shown to hold well in typical queuing analysis problems.

To use this theorem, the first step is to calculate the mean and variance of the resulting response time by adding the delay times for each of the components:

$$\overline{T} = \overline{T}_1 + \overline{T}_2 + \ldots$$

and

$$\mathrm{var}(T) = \mathrm{var}(T_1) + \mathrm{var}(T_2) + \ldots$$

Then, for a given probability, as given in Table 4-2, simply add the standard deviation, i.e., the square root of the variance, weighted by the factor p to the mean to obtain the maximum value of response time below which actual response times will fall with the given probability.

For instance, if mean response time is 4 seconds, and if its standard deviation is found to be 3 seconds, then with 99.9 percent probability, the response time will be less than $4 + 3.09 \times 3 = 13.27$ seconds.

TABLE 4-2.   NORMAL DISTRIBUTION

Probability	p
.90	1.28
.95	1.65
.99	2.33
.999	3.09
.9999	3.71

For random distributions in which the standard deviation is equal to the mean, Table 4-2 indicates that the maximum response time for a given probability is $(p + 1)$ times the mean response time.

Comparing Tables 4-1 and 4-2, the normal distribution technique equates approximately to $R = 2$ to 3 when random distributions are assumed.

Variance of response times.   For a queuing system in which inputs are random with arrival rate, R, and in which the distribution of the service time, T, is arbitrary, i.e., the Khintchine-Pollaczek M/G/1 case, the variance of the delay time, T_d, is given by*

$$\mathrm{var}(T_d) = \mathrm{var}(T_q) + \mathrm{var}(T)$$

or

$$\mathrm{var}(T_d) = \frac{R\overline{T^3}}{3(1-L)} + \frac{R^2\overline{T^2}^2}{4(1-L)^2} + \overline{T^2} - \overline{T}^2 \tag{4-71}$$

where

$\overline{T}$ is the mean of the service time, T
    (Note: elsewhere, this is noted simply as T.)

*This relation may be found in Martin [19], Martin [20], and IBM [11], each of which differs from the others and contains minor errors.

$\overline{T^2}$ is its second moment

$\overline{T^3}$ is its third moment

R is the arrival rate to the queue

L is the load on (occupancy of) the server

This is solved for the three following cases of interest:

1. *Exponential service time.* In this case,

$$\overline{T^2} = 2\overline{T}^2$$

and

$$\overline{T^3} = 6\overline{T}^3$$

Substituting these expressions into equation 4-71 yields the delay time variance for a server with exponentially distributed service time:

$$\text{var}(T_d) = \frac{\overline{T}^2}{(1-L)^2} \tag{4-72}$$

Note that this is the square of the mean service time as to be expected (see equation 4-11).

2. *Uniform service time.* If the service time may fall with equal probability between two limits (disk seeking is close to this), then

$$\overline{T^2} = \frac{4}{3}\overline{T}^2$$

$$\overline{T^3} = 2\overline{T}^3$$

and

$$\text{var}(T_d) = \frac{\overline{T}^2}{(1-L)^2}\left(\frac{1}{3} + \frac{L^2}{9}\right) \tag{4-73}$$

3. *Constant service time.* If the service time is constant (such as a polled communication line with a fixed-length message), then

$$\overline{T^2} = \overline{T}^2$$

$$\overline{T^3} = \overline{T}^3$$

and

$$\text{var}(T_d) = \frac{\overline{T}^2}{(1-L)^2}\left(\frac{L}{3} - \frac{L^2}{12}\right) \tag{4-74}$$

A reasonability check can be made on these variances by letting the load, L, approach zero. The delay time variance should approach the variance of the service time.

The results of this exercise are

$$\text{var}(T_d) \longrightarrow \overline{T}^2 \qquad \text{for exponential service}$$
$$\text{var}(T_d) \longrightarrow \overline{T}^2/3 \qquad \text{for uniform service}$$
$$\text{var}(T_d) \longrightarrow 0 \qquad \text{for constant service}$$

All of these are as to be expected, using var $(T) = \overline{T^2} - \overline{T}^2$ in each case.

Using the fact that the variance of a sum of random variables is the sum of the variances (equation 4-33), one can calculate the variance of the delay times, i.e., the variance of the response times, of a tandem queue in which a transaction flows through a series of servers. For instance, assume a transaction is processed by a communication line with constant service time, then by an application process with exponential service time, then by a disk with uniform service time, and finally by a communication line with constant service time. This situation is reflected in the following table with some sample values for service times and server loads. Service time variances are calculated according to the previous expressions.

TABLE 4-3. EXAMPLE TANDEM QUEUE

Step	Service time (t) distribution	Mean of T	Server load	Variance of T_d
Communications	Constant	.2	.2	.004
Process	Exponential	.3	.4	.250
Disk	Uniform	.4	.6	.373
Communications	Constant	.1	.2	.001
		1.0		.628

We see that the tandem queue provides us with a mean response time of one second and a variance of .628, i.e., a standard deviation of .792 seconds.

If we wished to use the Gamma distribution to determine the probability of a long response, we would calculate R as

$$R = \overline{T}^2/\text{var } (T) = 1^2/.628 = 1.6$$

Interpolating Table 4-1 for a 99.9 percentile, we find a value for k of 5.5. Multiplying the one-second mean service time by that number allows us to state that 99.9 percent of all transactions will be completed in less than 5.5 seconds.

As an alternative, we could use the Central Limit Theorem. At the 99.9% percentile, we see that we should move 3.09 standard deviations out from the mean. Thus, we can make the statement that 99.9 percent of all transactions will complete in less than (1 + 3.09 × .786) = 3.4 seconds.

The Gamma distribution gave us a more conservative result (5.5 seconds) than the Central Limit Theorem. In general, the more conservative result should be used. This will be given by the Gamma function for large, normalized standard deviations, i.e., the ratio of the standard deviation to its mean, and by the Central Limit Theorem for small, normalized standard deviations (typically, less than .6).

Properties of M/M/1 Queues

Queue lengths.   Queues formed by random arrivals at a server with random service times (an M/M/1 system) are the easiest to analyze. For an M/M/1 system, the probability that a queue will be a particular length can be derived through what is called a birth-death process. We used the birth part of this to derive the Poisson distribution.

We consider an M/M/1 queuing system, i.e., a single server with random arrivals and random service times, in which the average arrival rate is r and the average service rate is s. The probability that the queue will have length n is p_n, where the queue includes all items waiting in line plus the item being serviced.

If we consider a very short time interval, Δt, then the probability that an item will arrive at the queue is $r\Delta t$; this is a birth. Likewise, the probability that an item will leave the queue (assuming there is a queue) is $s\Delta t$; this is a death.

We observe the queue at some point in time and note with probability p_{n-1}, p_n, or p_{n+1} that there are $n-1$, n, or $n+1$ items, respectively, in the queue. If we come back at a time that is Δt later, we will find n items in the queue under the following conditions:

1. If there had been n items on the first observation and if there had been no arrivals or departures in the subsequent interval, Δt. Since the probability of no arrival is $(1-r\Delta t)$, and since the probability of no departure is $(1-s\Delta t)$, then this will occur with a probability $p_n (1-r\Delta t)(1-s\Delta t)$.

2. If there had been n items on the first observation and if there had been one arrival and one departure in the time interval Δt. This will occur with probability $p_n(r\Delta t)(s\Delta t)$.

3. If there had been $n-1$ items on the first observation and if there had been one arrival during the interval Δt, with no departures. This will occur with probability $p_{n-1}r\Delta t(1-s\Delta t)$.

4. If there had been $n+1$ items on the first observation and if there had been one departure during the interval Δt, with no arrivals. This occurs with probability $p_{n+1}s\Delta t(1-r\Delta t)$.

Ignoring terms with Δt^2, since these will disappear as Δt goes to zero, we have

$$p_n = p_n(1 - s\Delta t - r\Delta t) + p_{n-1}r\Delta t + p_{n+1}s\Delta t \qquad (4\text{-}75)$$

Accumulating p_n terms, this becomes

$$(s + r)p_n = rp_{n-1} + sp_{n+1} \qquad (4\text{-}76)$$

The load on the system, L, is

$$L = r/s$$

Thus, equation 4-76 can be rewritten as

$$p_{n+1} = (1 + L)\, p_n - Lp_{n-1} \qquad (4\text{-}77)$$

For $n=0$, there is no p_{n-1}, and there can be no departure if the initial value of n is zero. Thus, equation 4-75 can be manipulated for the case of $n=0$ to give

$$p_1 = Lp_o \tag{4-78}$$

Using equations 4-77 and 4-78 iteratively, we find

$$p_2 = L^2 p_o$$

$$p_3 = L^3 p_o$$

and

$$p_n = L^n p_o$$

Since L is the load on the server, it represents the probability that the server is occupied. Thus, the probability that the server is unoccupied is $1-L$. This is the probability that there are no items in the system (no queue):

$$p_o = 1-L \tag{4-79}$$

The probability of the queue length being n is

$$p_n = L^n(1-L) \tag{4-80}$$

We can perform some checks on this result as follows. First, the sum of these probabilities should be unity:

$$\sum_{n=0}^{\infty} p_n = \sum_{n=0}^{\infty} L^n(1-L) = (1-L)\sum_{n=0}^{\infty} L^n = \frac{1-L}{1-L} = 1$$

Next, we can calculate the average queue length, Q:

$$Q = \sum_{n=0}^{\infty} nL^n(1-L) = (1-L)\sum_{n=1}^{\infty} nL^n$$

Using equation 4-50, this becomes

$$Q = (1-L)\frac{L}{(1-L)^2} = \frac{L}{1-L} \tag{4-81}$$

This is just what Khintchine-Pollaczek predicted (see equation 4-10). The other results can be similarly verified.

Finally, the variance of the queue length is given by

$$\text{var}(n) = Q + Q^2 = \frac{L}{(1-L)^2} \tag{4-82}$$

(The derivation of this is complex; see Saaty [24], 40.)

The probability that a queue will exceed n items, $P(q > n)$, is

$$P(Q>n) = \sum_{n=n+1}^{\infty} L^n(1-L) = (1-L)\sum_{n=n+1}^{\infty} L^n = (1-L)\frac{L^{n+1}}{1-L}$$

from equation 4-47. Thus,

$$p(Q > n) = L^{n+1} \tag{4-83}$$

Summarizing what we have just deduced about the properties of M/M/1 queues, we have

Probability of queue length being n:

$$p_n = L^n(1-L) \tag{4-84}$$

Average queue length:

$$Q = \frac{L}{1-L} \tag{4-85}$$

Variance of queue length:

$$\mathrm{var}(Q) = \frac{L}{(1-L)^2} \tag{4-86}$$

Probability of queue length exceeding n:

$$P(Q > n) = L^{n+1} \tag{4-87}$$

Also, from equations 4-20 through 4-22:

$$W = Q - L = \frac{L^2}{1-L} \tag{4-88}$$

$$T_q = \frac{WT}{L} = \frac{L}{1-L} T \tag{4-12}$$

and

$$T_d = \frac{QT}{L} = \frac{1}{1-L} T \tag{4-11}$$

As noted by the equation numbers, the expressions for T_q and T_d are the same as those previously derived.

Properties of M/G/1 Queues

We have already derived the properties of queues formed by random arrivals to a server with a known, though not necessarily random, service time distribution. These are the Khintchine-Pollaczek equations, which are repeated here for convenience.

$$W = \frac{kL^2}{1-L} \tag{4-4}$$

$$Q = \frac{L}{1-L} [1 - (1-k)L] \tag{4-6}$$

$$T_d = \frac{1}{1-L} [1 - (1-k)L]T \tag{4-8}$$

$$T_q = \frac{kL}{1-L} T \tag{4-9}$$

$$k = \frac{1}{2} \frac{E(T^2)}{T^2} \tag{4-16}$$

Single-Channel Server with Priorities

In many of our systems, the server is serving a queue organized by priorities. When the server becomes free, it next services the item that has the highest priority and has waited the longest in its priority class.

There are two types of priority service disciplines of interest to us. One is nonpreemptive servicing, in which the service of an item is completed before the service of another item is started, even though a higher priority item may have arrived after servicing started. On the other hand, a preemptive service discipline requires that the servicing of an item be suspended if a higher priority item arrives. When the higher priority item has been serviced, servicing of the original item resumes where it left off.

The impact of priority service can be deduced intuitively by noting that, so far as an item being serviced is concerned, the capacity of a server is reduced by the time which it must spend servicing higher priority items. Let L_h be the load imposed on the server by items of higher priority than the one we are considering. The amount of time left to service an item at the considered priority is $(1-L_h)$ of the total time. The average amount of time required to service an item at priority p, T_p', is

$$T_p' = T_p + L_h T_p'$$

Here T_p is the time to service an item at priority p if there were no higher priority interference. This equation states that T_p of the server's time is actually spent servicing the item. However, during the total time, T_p', that the item is being serviced, the server spends L_h of that time tending to higher priority duties. Thus, the effective time to service the item is

$$T_p' = \frac{T_p}{1-L_h}$$

In effect, the service time at priority p has been lengthened by the factor $1/(1-L_h)$. The world has slowed down at priority p.

We found earlier (equation 4-9) that the time an item must wait in a queue for a single priority server carrying a load L is $T_q = kLT/(1-L)$. However, if the server must also process a higher priority load of L_h, we now know that the time that an item will wait in the queue at priority p, T_{qp}, is

$$T_{qp} = \frac{kLT}{(1-L)(1-L_h)} \tag{4-89}$$

Note that the term kLT is, in fact, the amount of service time left for the item currently being serviced when a new item arrives at the queue. Let us call this term T_o. Then

$$T_{qp} = \frac{T_o}{(1-L)(1-L_h)}$$ (4-90)

where

T_{qp} = average queue wait time at priority p.

T_o = average service time remaining for the item being serviced when a new item arrives at the queue.

L = load imposed on the server by items at priority p and higher.

L_h = load imposed on the server by items at priorities greater than p.

If we number our priorities from 1 to $p_{\max}$, with the convention that items with higher priority numbers have precedence over items with lower priority numbers, the above definitions for L and L_h can be expressed as follows:

$$L = \sum_{i=p}^{p_{\max}} L_i$$

$$L_h = \sum_{i=p+1}^{p_{\max}} L_i$$

where

$$L_i = \text{load imposed on the server by items at priority } i.$$

Equation 4-90 is quite general and is, in fact, applicable to most server systems. This result is rigorously derived by Saaty [24] and Kleinrock [15] (see Appendix 7). Let us now apply this quite general result to nonpreemptive and preemptive servers.

Nonpreemptive server.   For a nonpreemptive server, the average service time remaining for the item being serviced when a new item enters the queue is the average of such times over all priorities:

$$T_o = \sum_{i=1}^{p_{\max}} k_i L_i T_i$$

That is, the remaining service time at priority i is $k_i T_i$, and a priority i item will be in the server L_i of the time. Let L_t be the total load on the server and T_t be the service time averaged over all priorities. Then the probability that an item being serviced is at priority i is L_i/L_t. If k_i is independent of priority, i.e., the nature of the service is the same regardless of priority, then we can assign $k_i = k$ and rewrite T_o as

$$T_o = kL_t \sum_{i=1}^{p_{\max}} \frac{L_i}{L_t} T_i$$

or

$$T_o = kL_tT_t$$

Thus,

$$T_{qp} = \frac{kL_tT_t}{(1-L)(1-L_h)} \tag{4-91a}$$

where

L_t = total load imposed on the server by items at all priorities.

T_t = service time averaged over all priorities.

Once an item is given to the server, its service is not preempted. Therefore, from equation 4-22,

$$T_{dp} = T_{qp} + T_p \tag{4-91b}$$

where

T_{dp} = delay time through the server (queue wait time plus service time) at priority p.

T_p = service time at priority p.

Preemptive server.   For preemptive service, the activity at lower priorities is transparent to an item, since the service of lower priority items is immediately suspended and not resumed so long as a higher priority item is in the system. Therefore, using an argument similar to that used for nonpreemptive servers,

$$T_o = \sum_{i=p}^{p_{max}} k_i L_i T_i = kL \sum_{i=p}^{p_{max}} \frac{L_i}{L} T$$

or

$$T_o = kLT$$

where

T = service time averaged over all priorities at priority p and higher.

When an item is given to the server, it will be interrupted by higher priority activity. Thus, service time at priority p is $T_p/(1-L_h)$, and

$$T_{qp} = \frac{kLT}{(1-L)(1-L_h)} \tag{4-92a}$$

$$T_{dp} = T_{qp} + \frac{T_p}{1-L_h} \tag{4-92b}$$

Multiple-Channel Server (M/M/c)

A multiple channel queuing system comprises c channels serving a single queue into which items are arriving at a rate R. As soon as a server channel finishes processing an item, it starts servicing the next item at the head of the queue. Each server has an average service time, T.

The distribution of the queue lengths, p_n, is as follows, where n is the total number of items in the system, including those being serviced (Saaty [24], 116):

$$p_n = p_o(cL)^n/n! \ , \ 1 \leq n \leq c \tag{4-93}$$

and

$$p_n = p_o(L)^n c^c/c! \ , \ c \leq n \tag{4-94}$$

p_o is calculated from $\sum_{n=0}^{\infty} p_n = 1$:

$$p_o^{-1} = \sum_{n=0}^{c-1} (cL)^n/n! + (cL)^c/c!(1-L) \tag{4-95}$$

In the above expressions, L is the average load on each server. The total system load is

$$cL = RT \tag{4-96}$$

The average number of items waiting in the queue for service, W, is equal to the average number of items in the system in excess of the number of servers, c. From equation 4-94:

$$W = \sum_{n=c+1}^{\infty} (n-c)p_n = \sum_{n=c+1}^{\infty} (n-c)p_o(L)^n c^c/c!$$

Changing the summation index to $x = n-c$, we have

$$W = \frac{p_o c^c}{c!} \sum_{x=1}^{\infty} x(L)^{x+c} = \frac{p_o(cL)^c}{c!} \sum_{x=1}^{\infty} x(L)^x$$

From equation 4-50, W may be expressed as

$$W = \frac{L(cL)^c}{c!(1-L)^2} p_o \tag{4-97}$$

The average number of items in the system, Q, including those being serviced, is, from equation 4-20,

$$Q = W + cL \tag{4-98}$$

The average waiting time in the queue, T_q, is obtained from equation 4-21:

$$T_q = \frac{WT}{cL} = \frac{(cL)^c}{c(c!)(1-L)^2} p_o T \tag{4-99}$$

The average delay time through the system, i.e., queue time plus service time, is, from equation 4-22,

$$T_d = T_q + T \qquad (4\text{-}100)$$

The above equations apply for exponential service times. However, Martin points out (Martin [20], 461) that simulation studies have shown that the waiting line size, W, and waiting time, T_q, do vary in about the same way as does the Khintchine-Pollaczek distribution coefficient k, just as do single server queues. Thus, for general service time distributions,

$$W \approx \frac{kL(cL)^c}{c!(1-L)^2} p_o \qquad (4\text{-}101)$$

$$Q \approx W + cL \qquad (4\text{-}102)$$

$$T_q \approx \frac{k(cL)^c}{c(c!)(1-L)^2} p_o T \qquad (4\text{-}103)$$

and

$$T_d \approx T_q + T. \qquad (4\text{-}104)$$

Note for $c=1$, equations 4-95, 4-97, and 4-99 reduce to

$$p_o = \frac{1}{1 + L/(1-L)} = 1-L$$

and

$$W = \frac{L^2}{1-L}$$

$$T_q = \frac{LT}{1-L}$$

which are the single-server Khintchine-Pollaczek equations 4-4 and 4-9 for $k=1$. Q and T_d also reduce to equations 4-6 and 4-8 for $k=1$.

Multiple-Channel Server with Priorities

Equation 4-90 is quite general and applies to multiple-channel servers as well as to single-channel servers (see Saaty [24], p. 234). Equation 4-90 states that $T_q = T_o/(1-L)$ for a single priority server. Thus, from equation 4-99 for a multiple channel server,

$$T_o = \frac{(cL)^c}{c(c!)(1-L)} p_o T \qquad (4\text{-}105)$$

Nonpreemptive server.   For nonpreemptive service, T_o is averaged over all priorities:

$$T_{qp} = \frac{(cL_t)^c}{c(c!)(1-L_t)(1-L)(1-L_h)} p_o T_t \qquad (4\text{-}106\text{a})$$

$$T_{dp} = T_{qp} + T_p \qquad (4\text{-}106\text{b})$$

$$p_o^{-1} = \sum_{n=o}^{c-1} (cL_t)^n/n! + (cL_t)^c/c!(1-L_t) \qquad (4\text{-}106\text{c})$$

Preemptive server.   For preemptive service, lower priority service is transparent, and T_o is therefore averaged over all priorities from the considered priority and higher:

$$T_{qp} = \frac{(cL)^c}{c(c!)(1-L)^2(1-L_h)} p_o T \qquad (4\text{-}107\text{a})$$

$$T_{dp} = T_{qp} + \frac{T_p}{1-L_h} \qquad (4\text{-}107\text{b})$$

$$p_o^{-1} = \sum_{n=o}^{c-1} (cL)^n/n! + (cL)^c/c!(1-L) \qquad (4\text{-}107\text{c})$$

FINITE POPULATIONS

As discussed previously, queues formed from finite populations have the characteristic of *graceful degradation*: as the load on the system increases, the arrival rate decreases because of a reduced active population. In general, the population should be considered finite unless it is much larger than the expected queue lengths.

Common applications in TP systems include the following:

- Terminals on a multidropped communication line which contend for that line,
- Multiple servers (in the requestor-server sense) accessing a data base,
- Processors in a multiprocessor system contending for main memory.

The following is based on IBM [11], with some corrections and much enhancing. In general, we think of a user as doing some work before entering the queue. This time is called the availability time, T_a, and is assumed to be exponentially distributed. It is the time that a terminal is used prior to bidding for the line (often called "think time," since it represents the time that the user is thinking before entering the next transaction) or the time that a data-base manager spends processing a request before getting in line for the disk or the time spent actively processing by a processor before requesting its next common memory access.

Once in line, the user must wait a time, T_q, prior to being serviced and then an average exponentially-distributed service time of T. Thus, on the average, each user will cycle through the system every $(T_a + T_q + T)$ seconds. The user's availability time, T_a, is independent of the system, and T is unaffected by system load. However, as the system becomes loaded, the waiting time, T_q, increases, thus slowing down the arrival rates of the users. This is the graceful degradation effect.

Let us define a *service ratio*, z, as the ratio of availability time, T_a, to the average service time, T:

$$z = T_a/T \tag{4-108}$$

If the user is almost always available, i.e., not in the queue, the user's service ratio may be arbitrarily large. If the user is almost always in the queue, the service ratio may approach zero.

Since each user arrives at the queue every $(T_a + T_q + T)$ seconds on the average, and since there are m users, then the arrival rate, R, of users to the queue is

$$R = \frac{m}{T_a+T_q+T} = \frac{m/T}{z+T_q/T+1} \tag{4-109}$$

and the load, L, on the system is

$$L = RT = \frac{m}{z+T_q/T+1} \tag{4-110}$$

As an aside, equation 4-109 can be solved for $T_d = T_q + T$ as

$$T_d = \frac{m}{R} - T_a$$

This is known as the Response Time law (Lazowska [16]) and relates the system response time, T_d, to the individual interarrival time, m/R, and the think time, T_a. That is, the response time is the individual interarrival time minus the availability time—an intuitively obvious relationship.

From equation 4-21,

$$T_q = \frac{WT}{L} = \frac{WT}{m}(z+T_q/T+1) \tag{4-111}$$

Solving equation 4-111 for T_q gives

$$T_q = \frac{W(z+1)}{m-W}T \tag{4-112}$$

From equations 4-21 and 4-112, system load, L, can be expressed as

$$L = \frac{m-W}{z+1} \tag{4-113}$$

Solving for W,

$$W = m - (z+1)L \tag{4-114}$$

From equations 4-20 and 4-114,

$$Q = W + L = m - zL \tag{4-115}$$

and from equation 4-22,

$$T_d = T_q + T \tag{4-116}$$

Equations 4-112 through 4-116 express the queuing relationships for a finite population and for any number of servers as a function of the service ratio, z. Note that these relationships apply to both single-server and multiple-server queuing systems by substituting cL for L, where c is the number of servers, and L is the load on each server. The only assumption is that the availability time, T_a, and the service time, T, are exponentially distributed. However, L and W are functions of each other, and their solution depends on the number of servers. The evaluation of these terms is discussed in the next sections.

One other general relationship of interest is the probability that a user is busy, i.e., is in the queue or is being serviced. Since users arrive in the queue at a combined rate of R, each user will arrive once every m/R seconds, on the average, and will spend an average time of T_d seconds in the system. Thus, the probability that a single user is busy waiting for the server or being serviced is

$$P(\text{busy}) = \frac{RT_d}{m} = \frac{L}{mT}(T_q + T) = 1 - \frac{zL}{m} \tag{4-117}$$

using equations 4-112 and 4-114 for the simplification.

These relationships will be used to study the single-server and multiple-server cases.

Single-Server Queues (M/M/1/m/m)

For a single-server queue with random service times serving a finite population of size m with random availability times, the probability that n items will be in the system (including the one being serviced) can be shown to be the following (IBM [11]):

$$p_n = \frac{\dfrac{z^{m-n}}{(m-n)!}}{\displaystyle\sum_{j=0}^{m} \dfrac{z^j}{j!}} \tag{4-118}$$

The server utilization (or load), L, is the probability that the server is busy, i.e., the queue length is nonzero:

$$L = \sum_{n=1}^{m} p_n = \sum_{n=1}^{m} \frac{\dfrac{z^{m-n}}{(m-n)!}}{\displaystyle\sum_{j=0}^{m} \dfrac{z^j}{j!}} \tag{4-119}$$

As a sanity check, the case for $z=0$ represents full loading. The significant terms in equation 4-119 as z approaches zero occur for $n=m$ and $j=0$. In this case, L becomes 1 as would be expected.

For very large values of z, the significant terms are for $n=1$ and $j=m$. In this case, L approaches m/z. For an unloaded system (z infinite), L becomes zero as expected.

Equations 4-114, 4-115, 4-112, and 4-116, respectively, may be used with this expression for L to calculate W, Q, T_q, and T_d.

Multiple-Server Queues (M/M/c/m/m)

The finite population system has been solved for the finite-population, multiple-channel case. This is probably the most general solution of practical usefulness that exists as of the time of this writing. As with the single-channel case, it is assumed that both service time, T, and availability time, T_a, are exponentially distributed.

A typical (and very important) example of this type of queuing system in TP systems is the case in which multiple application programs access a data base via multiple copies of a data-base manager. In this case, the application programs are the users, and the data-base managers are the servers.

Again, the service ratio, z, is defined as

$$z = T_a/T$$

Let c be the number of servers and m the number of users. Then the probability, p_n, of there being n users in the queue can be shown to be the following (IBM [11], 45–46):

$$p_n = \binom{m}{n} \frac{1}{z^n} p_o, \ 1 \le n \le c \tag{4-120}$$

and

$$p_n = \frac{n!}{c!c^{n-c}} \binom{m}{n} \frac{1}{z^n} p_o, \ c \le n \le m \tag{4-121}$$

where $\binom{m}{n}$ is the binomial coefficient:

$$\binom{m}{n} = \frac{m!}{n!(m-n)!} \tag{4-122}$$

p_o is such that it satisfies

$$p_o = 1 - \sum_{n=1}^{m} p_n \tag{4-123}$$

W is the average number of users in the system exceeding the number of servers, c. Thus,

$$W = \sum_{n=c+1}^{m} (n-c)p_n \tag{4-124}$$

Knowing W as a function of z (the only variable in p_n) allows us to evaluate Q, T_q, and T_d from equations 4-113 (which gives the load L) and from equations 4-115, 4-112, and 4-116, respectively.

A different and somewhat more complex solution to this problem is given by Saaty [24], 326–327.

Computational Considerations for Finite Populations

The expressions for finite populations do not generally lend themselves to manual calculation. This is because they must be solved iteratively for many cases. This can be seen by the following reasoning.

The length of the waiting line, W, is a function of the service ratio, z. z is a function of the availability time, T_a. In many of our analyses, the average arrival rate at the queue is fixed as R, where R/m is the transaction rate per user. The availability time, T_a, is then $T_a = m/R - T_q - T$ (see equation 4-109). Thus, T_a is a function of T_q, which is a function of W. Thus, W is a complex function of itself.

Consequently, these expressions are best evaluated iteratively by computer. Typically, a choice for z will be made, and W will be calculated. Using W, T_q can be calculated from equation 4-112 and then T_a from equation 4-109. z can now be calculated, and if this value does not equal the starting value for z, a new value for z is chosen. This process continues until it converges on a common value for z.

Of course, if the model being evaluated has a determined average availability time, T_a, then these expressions can be calculated manually.

COMPARISON OF QUEUE TYPES

As we have seen, the delay time of a queuing system is sensitive to several parameters, most notable of which are the following:

- Load on the server(s).
- Distribution of service times.
- Number of servers.
- Size of population serviced by the system.

We generally assume that arrivals are Poisson-distributed.

It is useful to obtain a graphic feel for the effect of these parameters. We first consider the distribution of service times. Figure 4-5 shows the normalized response time, T_d/T, of single-server queues with a variety of response-time distributions:

- Exponential (M/M/1).
- Uniform (M/U/1).
- Constant (M/D/1).

As was previously discussed, a server with constant service time performs better than one with a uniformly distributed service time and even more so relative to a server with an exponentially distributed service time. Though the server performance curves of Figure 4-5 appear to be close, this can be misleading. It is true that differences at low

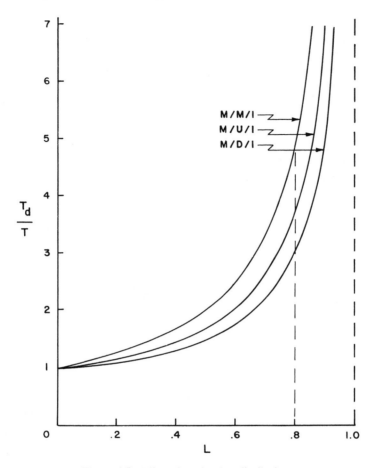

Figure 4-5   Effect of service-time distribution.

loads may not be significant. However, consider heavily loaded servers, as shown in the following table.

TABLE 4-4.   NORMALIZED
DELAY TIME (T_d/T)

	Server load		
	.7	.8	.9
Exponential	3.3	5.0	10.0
Uniform	2.6	3.7	7.0
Constant	2.2	3.0	5.5

At 90 percent server load, the response time, T_d, for a server with exponential service time is nearly twice that of a server with constant service time.

Another practical consideration for a queuing system can also be noted with reference to Figure 4–5. Consider an M/M/1 system that is 50 percent loaded. Its normalized delay time, T_d/T, is $1/(1 - L) = 2$. If the load imposed on this server increases by 10 percent to .55, then its normalized delay time becomes 2.22, or an 11 percent increase. At an 80 percent load, the normalized delay time is 5. A 10 percent load increase to 88 percent causes the delay time to increase to 8.33—a 67 percent increase. At 90 percent load, a 10 percent load increase to 99 percent causes a normalized delay time increase of 1000 percent!

This effect is called *amplification*. As the load on the system is increased, small changes in load cause ever greater amplification of delay-time changes. The range of response times as seen by a user fluctuates over a wider range, usually increasing levels of frustration.

For this reason, a common rule of thumb is to keep resource loading to a level less than 60 to 70 percent. At this level of loading, a system will be reasonably well-behaved in the presence of small load variations.

The comparison of systems with multiple servers or with finite populations or with both is more complex. However, a feel for the impact of these parameters can be obtained by studying Figure 4–6. This figure shows normalized response time, T_d/T, as a function of individual server load, L, for four cases:

1. The simple M/M/1 case of a single server serving an infinite population of users.
2. Three servers serving an infinite population (M/M/3).
3. A single server serving a population of only 10 users (M/M/1/10/10).
4. Three servers serving a population of 10 users (M/M/3/10/10).

Note the following characteristics:

- Having n servers serving a common queue of users (M/M/3 in Figure 4–6) is more efficient than having n servers each serving $1/n$ of the users (each being an M/M/1 server in Figure 4–6). We would rather wait in a common line for several bank tellers than have to pick a teller and then wait in a line dedicated to that teller.
- Response time improves for a queuing system as the population served by that system becomes smaller. This is because queues cannot grow as large or as quickly.
- The response time characteristic of finite populations approximates that for infinite populations when the population is much greater than the average queue length would be for infinite populations, i.e., for small loads. In Figure 4–6, a queue length of 1 occurs in the M/M/1 system for a load, L, of 0.5. At this point, the delay time for the finite population case M/M/1/10/10 is within 10 percent of the infinite population case M/M/1. Though not shown, a queue length of 1

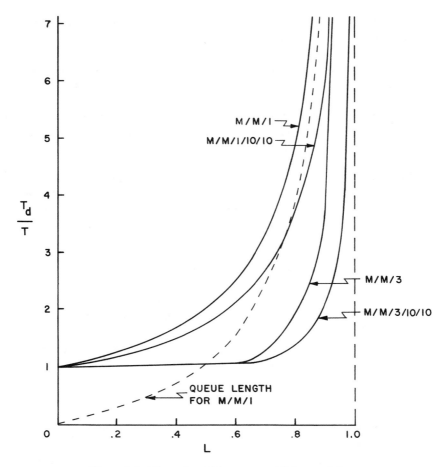

Figure 4-6   Effect of multiple servers and finite populations.

occurs for the M/M/3 system at a load, L, of .67. Again, the response times for the M/M/3 and M/M/3/10/10 systems are within 10 percent at this point. In both cases, so long as the finite population is an order of magnitude greater than the queue length, $(10 \gg 1)$, the infinite population solution is a reasonably accurate approximation.

An interesting rule of thumb follows from this observation and from the 60 to 70 percent load rule suggested earlier. At 2/3 load (66.7 percent), the average queue length is $L/(1 - L) = 2$. Since in most cases we do not want to exceed this load, we will not normally expect average queue lengths to be greater than 2. Therefore, a population of 20 will generally suffice to qualify as an infinite population. For population sizes less than 20, or for those cases where loads will exceed 67 percent, it may be advisable to consider the system as one with a finite population.

Figure 4–6 fails to answer one other important question. Given the need for a specific capacity, is it better to use a single high-capacity server or several lower capacity servers operating from the same queue?

Let us say that we decide that a resource must have an ultimate capacity to service 10 items per second. Figure 4–7 shows two solutions to this need:

- A more powerful single server with a service time of 0.1 second (M/M/1).
- Three less powerful servers operating in parallel serving the queue of items, each of these having a service time of 0.3 seconds (M/M/3).

In either case, a maximum of 10 items per second can be serviced.

As shown by Figure 4–7, the single-server system is decidely better at all loads, since its service time is much smaller, resulting in shorter delay times. If more servers were used in the multiserver case, then each would only get slower and aggravate the situation.

Thus, from Figures 4–6 and 4–7, we can make the following observations relative to the applicability of single-server and multiserver systems:

- If the choice to be made is the organization of n like servers, then it is better to feed them from a common queue rather than from individual queues (Figure 4–6).
- If the choice to be made is between one high-speed server and many lower speed servers, choose the high-speed server (Figure 4–7).

Typical examples of these situations follow.

- A replicated set of server processes should be driven from a common queue.
- A multiprocessor system with n processors sharing a common memory and serving a common task queue will outperform a multicomputer system with n computers if all processors have the same power.
- A single high-speed computer will outperform a multiprocessor system or a multicomputer system with the same cumulative capacity.
- A single high-speed disk unit will outperform multiple lower speed disk units with the same combined capacity.

SUMMARY

The queuing models described in this chapter are summarized in Appendix 2, with notational symbology being summarized in Appendix 1. The queuing expressions are grouped according to their Kendall classifications, where the author has defined certain classification types for the terms $A/B/c/k/m/z$ to meet the needs of the models presented.

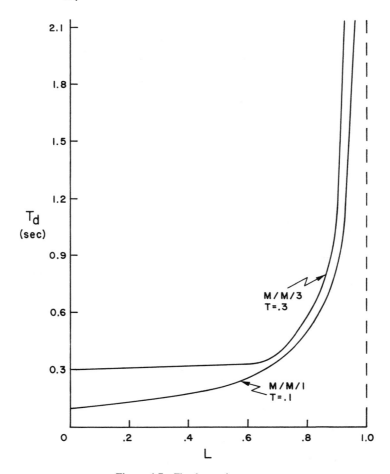

Figure 4-7   Fixed-capacity systems.

For arrival and service time distributions (A/B), the following classes have been presented:

M—random (Poisson, expontential)
U —uniform
D —constant
G —general

For the number of servers (c), we have

1—single server
c—finite servers

For the maximum queue length, k, we have always assumed an infinite queue ($k = \infty$). For finite queues, most models provide the probability distribution of queue lengths so that the probability of queue overflow can be considered.

For m, the number of potential users in the system, we have

m—a finite population of users

∞—an infinite population of users

Finally, for type of queue discipline, we have

A   —any

FIFO—first-in, first-out

PP   —preemptive priority

NP   —nonpreemptive priority

If any of the last three classification terms $/k/m/z$ are left off a queue system classification, it implies an infinite queue, infinite population, and a first-in, first-out service ($/k/m/z = /\infty/\infty/$FIFO). Also note that if a finite population of size m is considered, the maximum queue length is also m.

The queue systems we have studied include

$M/G/1/\infty/\infty/A$ (The Khintchine-Pollaczek case)

$M/M/1/\infty/\infty/A$

$M/U/1/\infty/\infty/A$

$M/D/1/\infty/\infty/A$ (These three are derivatives of $M/G/1$)

$M/G/1$ (for delay time variance)

$M/M/1$ (for queue distributions)

$M/G/1/\infty/\infty/PP$ (preemptive priorities)

$M/G/1/\infty/\infty/NP$ (nonpreemptive priorities)

$M/M/c$ (multichannel server)

$M/G/c$ (an approximation)

$M/M/c/\infty/\infty/PP$ (multiserver with preemptive priorities)

$M/M/c/\infty/\infty/NP$ (multiserver with nonpreemptive priorities)

$M/M/1/m/m$ (single-channel limited population)

$M/M/c/m/m$ (multichannel limited population)

Though many other cases have been studied in the literature, these are the ones that have useful solutions and which are of most interest to us.

The remainder of the book deals with the application of these concepts to the performance analysis of transaction processing systems. The intent is to show how to use these tools to create solutions to real-life problems. Though some application results are general, their intent is not to form a cookbook. Rather, the goal is to be able to look at a new and unique problem and determine an adequate, if approximate, solution.

5

Communications

The processing of a transaction begins with some pertinent event outside of the transaction processing system. This event could be a customer making a request to a teller or ticket salesperson, a status change in a power network, or an alarm generated by a patient-monitoring unit in a hospital. The first thing that must be done is to send the data describing this event to the TP system. This is the role of *communications*.

The study of communication facilities fills many volumes. The communication industry is a multibillion dollar industry with nearly a century of history. It is highly regulated and well-understood technically. It is a subject of intense standardization by organizations such as the American National Standards Institute (ANSI) and the European International Telegraph and Telephone Consultative Committee (CCITT). (Compare this state of affairs to that of the large but still fledgling computer industry, where we continue to dabble in seeking to understand what we are doing.)

Therefore, we can only scratch the surface of this massive body of knowledge. And we will do so only to the extent that we can understand and account for the performance issues involved in communicating a transaction to the TP system and in returning a reply.

The first half of this chapter consists of sections that provide the communication background for the performance sections that follow. For the communication novice, these initial sections range from the simple to the sublime, covering characteristics of communication channels, methods of data transmission, protocol concepts, and modern open systems via layered protocols. Those well-versed in communications may want to simply skim these sections for the terminology used later.

The later sections use examples to develop performance-analysis techniques for message transfer and establishment/termination procedures. These include half-duplex and full-duplex message transfer, point-to-point and multipoint (LAN) contention networks, and multipoint polled networks.

PERFORMANCE IMPACT OF COMMUNICATIONS

In a TP system, a communication line is a server. It is a resource of finite capacity that must pass data between the user and the TP host. The average time that it takes to pass this data is its *service time*.

Communication lines are often shared by many user terminals. Therefore, what may form are queues of user transactions awaiting access to the line.

The role of the communication facility in TP system performance is shown generally in Figure 5-1. The data describing the transaction arrives at the facility but must wait for access to it (1). The transaction data is then transmitted over the communication line (2) and enters a queue (3) of work waiting to be processed by the host (4). When the host has generated a reply (which is a performance study in itself), it enters that reply into a queue (5) to await access to the outgoing line. Finally, the reply is returned to the user (6) via the communication facility.

So far, simple. However, the analysis of waiting times and service times has many complexities not evident in this simple description. Communication queues, for example, are often not first-in, first-out queues. Rather, access is granted to the line in an orderly fashion by polling terminals in a round-robin fashion or in a disorderly fashion by letting a terminal grab the line and see if it is successful in transmitting without colliding with another terminal's transmission.

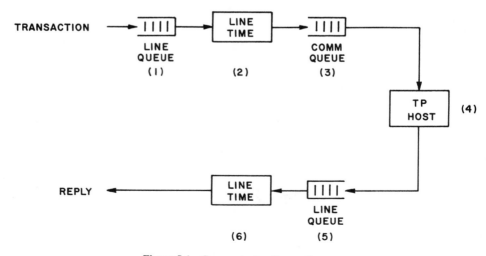

Figure 5-1 Communication line performance.

Line service times are complicated by the fact that considerable overhead may be required to pass one block of data. This overhead is created by the protocol procedures necessary for ensuring proper identification of communication traffic and its protection against errors. Furthermore, line service time can be a function of the line error rate, as blocks in error may have to be retransmitted.

In the following sections we will discuss the various communication techniques, message protocols, and network concepts which make up a TP communication facility and which can have an impact on TP performance.

COMMUNICATION CHANNELS

The first level in the communication hierarchy is the physical communication channel itself, which can take many forms. Some forms are obtainable from public networks, and others may be privately furnished.

Dedicated Lines

The simplest of all communication channels is the dedicated line (Figure 5-2a). This channel is permanently established and may support a single terminal or multiple terminals. If the line supports a single terminal (a point-to-point connection), then communication may be under control of the host, i.e., the host is the "master," and the terminal is the "slave." As an alternative, the terminal and host may both act as master and contend for the line.

If many terminals are *multidropped* on the line (a terminal connection is referred to as a *drop*), then they are usually controlled by a polling protocol in which the host master queries each terminal for incoming data on a round-robin basis or according to some other poll schedule. The host also directs outgoing traffic to a specific terminal or group of terminals.

Dedicated lines are highly efficient, as no time is spent in establishing the connection; the connection is permanent. However, dedicated lines are also quite costly and are generally justified only if they can be highly utilized.

Dialed Lines

For occasional use, dialed connections via a public network are often used (Figure 5-2b). When a user wishes to communicate with the TP host, he dials the host manually or via an automatic terminal dialing function and establishes a point-to-point connection for the duration of his session with the host.

Dialed connections can be quite economical for occasional use. However, connection-establishment time can be significant (many seconds); even worse, all host ports could be found busy. Only one terminal per dialed connection can be supported, and data rates are significantly less than those achievable on dedicated lines. Compounding the data-rate limitations are the higher error rates found on dialed lines (typically an order

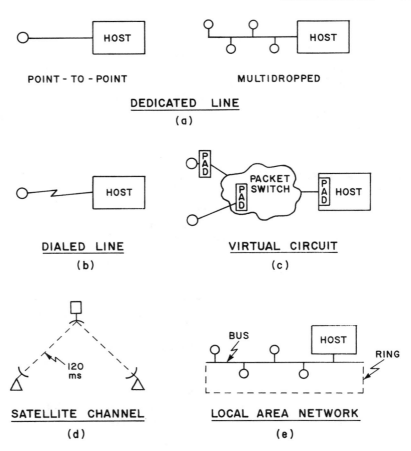

Figure 5-2 Communication channels.

of magnitude greater than those found on dedicated lines). These error rates slow the line even further because of retransmission requirements.

Virtual Circuits

The dedicated and dialed connections described above have one characteristic in common: once the connection is established, equipment is dedicated to that conversation from source to destination until the circuit is broken. Therefore, valuable communication equipment lies idle during pauses in the data conversation, equipment that could in principal be used to support other conversations, thereby increasing the capacity of the network and reducing the cost to the user.

The emergence of public and private packet switching networks has addressed this dilemma (Figure 5-2c). Using this technology, a user's data message is broken up into fixed-length packets. Each packet is routed independently through the network to its destination. Thus, each physical circuit connecting switching nodes in the network actually carries traffic from several users on an as-needed basis. In fact, if a node gets very busy, many networks will route packets around that node using alternate routes.

Thus, the packets comprising a message may, in fact, take different paths through the network to their common destination. The different transmission times imposed by these various paths, compounded by random delays caused by queuing and line errors, mean that there is no guarantee that the packets will arrive at their destination in the same order in which they were sent.

The proper disassembly of the message into packets at its source and the subsequent reassembly of the packets to reconstitute the original message at its destination is the function of a specialized piece of terminal equipment called a *PAD* (Packet Assembly and Disassembly). PADs may either be furnished by the customer and be located on the customer's premises or may be furnished by the network operator at the switch sites. In the latter case, customers communicate with the PAD over a standard dedicated or dialed communication line, as described above.

The host PAD is often implemented within the host via software, thus eliminating the need for special PAD hardware.

The connection between customers through a packet-switched network is called a *virtual circuit*, since it is logically there (what I send, you receive) but not physically there. That is, one cannot point to specific equipment and say that equipment is devoted to a particular connection.

Just as in standard telephone technology, virtual circuits can be dedicated (permanent virtual circuits) or "dialed" (switched virtual circuits). The dedication or sharing of these circuits relates to the use of logical resources in the switches that act to define the circuits, rather than relating to specific communication lines.

The use of packet-switched virtual circuits brings with it significant economics. The one disadvantage is a somewhat longer propagation time through the network (the "line time" of Figure 5-1).

Satellite Channels

Another medium for transmission of data is the *satellite channel* (Figure 5-2d). Functionally, a satellite channel is much like a dialed or dedicated line. Channels can be dynamically allocated to users as they need them (like a dialed connection) or can be dedicated to a pair of users.

Satellite channels are inherently one-way. In a TP application, two channels are needed, one to send the transaction and one to receive the reply. Satellite channels can have very high bandwidths and consequently can support large data rates. An interesting possibility is that the signals relayed by a satellite can be received by any receiver in the "footprint" of the satellite, thus opening the way to a variety of broadcast opportunities, such as distributing summary data of interest to all users of a TP system.

There is, however, an important performance issue that relates to satellite channels. That issue is its "line time," or propagation delay. A typical geostationary satellite is about 36,000 kilometers from its earth stations. At the speed of light (300,000 km/sec.), the propagation time between an earth station and its satellite is 120 msec., or 240 msec. from the transmitting earth station to the receiving earth station.

Satellite propagation delays coupled with comparable packet-switch delays can cause serious performance problems in a TP application using a packet-switched service, if satellite channels are used by the packet switch.

Local Area Networks

A *local area network* (Figure 5-2e) interconnects multiple users via a high-speed channel to which all users connect. The network medium usually comprises twisted-pair cable or coaxial cable configured as a bus or a ring. Contemporary local area networks typically support data rates in the one- to ten-megabit/second range. More complex networks can support multiple channels of these capacities or greater.

Usually, all users on a local area network are equals—that is, there is no master on the network that controls access to the network. Network access is either by contention (start transmitting if no one else is and hope no one else does) or by a masterless form of polling known as token passing. These protocols are discussed in a later section.

Local area networks can provide very high speed communication channels between large numbers of users over limited geographical range. Typical local area networks will span a building and perhaps even a college campus or industrial park.

Multiplexers and Concentrators

The efficiency of dedicated circuits often can be improved by combining the traffic from multiple users onto a single line in a manner more efficient than the use of simple polling techniques. One way to accomplish this is through the use of multiplexers.

Multiplexing is the sharing of a channel by several users in a way that is substantially transparent to the users. In effect, the channel is broken up into subchannels. The subchannels are then available as independent channels to individual users as shown in Figure 5-3a. Of course, the combined data requirements of the users must be somewhat less than the capacity of the channel.

There are several established techniques for multiplexing:

- *Frequency Division Multiplexing (FDM)* divides the channel into separate channels in the frequency domain, as shown in Figure 5-4a. A wide bandwidth is carved into several subchannels of smaller bandwidths. Since the data rate that is supportable over a channel is proportional to its bandwidth, then the capacity of each subchannel is only a fraction of the main channel capacity. This very important characteristic of the data capacity of a bandwidth-limited channel derives from the well-known Nyquist theorem (Nyquist [22]).

  FDM is very economical in terms of the equipment required to support it. However, it is an inefficient use of the main channel because of the guard bands required to prevent interference between subchannels. This is wasted bandwidth, not available for data transmission.

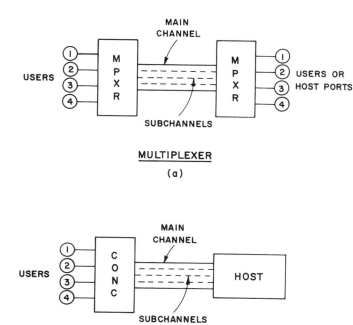

Figure 5-3 Shared channel use.

- *Time-Division Multiplexing (TDM)* divides the channel in the time domain (Figure 5-4b) rather than in the frequency domain. The high-speed data stream of the main channel is divided into time slots which are preallocated to subchannels. The time slots may be one bit wide, one byte (character) wide, or some other size.

  Data received from a user owning one of the subchannels is inserted into that subchannel at the transmitting end and is extracted and reconstructed into the user's message at the receiving end. Except for some synchronizing overhead needed to guarantee that the receiver can determine the beginning of a subchannel sequence (known as a frame), the TDM technique is highly efficient in its use of main channel capacity.

- *Statistical Multiplexing* further increases the utilization of the main channel when the subchannel users are casual. Casual users use a subchannel when they need to, but these users are idle a substantial amount of the time. Most TP system users are casual.

  A problem with both the FDM and TDM approaches just described when users are casual is that the subchannels are often idle. Available capacity is not being used.

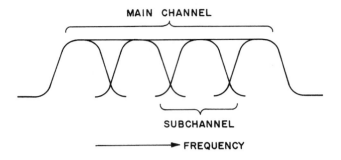

FREQUENCY DIVISION MULTIPLEXING
(a)

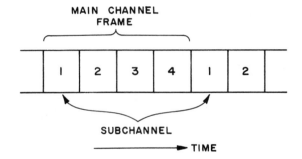

TIME DIVISION MULTIPLEXING
(b)

Figure 5-4   Multiplexing.

Statistical multiplexing is a TDM variant that solves this problem. With statistical multiplexing, subchannel time slots are not preallocated to users. In fact, there are many more users than time slots. When data is received at the transmitter, it is placed in the next available time slot and is sent to the receiver with some data identifying the sending user.

In this way, many casual users can be serviced by fewer subchannels. Statistical multiplexing does have the problem of overload when data bursts arrive that cannot be handled. In this case, the multiplexer must buffer the excess data until it can catch up. If its buffers fill, then the multiplexer must execute flow control procedures to stall the users sending data or else it will lose data and will have to request retransmission.

In any event, statistical multiplexing will impose delays on transaction and reply traffic during peak periods when it cannot handle the peak traffic. However, properly engineered, the statistical multiplexer can significantly reduce channel costs while remaining substantially transparent to the user.

The above discussion has reviewed the primary techniques for multiplexing. In most cases, these techniques will have minimal if any impact on performance.

There is another device, a *concentrator*, which is often used to perform a similar function (Figure 5-3b). Essentially just half of a TDM multiplexer, the concentrator combines traffic from many users into a single data stream for the host to untangle. In the case of the concentrator, the time slot size often is large enough for an entire message or at least for a significant packet of data from a message. In this case, there is a performance penalty equal to the message (or packet) transmission time over the main channel, since the message must be completely received at the transmitting end before it is sent to the receiver.

Modems

So far we have discussed communication channels without concerning ourselves very much with how data gets passed over them. Though this is the topic for the next section,

DIGITAL CHANNEL

(a)

ANALOG CHANNEL

(b)

Figure 5-5   Modems.

there is a very important device that is often needed to convey a data stream over a physical communication channel.

Though there are purely digital channels available today on which the user can directly impress his binary data stream (Figure 5-5a), most data channels are analog channels that are derivatives of voice channels (see Figure 5-5b). They can carry tones but cannot carry binary levels as we know them inside the terminal or computer.

Therefore, a device is needed to convert the data signals into tones suitable for the channel. This can be done by sending a loud tone for a one and a soft tone for a zero (changing the amplitude of the tone, or *amplitude modulation*). As an alternative, the pitch of the tone can be altered to designate a one or a zero *(frequency modulation)*. There is also a technique similar to frequency modulation known as *phase modulation.*

Because of various considerations, such as error performance and cost, frequency modulation is most often used, though phase modulation is also common. A device is needed at the user and host ends to modulate the data stream in order to create the analog tones and to demodulate received tones in order to recreate the original data stream sent from the other end. The device that performs this *mod*ulation and *dem*odulation function is known as a *modem.*

Usually, the modem is transparent so far as performance is concerned. However, there is a very important case in which it may have a significant performance impact. This case is that of half-duplex communication, especially for dialed connections, and is discussed in more detail later.

Propagation Delay

One final note is in order about communication channel performance; it concerns propagation delay over the circuit. We have already discussed propagation delay over satellite channels and through packet switched networks. But what about simple dedicated and dialed telephone channels? Can these delays be significant?

We can begin by looking at the simple propagation delay of the signal over a wire connecting the user to the host. Depending upon the type of wire (from loaded rural circuits to coaxial cable), the speed of a signal over wire can vary between about 0.5 to 0.9 of the speed of light. Even at the speed of light, a signal will take 16 msec. to traverse the 3000 miles across the USA or 65 msec. to go halfway around the world. More typical times might be twice as large.

Add to this the fact that every time the signal goes through an electronic repeater or filter, another few milliseconds are added. Long-haul circuit delays of several tens of milliseconds are definitely to be expected. Dialed lines typically will be worse than leased lines, since they may go through more central offices (and their associated equipment) than conditioned leased lines. Furthermore, their lower bandwidth usually goes hand-in-hand with longer propagation delays.

Long propagation delays can be of special concern in large polled networks in which each transaction must be charged with some poll overhead. If each poll requires two propagation delays (one to send the poll request and one to receive the response), polling can be quite slow, whether it is successful or not. This is discussed in more detail later.

DATA TRANSMISSION

Once we have a data channel over which we can feed a data stream, we must then agree on how the data will be represented on the channel. It is not enough to just send a message comprising a string of binary bits. We must know where the message begins and ends and how to interpret the bit patterns contained in the message.

Character Codes

Typically, messages in TP systems are made up of strings of characters: alphabetic characters, numeric characters, and special characters, such as punctuation marks. This is not true in all applications. Scientific data might be sent as large binary numbers in scientific notation (mantissa plus exponent). Satellite telemetry data might be long streams of binary data, as would a computer object program file being downloaded over a circuit.

We are interested in the alphanumeric data of TP system messages in which a character can be represented by a specified set of bits. Early teletype systems used 5 bits per character (32 combinations). This was the Baudot code. Two special characters (FIGS and LTRS) shifted between alphabetic meaning and numeric/special symbol meanings of the remaining 28 combinations (all 0s and all 1s had special meaning). In the 1950s, 6 bits was a popular definition of a character. This character size provided 64 combinations covering the alphanumeric character set (36 characters) plus ample special characters.

However, it soon became apparent that this was not enough. Upper-case and lower-case characters were desired. Furthermore, modern protocols required a rich set of control characters (this topic is discussed in more detail later). Seven-bit characters (128 combinations) were more appropriate to meet these needs.

Thus was born the ANSI standard ASCII code (American Standard Code for Information Interchange). The ASCII code set is a seven-bit code plus an error-detecting parity bit, as shown in Figure 5-6a. The parity bit may be unused (always set to 0 or 1), or it may be set such that the total number of bits in the character is odd (odd parity) or even (even parity). If either an even or odd parity bit is used, then the resulting eight-bit code is error-detecting. This is because the changing of any one bit in the character because of noise will cause the parity test to fail.

A competing code set is IBM's EBCDIC (Extended Binary Coded Decimal). This is also an 8-bit code in which all 256 combinations are used (see Figure 5-6b).

Thus, modern technology has settled on an 8-bit character code. This grouping of 8 bits is called a *byte*. (Four bits is enough to represent a number and is used in some applications. Four bits is called a *nibble*). Note that today's computers typically use word sizes that are multiples of bytes—word sizes of 16 bits or 32 bits.

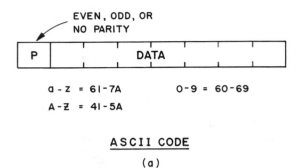

EVEN, ODD, OR
NO PARITY

a - z = 61-7A   0-9 = 60-69
A - Z = 41-5A

ASCII CODE

(a)

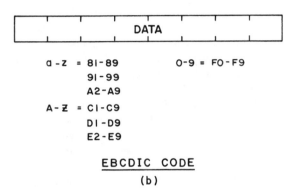

a - z = 81-89   0-9 = F0-F9
        91-99
        A2-A9
A - Z = C1-C9
        D1-D9
        E2-E9

EBCDIC CODE

(b)

NOTE : Character codes are in hexadecimal   **Figure 5-6** Code sets.

Asynchronous Communication

Having defined an eight-bit byte as a basic unit of information in a TP system, we must now be able to send a string of bytes over a communication channel in an intelligible fashion. Simply sending a long string of bits is not satisfactory, since we would never know where the byte boundaries were (see Figure 5-7a). Clearly, additional information must be embedded in the string of bits so that the receiver can determine where a byte starts.

One technique for doing this is called *asynchronous communication*. As shown in Figure 5-7b, a steady "1" signal is transmitted between characters (a *marking* signal). This interval is called the *stop* interval. When it is desired to send a byte, a *start* bit comprising a single "0" bit (a *spacing* signal) is sent, followed by the eight data-bits. Then the line returns to marking for the next stop interval. The stop interval is guaranteed to be of a minimum length (typically 1, 1.5, or 2 bits in length).

Thus, each byte is framed by a 1-bit start signal at its beginning and by a stop signal at its end (which is at least one bit in length). To recognize byte boundaries, the receiver

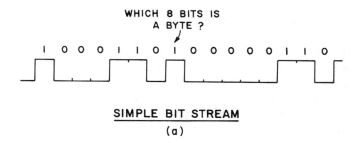

SIMPLE BIT STREAM

(a)

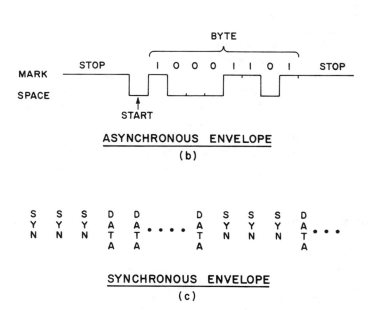

ASYNCHRONOUS ENVELOPE

(b)

SYNCHRONOUS ENVELOPE

(c)

Figure 5-7 Byte transmission.

simply looks for a stop-start transition (a mark-space transition), discards the first bit as the start bit, and stores eight bits. The next bit should be a stop bit, and the next start bit is awaited.

To achieve byte recognition, the asynchronous communication technique has created a 2-bit envelope around each byte (assuming a 1-bit stop interval). A byte being transmitted over an asynchronous communication channel therefore requires 10 bits to pass 8 bits of information—a 25 percent overhead.

One interesting characteristic of this technique is that the transmitter may transmit a character at any time, since the stop interval between characters can be arbitrarily long. This characteristic is particularly useful for data that is randomly generated (e.g. from a keyboard) and gives rise to the term *asynchronous*, applied to this technique for communications.

Synchronous Communication

Synchronous communication takes advantage of blocks of data that can be transmitted as uninterrupted byte streams to achieve a reduction in enveloping overhead (and also to achieve an improvement in error performance, as described later). Basically, one or more special synchronization characters (SYN) are inserted periodically in the byte stream. The receiver can search for the synchronization sequence and then can count out 8-bit bytes thereafter.

A typical synchronous sequence is shown in Figure 5-7c. The transmission is initiated with 3 SYN characters (the ASCII SYN character is hexidecimal 16). If the receiver is not in synchronization, it will look for a SYN character by continuously evaluating the last 8 bits received. When it finds a SYN character, the receiver then starts accumulating 8 bits at a time as data bytes (the next two should also be SYN characters, a condition that can be used as a sanity check).

Periodically, the transmitter will insert additional SYN characters to allow the receiver to ensure itself that it is still in synchronization. When the data has been sent, the transmitter can go idle, or it can send a steady stream of SYN characters to maintain synchronization with the receiver.

A typical interval between SYN characters is 128 data bytes. If 3 SYN characters are sent after every 128 data bytes, then the envelope overhead required for byte recognition is $3/128 = 2.3\%$. This is an order of magnitude better than asynchronous communication.

Error Performance

Noise on the communication line as well as phase, frequency, and amplitude distortion caused by line characteristics will distort the data signal as it travels over the channel. This is evidenced in the demodulated signal by a phenomenon known as *jitter*.

If successive received bits are viewed overlapped on an oscilloscope, the resulting pattern will appear as shown in Figure 5-8a. Each bit transition will generally not occur exactly at the time that it should. Rather, it will be a little early or a little late, appearing to "jitter" back and forth as successive bits are viewed. Though the relation between jitter, line distortion, and line noise is quite complex, the amount of jitter can be used as a measure of the intensity of the noise and distortion on the line.

Figure 5-8b shows the effect of jitter on an asynchronous signal. Let T_b be the duration of a bit interval. The appropriate strategy for asynchronous reception is as follows:

1. Look for a stop-start transition.
2. Wait for a one-half-of-a-bit interval ($T_b/2$).
3. Sample the received signal. This should be the start bit (otherwise, declare a false character and return to 1).
4. Sample eight more times at the bit interval, T_b, to obtain the eight data bits.

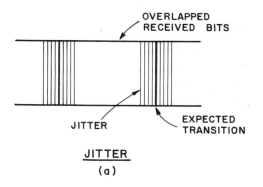

JITTER

(a)

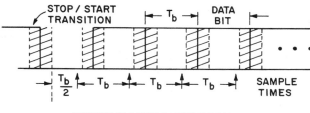

ASYNCHRONOUS TOLERANCE

(b)

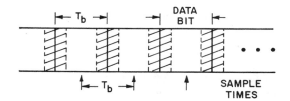

SYNCHRONOUS TOLERANCE

(c)   **Figure 5-8**   Noise tolerance.

5. Sample one more time after an interval of T_b to ensure that a proper stop interval has been received (otherwise, declare a synchronization error).

6. Repeat 1 through 5 for each successive character.

From Figure 5-8b, it is seen that a jitter of magnitude $T_b/4$ can move the start-stop transition 1/4 of a bit to the right and the transition of any data bit 1/4 of a bit to the left. At this point, the sample of the bit may be in error. Thus, the maximum jitter that can be tolerated by an asynchronous channel is $T_b/4$.

Figure 5-8c shows the equivalent case with a synchronous stream. For synchronous communication, the sample time is not determined by a single transition as it is in the asynchronous case. Rather, the sampling time is based on the long-term averaging of many data transitions (or in some cases is derived from the modulated signal itself) and is therefore quite accurate relative to the expected transition times.

Given accurate sampling times, it is evident from Figure 5-8c that it would take jitter of a magnitude equal to $T_b/2$ to create an error. Therefore, a synchronous channel can tolerate twice the jitter that can be tolerated by an asynchronous channel.

We have now seen that asynchronous techniques incur a byte-identification overhead which is an order of magnitude more than synchronous channels and that they can only tolerate half the noise. The reduced noise tolerance means a higher incidence of retransmissions and a further reduction in efficiency. So why is asynchronous communication even used?

The reason is cost. The requirements for more accurate clocking and for a more complex byte boundary recognition algorithm (recognizing a SYN character rather than a simple transition) make synchronous transmission more expensive than asynchronous transmission. Therefore, asynchronous techniques tend to be used for lower-speed applications (up to 2400 bits per second), and synchronous techniques tend to be used for higher-speed applications, where getting as much out of a channel as possible is desirable.

Error Protection

We have discussed the generation of errors because of line noise and distortion that cause jitter in the received signal. We have also seen one example of an error-detecting code to protect against such errors: the parity bit used in the ASCII character set. This is commonly known as a *vertical redundancy check* (VRC).

Unfortunately, errors on communication lines are not isolated. They tend to occur in short bursts. Therefore, it is quite possible that an even number of errors will occur within a character. In this event, the character parity check, or VRC, will still be satisfied; and the error will go undetected.

For this reason, a stronger error-detection scheme is often required. This is typically done by protecting the message (or transmission block) with additional error-detection codes placed at the end of the message. There are two in common use.

1. The longitudinal redundancy check (LRC) adds one byte to the message that is itself a parity byte. Each bit is set so that the sum of all corresponding bits in all bytes of the message is even (or odd, as the case may be).

2. The cyclical redundancy check (CRC) is a much stronger error detection code. It is typically a 16-bit code added to the end of the message, though longer codes give better protection. Though the theory behind CRC codes is quite extensive and complex (see Hamming [8]), the CRC is essentially that sequence of bits that, if appended to the message, creates a binary number that is exactly divisible by some predetermined number.

CRC codes can be extended to provide forward error correcting systems. In these systems, there is so much redundancy provided by the error correction code (often up to 50 percent—see Stallings [25]) that not only can an error be detected but also the specific bit in error can be identified. Therefore, that bit can be corrected. In this case, the code is a single-bit error-correcting code and may, in fact, correct many multiple-bit errors. Codes can be defined that will correct up to e errors and detect up to d errors, where $d > e$ (see Gallagher [6]).

However, the price that is paid is efficiency. As error codes get more powerful, they impose a higher overhead on the system. In the current art, error-correcting codes are used only in situations where retransmission is very expensive or impossible. Satellite channels are a good example of the use of these techniques, since retransmission uses expensive channel capacity. Broadcast systems are an example in which retransmission may be impossible, since there may be no return path.

Half-Duplex Channels

So far, we have concerned ourselves with the encoding of data so as to be able to identify it (byte identification) and to protect it against errors. There is one other major performance consideration at the data transmission level, and that is whether the communication channel is simplex, half-duplex, or full-duplex.

A *simplex* channel can transmit information in only one direction. A *half-duplex* channel can transmit in either direction but only in one direction at a time. A *full-duplex* channel can transmit in both directions simultaneously. We will ignore simplex channels, since they are not usually of use in TP systems. If they are used, they behave, for performance purposes, as half of a full-duplex channel.

A half-duplex channel creates several performance considerations. Not only is traffic in one direction affected by traffic in the other direction, but there also can be significant delays in turning a channel around.

Channel turnaround time comprises two components:

1. *Channel settling time*. When a channel is relinquished by one transmitter and acquired by another transmitter, there is a period during which the energy imparted to the channel by the first transmitter is decaying, and the energy imparted by the second transmitter is building. Only when the new transmission energy is greater than the old transmission energy by a significant amount can the line be used for reliable communication. This time is typically a few byte intervals.

2. *Echo suppressors*. Long telephone lines tend to develop echoes because of impedance mismatches along their length. To prevent this from becoming a nuisance to telephone users, echo suppressors have been installed throughout the telephone network. These devices determine the direction of predominant transmitted energy and suppress transmissions in the reverse direction. When the direction of transmission reverses, the echo suppressors reverse direction. This can take a few tens or even a few hundreds of milliseconds. (Have you ever noticed the first syllable of the conversation from the other end being cut off?) On a half-duplex channel, reliable communication cannot be achieved until the

echo suppressors on the channel are all reversed. Though the telephone companies have undertaken a program to upgrade their equipment in order to eliminate echo suppressors, many remain and probably will remain for the foreseeable future. This is primarily a problem for dialed lines, as dedicated lines are conditioned in many ways which preclude the need for echo suppressors.

The turnaround delays required by channel settling time and by echo suppressors may be established by timers in the terminal or host equipment or may be compensated for in the modem itself. The modem provides two signals for this purpose:

1. A Request To Send (RTS) signal to the modem, requesting permission to send data.
2. A Clear To Send (CTS) signal from the modem, indicating that data may now be sent.

In actual fact, the only logic that links the CTS signal to the RTS signal is a timer in the modem. The time-out is set by the user to the minimum safe time determined for channel turnaround. Typical timer values range from tens of milliseconds to hundreds of milliseconds.

Clearly, channel turnaround delays can have a significant impact on communication channel performance. A 100-msec. turnaround penalty for every 200-byte block over a 2400-bit/sec. channel requiring $(8)(200)/2400 = 667$ msec. per block is not to be taken lightly. This becomes even worse for a polled channel, wherein a typical poll sequence might be 3 characters and a poll response 1 character (10 msec. and 3.3 msec., respectively, at 2400 bits/sec.). Adding 100 msec. to each of these completely distorts the performance picture.

Full-Duplex Channels

A full-duplex channel is conceptually simple. Both sides of the conversation can transmit simultaneously. Full-duplex channels can be derived in several ways from physical channels. For instance, two separate channels may be provided, one to be used for each direction. This is usually the technique used for higher speed communications.

For lower data rates, a single physical channel may be divided into two logical channels using Frequency Division Multiplexing (FDM), as described earlier. The lower half of the frequency spectrum supported by the channel may be used to send data in one direction, and the upper half of the frequency spectrum may be used to send data in the opposite direction. This technique is used by low speed (300 bit per second) modems. One significant advantage of this technique is that a full-duplex connection can be established over a dialed line.

Though full-duplex channels are conceptually simple, the message transfer protocols required to take maximum advantage of the full-duplex capability can be quite a bit more complex than those used with half-duplex channels. These protocols are discussed in detail in the next section.

PROTOCOLS

The previous discussions can be perceived as describing the process of *data transmission*. The facilities and techniques described allow sequences of bytes to be delivered between users. Let us now discuss *data communications*.

In order to have a meaningful communication of data between a sender and a receiver, the data must be identifiable and transferred reliably. The procedure for accomplishing this is called a *protocol*.

A protocol is an agreement between the sender and receiver of data as to exactly how that data will be transferred. Protocols provide three primary functions:

1. *Message identification*—They identify the bounds of messages carrying the transaction and response data.
2. *Data protection*—They protect data against error, ensuring its reliable delivery.
3. *Channel allocation*—They provide the mechanism for allocating the channel in an orderly manner to the various competing users of the channel.

Protocols typically have three distinct parts:

1. The *establishment procedure*, which serves to establish a virtual connection between two users (or many users in the case of a broadcast).
2. The *message transfer procedure*, which describes the form of message transfer.
3. The *termination procedure*, which breaks the virtual connection.

The establishment and termination procedures satisfy the channel allocation function. The message-transfer procedure is the message-identification function. Data protection spans and significantly complicates all procedures.

There are many standardized protocols, and their study alone would fill volumes. Our concern is to understand the basics of protocols from a performance viewpoint so that, given a protocol specification, we can evaluate its performance within a given communications environment. Therefore, we will study some classes of protocols and relate them generally to some of the more popular protocols in use today.

Message Identification and Protection

Just as start-stop bits and synchronization bytes are used to identify the boundaries of data bytes in a bit stream, so must there be a mechanism to identify messages in a byte stream. This is typically accomplished with control characters that are chosen to be unique in the byte stream.

Quite simply, a unique start-of-text byte may indicate the start of a message, and an end-of-text byte may indicate the end of a message. These are commonly designated STX and ETX, and are, for instance, found in the ASCII control set.

Error-protection (and in some instances, error-correction) bytes follow the ETX byte. As discussed earlier, these include LRC (longitudinal redundancy check) or CRC (cyclical redundancy check) codes.

A typical message protected by a sixteen-bit CRC code would be formatted as follows:

STX (data) ETX CRC CRC

Message Transfer

Let us next look at the major function of any protocol: the reliable transfer of a message from its source to its destination. Just as with communication channels, we may dichotomize protocols into half-duplex and full-duplex protocols. When using a half-duplex protocol, transmission occurs in only one direction at a time. A full-duplex protocol supports simultaneous communication in both directions. Half-duplex protocols may be implemented using either half-duplex or full-duplex communication channels. However, full-duplex protocols require a full-duplex channel.

Half-Duplex Message Transfer. In a typical half-duplex protocol, user A sends a message to user B and then awaits a response from user B, as shown in Figure 5-9a. This response may be a positive acknowledgement that the message was received correctly (ACK) or a negative acknowledgement indicating that the message was received in error (NAK). If user A receives an ACK, the next message is sent. However, if user A receives a NAK, the previous message must be retransmitted and the above process repeated.

This protocol causes the transmitter to pause between messages in order to receive an acknowledgement from the receiver. This pause is required because the half-duplex channel supports only one transmission at a time.

Full-Duplex Message Transfer. A full-duplex channel allows the transmitter to send continuously, since acknowledgements can be returned over the reverse channel while message transmission continues. In fact, the other end can be transmitting its own series of messages at the same time. The problem is the coordination of acknowledgements with messages, since the transmitter may be able to send many messages before it gets an acknowledgement to a previous message (especially over channels with long propagation times, such as satellite or packet-switched channels).

The solution to this problem is to number messages and then to acknowledge by message number. In fact, to allow both ends to transmit simultaneously, the ACK or NAK can be piggybacked into each message. Figure 5-9b shows this procedure. User A is sending messages A1, A2, etc., while user B is sending messages B1, B2, and so on. Each piggybacks an acknowledgement of the last message received correctly or the first message received incorrectly.

For instance, by the time user B is ready to send its fourth message, B4, it still has only been able to process user A's message A1 and so sends an ACK1 (just as it had with

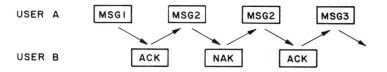

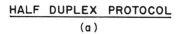

HALF DUPLEX PROTOCOL
(a)

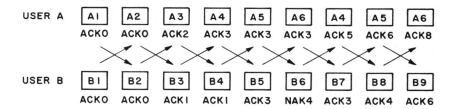

FULL DUPLEX PROTOCOL
(b)

Figure 5-9   Basic protocols.

its previous message, B3). By the time user B is ready to transmit its next message, B5, it has approved two more messages from user A and so sends an ACK3.

However, user B now finds user A's message A4 in error. Therefore, user B sends a NAK4 with its next message, B6. When user A receives the NAK4, it resets itself to start sending at its message A4, and the process continues.

This is obviously a more complex protocol than that required for half-duplex channels. It also requires storage at the transmitter for several messages to support the potential retransmission of these messages. This can be compared to a storage requirement of only one message for the simpler half-duplex channel. However, in return for this added cost, the full-duplex channel is utilized to a much greater extent.

Note that in this example the transmitter was required to back up to the message in error and to retransmit all data from that point on. We will refer to this as the *Go-Back-N protocol*. An alternative strategy that is also used is *selective retransmission*, in which only the message in error is retransmitted. In this case, referring to Figure 5-9b, user A's message sequence would have been (. . . A4, A5, A6, A4, A7, A8 . . .). However, this technique requires storage not only at the transmitter but also at the receiver, since later messages must be held until the message in error is received properly. Again, higher cost yields higher performance.

Channel Allocation

In order to send a message from a source to a destination, the sender must acquire the sole use of the channel and must then be able to address the receiver. This is the establishment procedure.

When the message (or perhaps a block of data representing a partial long message) has been sent, the sender must release the channel. This is the termination procedure.

In order for a channel to be allocated to a sender, one of two procedures may be used:

1. Assignment of the channel by an orderly procedure.
2. Uncontrolled contention for the channel by all users.

Orderly procedures for channel assignment include polling of users by a master station or the passing of a token giving the current token holder the right to use the channel. If a contention protocol is used, then provision must be made to detect collisions and to recover the lost data.

There is one further dichotomy to be recognized when considering establishment/termination procedures, and that is the number of users of the channel. If there are only two users, then the channel is a point-to-point channel. If there are more than two users, then the channel is a multipoint channel.

Bit Synchronous Protocols

So far, the protocols we have discussed are byte-oriented. Control characters are taken from a byte set, and error control characters are based on a byte structure. In fact, data is expected to be in bytes.

There are many applications in which a byte structure is not native to the data. A good example is public networks, which must be transparent to any data structure. Data channels derived from telephone lines meet this criterion as the particular form of data representation and the protocol are up to the user.

The situation becomes more complex for packet-switching networks, since by their very nature they must break the user's data into packets. They use their own data structures and protocols, and these must be transparent to any user data structure.

The protocols used for such applications are bit-oriented, as they must deal with data at the bit rather than the byte level. Since synchronous lines are typically used with these protocols for performance considerations, these protocols provide synchronization procedures. Therefore, we refer to such protocols as *bit synchronous protocols*. Bit synchronous protocols use full-duplex channels and are full-duplex protocols. Message transfer procedures and establishment/termination procedures are entwined in these protocols.

The two most commonly used bit synchronous protocols are HDLC (a CCITT standard) and SDLC, IBM's offering. HDLC stands for High-Level Data Link Control, and SDLC stands for Synchronous Data Link Control. The ANSI ADCCP and CCITT LAP-B protocols are other examples.

HDLC and SDLC are quite similar, especially concerning our needs for performance consideration. They are described in some detail in Stallings [25], Meijer [21], and Hammond [9]. We will take a high-level look at HDLC below as an example.

Under HDLC, a message is broken up into packets, or frames. Each frame is enveloped with synchronization, control, and error protection information as shown in Figure 5-10a. Frame elements include:

- Leading and trailing flag fields that provide synchronization. Each flag is an eight-bit field containing the bit sequence 01111110.

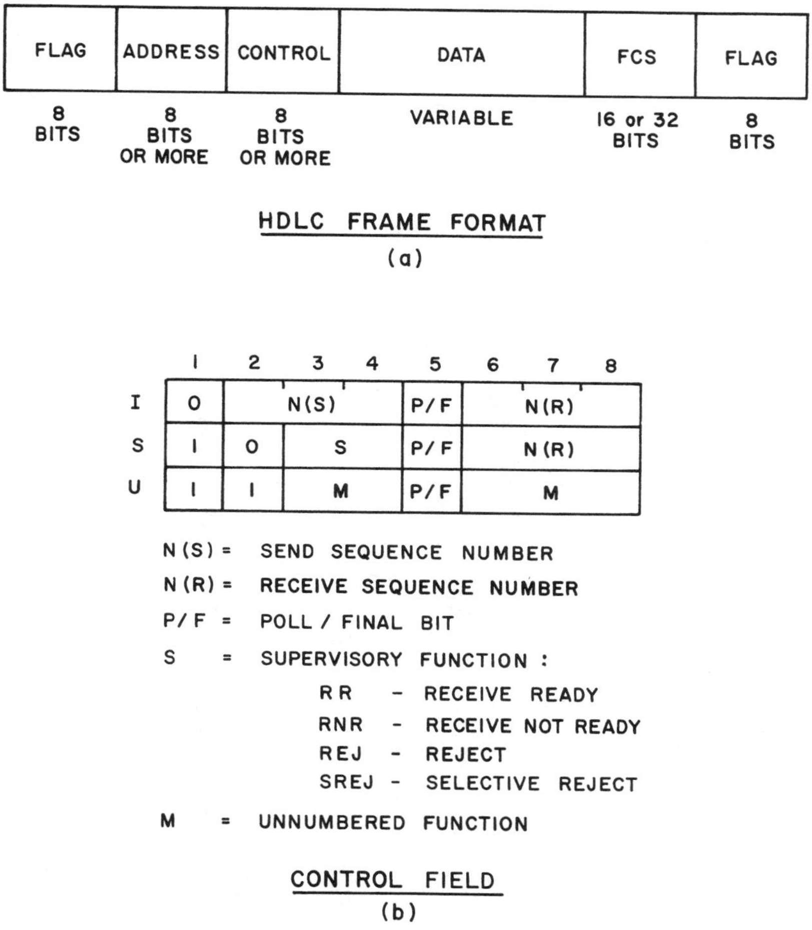

FLAG	ADDRESS	CONTROL	DATA	FCS	FLAG
8 BITS	8 BITS OR MORE	8 BITS OR MORE	VARIABLE	16 or 32 BITS	8 BITS

HDLC FRAME FORMAT
(a)

	1	2	3	4	5	6	7	8
I	O		N(S)		P/F		N(R)	
S	I	O	S		P/F		N(R)	
U	I	I	M		P/F		M	

N(S) = SEND SEQUENCE NUMBER

N(R) = RECEIVE SEQUENCE NUMBER

P/F = POLL / FINAL BIT

S   = SUPERVISORY FUNCTION :

       RR   – RECEIVE READY

       RNR – RECEIVE NOT READY

       REJ – REJECT

       SREJ – SELECTIVE REJECT

M   = UNNUMBERED FUNCTION

CONTROL FIELD
(b)

Figure 5-10   HDLC.

- An address field of eight or more bits to identify the recipient of the frame.
- A control field of eight or more bits that defines the type of frame (information, supervisory, or unnumbered).
- The data field, which may be of any length (in some implementations, it is constrained to be a multiple of eight bits).
- A frame check sequence (FCS) field that contains a 16-bit or 32-bit CRC character for error detection.

The flag fields provide synchronization by including a unique bit sequence in each frame. The uniqueness of this flag sequence must be preserved in that it must not appear in the rest of the frame. Should a sequence of six 1s that can be misinterpreted as a flag field be found in the frame, the sequence is broken up by a technique called *bit stuffing*. The transmitter simply inserts a 0 after every sequence of five 1s (except, of course, in the flag fields). The receiver, upon receiving five 1s, checks the next bit. If it is a 0, the receiver deletes it. If it is a 1, and the seventh bit is a 0, the receiver interprets the sequence as a flag field (seven 1s signal a special abort condition).

The control field provides for three frame types:

1. *Information frames* (I-frames), which carry the data.
2. *Supervisory frames* (S-frames), which provide flow control and error control.
3. *Unnumbered frames* (U-frames), which are used for a variety of channel control functions.

The information and supervisory frames are used for the establishment and error recovery functions in which we are interested. Many of these functions are implemented in the frame's control field, as shown in Figure 5-10b.

The first one or two bits define the type of frame to follow. If this is an information frame, a pair of three-bit sequence numbers is provided. One sequence number, N(S), specifies the sequence number of the current frame being sent. The other, N(R), specifies the sequence number of the next frame anticipated. In other words, N(R) tells the other end that all previous frames have been received properly and that the other end may flush these messages from its buffers. Thus, message acknowledgement is piggybacked onto information packets as they flow through the system.

If an acknowledgement is due to be sent to the other end, but no information frame is available, then a supervisory frame may be sent instead. An RR frame (Receive Ready) is sent with the next expected frame number in N(R) if this end is in a position to receive a frame. Otherwise, an RNR (Receive Not Ready) supervisory frame is sent. This also indicates the next frame to be expected but forces the other end to delay its transmission until a subsequent RR frame is sent. Thus, RNR/RR couples provide flow control over the link.

If a frame is received in error, then a supervisory REJ (Reject) frame is sent, indicating in N(R) the frame from which retransmission is to begin. This is the Go-Back-N protocol. If selective retransmission is desired, the supervisory SREJ (Selective Reject) frame is sent instead. In this case, only the frame indicated by N(R) is retransmitted.

Note that the sequence number fields are three bits in length and provide sequence numbers 0–7. This means that the window size, W, on the channel is seven messages. That is, the receiver can get up to seven messages behind the sender before the sender must wait for an acknowledgement.

A window size of 7 is used instead of 8 to prevent confusion over message numbers. To understand the reason for this, let us consider the following example. Assume that the sender has sent messages 0 through 7 and is waiting for an acknowledgement while it is holding these eight messages. It then receives an acknowledgement with N(R) = 0, indicating the next message the receiver is expecting. Is it the message 0 currently being held by the transmitter, or is it the message 0 which the transmitter is due to send next? This confusion is avoided by always limiting the window size to one less than the sequence number range (the window size may, of course, be further limited by other factors, such as available buffering).

Though the HDLC protocol described here limits the window size to 7, an extension to a window size of 127 is available through HDLC. This can be important for high-speed, long-delay channels such as satellite channels.

Let us now look at the establishment functions built into HDLC. These are controlled via two fields in the frame, the P/F bit in the control field and the address field. The P/F bit is the poll-final bit. The host uses this bit to poll a terminal, the terminal uses this bit to indicate to the host that it has nothing more to send. The specific terminal is addressed by the host via the address field.

In order to select a terminal for transmission, the host simply addresses a message to it via the address field.

In order to poll a terminal, the host sends a frame containing that terminal's address with the P/F bit set. If an information frame is due to be sent to the terminal, the poll bit in that frame is set. Otherwise, a supervisory RR frame is sent.

If the terminal has no data to send, it will return an RR frame with the P/F bit set. If it has data, it will return information frames to the host. All but the last I-frame will have a zero P/F bit. A one P/F bit in the last frame indicates to the host that the terminal has finished its transmission.

BITS, BYTES, AND BAUD

A passing comment on some communication terminology is appropriate at this point. Let us take a 2400 bit-per-second synchronous communication line. Some refer to this as a 2400-bit-per-second line, others as a 2400-baud line, and still others as a 300-byte-per-second line. Are these all equivalent? I think so, but I doubt it.

And if that sounds confusing, it's because we have let ourselves get sloppy with nomenclature. Let us first take the term *baud*.

Baud is technically a measure of the number of state transitions per second that a communication line is capable of achieving while still having the receiver accurately detect the state sequences. In many cases, the line shifts between only two states: one and zero. In this case, baud is the measure of bits per second that the line can handle.

However, many transmission schemes use more than 2 values per transition. A common modulation technique is 4-phase modulation. With this technique, each transition is to one of 4 states and thus represents 2 bits. In this case, a 2400-baud line supports 4800 bits per second.

In general, if each state can be one of M values, then baud and bits per second are related as follows:

$$\text{Bits per second} = \text{baud } x \log_2 M$$

The term *bits per second* is not all that clear either. From a purely information theory viewpoint, a *bit* is a unit of information. There is no information carried in asynchronous start/stop bits. Since a 1200-baud asynchronous line (in the loose sense) transmits 120 10-bit characters per second, with each character containing only 8 information bits, is it a 1200-bit-per-second line or only a 960-bit-per-second line?

Well then, we say, let us use bytes as our measure. But again, there is no information carried in synchronous SYN bytes nor in control bytes such as STX, ENQ, or error control characters. Do we eliminate these from our measure of line capacity?

Enough said. Modern usage has become somewhat sloppy, and all forms are accepted. Let's make sure that our use is clear, either by context or by explicit definition.

LAYERED PROTOCOLS

In the previous sections, as we discussed communications from the physical channel level up to some fairly complex protocols, we described how each lower layer adds its own information to the data in order to communicate. An application might start out with a message to send. This gets passed to a protocol handler, which frames the message with start-of-text and end-of-text identifiers and which adds some error control and channel control information. Finally, this expanded message is handed to a transmitter, which may add start/stop bits or SYN characters to get the data across the line.

At the other end, the receiver strips out the synchronization bits and hands the message in its protocol envelope to the protocol handler. The protocol handler extracts the message and hands it to the application program.

This procedure is diagrammed in Figure 5-11. In effect, the application program at the source end is acting as if it is communicating directly with the application program at the destination end. Each does so by passing data between itself and a protocol handler. The details of the protocol handler are of no concern to the application programs.

The protocol handler also acts as if it is talking directly to its companion protocol handler. On the one hand, each passes data between itself and a mysterious application program. On the other hand, each exchanges data with a line handler. The protocol handler needs no information about the inner workings of either the application programs

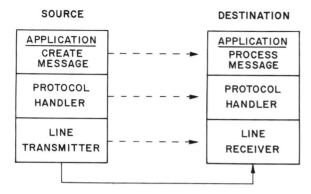

Figure 5-11   Layered protocol.

or the line handlers. Only the interfaces need be defined. However, the protocol handler must have intimate knowledge of and cooperate with its companion protocol handler.

The same description applies to the line handlers (the transmitter and receiver). They talk to each other but have no knowledge of higher layers.

Thus is born the concept of *layered protocols*. Each lower layer deals in a greater abstraction relative to the data being handled. It provides services to the next higher layer by using the primitives of the next lower layer. Each layer acts as if it is communicating with a copy of itself via its own layer protocol. It has no knowledge of higher or lower layers, except for the immediate interfaces.

Major networks today are based on layered protocols. The two most common are the International Standard Organization's Open System Interconnect (ISO/OSI) and IBM's Systems Network Architecture (SNA). The popular X.25 protocol used widely in packet-switching networks implements the lower three levels of ISO/OSI.

ISO/OSI

OSI is more of a model for layered architectures than it is a specification. In fact, it is called the *OSI Reference Model* (ISO [12]).

The OSI Reference Model establishes seven layers, as shown in Figure 5-12. Each layer has its own defined responsibilities and provides services relative to these responsibilities, as shown in Figure 5-13, to the layer above it (except for the application layer, which is the highest). It can communicate with its peer layer, which is typically in a separate system, via a communication channel provided by the next lower layer. Each peer layer has a protocol it uses to intercommunicate; this protocol is of no concern to other layers (though protocols often are designed with other protocols in mind to simplify the system). The lowest layer, the physical layer, has direct access to the physical communication channel.

We discuss now the seven OSI layers.

Application layer.   The *application layer* is the layer at which the application processes execute and at which users interact with the system. System and network management functions also reside at this level.

LAYER

7	APPLICATION
6	PRESENTATION
5	SESSION
4	TRANSPORT
3	NETWORK
2	DATA LINK
I	PHYSICAL

Figure 5-12   OSI reference model.

Presentation layer.   The lower layers under the application layer serve to allow diverse applications running on different equipment to converse with each other. This requires that the differences in the way these applications communicate must be made transparent to the applications.

At the highest level, these differences may include the code used, number representation, compression of repetitive data, message structure, and terminal formats. The resolution of these differences is the responsibility of the *presentation layers* and may be considered the syntax of the conversation between application layers.

There are three syntax versions to be considered for the data: that syntax used by each of the two application processes and that syntax provided to the presentation layer by

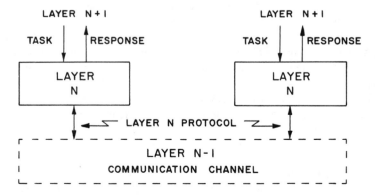

Figure 5-13   Layer communications.

the channel comprising the lower layers. It is the responsibility of the presentation layer at each end to convert between the application layer syntax and the lower level channel syntax.

Session layer.   The *session layer* is responsible for establishing a connection between application entities and for managing the session. Session establishment is done at the request of an application and may involve requesting an appropriate channel from the transport layer, establishing the availability of the destination application, identifying the source application for the destination, and obtaining permission from the destination application to communicate with the source application. At the end of the session, the session layer must terminate the session.

Session management includes the enforcing of the interaction between the applications, whether it be full-duplex, half-duplex, or simplex. It may be responsible for ensuring the proper sequence of messages if the lower levels might interchange, add, or delete messages. This may occur especially if the physical communication channels fail and are recovered by lower layers. If system usage is to be accounted for, this is a valid function for the session layer.

Transport layer.   The session layer is aware of which application it is to talk to, but it has no knowledge of where that application is. The establishment of a channel to that application begins with the *transport layer*.

The primary function of the transport layer is to provide a transparent means of data transfer for a session. If messages from the session layer need to be broken up into packets, then the transport layer is responsible for disassembling the message into outgoing packets and assembling incoming packets into messages (the PAD function). It interacts with the network layer to provide flow control if necessary, ensuring that no more data is passed to the network than the network can handle.

The transport layer also may be responsible for providing a certain class of service demanded by the session layer. Classes of service include priority, delay, and security specifications, as well as services such as multiple addressing.

Network layer.   The *network layer* relieves the transport layer of any concern over how the systems are interconnected. It is the network layer that knows the topology of the system, and it is the network layer's responsibility to see that packets submitted by the transport layer are routed properly to their destinations.

There are a variety of routing mechanisms that may be used. *Fixed routing* defines a specific path between each pair of endpoints. *Alternate routing* defines a primary path for each endpoint and one or more alternate paths in case of failure or congestion on the primary path. *Dynamic routing* allows packets to be routed through the network along a path which makes best use of the network facilities at that instant in time.

The network layer is responsible for flow control in the network and interacts with the transport layer to restrict incoming data if it cannot be handled by the network. The network level may or may not be responsible for the proper ordering of received packets, depending upon the characteristics of the channel. It must be responsive to class-of-service requests from the transport level.

Note that the routing of a packet may carry it through several nodes in a network. How does the reference model apply to a node in which an application for this session is not active? The answer is that the network layer is responsible for routing, as shown in Figure 5-14. A message originates at an application layer and is broken into packets by the transport layer in that system. The packets then flow through the network layers of all intervening nodes until they arrive at the destination system. There the network layer passes the packets to the transport layer, where the message is reassembled and delivered to the application layer via the session and presentation layers.

Data link layer.   The purpose of the data link layer is to provide virtually error-free communication across a link connecting two nodes in the network. It must do so in a manner which imposes no restriction on the data (data transparency). As such, the data link layer provides the following primary functions:

- Synchronization, so that packets (frames) may be identified.
- Error detection.
- Error correction, either through forward error correction or via retransmission.

Note that it must be assumed that a connection spans several nodes. The data link layer guarantees error-free communication only across the separate links in the connection—it cannot guarantee error-free operation across the channel. That is why higher layers are also involved in error control.

The HDLC protocol which we have described earlier is a contemporary example of a data link layer.

Physical layer.   The physical layer is responsible for the management of the physical communication link. This includes the electrical characteristics of the channel

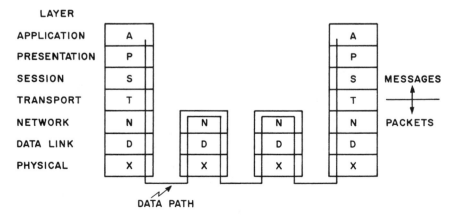

Figure 5-14   OSI multinode communication.

and the mechanical specification of the connectors to the channel. It also includes the modem interfaces and the functions and usage of modem signals.

SNA

The IBM *Systems Network Architecture (SNA)* is a specific implementation of a layered protocol. Though its layers are somewhat different from the ISO Reference Model, there is a strong similarity.

Under SNA, there are five layers. They are shown in Figure 5-15 with their general correspondences to the OSI model.

Under SNA, there is no defined physical layer; the existence of a suitable physical connection is implied.

The *data link control layer* is very much like the OSI data link level. SDLC, which is more or less a subset of the HDLC protocol described earlier, is specified for this level.

The *path control layer* provides services similar to the OSI network layer. It provides logical channels and flow control between entities known as Network Addressable Units (NAUs). Since dynamic routing is supported at this level, path control is responsible for the delivery of data units in proper order even if they are received from the data link control layer in improper order.

The *transmission control layer* is similar to the OSI transport layer except that it has some responsibilities related to session management. A session under SNA is a logical

OSI	SNA
APPLICATION	FUNCTION MANAGEMENT DATA SERVICES
PRESENTATION	
SESSION	DATA FLOW CONTROL
TRANSPORT	TRANSMISSION CONTROL
NETWORK	PATH CONTROL
DATA LINK	DATA LINK CONTROL
PHYSICAL	

Figure 5-15   SNA layers.

connection between NAUs. Transmission control is responsible for establishing and terminating a session and for maintaining the connections required during the session.

The *data flow control layer* is the other part of session control and corresponds to the OSI session layer. It is responsible for managing the session, including half-duplex or full-duplex data flow, for ensuring all-or-none data delivery, and for bracketing transactions so that the range of a transaction comprising several messages can be identified.

The *function management data services layer* provides services to the end user. It is similar to OSI's presentation layer and spills into the application layer. It provides OSI presentation services such as data reformatting and data compression. It also provides network management functions such as network reconfiguration, collection of network statistics, and fault identification and isolation.

Reference may be made to Meijer [21] for a more detailed discussion of SNA.

X.25

X.25 is a protocol that is widely used internationally. It is packet-oriented and is therefore used widely in packet-switching networks.

It corresponds roughly to the OSI Reference Model layers 1, 2, and 3 (physical, data link, and network). The data link layer is a subset of the HDLC protocol described earlier. The network layer is designed specifically to interface easily with the HDLC protocol.

The following description of X.25 is a condensation of material found in Stallings [25] and Meijer [21]. Under X.25, a user always communicates with a communication facility. The user's equipment is called Data Terminal Equipment (DTE), and the communication facility is called Data Circuit-Terminating Equipment (DCE). Figure 5-16 shows the use of X.25 in a packet-switched environment. Users connect their DTEs to the packet-switched network via a DCE provided by the network and communicate with that DCE over an X.25 line. The DCE is responsible for establishing a virtual connection through the switch to the destination-user's DCE, which talks to the destination-user's

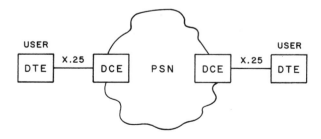

DTE - DATA TERMINAL EQUIPMENT

DCE - DATA CIRCUIT - TERMINATING EQUIPMENT

PSN - PACKET SWITCHED NETWORK   **Figure 5-16**   X.25 in a network.

DTE via an X.25 link. There is no requirement that X.25 be used within the packet-switched network itself.

Data must be submitted to the X.25 link in packets. The maximum packet length is specified—128 bytes is typical. (It would be more accurate to use "octets" instead of bytes, as the X.25 protocol implies no structure of the data.)

Packets of data are enveloped with a three-byte X.25 header shown in Figure 5-17. The fields are as follows:

- The *qualifier bit*, Q, which allows the distinction between data flows—for instance, information or control.

- The *delivery bit*, D, which requests a delivery confirmation from the destination.

- The *modulo*, a field that specifies whether a window size of 7 or 127 is to be used, i.e., a sequence number range of 8 or 128. It also specifies certain format extensions.

- The *group field* and *channel number field*, which, when concatenated, allow the designation of up to 4095 logical channels.

- The *receive*—N(R)—and the *send*—N(S)—sequence numbers, analogous in their use to the same HDLC fields described earlier.

- The *more-data bit* (M), which signifies that the current packet is an intermediate packet in the message. The last packet sets this bit to zero.

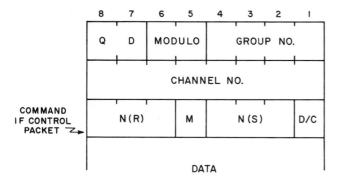

Q   -   QUALIFIER
D   -   DELIVERY
MODULO   -   SEQ. NO. RANGE = 8 OR 128
GROUP NO.   -   LOGICAL CHANNEL GROUP NO.
CHANNEL NO. - LOGICAL CHANNEL NO.
N(R)   -   RECEIVE SEQUENCE NO.
N(S)   -   SEND SEQUENCE NO.
M   -   MORE DATA
D/C   -   DATA (0) OR CONTROL (1)   **Figure 5-17** X.25 header.

- The *data/control bit* (D/C), which specifies whether this is a data (information) packet or a control packet.

Control packets have the same format in the first two bytes as a data packet. However, bit 1 of the third byte is set to 1; and bits 2–8 are used as a command. The commands are shown in Figure 5-18. Their interpretation is always in pairs, depending upon whether the control packet was sent by a DTE or a DCE.

X.25 supports two types of connections. One is a permanent virtual circuit (PVC). This is a dedicated circuit that requires no call establishment or disconnection. The other is a virtual call (VC), which establishes a virtual circuit and then disconnects it at the end of the call.

The establishment and disconnection procedures are shown in Figure 5-19, using some of the control packets listed in Figure 5-18. The originating DTE first sends a Call Request packet, which is passed through the network and received by the destination DTE as an Incoming Call packet. If it can handle the call, the destination DTE responds with a Call Accepted packet, which is delivered to the originating DTE as a Call Connected packet.

At this point, the two DTEs can communicate. The message transfer procedures of the HDLC protocol described earlier are used for data communication.

When one DTE is ready to clear the call, it sends a Clear Request packet, which is received by the other DTE as a Clear Indication packet. It responds by returning a Clear Confirmation packet.

It is interesting to note the multiple encapsulations of data in layered protocols, using X.25 as an example. In Figure 5-20 a data packet is shown as it is received for transmission over the physical channel. The data message (which itself may have higher-level headers and trailers) is appended with an X.25 header at the network layer. This packet is then transferred to the data-link layer, where the HDLC envelope is added (as shown in Figure 5-20).

At the receiver, the data-link layer strips the HDLC envelope from the packet. The X.25 envelope is stripped by the network layer before sending the packet up the layer structure.

MESSAGE TRANSFER PERFORMANCE

Let us now look at some performance considerations for message transfer. In the following sections, we consider the line efficiency and transit time for both half-duplex and full-duplex message transfer procedures.

Half-Duplex Message Transfer Efficiency

The efficiency of message transfer is affected by two considerations:

1. The overhead created by the protocol for message identification and error detection.

FUNCTION	DCE TO DTE	DTE TO DCE
CALL SETUP	INCOMING CALL CALL CONNECTED	CALL REQUEST CALL ACCEPTED
CALL CLEARING	CLEAR INDICATION DCE CLEAR CONFIRMATION	CLEAR REQUEST DTE CLEAR CONFIRMATION
DATA AND INTERRUPT	DCE DATA DCE INTERRUPT DCE INTERRUPT CONFIRMATION	DTE DATA DTE INTERRUPT DTE INTERRUPT CONFIRMATION
FLOW CONTROL	DCE RR DCE RNR	DTE RR DTE RNR DTE REJ
RESET	RESET INDICATION DCE RESET INDICATION	RESET REQUEST DTE RESET CONFIRMATION
RESTART	RESTART INDICATION DCE RESTART CONFIRMATION	RESTART REQUEST DTE RESTART INDICATION

Figure 5-18   X.25 control packets.

2. Retransmission of messages in error.

Stallings [25] presents a very understandable description of message-transfer efficiency, which we will follow in principle. Let us make the following definitions:

U = message transfer efficiency.

t_m = average time required to transmit a message (sec.).

t_{pro} = overhead time per message imposed by the protocol (sec.).

k_r = the average number of times that a message must be sent (retransmission factor) due to errors and the successful transmission.

Then the efficiency of message transfer, U, can be expressed as

$$U = \frac{t_m}{k_r(t_m + t_{pro})} \tag{5-1}$$

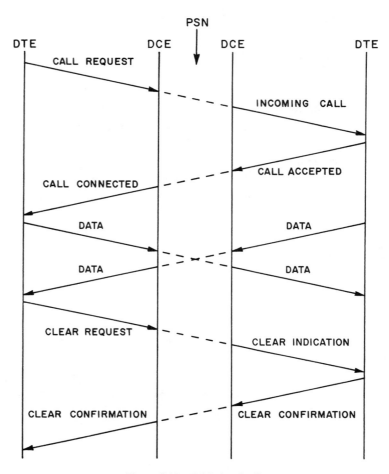

Figure 5-19 X.25 virtual call.

That is, it is the ratio of the basic message time, t_m, to the actual time spent delivering the message, $k_r(t_m + t_{pro})$. Note that errors in protocol control blocks (ACK, NAK) are ignored, as these are typically small blocks less subject to error. Also note from equation 5-1 that the actual communication channel time used to send a message is t_m/U.

To understand protocol overhead, let us trace the path of a half-duplex message transfer using Figure 5-21. The first step is to transmit the message; this requires a time, t_m, as defined above.

The message must propagate over the communication channel. To do so requires a time, t_{prop}. It must then be processed by the receiver, t_{prc1}, which will transmit an ACK if the message is correct. The ACK will require a transmission time of t_{ack}. Finally, the ACK will propagate to the transmitter (a time of t_{prop}) and will be processed by the transmitter, t_{prc2}. At this point, message transfer is complete.

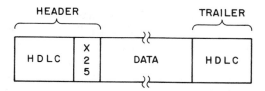

Figure 5-20   X.25 data encapsulation.

From this description, the protocol overhead time, t_{pro}, can be expressed as

$$t_{pro} = 2t_{prop} + t_{prc} + t_{ack} \tag{5-2}$$

where

t_{prop} = one-way channel propagation time (sec.),

t_{prc} = processing time for the message and for the ACK ($t_{prc1} + t_{prc2}$),

t_{ack} = time to send the ACK.

Let us define the following term, a, such that

$$a = \frac{t_{pro}}{2t_m} = \frac{t_{prop} + (t_{prc} + t_{ack})/2}{t_m} \tag{5-3}$$

That is, a is the average protocol delay per transmission and is normalized by the message time. There are two transmissions per message transfer: one for the message itself and one for the acknowledgement.

Using equation 5-3, equation 5-1 can be rewritten as

$$U = \frac{1}{k_r(1 + 2a)} \tag{5-4}$$

The retransmission factor, k_r, can be evaluated as follows: Let

p_b = probability of a bit error in the communication channel,

p_m = probability that a message contains one or more errors,

M = message size, in bytes, and

H = message overhead, in bytes.

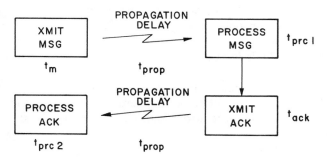

Figure 5-21   Protocol overhead.

Typical values for p_b are 10^{-5} for dialed lines and 10^{-6} for dedicated lines.

We assume that bit errors are random and independent. This is hardly the case in typical communication channels, where errors tend to occur in bursts. However, the assumption of independence is conservative and will lead to somewhat higher message error rates than will actually be observed. We also assume that our error detection algorithm is perfect.

The message overhead of H bytes includes header and trailer data which frame a message. Examples of this overhead will be given later.

For synchronous transmission, the total number of bits in a message is $8(M+H)$. (The multiplier will be 10 or more for asynchronous transmission.) The probability that a particular bit is error-free is $(1-p_b)$. The probability that all bits are error-free is the probability that the message is error-free and is $(1-p_b)^{8(M+H)}$. Thus,

$$p_m = 1 - (1 - p_b)^{8(M+H)} \tag{5-5}$$

A message must always be transmitted at least once. It will be transmitted a second time with probability p_m, a third time with probability $p_m{}^2$, etc. It will be transmitted on the average k_r times, where

$$k_r = 1 + p_m + p_m{}^2 + \ldots$$

or

$$k_r = \frac{1}{1-p_m} \tag{5-6}$$

Substituting this result into equation 5-4 yields

$$U = \frac{1 - p_m}{1 + 2a} = \frac{(1-p_b)^{8(M+H)}}{1 + 2a} \tag{5-7a}$$

If the bit error probability is sufficiently small, then

$$(1-p_b)^{8(M+H)} \approx 1-8(M+H)p_b$$

and

$$U \approx \frac{1-8(M+H)p_b}{1+2a} \tag{5-7b}$$

This approximation is valid if $8(M+H)p_b \ll 1$. For values of p_b in the order of 10^{-6} and for reasonable message sizes, this approximation holds.

Full-Duplex Message Transfer Efficiency

The analysis of the efficiency of a full-duplex protocol is complicated by the fact that there are two cases to consider, both based on the extent of the protocol delay, a. To understand these cases, we must add one additional concept to our knowledge of protocols: the window, in particular, the window of size W.

As we mentioned earlier, the transmitter must be able to buffer messages so that it can retransmit from the point at which the receiver received a message in error. Furthermore, the receiver must provide equivalent buffering if selective retransmission is used. But how much buffering is required?

The number of messages that the transmitter can get ahead of its acknowledgements from the receiver is called the *window*. It, in fact, is specified by the protocol, as the window size relates to the size of the message number that can be specified in an ACK or NAK message. (See Stallings [25] for a more thorough discussion of this.) A typical window size, W, is 7, though larger windows are sometimes used for channels with very long propagation times.

Since the difference between the transmitter and receiver can be no greater than W messages, this is the amount of buffering required. Messages are held in the buffer until they are acknowledged, at which time they are flushed. (For selective retransmission, messages must remain in the receive buffer until all previous messages have been properly received.)

Now let us assume that the time required for the transmitter to send W messages is greater than the total propagation time to receive an acknowledgement. That is,

$$Wt_m \geq (1 + 2a)t_m$$

Then the transmitter will always receive an acknowledgement to a message before it fills up its buffers with unacknowledged messages. Therefore, the transmitter can continually use the channel for transmission; efficiency, U, is affected only by retransmissions:

$$U = 1/k_r , \ W \geq 1 + 2a$$

However, if the transmission time for W messages is less than the total propagation time, then after W messages are sent, the transmitter must wait a time $(1+2a)t_m - Wt_m$ before it can start sending again. This cycle will repeat every W messages. Thus, only W messages will be sent every $(1+2a)t_m$ seconds, and

$$U = \frac{W}{k_r(1+2a)}, \ W < 1+2a$$

Restating the above results, the efficiency for a full duplex protocol can be expressed as

$$\begin{aligned} U &= 1/k_r & W \geq 1+2a \\[2mm] &= \frac{W}{k_r(1+2a)} & W < 1+2a \end{aligned} \qquad (5\text{-}8)$$

It remains now to evaluate k_r. For the selective retransmission case, the procedure is simple, since only the message in error needs to be retransmitted. This is equivalent to the half-duplex protocol case, and equation 5-6 holds. Thus, *for selective retransmission:*

$$\begin{aligned} U &= 1 - p_m & W \geq 1+2a \\[2mm] &= \frac{W(1-p_m)}{1+2a} & W < 1+2a \end{aligned} \qquad (5\text{-}9)$$

The technique in which all blocks after the block in error are retransmitted is called the Go-Back-N technique; let us evaluate its efficiency. With this technique, N messages must be retransmitted. In a manner similar to the derivation of equation 5-6, we note that a message must always be transmitted once. With probability p_m, N messages will have to be retransmitted; with probability p_m^2, N messages will have to be transmitted a second time, and so on. (We ignore here the probability of error in other than the first message being retransmitted, as this will simply initiate a new retransmission sequence). Thus, the retransmission factor, k_r, is

$$k_r = 1 + Np_m + Np_m^2 + \ldots$$

or

$$k_r = 1 + \frac{Np_m}{1-p_m} \tag{5-10}$$

For the case in which the transmission time of W messages is greater than the total propagation time to receive a message ($W \geq 1+2a$), the number of messages that the transmitter leads the receiver by is $N = (1+2a)$. This is because it will take $(1+2a)t_m$ seconds for an acknowledgement to be returned to the transmitter for a message that is just beginning its transmission. During this time, $N = (1+2a)t_m/t_m$ messages will be sent, including the message for which the acknowledgement is being returned. If that acknowledgement is a NAK, then $(1+2a)$ messages must be retransmitted.

Likewise, if W messages take less time than the round-trip time to receive the acknowledgement ($W < 1+2a$), then the transmitter must pause after W messages and must wait for the acknowledgement. If it is a NAK, then $N = W$ messages must be retransmitted.

Substituting these values for N into equation 5-10 to obtain k_r, and then combining that result with equation 5-8 yields, *for Go-Back-N retransmission:*

$$
\begin{aligned}
U &= \frac{1-p_m}{1+2ap_m} & W &\geq 1 + 2a \\[2ex]
&= \frac{W(1-p_m)}{(1-p_m+Wp_m)(1+2a)} & W &< 1 + 2a
\end{aligned}
\tag{5-11}
$$

Message Transit Time

From a system performance viewpoint, we are as interested in the transit time of a message as we are in line efficiency. Let us evaluate message transit time for the three cases discussed above.

Let

t_m' = message transit time (sec.), or the average time required to send a message and to have it successfully received.

For half-duplex protocols, we note that the first copy of a message passes through the receiver in a time $t_m(1+a)$. Subsequent retransmissions require a time $t_m(1+2a)$.

Since the average number of retransmissions per message is $p_m/(1-p_m)$, then

$$t'_m = t_m(1+a) + t_m(1+2a)p_m/(1-p_m)$$

This can be rearranged as follows:

$$t'_m = \frac{(1+2a) - a(1-p_m)}{1-p_m} \, t_m = \left(\frac{1+2a}{1-p_m} - a\right)t_m \qquad (5\text{-}12)$$

Using equation 5-7a, this becomes the *half-duplex message transit time*,

$$t'_m = \left(\frac{1}{U} - a\right)t_m \qquad (5\text{-}13)$$

This intuitively obvious result is that the message transit time is the total round-trip message time, t_m/U, minus one propagation time (since the successfully received message does not have to await an acknowledgement).

For the case of selective retransmission with a full-duplex protocol, the same argument holds. An error-free message will require $t_m(1+a)$ time to pass through the receiver. A retransmitted message occurs with probability $p_m/(1-p_m)$ and requires a time of $t_m(1+2a)$. Thus, equation 5-12 holds. However, this cannot be written in the form of equation 5-13, since the efficiency, U, of a selective retransmission line is a different expression, one given by equation 5-9. We therefore use equation 5-12 for the *full-duplex selective retransmission message transit time:*

$$t'_m = \left(\frac{1+2a}{1-p_m} - a\right)t_m \qquad (5\text{-}14)$$

For the half-duplex and selective retransmission cases, we have not been concerned with the effect of errors on other messages. When a communication line accepts a message for transmission, it is sent forthwith and is received by the receiver in a time independent of other errors. Error retransmission time affects the average service time t_m/U, and thus is a factor in the communication line load. This will affect the queue delay but not the transit time for a message.

However, for the Go-Back-N protocol, the situation is not so simple. If a message must be retransmitted, all $N-1$ messages following it must also be retransmitted. Thus, N messages are delayed by a time $t_m(1 + 2a)p_m/(1-p_m)$, and the average message transit time is

$$t'_m = t_m(1 + a) + Nt_m(1 + 2a)p_m/(1-p_m)$$

Using the manipulation that led to equation 5-12, this can be written as

$$t'_m = \left[\left(\frac{1+2a}{1-p_m}\right)(1 + (N - 1)p_m) - a\right]t_m$$

As was done intuitively for the half-duplex case of equation 5-13, equation 5-14 for selective retransmission can be interpreted as the round-trip delay of an average message minus one propagation time, a, since the message receipt does not have to wait for its acknowledgement. For the Go-Back-N protocol, the average round-trip message time, including error retransmissions, is increased by $N - 1$ retransmissions for p_m of the time.

As noted earlier for this case:

$$N = 1+2a \qquad W \geq 1+2a$$

$$N = W \qquad W < 1+2a$$

Thus, for *full-duplex Go-Back-N message transit time:*

$$t'_m = \left[\left(\frac{1+2a}{1-p_m} \right)(1 + 2ap_m) - a \right] t_m \qquad W \geq 1+2a$$

$$\text{(5-15)}$$

$$t'_m = \left[\left(\frac{1+2a}{1-p_m} \right)(1 + (W - 1)p_m) - a \right] t_m \qquad W < 1+2a$$

It is important to note that if a communication line is to be considered a server serving a queue of waiting messages, then its service time is its effective channel utilization, t_m/U, not the message transfer time, t'_m.

Message Transfer Example

Let us look at a typical line and evaluate line utilization and message transit time for the above three protocols. Our example line will be a long-haul dedicated full-duplex synchronous line with the following parameters:

p_b = bit error rate = 10^{-5}

$M+H$ = message length = 300 bytes

t_{prop} = propagation time = 50 msec.

t_{prc} = processing time = 20 msec.

s = line speed = 19,200 bits/sec. = 2,400 bytes/sec.

t_{ack} = acknowledge packet time = 6 bytes @ 2,400 bytes/sec = 2.5 msec.

t_m = message time of 300 bytes @ 2,400 bytes/sec. = 125 msec.

W = window size for full-duplex protocols = 7

From equation 5-5, the probability of a retransmission, p_m, is

$$p_m = 1 - (1 - 10^{-5})^{8(300)} = .0237$$

From equation 5-3, the average normalized protocol delay, a, is

$$a = \frac{50 + (20+2.5)/2}{125} = .49$$

Thus, $W > 1+2a$; that is, a full-duplex acknowledgement will be returned before the window is exhausted.

Using these values, Table 5-1 is constructed. It shows the line efficiencies, message transit times, and communication line service times for all three protocol classes as well as for an ideal line, i.e., no delay and no errors.

TABLE 5-1.   MESSAGE PROTOCOL EXAMPLE

	U Line efficiency	t'_m Message transit time (msec.)	t_m/U Line service time (msec.)
Ideal line	1.0	125	125
Half-duplex	0.493	192	254
Selective retransmit	0.976	192	128
Go-Back-N	0.954	198	131

Note the relationship between the message transit time and the line service time. For a half-duplex line, the service time is much greater than the transit time, since the line must be held until an acknowledgement is received, though the message has already been delivered. For full-duplex lines, messages are not delayed for prior acknowledgements. The next message is sent before the prior message may have propagated to the receiver. Thus, service time is less than transit time.

The superiority of the full-duplex protocols is apparent. Though the message transit time is substantially the same for all cases, full-duplex protocols make use of the line twice as efficiently. Therefore, they can handle twice as much traffic as the half-duplex protocols under the conditions assumed in this example. The efficiency of the half-duplex line is further compromised by the fact that transmission can occur in only one direction at a time. Therefore, if the traffic in both directions is equivalent, the capacity of a half-duplex line is reduced by a further factor of two relative to a full-duplex line.

ESTABLISHMENT/TERMINATION PERFORMANCE

The assignment of a channel to a data communication session adds additional overhead to message transmission. If the session is long, this overhead may be minor. However, for short sessions, channel establishment and termination overhead may be quite significant.

Two common cases are considered by example in the following sections. In the first example, a dedicated line connects two users who are peers. Either may try to use the line, and collisions must be resolved. This is an example of a contention protocol.

The other example is for a multipoint line in which a master station polls the other users (slaves) in an orderly manner. Communication is allowed only between the master and a selected (polled) slave.

There are many other types of protocols in use. The role of master station may be transferred between users in some networks. The line may be held for a reply in some cases but released after the transmission of a transaction in other cases. The techniques used in the following examples are extendable to these and other protocols.

A more complex class of protocols are those that provide multipoint contention. These are discussed in the subsequent section about local area networks.

Point-To-Point Contention

The first procedure to be discussed is a half-duplex contention protocol on a point-to-point channel. This is a typical case in TP systems in which a terminal is connected to the TP host via a dedicated line. Usually, the terminal will initiate the transmission of a request to the host and will await a reply. However, on occasion the host may want to send an unsolicited message to the terminal.

An important characteristic of this example is that the line is not heavily utilized. Therefore, if either the terminal or the host simply seizes the line whenever it wants to send, the probability of colliding is quite low.

An example of this sort of protocol is provided by the ANSI X3.28 protocol described in ANSI [2]. Subcategory 2.3 (Two-Way Alternate Nonswitched Point-To-Point) describes the contention protocol, which typically is used with the X3.28 subcategory B1 message transfer protocol (Message Associated Blocking with Longitudinal Checking and Single Acknowledgement).

A simplified representation of this protocol is shown in Figure 5-22 via the "railroad" diagram used so successfully in the ANSI specification. This diagram shows the flow of control information and data in an unambiguous and compact form. Actions taken by one user are shown in blocks; actions taken by the other user are unblocked. The main flow is indicated by heavy lines.

Let us denote our two users as user A and user B. When user A wants to acquire the channel, it sends an ENQ character (1) (one of the ASCII control characters). If user B is

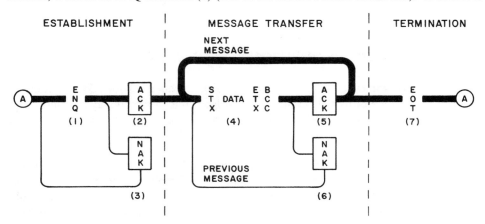

Figure 5-22   Point-to-point contention.

ready to receive the message, it responds with an ACK (2). If it is not ready, it responds with a NAK (3).

When user A receives the ACK, the channel belongs to it (this is the establishment procedure). User A then can send one or more messages (4), pausing at the end of each to await an acknowledgement from the receiver (5). If a NAK is received (6), the message must be retransmitted.

When user A is finished, it releases the channel by sending an EOT character (7). This termination procedure completes the sequence. At this point, either user may seize the channel.

Of course, if both users attempt to seize the channel at the same time by sending simultaneous ENQ characters, a collision occurs. The contention is resolved by having both users wait different times for a response before giving up and trying again. The user with the shorter time-out wins.

The probability of a collision can be determined as follows. As defined earlier, let

$$t_{prop} = \text{channel propagation time between the two users}$$

Also let

$$R_a = \text{message rate of user A (messages/sec.)}.$$

$$R_b = \text{message rate of user B (messages/sec.)}.$$

$$t_a = \text{delay time for user A after a collision.}$$

$$t_b = \text{delay time for user B after a collision.}$$

$$t_{ca} = \text{channel acquisition time for user A (sec.)}.$$

$$t_{cb} = \text{channel acquisition time for user B (sec.)}.$$

One user (say user A) attempts to seize the channel by sending an ENQ. On either side of its seizure attempt time, there is a critical time slot, t_{prop}, during which user B may seize the channel and cause a collision. If user B sends an ENQ before user A but within one propagation time, user A will not see it before it sends its ENQ. Likewise, user B will not see user A's ENQ for one propagation time and may send its ENQ during that time.

The probability that user B will collide with a user A seizure attempt is $2t_{prop}R_b$. Likewise, the probability that user A will collide with a user B seizure attempt is $2t_{prop}R_a$.

In the event of a collision, one user will win the time-out race. Let us say that it is always user A. That is,

$$t_a < t_b$$

We now can calculate the channel acquisition times for user A and user B. In either case, a wait time of $2t_{prop}$ always occurs as the ENQ propagates to the other end and as an

ACK is returned. With probability $2t_{prop}R_x$ ($x = a, b$), a collision occurs. User A must wait a time t_a before trying again and is guaranteed success. Thus, the user A channel acquisition time, t_{ca}, is

$$t_{ca} = 2t_{prop} + 2t_{prop}R_b \ (t_a + 2t_{prop})$$

or

$$t_{ca} = 2t_{prop}[1 + R_b(t_a + 2t_{prop})], \ t_a < t_b \qquad (5\text{-}16)$$

t_{ca} can be added to the message time, which is calculated according to the procedures in the previous section. This gives total message time from a performance viewpoint. Total line utilization is obtained by also adding in the termination time required to send an EOT, which is simply another t_{prop} time.

Following a collision, user B must wait user A's delay time plus its message time. It then must reacquire the channel. Let

$$t'_{ma} = \text{message transit time for user A}$$

Also let

$$k_a = \text{number of messages sent by user A}$$

Then user B's channel acquisition time, t_{cb}, is

$$t_{cb} = 2t_{prop} + (2t_{prop}R_a)(t_a + k_a t'_{ma}) + (2t_{prop}R_a)(2t_{prop})$$

The first term is user B's first attempt at channel seizure. The second term represents the delay of user B's request while user A seizes the channel ($t_a + k_a t'_{ma}$), which occurs with probability $2t_{prop}R_a$. The third term represents the second acquisition attempt after user A has released the channel. This occurs with probability $2t_{prop}R_a$ and takes a time $2t_{prop}$.

t_{cb} can be written as

$$t_{cb} = 2t_{prop}[1 + R_a(t_a + 2t_{prop} + k_a t'_{ma})], \ t_a < t_b \qquad (5\text{-}17)$$

As an example, consider the following case:

t_{prop} = channel propagation time = 50 msec.

R_a = 1 message per 30 seconds (transaction).

R_b = 1 message per 30 seconds (reply).

t_a = user A delay time = 200 msec.

k_a = number of user A messages = 1.

t'_{ma} = user A message time = 1 second (say, a 300-byte message over a 2400-bit/sec. line).

Then,

$$t_{ca} = \text{user A channel acquisition time}$$

$$= .101 \text{ seconds.}$$

$$t_{cb} = \text{user B channel acquisition time}$$

$$= .104 \text{ seconds.}$$

Since the ideal time is a round-trip propagation time of 0.1 seconds, the contention protocol behaves well in this case.

Multipoint Poll/Select

Another common configuration in TP systems is a multipoint channel in which terminals are polled by the TP host. Typical of these protocols are the ANSI X3.28 Subcategory 2.4 and 2.5 and IBM's bisync (binary synchronous, or BSC) protocol. Both are quite similar, and a simplified representation of the bisync protocol is shown in Figure 5-23.

This protocol supports two functions. One is polling, in which the host invites one of the terminals to send a message. To do so, the host sends a poll sequence (1) comprising the terminal's identification in upper-case characters followed by an ENQ character. If the terminal has no message to send, it returns a NAK (2). If the terminal has a message to send, it sends that message (3) (according to some message-transfer protocol not shown).

Following either event, the host terminates the process by sending an EOT character (4). At this point, the host is free to initiate its next function.

The other protocol function is that of selection, which is used to send a message to a terminal. To do so, the host sends a selection sequence (5) comprising the terminal iden-

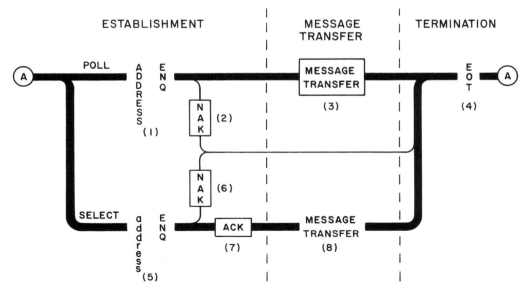

Figure 5-23 Multipoint poll/select.

tification in lower-case letters followed by an ENQ. If the terminal is not ready to receive the message, it returns a NAK (6). If it is ready, it returns an ACK (7), and the host then sends the terminal its message (8). Again, the message transfer protocol is not shown.

An alternate selection sequence is called *fast select*. With fast select, the terminal is assumed to be ready at any time. The selection sequence (5) and message (8) are sent together, with no intervening ACK (7) or NAK (6) being returned by the terminal.

After either event, the host sends an EOT (4) to terminate the process.

From a performance viewpoint, the interesting question is the frequency of negative polls (a poll with no response) and the consequent poll cycle time. Martin [19] presents a solution to this as follows. Let

Q = number of terminals which have a message to send and which are awaiting a poll.

V = total number of terminals on the line.

$P(n)$ = probability that the nth terminal being polled is the first to respond with a message.

The probability that the first terminal to be polled has a message is

$$P(1) = Q/V \qquad (5\text{-}18)$$

The probability that the second terminal is the one to respond is the probability that the first terminal has no message and that the second terminal does. Thus,

$$P(2) = \left(1 - \frac{Q}{V}\right)\frac{Q}{V-1} = \frac{Q}{V}\frac{V-Q}{V-1}$$

$$= P(1)\frac{V-Q}{V-1}$$

Similarly,

$$P(3) = \left(1 - \frac{Q}{V}\right)\left(1 - \frac{Q}{V-1}\right)\frac{Q}{V-2}$$

$$= \frac{Q}{V}\frac{V-Q}{V-1}\frac{V-Q-1}{V-2}$$

$$= P(2)\frac{V-Q-1}{V-2}$$

and

$$P(N) = P(N-1)\frac{V-Q-N+2}{V-N+1} \qquad (5\text{-}19)$$

Let

M = the number of terminals that must be polled in order to get a message.

We know that in the worst case, the first $V-Q$ terminals will be idle and that the first terminal with a message will be $V-Q+1$. Therefore, the average number of terminals that must be polled to get the first message, M, is

$$M = \sum_{N=1}^{V-Q+1} NP(N) \tag{5-20}$$

where $P(1)$ is given by equation 5-18 and $P(N)$ is given by equation 5-19. It can also be shown that

$$\sum_{N=1}^{V-Q+1} P(N) = 1$$

as would be expected.

Equation 5-20 gives the establishment procedure overhead for polling, since $(M-1)$ negative polls are associated with each message. It is based on the assumption that at least one terminal is always active.

What about a lightly loaded line which only occasionally sees a message from a terminal—and when there is a message, there is only one terminal on the line with a message? In this case we can expect the number of negative polls to be about half the total number of terminals. More precisely, the probability that any one terminal will have the message is $1/V$. The average number of terminals that will be polled to get the message once the message is ready is, from equation 5-20,

$$M = \sum_{N=1}^{V} N\left(\frac{1}{V}\right) = \frac{1}{V} \frac{V(V+1)}{2} = \frac{V+1}{2} \tag{5-21}$$

In order to determine whether to use equation 5-20 or 5-21, and in order to evaluate equation 5-20, we need to know the number of waiting terminals, Q. Q will depend upon the line load, which depends upon the negative poll load, which depends on Q. This circular relationship requires that we guess initially at Q, make a calculation, and perhaps iterate to obtain more accurate results.

One way to approach this is to use the M/G/1 queuing model as an initial guess. If this results in a value of Q less than 1, use the simpler equation 5-21. Otherwise, use equation 5-20.

Let us illustrate this with an example. Consider a line for which

V = total number of terminals = 8.

Transaction rate = 1 transaction/15 seconds/terminal.

Transaction message time = 1 second, a constant, sent in response to a poll.

Response message time = 0.5 seconds, a constant, sent via fast select.

t_{poll} = time to send a poll or select sequence = 30 msec.

t_{prop} = channel propagation time = 15 msec.

Terminals send a transaction message of fixed length (say, 300 bytes at 2400 bits/sec., requiring one second to transmit as assumed). The reply is also a fixed-length message (say, 150 bytes at 2400 bits/sec., requiring 0.5 seconds). A terminal sends its transaction to the host in response to a poll. The host responds later with a reply via a select sequence. Every transaction is followed by one and only one reply.

As an initial cut, the load on the line is calculated using just the transaction and reply load:

$$L = \frac{8(1+.5)}{15} = .8$$

The distribution coefficient for the M/G/1 model is given by equation 4-18:

$$K = \frac{1}{2}\frac{E(T^2)}{T^2} = \frac{1}{2}\frac{(.5)(1)^2 + (.5)(.5)^2}{[(.5)(1) + (.5)(.5)]^2} = .56$$

The average number of terminals, Q, waiting for the line (including the one being serviced, if any) is from equation 4-6:

$$Q = \frac{L}{1-L}[1 - (1-k)L] = 2.6$$

Since Q must be an integer, let us use $Q = 3$. Equation 5-20 applies, which yields

$$M = (.375) + 2(.268) + 3(.179) + 4(.107) + 5(.054) + 6(.018)$$
$$= 2.25$$

Thus, each successful poll requires a total of 2.25 polls (1.25 negative polls plus one successful poll), each requiring $(2t_{prop} + t_{poll}) = 60$ msec. Since the transaction rate is 8/15 transactions per second, poll load is $(8/15)(2.25)(.06) = .07$.

When added to the .8 load imposed by the messages, total line load is .87.

This load can be used to repeat the above calculation until the integral number of busy terminals remains constant. For instance, successive iterations for this case give

TABLE 5-2. POLLING EXAMPLE

Iteration	Q	Load (L) Initial	Load (L) Final	M
1	3	.80	.87	2.25
2	5	.87	.85	1.50
3	4	.85	.86	1.80
4	4	.86	.86	1.80

The iteration has converged nicely, resulting in 1.8 polls on the average being required to receive a message (.8 negative polls plus one successful poll).

Establishment and termination times now directly follow for this example. To establish the channel for an incoming (polled) transaction requires 1.8 poll times (which include the message propagation times by our definition). This is $1.8 \times 60 = 108$ msec. Thus, to receive our 1 second message actually requires 1.1 seconds due to polling.

Termination is effectively transparent, as the EOT termination character can be simply piggybacked onto the next poll or select sequence.

LOCAL AREA NETWORK PERFORMANCE

The connection of user terminals to a TP host via a *local area network* (LAN) is rapidly gaining popularity, especially if the terminal population is fairly close geographically to the host. Also, remote terminal clusters may be interconnected by a LAN and then connected to the host by a LAN gateway. A gateway is another device on the LAN which passes LAN data to the host and which distributes host data to the LAN.

We now consider techniques for managing data on a LAN. A local area network is a high-speed data link generally comprising twisted pair wires, coaxial cable, or a fiber optic link (Figure 5-24a). It may span a building, a college campus, or an industrial complex. Users attach directly to the LAN and can communicate with any other user of the LAN according to a specific protocol. In fact, when one user transmits, all other receivers receive that transmission. The transmitted data contains addressing information identifying the intended receiver(s).

In this section we discuss certain protocols that are popularly used for LANs. These protocols tend to combine the establishment/termination procedures and message transfer procedures of classical protocols and for this reason are treated separately.

It is noted that the family of IEEE 802.x standards describe contemporary LAN protocols.

Multipoint Contention: CSMA/CD

In a previous section we considered point-to-point contention protocols, in which either one of the two terminals could attempt to seize the line and transmit. In the event of a collision, procedures were established so that each terminal would back off and try again at different times to resolve the contention.

There is an important class of multiuser local area networks in which all users contend for the network. Various procedures are used to resolve conflicts. One of the popular LAN contention protocols is a protocol known as CSMA/CD, which stands for Carrier-Sense Multiple-Access with Collision Detection.

Under this protocol, any user of the LAN can transmit at any time so long as three rules are obeyed. The first two rules are

1. The user first listens to the network to see if it is idle. If the network is busy, the user waits a random time and tries again.
2. If the channel is idle, then the user can transmit his data.

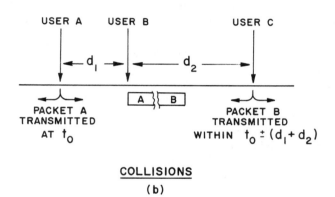

Figure 5-24 CSMA protocol.

This protocol in its basic form is called CSMA. *CS* stands for carrier sense. That is, the user listens before talking. *MA* means multiple access—many users can use the network.

The protocol is enriched if a transmitter can monitor the line while it is transmitting. In this case, if another user starts transmitting, both transmitters will read the garbled signal on the line and will stop transmission without wasting further valuable channel time. This third rule adds collision detection to the protocol, giving the protocol the name CSMA/CD. The third rule can be restated thus:

3. While transmitting, monitor the channel. If the signal is garbled, transmit a short jamming burst to ensure that all users detect the collision, and then stop transmission. Wait a random time, and try again.

Collision detection is useful because even listening to the channel before transmitting does not guarantee collision-free operation. This is illustrated in Figure 5-24b, where three users are shown on a LAN. User A is a distance of d_1 from user B, and user C is a distance of d_2 from user B. For our purposes, we will measure d_1 and d_2 in terms of channel propagation time, i.e., d_1 is the time it takes for a signal to propagate from user A to user B.

Now let us assume that user A transmits a packet at time t_o. It will not reach user C until time $t_o + d_1 + d_2$. Therefore, user C can legitimately decide to send a packet during this time, as it has not yet heard user A's transmission. In fact, user C can send a packet at any time during the interval $t_o \pm (d_1 + d_2)$, using the reverse argument for the minus sign. Should user C do so, a collision will result. All users will eventually see a jamming signal.

The evaluation of collision probabilities and the resulting LAN performance have been heavily analyzed and are thoroughly covered in Hammond [9]. Only the results are given here.

Let

S = the rate of packets successfully transmitted per packet transmission time.

G = the rate of packets offered to the network (successful transmissions plus retries) per packet transmission time.

a = normalized end-to-end propagation delay of the channel, defined as the ratio of the end-to-end propagation delay to the packet transmission time, in short:

$$a = \frac{\text{end-to-end LAN propagation time}}{\text{packet transmission time}}$$

Note that S, G, and a are all normalized to the packet transmission time, which is assumed fixed.

Is the term a significant? Are propagation delays significant relative to packet time? Hammond [9] notes that signals propagate over a coaxial cable at about .65 of the speed of light. This is about 5 nanoseconds (5×10^{-9} seconds) per meter. To travel a kilometer (a typical LAN length) requires about 5 microseconds. A typical LAN data rate is 10 megabits/second. Thus, signal propagation time is about 50 bit times. A user at one end of the LAN can send 50 bits before a user at the other end will hear it. Electronic delays in the transmitters and receivers can be even more significant. Thus the ratio a is the primary factor in LAN performance.

Note that G/S is the average number of transmissions required per packet. This is the number we would like for performance analysis. Unfortunately, as we shall see below, LAN analysis is not so kind to us since the expressions do not lend themselves to obtaining G/S. Computer computation is required.

Hammond [9] gives the following results for the CSMA and CSMA/CD protocols described above, assuming random arrivals:

CSMA:

$$S = \frac{Ge^{-aG}}{G(1+2a) + e^{-aG}} \tag{5-22}$$

CSMA/CD:

$$S = \frac{Ge^{-aG}}{Ge^{-aG}+jaG(1-e^{-aG})+2aG(1-e^{-aG})+(2-e^{-aG})} \tag{5-23}$$

where

$$j = \frac{J}{t} \tag{5-24}$$

and

J = jamming interval (seconds).

t = propagation time between stations (sec.) (assumes stations are equidistant).

Another case to be noted is a simpler protocol in which the transmitter does not listen before sending. In this case, collisions, of course, will be significantly more frequent. This simpler protocol is used in some radio networks and is called the Aloha protocol after the first major network in which it was used (in Hawaii, of course). For this case:

Aloha:

$$S = Ge^{-2G} \tag{5-25}$$

In none of these expressions can we easily find G/S, the probability of retransmission that we would like to have. In fact, we usually know S (the traffic to be carried) and must find G, just the opposite of what these expressions allow.

The obvious technique is to calculate tables or graphs and to use them to find G for a given value of S. To some extent, Hammond [9] presents graphs that could be quite helpful.

However, the graphical representations of S vs. G expose another interesting problem. A typical S–G relationship is shown in Figure 5-25. Note that initially, as system throughput S increases, the network load G increases linearly. Then network load starts to rise at a faster rate as retransmissions occur. Ultimately, the network cannot support the level of retransmissions, and throughput S falls off even as network load increases further. The network is thrashing.

In fact, at any given throughput value, S, there are two network load values, G, one for proper operation and one for thrashing. Two points are to be made:

1. Use the lower value of G to obtain the probability of retransmission G/S, since it must be assumed that the network is not thrashing.
2. Don't operate the network near its peak throughput S, as it may go over the hump and start thrashing.

Token Rings

A *token ring* is another organization of a local area network. To use this protocol, the LAN must be structured as a closed ring, as shown in Figure 5-26a.

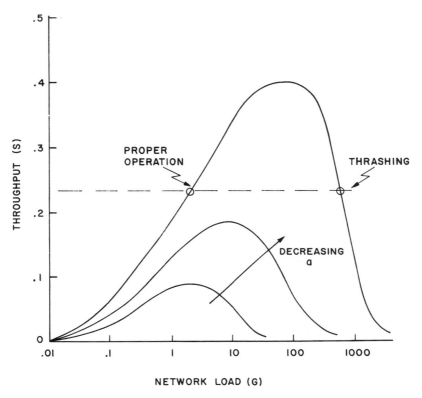

Figure 5-25   Performance characteristics of multipoint contention protocols.

Stations connect to the ring in such a way that they can listen to traffic on the ring as it passes by and modify that traffic on the fly. To do this, each data packet is necessarily delayed in the station-connecting equipment, typically by a few bits. For instance, data may be passed through a shift register of sufficient length (Figure 5-26b) to allow the station to do the following:

- Interpret data entering from the ring.
- Modify the data before retransmitting.
- Insert data before retransmitting.
- Delete data to prevent retransmission.

Data packets circulating around the ring incur two types of delays:

1. The propagation time over the link between channels
2. The station latency, or delay incurred as the data circulate through the station connection

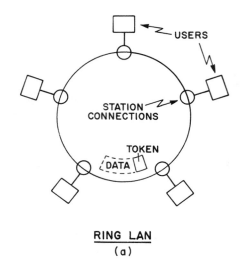

RING LAN
(a)

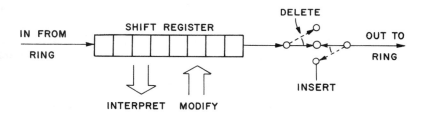

STATION CONNECTION
(b)

Figure 5-26 Token ring.

In the simple (and most popular) token ring, a single token circulates around the ring. It is, in fact, a small packet of control data that includes, among other things, a free/busy indicator. As it circulates, each station in turn can receive it, evaluate it, and pass it on to the next station.

On an idle ring, the token is marked as free. If a station has a message to send, it waits for the idle token. When it receives the idle token, the station marks it busy and adds its data to the end of the token. It also fills in an address field in the token.

The busy token with data now circulates around the ring and is read by each station. When a station reads a busy token, it checks to see if the data is addressed to itself. If so, it captures the data. In either event, the busy token is passed on to the next station.

Finally, the token returns to the station that sent the data. That station sets the token to idle and deletes the data from the token as it passes by.

An approximate pass at token ring performance can be taken as follows:

Let

$$t_{prop} = \text{propagation time between stations}$$

$$t_{sta} = \text{station latency time}$$

The time to pass the token from one station to the next is $t_{prop} + t_{sta}$. This time is, in every respect, a poll cycle as previously described. The only difference is that the system is self-polling rather than requiring a master station to do the polling. As described earlier, of the V stations on the network, Q will be waiting with data to send. On the average, M stations will be polled in order to find a terminal with a message. M, Q, and V are related by equations 5-20 or 5-21, as appropriate.

Once a sending station has been found, the data packet must travel, on the average, halfway around the ring to its destination. That is, if there are V users, $V-1$ of which are possible receivers, then the probability that any particular user will be the receiver for a packet is $1/(V-1)$. The average number of users that the packet must pass before the receiver is found is

$$\sum_{i=1}^{V-1} i/(V-1) = \frac{1}{(V-1)} \frac{V(V-1)}{2} = \frac{V}{2}$$

The packet must pass all stations and return to its transmitter before the token is freed.

Thus, the total network time to send the next message, given that one is available, is the sum of the polling time, $M(t_{prop} + t_{sta})$, and the transmission time, $V(t_{prop} + t_{sta})$. Let the rate of arrival of messages to be transmitted be R messages per second. In a busy system, the rate of message transmission over the network will equal the arrival rate of messages to the network:

$$(M + V)(t_{prop} + t_{sta}) = 1/R \tag{5-26}$$

where

$$R = \text{message rate (messages per second)}$$

Equation 5-26 can be solved for the average number of terminals, M, that must be polled:

$$M = \frac{1}{R(t_{prop} + t_{sta})} - V \tag{5-27}$$

If equation 5-27 indicates a value of M greater than $(V+1)/2$ (a lightly loaded network), then equation 5-21 governs, and M is taken as $(V+1)/2$. In this case, there is only one transaction on the ring awaiting service. On the average, the token will pass by half the terminals to find the message and half the terminals to deliver the message. The total time to deliver the message from the time it was submitted, t_s, is

$$t_s = V(t_{prop} + t_{sta}),\ M \geq (V+1)/2 \tag{5-28}$$

where

$$t_s = \text{message delay time.}$$

If equation 5-27 indicates a value of M less than $(V+1)/2$, then the number of messages, Q, waiting for service on the LAN is obtained from equation 5-20. (An iterative calculation is required.) Though service is round-robin, it is conservative to assume first-in, first-out servicing. In this case, message delay time is

$$t_s = Q(M+V)(t_{prop}+t_{sta}) - \frac{V}{2}(t_{prop}+t_{sta}),\ M < (V+1)/2 \tag{5-29}$$

The first term represents the time to pass the idle token to the next active device for each of the Q messages in line and then to pass the busy token completely around the ring. The second term represents the fact that the message in question needs to pass only $V/2$ terminals to reach its receiver.

Using equation 5-26, equation 5-29 can be rewritten as

$$t_s = \frac{Q}{R} - \frac{V}{2}(t_{prop} + t_{sta}),\ M < (V+1)/2 \tag{5-30}$$

SUMMARY

The material contained in this chapter, though voluminous, hardly scratches the surface of communication technology. However, it provides us with the basics required to understand and evaluate performance of communication channels, protocols, and networks.

In-depth discussions of many more networks and standards may be found in the various references cited, including Kleinrock [15] on ARPANET, Meijer [21] on standards and protocols, Hammond [9] on local networks, and Stallings [25] on networks.

6

Processing Environment

Now that we can receive a request from a user and have a mechanism for returning a reply, how do we get from here to there? The computer—viewed as the central processing unit (the CPU), its memory, its I/O ports, and its operating system—is the transaction-processing engine that provides the environment in which the application programs can process a request and can return a reply.

In this chapter we review issues related to hardware and operating system design. Of particular importance to performance analysis is contention created in multiprocessor systems and thrashing caused by operating system activities.

For purposes of analysis, we will consider the processing environment in terms of two levels: the physical level and the operating system level.

At the physical level, the CPU, memory, I/O controllers, and, in the case of a distributed system, the interprocessor or intercomputer bus act together to execute the instructions submitted by the operating system and by the application programs. In many performance analyses, the detailed characteristics of the physical level are hidden by, and in fact are take into account by, the operating system. However, it is often desirable to deal at the physical level, and we will view some of the performance issues of that level.

The role of the operating system level is to hide the physical characteristics of the computer from the user and to provide a more comfortable (if less efficient) environment for the development of new applications. As modern operating systems become more powerful and do more for the application programmer, they often exact a greater toll in performance. The performance of many TP systems today is limited more by operating system characteristics than it is by the hardware or by the application programs.

PHYSICAL RESOURCES

The physical resources with which we should be concerned are the CPUs, memories, I/O controllers, and interconnecting bus structures that make up a computer. Actually, a single computer architecture does not create a very interesting exercise for the performance analyst. We will, therefore, take as an example a multiprocessor distributed system and will look at its performance characteristics as the load imposed upon it increases. This example is structured to illustrate performance modeling techniques for a variety of hardware considerations. Once understood, these techniques can then be used by the analyst as a foundation for modeling other multiprocessor systems.

Much of the material for the following multiprocessor example was taken from studies performed for Concurrent Computer Corporation. The author would like to express his appreciation to Concurrent Computer for its permission to use this material.

A typical multiprocessor system is shown in Figure 6-1. Though this is a fairly simple representation of such a system, it highlights the performance issues with which we will want to deal. In this system, several processors are connected via a single full-duplex (i.e., two-way) bus to a plurality of memory units. Each processor also handles certain I/O devices on behalf of the entire system.

Several manufacturers currently offer systems with multiprocessor architectures, including Concurrent Computer (Tinton Falls, New Jersey), Stratus (Marlboro, Massa-

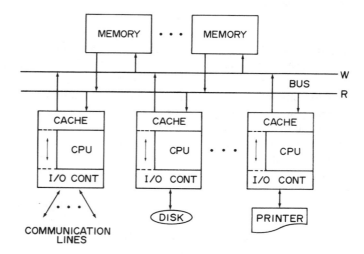

Figure 6-1 Multiprocessor system.

chusetts), and Sequoia (Marlboro, Massachusetts). Some of these systems can become quite large and may include several hundred processors.

Let us add some characteristics to our hypothetical system to give us something to analyze.

Processors

The industry today likes to characterize processor power in MIPS, or millions of instructions per second. Unfortunately, this is not a very meaningful term. First of all, there is a big difference between what is done with a 16-bit instruction and what is done with a 32-bit instruction. Second, in today's sophisticated architectures with variable-length instructions, pipelining, and so on, the actual rate of instruction execution is very much a function of the program being run.

Rather than predicting how fast a given program will run, we will look at performance degradation under various conditions compared to the system's ideal performance. This will be done by defining a *processor performance factor*, P_{pf}, which is unity under ideal conditions, and which decreases as system load causes performance degradation. More about this later. We will accept from the designers that the average execution rate for a processor is M instructions per second:

$$M = \text{processor speed (instructions per second)}$$

As shown in Figure 6-1, each processor contains, in addition to its CPU, a cache memory (to make more efficient use of the main memory resource) and one or more I/O controllers.

Cache Memory

The *cache memory* is a small high-speed memory (generally faster than main memory) that is used to store the more recent data accessed by the CPU. The hope is that most data or instructions that the program will need to access will be found in cache. This has proved to be quite effective in practice, as programs tend to operate within small loops of instructions and within small local areas of data for significant periods before moving on.

When data or instructions must be moved into cache, they must overwrite information currently in cache. The decision of what information to overwrite is a decision made by the cache controller. Usually, cache information is aged; the information that has not been used for the longest time is chosen to be overwritten.

Since cache memories tend to be implemented with higher speed components than main memories, they are more costly and therefore smaller. Cache memories tend to be in the 4 to 64 kilobyte range, whereas main memories tend to be in the range of 1 to 64 megabytes—a thousand times bigger.

For purposes of our analysis, we will assume that our cache memory has the following characteristics:

- It has an access time of 100 nanoseconds (one nanosecond is one billionth of a second).

- Its word length is 32 bits, or 4 bytes.
- Data is moved to it from memory in 4 word blocks (16 bytes).
- Data that the CPU writes is written to cache memory as well as to main memory in whatever increments of whole words the CPU desires, up to a maximum of four words. This is called *cache write-through* and ensures that main memory is always up-to-date.
- While data is being read into cache or written through cache to main memory, the processor is paused.

Note that to the extent that the CPU has to access main memory, system performance will degrade. Not only is main memory slower, but there also is contention for its access from other processors. A processor will have to access main memory to read data not in its cache, and to write data. Therefore, to the extent that the program can be written to be highly modular and to make extensive use of local registers and stacks to write temporary results, the system will perform better. This is often the responsibility of an optimizing compiler.

When the CPU finds its data in cache, this is called a *cache hit*. If it has to access main memory to read data, this is called a *cache miss*. It is virtually impossible to predict what the average cache miss ratios will be, since cache activity is highly dependent upon the structure of the particular program being run. However, the performance analyst can predict the effects on performance caused by cache misses. This prediction can then serve as valuable information for the designers who are sizing cache, writing compilers, and so on. We will make these predictions in the following analysis.

For the time being, we can characterize the performance of the cache memory by a single parameter: the cache miss ratio, p_m:

p_m = cache miss ratio (the probability that a read will require a main memory access).

It might be noted that the cache memory described above is quite simple in today's technology. Some systems do not write through cache, thus saving significant main memory time. Rather, the cache memories of all processors are considered an extension of main memory, and the "ownership" of any piece of data is known to the memory system. If one processor wants a data item that is currently in another processor's cache, it receives it from that cache memory.

I/O System

Each processor may be responsible for handling I/O transfers between certain devices, such as terminals, disks, printers, etc., via I/O controllers connected to that processor. In some architectures, certain processors are designated as I/O processors—perhaps even as data-base processors, communication processors, etc.—and others are designated as application processors, which perform no I/O but which act upon data received by the I/O processors and which return data to them. In other architectures, all processors are amorphous—they may do anything. At a first level of approximation, this sort of structure can be ignored, as each processor is simply a member of the user population for the common memory resource.

I/O operations are typically either *programmed I/O* or *direct access I/O*. Under programmed I/O, data is written to and read from a device, a character at a time, under direct programmed control. This is usually used for very low-speed devices or to send commands to or receive status from an I/O device. For purposes of analysis, this load will be ignored. It is small and can be considered part of the application program.

Direct access I/O occurs when a device reads data directly from memory or writes it directly to memory without program intervention. This is often referred to as a DMA (direct memory access) transfer. The program, of course, must initiate the transfer and must be notified of its completion (usually via a hardware-generated interrupt).

Direct access is usually used for all high-speed devices (disks, tapes, high-speed communication lines, line printers) and can represent a significant load on the system. For purposes of our model, let us assume the following I/O characteristics:

- Data is transferred in direct access mode between main memory and a device in 4-word (16 byte) blocks (the same as for cache reads).
- The cache memory logic is used to accomplish the memory transfers.
- There are no freewheeling input devices, i.e., the rate of all input data flow can be controlled to prevent data loss in high load situations. (This usually implies that the I/O controllers have sufficient buffering to accommodate any outstanding read requests.)

The I/O system can then be characterized simply by the composite data rates from all devices. Let

$$D_i = \text{data input rate from all devices (bytes/sec.)}$$

$$D_o = \text{data output rate to all devices (bytes/sec.)}$$

These data rates are taken as those that would occur in an ideally operating system ($P_{pf} = 1$). However, since I/O transfers are initiated by the processors, it is assumed that actual I/O rates drop off with processor performance and are, in fact, $P_{pf}D_i$ and $P_{pf}D_o$.

Bus

A high-speed bus interconnects the processors with the main memory modules. This bus is a full-duplex bus comprising an R-bus (Read) and a W-bus (Write). The W-bus is used to send the address of the data to the memory. For write operations, it also then sends the data to memory. The R-bus is used to receive data read from memory during a read operation, the address of this data having been supplied previously on the W-bus.

Each bus is 32 bits wide (4 bytes) plus control signals. This is sufficient to send a full address or a full data word on each bus cycle. Thus, to read a block from memory, one W-bus cycle is required to send the address; four R-bus cycles are required to read the four-word block. To write a block requires two to five W-bus cycles—one for the address and one for each data word to be written (up to four words).

The bus speed is 100 nsec. (nanosecond) per word. This means that each bus has a capacity of 40 megabytes per second for a composite speed of 80 megabytes per second. Some of this capacity, though, is used for addressing.

The bus is a common resource for the system. Processors must contend for it to send addresses and data to memory, and memory units must contend for it to return data to the processors. There are several contention schemes that could be used, including round robin and priority schemes. This system uses a time-varying priority contention algorithm that increases the priority of a processor or memory as it waits. Thus, a user who has waited awhile is more likely to obtain the bus than one who has just arrived. This algorithm approximates first-in, first-out (FIFO) servicing.

Several questions can be addressed relative to the performance of the bus:

- Is it a significant bottleneck in the system?
- Is it balanced, or is one side (R or W) heavily used and the other lightly used? Should costs, therefore, be reallocated to make one side faster or wider than the other?

To summarize the bus characteristics:

- The bus is full-duplex (W-bus and R-bus).
- Each path is 32 bits wide (4 bytes) plus control data.
- Bus cycle time is 100 nsec.
- A write requires one W-bus cycle to send the address and one to four W-bus cycles to send the data.
- A read requires one W-bus cycle to send the address and four R-bus cycles to receive the data.

Main Memory

Main memory comprises one or more memory modules that operate independently. Each module provides, let's say, two megabytes of storage. Up to 32 memory modules can be provided for a total of 64 megabytes of memory.

Each memory module requires 400 nsec. to set up an address and 100 nsec. per word to read or write data. Thus, a read operation requires 800 nsec., and a write requires 500 to 800 nsec., depending upon its length. The entire 4-word block is read from memory before any data is returned to the requesting processor via the R-bus.

A queue with a capacity of eight items is provided in each memory module. Each item is five words in length and can hold anything from a read command and address to a write command with its address and data. As long as there is room in the queue, the memory can accept an access command. If the queue is full, the command is rejected; and the requesting processor must back off and try again later. Back-off time is typically a few microseconds. If queue overflows are frequent, back-off time might be a performance factor. If back-off time is long, processors will be delayed; if it is short, bus load and consequently queue delays for the bus will increase.

Summarizing main memory characteristics:

- Each memory module provides two megabytes of storage.
- Up to 32 memory modules may be configured in the system.
- Data is accessed one word at a time.
- Memory timing is 400 nsec. to set up and 100 nsec. per word to read or write data.
- A queue of eight items is provided to buffer incoming memory commands.

Note that since memory speeds and bus speeds are identical, the memory could request the R-bus as soon as it had accessed the first word, thus saving 300 nsec. Many common memory systems do this. We assume a full read here to simplify the analysis so as to more clearly present the underlying analytic principles.

Processor Performance Factor

We alluded previously to a processor performance factor, P_{pf}. Let us now define it. If a processor were running totally without access to main memory, i.e., all reads were from cache or from its own internal registers and stack, and all writes were to its internal registers and stack, then it would be operating at maximum speed. This speed has been defined as M million instructions per second. Instructions are being executed every $1/M$ microsecond.

However, to the extent that main memory must be accessed, additional overhead is incurred, which slows the system down. On the average, each instruction will be slowed by a time, T_i, so that instructions are actually being executed every $T_i + 1/M$ microseconds. The *processor performance factor* is defined as the ratio of the ideal instruction execution time to the actual execution time:

$$P_{pf} = \frac{1/M}{T_i + 1/M} = \frac{1}{MT_i + 1} \tag{6-1}$$

T_i is a direct function of the number of reads and writes that must be made to main memory. Since each of these main memory accesses may be delayed due to other system activity, then T_i is also a function of that other activity. In our example, that activity is generated by other processors and I/O devices.

Let

r = proportion of instructions which are reads.

w = proportion of instructions which are writes.

t_r = time to complete a read to main memory (μsec., i.e., one millionth of a second).

t_w = time to complete a write to main memory (μsec.).

p_m has been defined as the *cache miss ratio*, i.e., the probability that a read will have to be passed to main memory. Since T_i is the main memory read and write delays averaged over all instructions, it may be expressed as

$$T_i = p_m rt_r + wt_w \tag{6-2}$$

Traffic Model

A traffic model showing the progression of a read or write access through the system is shown in Figure 6-2. The processor (1) first waits for access to the W-bus (2) so that it can send its command and address word and the data if this is a write command. When the processor is granted access to the W-bus (3), it sends its data to the appropriate memory queue (4), where it awaits action by the memory. However, if the memory queue is full, the request is rejected (5), and the processor will have to try again later. If the request is accepted, and if it is a write access, the write operation is now complete; the processor can continue.

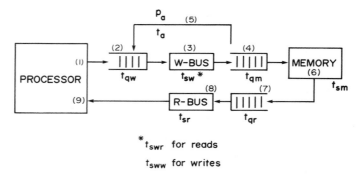

Figure 6-2   Multiprocessor traffic model.

If this is a read access, the processor must wait for the memory module (6) to work through its queue of work, access the data, and send it back to the processor via the R-bus. To do this, the memory module must wait for access to the R-bus (7), then send it via the R-bus (8) to the processor (9). At this point, the processor can proceed.

Queuing and service times that are identified in Figure 6-1 are

t_{qw} = waiting time for the W-bus (μsec.).

t_{sw} = service time for the W-bus (μsec.).

t_{swr} = time to send a read command on the W-bus (μsec.).

t_{sww} = time to send a write command on the W-bus (μsec.).

t_{qm} = queuing time for the memory (μsec.).

t_{sm} = service time for the memory (μsec.).

t_{qr} = queuing time for the R-bus (μsec.).

t_{sr} = service time for the R-bus (μsec.).

p_a = probability that memory queue is full (abort).

t_a = retry time (μsec.).

One complication in this model is the W-bus retry possibility, which is reflected by the probability p_a. If the W-bus must retry, it must wait a time, t_a, before trying again. Obviously, when it tries a second time, it will again fail with probability p_a. In fact, it will have to try a second time with probability p_a, a third time with probability p_a^2, and so on. The total number of tries is $1 + p_a + p_a^2 + \ldots$, or $1/(1 - p_a)$. The total number of retries is one less, or $p_a/(1 - p_a)$.

Thus, the read and write time delays can be expressed as

$$t_r = (t_{qw} + t_{swr} + p_a t_a)/(1 - p_a) + t_{qm} + t_{sm} + t_{qr} + t_{sr} \qquad (6\text{-}3)$$

$$t_w = (t_{qw} + t_{sww} + p_a t_a)/(1 - p_a) \qquad (6\text{-}4)$$

Note that W-bus queue times and memory queue times are independent of reading or writing, since both reads and writes are mixed in the queue. However, W-bus service time is different for reads and writes (one cycle for a read, two to five for a write); these are therefore expressed separately. W-bus queue time will depend on the average service time, which is

$$t_{sw} = \frac{R t_{swr} + W t_{sww}}{R + W} \qquad (6\text{-}5)$$

where R and W are the read and write access rates, including both processor activity and I/O activity. Since the rate of read/write processor accesses is $p_m r M$ and $w M$, respectively, and since the rate of read/write I/O accesses is $D_o/16$ and $D_i/16$, respectively (16 bytes/access for I/O), then

$$R = p_m r M + D_o/16 \qquad (6\text{-}6)$$

$$W = w M + D_i/16 \qquad (6\text{-}7)$$

Note that the subscripts o and i for data transfers reflect output and input relative to the device. Device outputs (D_o) are reads from memory and writes to the device, and device inputs (D_i) are reads from the device and writes to memory.

Performance Tools

It now remains for us to evaluate the terms in Figure 6-2. The analytical process is complex, as the traffic model does not fit any of our queuing models. It is true that the servicing order of all queues is substantially FIFO (First-In, First-Out). Since there are a limited number of users in each population (the processors on the one hand contending for the W-bus and memory, and the memories on the other hand contending for the R-bus), it seems that our finite population models ought to be useful. And this is, in fact, true for the multiple memories contending for the R-bus.

However, the processor-to-memory path is a tandem queue. A request must first wait for the W-bus. Then, if it is a read, it must wait for the memory. How does one define the availability time, T_a, and the service time, T, needed to calculate the service ratio, z, for a read operation? Furthermore, R-bus service times are constant. Memory and W-bus service times are probably more constant than random. How do we handle these? The answer to this is not apparent to the author. We could give up and look for another job. Or we could use the best tools we have for the job, invoking our cloak of devout imperfectionism.

In this case, the tools we can always fall back on are the Khintchine-Pollaczek relations. We will use these to characterize the delays in the system. If there are not many processors or memories in the system, at least the results will be conservative, since they should predict queues that are somewhat larger than the actual ones. On the other hand, if there are many processors or memories (say twenty or more), these relations will yield predictions that will be quite good.

Note that though the processors are sending data to multiple memories and the memories are sending data to multiple processors, these are both single-server situations. This is because each block of data is being routed to a specific memory or processor. Memories and processors are not load-sharing servers in this environment.

Performance Model

W-Bus.   The W-bus service time for read operations is a single cycle to send an address word:

$$t_{swr} = 0.1 \ \mu\text{sec}. \tag{6-8}$$

For a write operation, the average service time is a function of the distribution of write lengths. Let w_i be the probability that a processor write is i words long ($1 \leq i \leq 4$). Then

$$t_{sww} = \frac{wM \sum\limits_{i=1}^{4} w_i (0.1 + 0.1i) + (0.5)D_i/16}{wM + D_i/16} \tag{6-9}$$

where care has been taken to average in I/O writes. It is assumed that the distribution of W-bus retry service times is the same as the originally imposed service times.

Average W-bus service time is t_{sw}, as given by equation 6-5. The distribution coefficient, k_w, as defined by Khintchine and Pollaczek, is

$$k_w = \frac{R(0.1)^2 + wM \sum\limits_{i=1}^{4} w_i (0.1 + 0.1i)^2 + (0.5)^2 D_i/16}{2(R + W)t_{sw}^2} \tag{6-10}$$

(Note the use of equation 6-7 in the numerator to account for I/O load.)

The load on the W-bus, L_w, is the rate of accessing of that bus multiplied by the time of each access. Since accessing will slow down as the processors slow down, the load on the W-bus decreases proportionately with the processor performance factor, P_{pf}. However, W-bus load will increase with retries due to memory queue overflow. W-bus load is expressed as

$$L_w = P_{pf}P(R + W)t_{sw}/(1 - p_a) \qquad (6\text{-}11)$$

where

$$P = \text{number of processors}$$

Thus, the waiting time for the W-bus is

$$t_{qw} = \frac{k_w L_w}{1 - L_w} t_{sw} \qquad (6\text{-}12)$$

Memory.   The memory average service time is similar to that of the W-bus service time. A read requires a fixed 0.8 µsec., and a write requires $0.4 + 0.1i$ µsec., where i is the number of words to be written.

The average memory service time, t_{sm}, is

$$t_{sm} = \frac{0.8R + wM \sum\limits_{i=1}^{4} w_i\,(0.4 + 0.1i) + (0.8)D_i/16}{R + W} \qquad (6\text{-}13)$$

The distribution coefficient, k_m, is

$$k_m = \frac{R(0.8)^2 + wM \sum\limits_{i=1}^{4} w_i\,(0.4 + 0.1i)^2 + (0.8)^2 D_i/16}{2(R + W)t_{sm}^2} \qquad (6\text{-}14)$$

The load on the memory is

$$L_m = P_{pf}P(R + W)t_{sm}/S \qquad (6\text{-}15)$$

where

$$S = \text{the number of memories in the system (storage devices)}$$

The queuing delay for memory is

$$t_{qm} = \frac{k_m L_m}{1 - L_m} t_{sm} \qquad (6\text{-}16)$$

Note that we have assumed equal load across all memories. Usually, in systems such as these, there is not enough data to suggest any more detailed an allocation.

R-Bus.   The R-Bus service time is constant at 0.4 msec.:

$$t_{sr} = 0.4 \qquad (6\text{-}17)$$

The distribution coefficient is

$$k_r = 0.5 \qquad (6\text{-}18)$$

since the service time is constant.

R-bus load is

$$L_r = 0.4RP_{pf}P \qquad (6\text{-}19)$$

and the queue delay is

$$t_{qr} = \frac{k_r L_r}{1 - L_r} t_{sr} \qquad (6\text{-}20)$$

Memory Queue Full. Finally, we can approximate the memory-queue-full probability. For random arrivals and random service times, the probability that a queue will exceed n items is L^{n+1}, where L is the load on the server (this includes the item being serviced, which still takes queue space in this memory system). Since the service time of the memory is far from random, this result will be conservative. Therefore, it is conservative to state that the memory retry probability, p_a, is

$$p_a = L_m{}^9 \qquad (6\text{-}21)$$

since a memory queue of eight items is provided.

Model Summary

The model we have generated for this distributed processing system is summarized in Table 6-1 (parameter definitions) and Table 6-2 (equations).

Note that iterative calculation is required to calculate the results, since the load imposed on the memory system is a function of that same load. As the load increases, response time increases. The processors slow down, thus reducing the load. This shows up via the term P_{pf}, the processor performance factor we are attempting to calculate. P_{pf} is a function of T_i, which is a function of queue delays, which are functions of loads, which are functions of P_{pf}. Consequently, this set of results does not lend itself to manual calculation; it must be calculated by computer.

Note the similarity to the approach taken in chapter 4 for finite populations. There, system load was calculated as a function of delay time as given by equations 4-109 and 4-110 in a manner analogous to what we have done above. Since the finite population solution was not available to us because of the difficulty of establishing an availability time, T_a, we have accomplished an adequate result by using a similar technique.

Model Evaluation

Using this model, one could ask several questions about the projected performance of the system:

1. How many processors can be supported by the bus?
2. What is the optimum processor-to-memory ratio? (i.e., at what point does memory speed start to have an impact on performance?)
3. What is the effect of cache misses?

4. What is the effect of writes?

5. How does I/O affect performance?

6. Is memory queue overflow a factor?

7. Are the buses evenly loaded?

The model has been evaluated for a typical set of conditions to show how these questions could be answered in a real analysis.

Certain input parameters are assumed in order to allow calculation. Unless modified as a calculation parameter, the input values shown in Table 6-1 have been used to create the results. This table assumes that each processor executes at 3 MIPS. Thirty percent of

TABLE 6-1. MULTIPROCESSOR PARAMETERS

Input parameters

Parameter	Meaning	Value
D_i	Data input rate from all devices (bytes/sec.).	0
D_o	Data output rate to all devices (bytes/sec.).	0
M	Processor speed (instructions/sec.).	3×10^6
P	Number of processors.	varies
p_m	Cache-miss ratio.	0.1
r	Proportion of instructions that are reads.	0.3
S	Number of memory units.	4
t_a	Write bus back-off time (μsec.).	3
w	Proportion of instructions that are writes.	0.1
w_i	Proportion of all processor write accesses that are i words in length ($1 \leq i \leq 4$).	$w_i = 1 - 0.4$ $2 - 0.4$ $3 - 0.0$ $4 - 0.2$

Intermediate parameters

Parameter	Meaning
j	Resource index (used below): $j = m$–memory. $\quad r$–R-bus. $\quad w$–W-bus.
k_j	Distribution coefficient for resource j.
L_j	Load on resource j.
p_a	Probability of memory queue full.
P_{pf}	Processor performance factor.
R	Total processor and I/O read rate.
T_i	Average delay time per instruction due to main memory access (μsec.).
t_{qj}	Queuing delay for resource j (μsec.).
t_r	Time to complete a read to main memory (μsec.).
t_{sj}	Service time for resource j (μsec.).
t_{swr}	Time to send a read command on the W-bus (μsec.).
t_{sww}	Time to send a write command on the W-bus (μsec.).
t_w	Time to complete a write to main memory (μsec.).
W	Total processor and I/O write rate.

TABLE 6-2. MULTIPROCESSOR MODEL

$$P_{pf} = \frac{1}{MT_i + 1} \tag{6-1}$$

$$T_i = p_m r t_r + w t_w \tag{6-2}$$

$$t_r = (t_{qw} + t_{swr} + p_a t_a)/(1 - p_a) + t_{qm} + t_{sm} + t_{qr} + t_{sr} \tag{6-3}$$

$$t_w = (t_{qw} + t_{sww} + p_a t_a)/(1 - p_a) \tag{6-4}$$

$$t_{sw} = \frac{R t_{swr} + W t_{sww}}{R + W} \tag{6-5}$$

$$R = p_m r M + D_o/16 \tag{6-6}$$

$$W = w M + D_i/16 \tag{6-7}$$

$$t_{swr} = 0.1 \ \mu sec. \tag{6-8}$$

$$t_{sww} = \frac{w M \sum_{i=1}^{4} w_i (0.1 + 0.1i) + (0.5) D_i/16}{w M + D_i/16} \tag{6-9}$$

$$k_w = \frac{R(0.1)^2 + w M \sum_{i=1}^{4} w_i (0.1 + 0.1i)^2 + (0.5)^2 D_i/16}{2(R + W) t_{sw}^2} \tag{6-10}$$

$$L_w = P_{pf} P (R + W) t_{sw}/(1 - p_a) \tag{6-11}$$

$$t_{qw} = \frac{k_w L_w}{1 - L_w} t_{sw} \tag{6-12}$$

$$t_{sm} = \frac{0.8R + w M \sum_{i=1}^{4} w_i (0.4 + 0.1i) + (0.8) D_i/16}{R + W} \tag{6-13}$$

$$k_m = \frac{R(0.8)^2 + w M \sum_{i=1}^{4} w_i (0.4 + 0.1i)^2 + (0.8)^2 D_i/16}{2(R + W) t_{sm}^2} \tag{6-14}$$

$$L_m = P_{pf} P (R + W) t_{sm}/S \tag{6-15}$$

$$t_{qm} = \frac{k_m L_m}{1 - L_m} t_{sm} \tag{6-16}$$

$$t_{sr} = 0.4 \tag{6-17}$$

$$k_r = 0.5 \tag{6-18}$$

$$L_r = 0.4 R P_{pf} P \tag{6-19}$$

$$t_{qr} = \frac{k_r L_r}{1 - L_r} t_{sr} \tag{6-20}$$

$$p_a = L_m^9 \tag{6-21}$$

all instructions are reads, and 10 percent are writes. The cache-miss ratio for reads is 10 percent. Average write length is two words (the weighted average of the w_i's). No I/O is occurring except for the special I/O calculation shown below. Four memory units are provided unless this parameter is used as an input variable.

Figure 6-3 shows system performance as processors and memory are added. Note that with only 1 memory, the system is effectively limited to 6 processors (giving the power of 3.2 processors). With 8 memories, performance starts to flatten around 12 processors.

As a rough statement, one could say that each memory can support about four

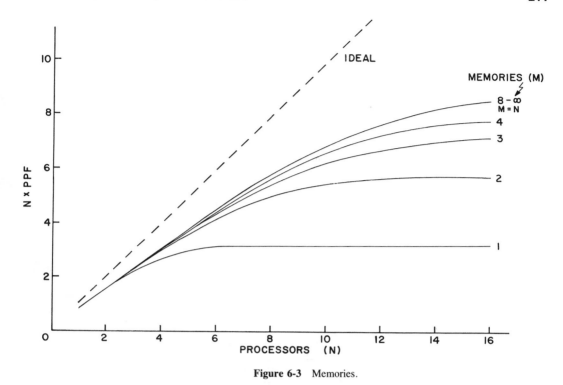

Figure 6-3 Memories.

processors. At this level, P_{pf} is running about 0.6. The addition of an extra processor gives less than 0.5 processor improvement in service and is hardly worth it. Beyond 8 memories and 12 processors, the system is bus-limited (note that an infinite number of memories gives about the same performance as 8). We have just answered the first two questions.

Figure 6-4 shows processor performance as a function of the cache-miss ratio, p_m. Above 5 percent, performance drops dramatically. Thus, compilers, cache size, and hardware architecture should be aimed at cache miss ratios smaller than 5 percent. Our third question is now answered.

Figure 6-5 shows processor performance as a function of the write ratio for a varying number of processors. This is a very sensitive factor—for even 6 processors, write ratios in excess of 10 percent impose significant load. Thus, the answer to our fourth question.

Figure 6-6 shows the effect on processor performance as I/O rates increase. I/O is assumed to be split evenly between input and output. Performance drops fairly uniformly with I/O rates. The system loses approximately a half processor of capacity with every 10 megabytes/sec. of I/O. So goes our fifth question.

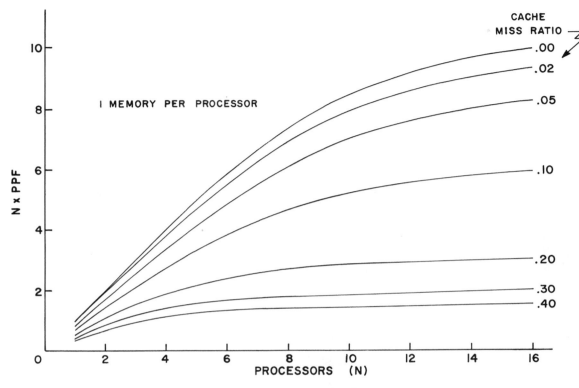

Figure 6-4   Effect of cache misses.

For any reasonable operation, memory modules should not be loaded beyond 80 percent load. In this case, the probability of queue overflow from equation 6-21 is $(.8)^9 = .013$ and is not a significant factor. Our sixth question answered.

Finally, Figure 6-7 shows the loading on the buses as a function of the number of processors. Our seventh question is answered. The loads on the R-Bus and W-Bus are reasonably balanced, at least for this mix of instructions.

It should be apparent that some pretty tough questions can be answered by a model that is fairly approximate. Notice that no attempt was made to give highly precise answers. The physical system being modeled is just too complex to ever allow this. However, the general statements that can be made are quite powerful, as can be seen.

How accurate are these results? We never know until we have a physical system to measure, and this particular one will probably never be built (after all, it was just a hypothetical system). However, my experience and that of many others in the field has

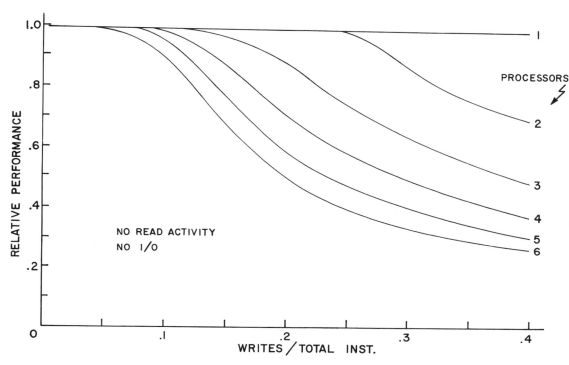

Figure 6-5   Effect of WRITES.

been quite encouraging in terms of modeling accuracy (see Martin [20] and the real-life case study presented in chapter 11). Once again, it is better to be able to make a reasonably useful statement about performance than to make no statement at all.

OPERATING SYSTEM

Unlike the physical environment that we have just discussed, the operating system environment does not lend itself to an example that can be solved in its entirety. Rather, the operating system provides certain environmental tools that the application processes use to perform their functions. Therefore, we will deal with an understanding of those tools in

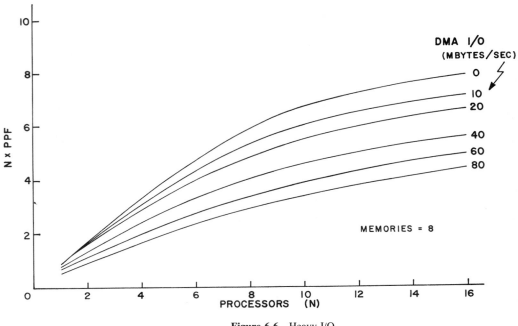

Figure 6-6 Heavy I/O.

this section and will apply them to different application architectures in the following chapters.

There are six operating system functions that typically have an impact and often need to be considered in a performance analysis:

- task dispatching
- interprocess messaging
- memory management
- I/O transfers
- O/S-initiated actions
- resource locking

Task Dispatching

When a process is ready to run, it must be placed in a queue (or Ready List) to await its turn to use the processor. The processor is the server, and the processes are the users in a classical queuing system. The number of processes running in a TP system is usually large enough to qualify as an infinite population; at least, that will be the case assumed herein.

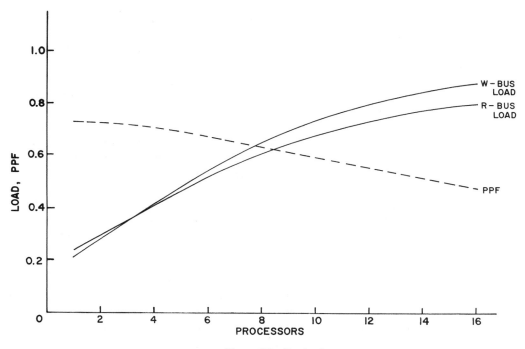

Figure 6-7 Bus loading.

Of course, if a specialized application has only a few processes, then the finite queuing system model can be used.*

Furthermore, the processing time required by the various processes varies so much that the assumption of randomly distributed processing times should be quite valid.

The time spent in the Ready List, or processor queue, is called the *dispatch time* and is referred to as t_d in these discussions. There is a second component of task dispatching time, and that is the operating system processing time required to switch processes, called *context switching*. This involves placing the current but expiring process on some list, removing the new current process from the Ready List, switching memory maps, modifying the processor environment registers, and so on, i.e., doing all the things required to put the old process to rest and to start up the new process. Depending upon the amount of hardware support available, context switching can take anywhere from a few microseconds to a few milliseconds; one to two milliseconds is typical. For purposes of performance analysis, this is a fixed time that can be bundled into the application process time and is handled throughout the text in this manner.

The time spent waiting for the processor—our dispatch time—is affected by two

*A more precise solution to this dispatching problem is given in Appendix 6, where it is shown that a reasonable approximation is obtained by simply ignoring the load imposed on the processor system by a given process when calculating its dispatch time.

other considerations. One is whether the application is running in a single computer or multicomputer environment (or in certain multiprocessor environments) in which it can only run in one processor. This is the classic single-server case, and queue delays are determined from the M/M/1 model. Alternatively, the application may run in a load-sharing multiprocessor environment in which, when it reaches the head of the Ready List, it is serviced by the next available processor out of c processors. This environment is a multiserver environment described by the M/M/c model.

The other consideration is that of priorities. Most TP systems provide many priority levels for processes (256 priorities is not atypical). If there is a processor load at higher priorities, it must be taken into account by the proper model, depending upon whether the operating system is preemptive or not (i.e., if it is preemptive, an executing process can be preempted by a higher priority process).

Within this framework, the calculation of dispatch time is straightforward. It is a "bean counting" exercise in which the dispatch rate and average running time for each process are set forth. A process will be dispatched typically on every I/O completion, whether it be the receipt of data to process, the completion of data that was sent, or the receipt of an interprocess message. Of course, I/O operations are often no-waited, or asynchronous (depending upon the manufacturer's terminology), which means that the process does not pause just because it has initiated an I/O operation but continues to do other work. In this case, actual dispatching may occur less frequently.

On the other hand, a process may be dispatched simply because a time-out that it has specified has occurred. In any event, determining the dispatch rate and the average execution time for a process requires a thorough understanding of the particular application and is a subject of the system description which should precede each performance analysis. Given that the performance analyst has done the necessary homework and has established the appropriate parameters for each process—its dispatch rate as a function of load, its average service time, and its priority—one can compute the following parameters. Let process i running at priority p have a dispatch rate of n_{ip} and an average service time of t_{sip}. Then the process dispatch rate at priority p, n_p, is

$$n_p = \sum_i n_{ip} \qquad (6\text{-}22)$$

The processor load imposed by all processes running at priority p is

$$L_p = \sum_i n_{ip} t_{sip} \qquad (6\text{-}23)$$

The average service time of processes running at priority p is the total processing time per second divided by the number of dispatches per second at priority p:

$$t_{sp} = \frac{\sum_i n_{ip} t_{sip}}{\sum_i n_{ip}} = L_p / n_p \qquad (6\text{-}24)$$

The processor load imposed by all processes running at a higher priority than priority

p is

$$L_h = \sum_{q>p} \sum_i n_{iq} t_{siq} \tag{6-25}$$

and the average dispatch rate for these processes, n_h, is

$$n_h = \sum_{q>p} \sum_i n_{iq} \tag{6-26}$$

Consequently, the average service time for those processes executing at a priority higher than p, t_{sh}, is

$$t_{sh} = L_h/n_h \tag{6-27}$$

The above has calculated average service time for processes at priority p and for processes with a priority greater than p. The average service time, t_s, for processes at priority p and higher is

$$t_s = \frac{L_p t_{sp} + L_h t_{sh}}{L_p + L_h} \tag{6-28}$$

This is true because of all process executions at priorities p or higher, $L_p/(L_p + L_h)$ will be processes executing at priority p with average service time of t_{sp}, and $L_h/(L_p + L_h)$ of these processes will be executing at a higher priority with an average service time of t_{sh}.

For all processes running at all priorities, the dispatch rate, n_t, load, L_t, and service time, t_t, are:

$$n_t = \sum_q \sum_i n_{iq} \tag{6-29}$$

$$L_t = \sum_q \sum_i n_{iq} t_{siq} \tag{6-30}$$

$$t_t = L_t/n_t \tag{6-31}$$

For a system in which only one processor can execute the above processes (single computer, multicomputer, or certain multiprocessor systems), the dispatch time in general is the queue time, T_q, taken from the M/M/1/∞/∞/PP model for a preemptive operating system and from the M/M/1/∞/∞/NP model for a nonpreemptive system. From chapter 4 and Appendix 2:

1. *Preemptive single server*

$$t_d = \frac{(L_p + L_h) t_s}{(1 - L_p - L_h)(1 - L_h)} \tag{6-32}$$

2. *Nonpreemptive single server*

$$t_d = \frac{L_t t_s}{(1 - L_p - L_h)(1 - L_h)} \tag{6-33}$$

For a multiprocessor load sharing system with c processors:

3. *Preemptive multiserver*

$$t_d = \frac{(L_p + L_h)^c p_o t_s}{c(c!)[1 - (L_p + L_h)/c]^2(1 - L_h/c)} \tag{6-34}$$

4. *Nonpreemptive multiserver*

$$t_d = \frac{L_t^c p_o t_s}{c(c!)(1 - L_t/c)[1 - (L_p + L_h)/c](1 - L_h/c)} \tag{6-35}$$

in the above equations,

$$p_o^{-1} = \sum_{n=0}^{c-1}(L')^n/n! + (L')^c/[1 - L'/c]c! \tag{6-36}$$

and

$L' = L_p + L_h$ for the preemptive case and L_t for the nonpreemptive case.

Note that L_p, L_h, and L_t in these equations comprise the total system load rather than the average server load, as used in Appendix 2 and chapter 4.

Of course, in all cases of a preemptive system, the actual process service time which is added to the dispatch time to obtain full delay time must be divided by $(I - L_h)$ to account for preemptive processing by the higher priority processes (see Appendix 2 and chapter 4).

If the system is a single priority system, L_h in the above equations becomes zero, with the corresponding simplifications.

Interprocess Messaging

Contemporary TP applications are organized as autonomous processes, each with their own scope of responsibility and all passing data to each other via messages. In some cases, these interprocess messages can represent a significant portion of the load on a TP system.

There are several ways in which the messaging facility can be implemented. All are suitable for distributed systems, but one—the mailbox—is suitable only for single computer or multiprocessor systems. These techniques are described briefly below. However, the only result of practical interest to the performance analyst is the bottom-line time required to pass a message from one process to another.

Global message network.   With this implementation, any process can send a message to any other process in the system without any specific effort on the part of one process to establish a path to the other process.

This technique is generally applied to multicomputer systems. All the sending process needs to know is the name of the receiving process.

The operating system knows the name of all processes in the system and their whereabouts. It assumes the responsibility for the message, usually moving it into a system-allocated buffer. It then routes it over the bus (or network, if necessary) to the computer in which the receiving process is running and queues it to the message queue for that process.

Even if the receiving process is running in the same computer as the sending process, this full procedure is often followed, except that the bus transfer is null, i.e., shortcuts are not taken.

This type of messaging facility is used by Tandem.

Directed message paths.   In other implementations, there are no general messaging facilities provided by the operating system. Rather, it is the responsibility of one process to establish a message path to another process via operating system facilities. Once established, the operating system knows of this path, and message transfer is similar to that used for global messaging.

This philosophy is found in the UNIX pipe structure and is used by Syntrex (Eatontown, New Jersey) in its distributed word-processing product.

File system.   The TP file system can also be used to pass messages between processes. A message file can be opened by two processes and can be used by one process to write messages to the other. The receiving process is alerted to the receipt of a message via an event flag and can read that message from its file.

On the surface, this can sound very time-consuming—writing to and reading from disk. However, disk transfers are cached in memory (in a cache similar to the memory cache described in the previous section). If messages are read shortly after they are written, they will still be in memory; the message time is equivalent to the above techniques. If they are not read for awhile, they are flushed to disk to free up valuable memory space.

Since the file system allows transparent access to all files across the system, this messaging concept supports distributed systems. This technique is used by Stratus in its multicomputer system.

Mailboxes.   Mailboxes are like message files except that they reside in common memory. They are adaptable only to single-computer or multiprocessor systems, since all processes must have direct access to the mailbox memory. Since there need be no physical movement of the message as with the other techniques, message transfer with mailboxes can be much faster.

Message transfer in multicomputer systems tends to be quite time-consuming because of multiple physical transfers of the message from application space to system space to the bus to a different system space and back to application space. Typical transfer times are measured as a few milliseconds to tens of milliseconds.

Direct memory transfer of messages in multiprocessor systems can be significantly faster, especially when mailboxes are used. Typical transfer times are measured in tenths of milliseconds.

In any event, the time required to pass messages between processes can usually be bundled in with the process service time for the sending and receiving processes.

Memory Management

Most TP systems today provide a virtual memory facility in which there is little relation to logical memory and physical memory. In principle, many very large programs can execute in a physical memory space much smaller than their total size. This is accomplished by page swapping, as discussed in chapter 2. When a process requires a code or data page that is not physically in memory, the operating system declares a page fault, suspends that program, and schedules the required page to be read into physical memory, overwriting a current page according to some aging algorithm. When the page has been swapped in, the suspended program is allowed to continue.

Page fault loads are very difficult to predict and analyze; but for the performance analyst, there is an easy out. Page faulting is so disastrous to system performance that we typically assume it does not exist. If it becomes significant, the cure is to add more memory (if possible).

Though this sounds like a cop-out, it is not without merit. If a system does not have enough memory, it will begin to *thrash* because of page faulting. This sort of thrashing will rapidly bring a TP system to its knees.

Contemporary wisdom and experience indicate that page faulting should not exceed one to two faults per second.

Overlay management is another technique for memory management and is controlled by the application program. It is less flexible than page management but avoids the thrashing problem (assuming that overlaid programs are not also running in a paged virtual memory environment). An application process is considered to have a root segment that is always in memory and one or more overlay areas. It is free to load parts of its program into its overlay area when it deems fit. When the application process makes such a request, it is suspended until the overlay arrives and is then rescheduled. The impact of overlay calls is simply the added overhead of the disk activity and the additional process dispatching, both of which can be accounted for using the normal techniques presented herein.

I/O Transfers

Once an I/O block transfer (as distinguished from a programmed I/O transfer) has been initiated, it continues independently of the application process. Processor cycles are used to transfer data directly to or from memory, following which the operating system responds to a transfer completion interrupt. At this time, it will typically schedule the initiating process so that this process can do whatever it needs with the data transfer completion.

Let

D_{io} = average I/O transfer rate in both directions (bytes/sec.).

B_{io} = average block transfer rate in both directions (blocks/sec.).

t_{dio} = processor time to transfer a byte (often just a portion of a processor cycle as data may be transferred in multibyte words) (sec.).

t_{bio} = operating system time required to process a data transfer completion (one per block) (sec.).

Then the processor load imposed by I/O at the data transfer and interrupt level, L_{io}, is

$$L_{io} = D_{io}t_{dio} + B_{io}t_{bio} \tag{6-37}$$

The application of this overhead value to system performance will now be discussed, along with other operating system functions that have a similar effect.

O/S Initiated Actions

Besides the functions just described, there are other operating system functions that impose an overhead on the system. These are primarily tasks that the operating system itself initiates, such as

- timer list management,
- periodic self-diagnostics,
- monitoring of the health of other processors or computers in the system.

Let

L_{os} = operating system load imposed on the system by O/S initiated functions.

L_{io} = I/O load on the system (as defined above).

L_o = total operating system overhead, including I/O transfers and self-initiated functions.

Then

$$L_o = L_{os} + L_{io} \tag{6-38}$$

Since L_o of the processor capacity is being consumed by nonapplication-process oriented activity, $(1-L_o)$ of the processor is available for application use. This has the effect of increasing all application service times by $1/(1-L_o)$:

$$\text{Apparent Service} = \frac{\text{Actual Service Time}}{(1 - L_o)} \tag{6-39}$$

That is, it appears that the application process is running on a machine that has only $(1-L_o)$ of its rated speed or capacity. If there are other higher priority processes running which also rob the application process of processing capacity, then L_o is simply another component of that higher priority processing load. (L_h would include L_o in equations 6-32 through 6-36, for example.)

Note that L_o is not meant to include data-base management overhead. Though the data-base manager is not an application process per se, from a performance viewpoint it is treated as such a process. This topic is discussed in the next chapter.

Locks

In a multiprocessor system, there will be contention for various operating system resources by the multiple processors in the system. For instance, more than one processor may try to schedule a new process, which means that each such processor will attempt to modify the ready list. Multiple processors may try to modify a block in disk cache memory as described in the next chapter.

To prevent such a resource (ready list, timer list, disk cache, etc.) from becoming contaminated, only one processor at a time must be allowed to use it. Therefore, each common resource is protected by a so-called *lock*. If a processor wants to use one of these resources, it must first test to see if this resource is being used. If not, the processor must lock the resource until it has finished with it so that another processor cannot use that resource during this time. Actually, this action of testing and locking must be an integrated action so that no other processor can get access to the lock for testing between the test and lock actions.

If a processor finds a lock set, it must pause and wait for that lock (i.e., enter a queue of processors waiting for that lock) before it can proceed. This queuing time for locks must be added to the process service time if it is deemed to be significant. And indeed, significant it can be. There are examples of contemporary systems in which resource locking is the predominant operating system bottleneck.

In some systems, if the lock delay is too long, the process will be scheduled for a later time. Though this frees up the processor for other work, it has a serious impact on the delayed process because the process must now await another dispatch time. Lock delay can also seriously affect processor load because of the extra process-context switching time that is incurred.

Thrashing

There are several possibilities for thrashing in systems of this sort. One common cause is page-faulting. Another cause in multiprocessor systems is long queues for locked resources, which can cause additional context switches. These effects can cause the processing requirements for a process to suddenly increase, with a significant increase in response time.

There are other, more subtle increases in processing requirements for TP systems. Memory and bus contention can cause process service times in multiprocessor systems to increase as load increases. Interprocess message queue lengths will increase as load increases, causing dumping to disk in some systems or rejection of messages in other systems. Either case causes an increase in process service time.

All of these factors cause a process's effective service time to increase as load increases. As service time increases, the capacity of the system decreases. In extreme cases (unfortunately not uncommon in multiprocessor systems), the system capacity can decrease beyond its current capacity, causing a "U-turn" in system performance. That is, the system can suddenly start thrashing and have a capacity *less than* the capacity at which it started thrashing. Response times can dramatically increase by an order of magnitude or more at this point.

Figure 6-8 illustrates this phenomenon. This figure is a little different from the response time curves with which we have previously dealt, as it shows response time as a function of throughput (i.e., transactions per second processed by the system) rather than load. Normally, the throughput of the system is the offered transaction rate, R, and is related to the load, L, by $L=RT$. However, in a thrashing system the system is 100% loaded (it is continually busy) and may not be able to keep up with the arriving transaction stream. For that reason, we observe response time as a function of the throughput of the system rather than its load.

With reference to Figure 6-8, as long as the system can keep up with the arriving

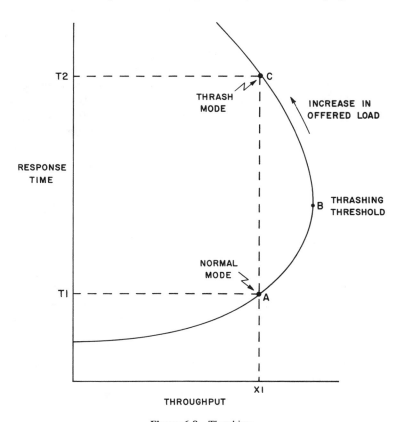

Figure 6-8   Thrashing.

transactions, it behaves properly. For example, while operating at point A, it can provide a throughput of $X1$ transactions per second with an average response time of $T1$.

However, as the incoming transaction rate approaches the "thrashing threshold," B, various system resources become seriously overloaded. Memory use is stressed to the point of creating excessive page faults; lock contentions cause processes to time out and be rescheduled; queues grow too long and are dumped from memory to disk. In short, service time per transaction dramatically increases. As a consequence, the capacity of the system is decreased (it is, in effect, the inverse of the service time), the response time is increased (it is proportional to the service time), and the system is operating at point C.

A further increase in the offered load (transaction arrival rate) to the system will only aggravate the situation, causing more thrashing, decreased capacity, and increased response time. This leads to the "U-turn" effect of Figure 6-8.

What is the practical impact of such a system characteristic? Consider a user interacting with the system while the system is operating at point A. A sudden, brief burst of activity will drive the system into thrashing mode; the user will suddenly find that the system is now operating at point C. Response time has suddenly increased from $T1$ to $T2$. In one typical system displaying this characteristic, the author measured response times which suddenly increased from 1 second to 30 seconds! So far as the user is concerned, the system has just died.

This condition will persist until the offered load decreases long enough for thrashing to cease and for the system to get its house back in order.

This is the second thrashing example that we have discussed. The first example related to local area networks using contention protocols (see Figure 5-25). As in that case, the main lesson is that systems with the potential for such severe thrashing should be operated well below the thrashing threshold. Normal operating loads should allow adequate margin for anticipated brief peak loads to ensure that these loads will not cause thrash mode operation.

SUMMARY

In this chapter we have looked at the physical hardware and its effect upon performance. The hardware was viewed as a complete analyzable system, and our performance analysis tools were used to make some wide-ranging statements about a typical system.

With respect to today's operating systems, we also reviewed many characteristics that may have a serious impact on performance. It is often true in contemporary systems that interprocess messages in multicomputer systems are the most predominant of all operating system functions. Task dispatching is also often important, especially for those cases in which processors are running heavily loaded. I/O and other O/S activity are usually less important (with the exception of data-base management activities, which are discussed in a later chapter). Memory management (page faulting) is either not a problem or is an insurmountable problem. The rapidity at which a system breaks when page faulting becomes significant is so awesome as to justify remaining well away from page faulting.

In chapter 8, we will look at system performance from the viewpoint of the application processes. This is where we will use some of the operating system concepts developed in this chapter.

7

Data-Base Environment

Most transaction processing systems obtain the information required to formulate a response from a base of data that is so large that it must be maintained on large, bulk-storage devices, typically disk units in today's technology. The data is so massive that it is very important to have efficient access paths to locate a particular data item with the minimal amount of effort. This is especially true when data is stored on disk, for as we shall see, each disk access requires a significant amount of time.

It appears that the future is rapidly bringing high-speed gigabyte RAM (Random Access Memory) technology into the realm of reality (a giga is a billion!). When this happens, many of today's concerns over rapid access will be replaced with equal concern over the logical ease of access and maintainability of the data base—a subject already addressed by today's relational data bases. Though data-base organization is not a topic for this book, we will address it briefly later in this chapter.

Of course, coming in parallel with gigabyte RAM is the development of kilo-gigabyte disks so that performance of these systems will probably always be an issue—just on a larger scale than today.

We consider in this chapter the performance of data bases stored on one or more disk units. Data is typically managed by a data-base manager that provides a "logical view" of the data base. "Logical view" means that the data is seen in the way the user wants to see it, no matter how the data is actually physically organized. For instance, one might want a list of all employee names by department. The data-base manager will provide a view of the data base as if it contains employees organized by department, even though the actual data in the data base might be organized in multiple lists, including a master employee list containing employee name, number, address, salary, etc., and a second list giving employee numbers for each department.

Data-base managers are large and complex and are usually implemented as a set of cooperating processes. As such, their analyses will follow the techniques described in the next chapter, which covers application processes. However, the performance of the data-base manager is very much a function of the system's ability to efficiently access and manipulate the various files (or tables) that constitute the data base. This is the role of the file system and is the subject of this chapter.

THE FILE SYSTEM

The file system in a contemporary TP system, viewed from a performance standpoint, comprises a hierarchy of components, as shown in Figure 7-1.

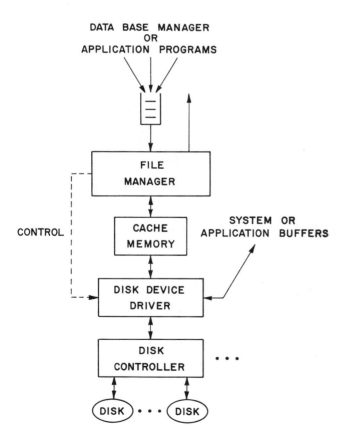

Figure 7-1 File system hierarchy.

Disk Drives

At the bottom of the hierarchy are the *disk drives* themselves. In most systems today, the disk drives use moving read/write heads that must first be positioned to the appropriate track or cylinder if multiple disk platters with typically one head per platter are used. A cylinder comprises all of the tracks on all platters at a particular radial of the disk unit. Once positioned, the drive must wait for the desired information to rotate under the head before reading or writing can be done.

Thus, to access data on a disk drive, two separate but sequential mechanical motions are required:

- *Seeking,* or the movement of the read/write heads to the appropriate cylinder.
- *Rotation,* or *latency,* which is the rotation of the cylinder to the desired position under the now-positioned heads.

This sequence of actions is necessary to position the disk heads and read data. Writing data is a bit more complex. It must first be understood that data is organized into sectors on the cylinder (a sector is typically 256 to 4096 bytes). Data can be read or written only in multiples of sectors. A sector typically contains many records. Thus, to write a record, the appropriate sector must be read according to the above sequence, the record must be inserted, and the sector must be rewritten. Since the heads are already positioned, this simply requires an additional disk rotation time relative to a read operation. Typical seek times are 20 to 40 msec.; latency time is, on the average, a half revolution time, or 8.3 msec., for a disk rotating at 3600 rpm (today's norm).

Seek plus latency time will be called *access time*. A good average access time to be used in the following discussions and examples is 35 msec. to read a record and 52 msec. to write a record (a rotational time of 17 msec. is added for a write).

Disk Controller

The *disk controller* is a hardware device controller that directly controls one or more disk drives. Typical controllers can control up to eight drives. A controller executes three basic classes of commands:

1. *Seek,* meaning to seek a specified cylinder on a specified drive.
2. *Read,* meaning to read a given sector or sectors on the currently positioned cylinder on the specified drive.
3. *Write,* meaning to write a given sector or sectors on the currently positioned cylinder on the specified drive.

Of course, there are other commands for status and diagnostic purposes, but these are the ones important for performance issues.

Most controllers can overlap seeks—that is, they can have multiple seeks outstanding so that several disk drives can be positioning themselves simultaneously to their next desired cylinders. The good news is that since seek time is the predominant factor in access time, this technique can significantly reduce access time and increase disk performance. The bad news is that it takes so much intelligence on the part of the software to be able to look ahead and predict cylinder usage (except in certain unique applications) that this feature is seldom supported by software. More about this later.

Some disk controllers provide buffering for the data to be read from, or written to, disk. That is, for a write operation the software will first transfer the data to be written to the disk controller buffer. The controller will then write the data to disk at its leisure. Likewise, for a read the data will be read from the disk into the controller's buffer, where it will be available to be read by the processor at its leisure.

Controller buffering is a mixed blessing. Without buffering, it becomes a real hardware performance problem to ensure that sufficient I/O capacity and processor memory time exist to guarantee the synchronous transfer of data between the disk and processor without data loss (once started, this data stream cannot be interrupted). On the other hand, with controller buffering, a disk transfer cannot exceed the buffer length (typically, anywhere from 256 to 4,096 bytes). Without controller buffering, data transfers can be as long as desired (at least, they can be as long as the processor's I/O channel will allow).

For our normal performance efforts at the application level, the problem of controller buffering usually is not considered. Disk transfer sizes are given, and we assume that they occur without data loss.

Disk Device Driver

The *disk device driver* is the lowest level of software associated with the file system. It accepts higher level commands from the file manager and executes these as a series of primitive commands submitted to the disk controller. It monitors status signals returned by the controller to determine success or failure of operations, takes such steps as it can to retry failed operations, and takes whatever other steps are necessary for guaranteeing the integrity of disk operations (such as replacing bad sectors with spare sectors from an allocated pool).

The most common commands handled by the device driver are read/write commands. The driver will select the appropriate disk drive, will issue an appropriate seek command, will ensure that the heads have positioned properly, and then will issue a data transfer command.

The memory location of data to be written to disk or of the destination of data to be read from disk is passed to the device driver along with the command from the file manager. Data may be transferred between the disk and buffers provided by an application program (or provided by the operating system on an application program's behalf), or data may be transferred into and out of disk cache memory.

The device driver, once initiated by a command from the file manager, operates substantially at the interrupt level. When it has successfully completed the transfer or has given up, it will schedule the file manager. The device driver execution time is typically included in the load L_{io}, discussed under O/S-initiated functions in the previous chapter.

Cache Memory

Most systems today provide a disk *cache memory* capability that functions much like the memory cache described in chapter 6. Basically, the intent is to keep the most recently used disk data in memory in the hopes that it will be reaccessed while in cache. Because of the slow speed of disk relative to the system's main memory, disk cache is usually allocated from main memory space (this part of memory is usually not a candidate for page swapping). Because memory sizes in today's TP systems can be quite large (many megabytes), disk cache is often not limited in size but rather is established by the application designers at system generation time.

The management of disk cache is similar in many respects to memory cache. Several factors are taken into consideration, such as

- *Transfers* likely to make ineffective use of cache are often allowed to bypass cache. Sequential file transfers by sector are a good example of this. If a file is read sequentially or written sequentially by sector, previous sectors will never be reaccessed and so do not need to be cached. However, if records within a sector are being accessed, sequential sectors are cached so that records blocked in that sector may take advantage of cache. In some systems, sequential sectors in cache are overwritten by the next sector, as the old sector will not be needed again.

- *The various records* in cache are aged and are also flagged if they have been modified (a dirty record). When a new record is to be read in, an appropriate area in cache must be overwritten. The caching algorithm will generally elect to overwrite the oldest area, i.e., an area that has not been used for the longest time. If there is a choice, a clean area will be overwritten as opposed to a dirty area, since a dirty area must be written to disk first before it can be overwritten (unless cache write-through is used as discussed next).

- In many TP systems, *modified data* will reside in disk cache memory until it is forced to disk by being overwritten with new data. However, in the event of a processor failure, that data may be lost, and the data base will have been corrupted. In some fault-tolerant systems, cache write-through is used. In this case, all writes to disk cause an update to cache and a physical write to disk (just like our earlier memory cache example) before the write is declared complete. In this way, all completed writes reside on disk in the event of a processor failure.

- *The size of cache memory required* is a direct function of the transaction rate to be supported by the system. Consider a transaction which reads a record and which may have to update that record at the operator's discretion 30 seconds later. If the system is handling 1 transaction per minute, then a cache size of 1 record is likely to give good performance. However, if the system transaction rate is 10 per second, then a minimum cache size of 300 records will be needed to guarantee any reasonable cache hit ratio, i.e., 10 records per second (300 records total) will have been read into cache during the 30 seconds it will have taken the operator to update the original record.

Disk cache memory is just another flavor of the concept behind virtual memory (page faulting) and main memory caching. As with these other mechanisms, disk cache hit ratios are very difficult to predict. As mentioned above, they are most effective when files are being accessed randomly (a common characteristic of TP systems) and are least effective when files are accessed sequentially (as with batch systems). In TP systems, disk cache hit ratios of 20 percent to 60 percent are common. This parameter is typically specified as an input to the model or is treated as a computational variant.

File Manager

The *file manager* usually runs as a high priority process in the TP system. In the simplest case, there is typically one file manager associated with each disk controller, although this is not a firm rule. A file manager may control several disk controllers, or as an alternative, there may be several file managers associated with a single disk controller. Multiple file managers are considered later.

Application processes (including a data-base manager, if any) submit requests to the file manager for disk operations, which are stacked up in the file manager input queue. These can be quite complex operations, such as

- *Open*. Open access to a file on behalf of the requesting process. Typically, a file control block (FCB) is allocated and assigned to the process-file pair. This instantiation of a file open is often given a file number so that later file requests by this process need only give a file number rather than a file name. The FCB keeps such data as current record position, end-of-file marker, and file permissions. A file open may be requested for various permissions, such as read only, modify privileges, or shared or exclusive access.
- *Close*. Close the access to the file by this process.
- *Position*. Position the record pointer to a particular record or to the end of the file.
- *Read*. Read a record.
- *Lock*. Lock the record being read (or file or record field, depending upon the file management system) so that no other process can lock this record or update it. Locking is used prior to an update to make sure that processes do not step on each other when trying to simultaneously update the same record.
- *Write*. Write a new record or a modified record.
- *Unlock*. Unlock the record being written.

This is only a partial list of file management duties. We have yet to talk about file structures, which would expand this list to include operations such as searching for blank slots in random files, keyed reads and writes, etc. The point is that the file manager is a highly intelligent process, and this intelligence costs time. Typical file manager execution times can run 10–50 msec. for 32-bit 1-MIP machines. Only for special applications today is processing time less than 10 msec. per file access.

When compared with the 30–50 msec. disk access time, it can be seen that the file manager time makes a bad situation even worse. Note that file manager time is substantially additive to disk time. When a request is selected for processing, the file manager must first do all the validation and processing required to submit one or more commands to the disk device driver. It then checks to see if the data item is in cache. If not, the file manager submits the first of a potential series of commands to the disk driver and then goes dormant until the disk driver has completed the operation and has returned the result (data or status). The file manager then must verify the result and, if necessary, submit the next command to the driver. This process continues until the request from the application process has been completely satisfied.

Some operations, such as file opens and keyed accesses, can require several disk operations to complete. In all of these operations, the disk is active while the file manager is dormant and vice versa. Thus, the actual time required to complete a disk operation is the sum of the physical disk times and the file manager processing times.

File System Performance

Let

t_{da} = disk access time (seek plus latency) (sec.).

t_{dr} = disk rotational time (twice latency) (sec.).

n_{dir} = number of disk read operations required for file operation i (open, close, read, write, etc.).

n_{diw} = number of disk write operations required for file operation i.

t_{fmi} = file manager time for operation i (sec.).

f_i = proportion of t_{fmi} required if data is in cache.

p_d = average disk cache miss ratio, i.e., the probability of requiring a physical disk access.

t_{fi} = file system service time for operation i (sec.).

Note that the disk time required to read a record is t_{da} and to write a record is t_{da} + t_{dr}. There are two cases to consider in terms of file system service time: caching of writes and cache write-through. If writes are cached, the sector to be updated is searched for in cache. If found, the sector is updated and left in cache. It eventually will be flushed to disk when it hasn't been used for awhile but may have had several updates made to it by then. The cache miss ratio, p_d, must take this into account.

If writes are not cached (cache write-through), each write modifies the sector to be updated if it is in cache, but that sector is unconditionally written to disk. The write will take advantage of cache to read the sector but will always physically write it back to disk (on the next disk spin if it had been physically read from disk). Thus, if the sector is found in cache, a disk time of t_{da} is required to write it.out. If it is not found in cache, a disk time of $t_{da} + t_{dr}$ is required to read it and then to write it out. A time, t_{da}, is required every time; a time, t_{dr}, is required p_d of the time.

For cached writes, file system service time for operation i is

$$t_{fi} = a_i t_{fmi} + p_d \left[n_{dir} t_{da} + n_{diw}(t_{da} + t_{dr}) \right] \tag{7-1}$$

For cache write-through,

$$t_{fi} = a_i t_{fmi} + p_d \left(n_{dir} t_{da} + n_{diw} t_{dr} \right) + n_{diw} t_{da} \tag{7-2}$$

The parameter a_i takes into account the effect of finding the desired data in cache. If $(1 - p_d)$ of the time data is in cache, and if the file manager time then required is $f_i t_{fmi}$, then the average file manager time for operation i is

$$(1 - p_d) f_i t_{fmi} + p_d t_{fmi}$$

or

$$(p_d + f_i - p_d f_i) t_{fmi}$$

Thus,

$$a_i = (p_d + f_i - p_d f_i) \tag{7-3}$$

Let

$$p_i = \text{probability of file operation } i.$$

$$t_f = \text{average file service time (msec.).}$$

Then the average file system service time is

$$t_f = \sum_i p_i t_{fi} \tag{7-4}$$

If

$$R_f = \text{rate of file requests (per second).}$$

$$L_f = \text{load on file system.}$$

$$n_f = \text{number of file requests per transaction.}$$

$$R_t = \text{transaction rate (per second).}$$

then the file system load is

$$L_f = R_f t_f = R_t n_f t_f \tag{7-5}$$

Assuming that file service time, t_f, is random and that the number of processes requesting file service functions is large, the file service delay time, t_{df}, including queue delays and servicing, is

$$t_{df} = \frac{t_f}{1 - L_f} \qquad (7\text{-}6)$$

Equations 7-1 and 7-2 above ignore the actual transfer time of the data between disk and memory. This is a small portion of a single rotation and is usually small enough so that it can be ignored. For instance, if there are 32 sectors per track, then the transfer of one sector will require $\frac{1}{32}$ of a rotation time. If rotation time is 16 msec., this amounts to 0.5 msec., which is small compared to average access times in the order of 30 to 50 msec.

FILE ORGANIZATION

Formal data-base structures are generally characterized as hierarchical, network, or relational. Though data-base structures are not the topic of this book, suffice it to say that each of these organizations is a further attempt at achieving ultimate flexibility and maintainability of the data base.

And as this goal is achieved, it exacts its toll: performance. Relational data bases are recognized today as being the most flexible and maintainable data bases—and often the worst performance hogs (though impressive strides in this area are being made). Many systems are first built as pure "third normal form" relational data bases and are then modified to compromise this structure in order to achieve adequate performance. (For an excellent discourse on data-base structures, see Date [5], a classic in this field.)

One characteristic that all of these data-base structures have in common is the need for keyed files. Thus, almost all of today's file systems support keyed files. They also support sequential files for batch processing, random files for efficiency, and unstructured files as the ultimate programmer's out. These file structures form the basis of TP system performance to a large extent and are described next.

Unstructured Files

An *unstructured file* is viewed simply as an array of bytes (see Figure 7-2a). The application process can read or write any number of bytes (up to a limit) starting at a particular byte position. Note that in general, a transfer operation will begin within one sector on disk and end within another sector.

Let

b_s = number of bytes in a disk sector.

b_u = number of bytes being transferred to or from an unstructured file.

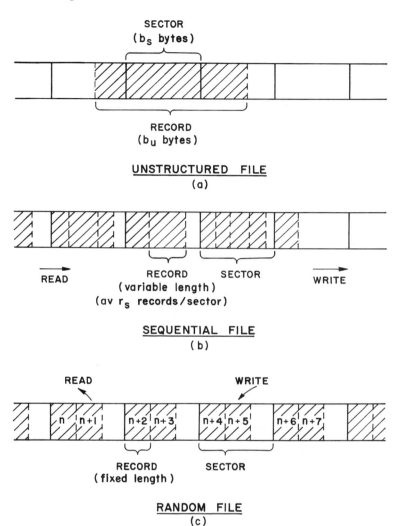

Figure 7-2 File structures.

If the transfer size is no greater than a sector, the probability of it falling directly within a sector is $(b_s - b_u + 1)/b_s$; otherwise, two sectors must be accessed, with probability $1 - (b_s - b_u + 1)/b_s = (b_u - 1)/b_s$. Thus, the average number of sectors to be accessed is

$$1\,\frac{(b_s - b_u + 1)}{b_s} + 2\,\frac{(b_u - 1)}{b_s} = \frac{b_s + b_u - 1}{b_s}, \; b_u \le b_s$$

If the transfer size, b_u, is greater than a sector length, b_s, then it will be less than an integral number of sectors by

$$\left(\left\lceil \frac{b_u}{b_s} \right\rceil b_s - b_u \right) \text{ bytes}$$

where $x\rceil$ is the ceiling operator, implying that x is rounded up to the next integer unless it already is an integer. This length plus 1, divided by the sector size, is the probability that the transfer will be found in $(b_u/b_s)\rceil$ sectors; otherwise, it will require one more sector.

Thus, for $b_u > b_s$, the average number of sectors required is

$$\left\lceil \frac{b_u}{b_s} \right\rceil + \left(1 - \frac{\left\lceil \frac{b_u}{b_s} \right\rceil b_s - b_u + 1}{b_s}\right), \quad b_u > b_s$$

The first term is the minimum number of sectors required; the second term is the probability of requiring one more sector. This reduces to

$$\frac{b_s + b_u - 1}{b_s}$$

which is the same result as that obtained for a transfer size less than a sector size.

Thus, to transfer a record to or from an unstructured file, the average number of sectors that must be accessed, n_{du}, is

$$n_{du} = \frac{b_s + b_u - 1}{b_s}. \tag{7-7}$$

A typical disk driver will treat an unstructured read or write of multiple sectors as a primitive operation and will transfer these sectors without interruption. This often means that only one seek is made to the proper cylinder, and then one sector is transferred on each spin of the disk (there not being enough time between sectors to issue a new set of disk access commands). In this case, equations 7-1 and 7-2 can be rewritten for the special case of unstructured files as follows:

For unstructured reads:

$$t_{fi} = a_i t_{fmi} + p_d t_{ua} \tag{7-8}$$

where t_{ua} is a single access time, t_{da}, to transfer the first sector plus $(n_{du} - 1)$ rotation times, each requiring a time of t_{dr} to transfer the remaining sectors:

$$t_{ua} = t_{da} + (n_{du} - 1)t_{dr} \tag{7-9}$$

For unstructured cached writes:

$$t_{fi} = a_i t_{fmi} + p_d(t_{ua} + n_{du}t_{dr}) \tag{7-10}$$

For unstructured uncached writes:

$$t_{fi} = a_i t_{fmi} + t_{ua} + p_d n_{du} t_{dr} \tag{7-11}$$

(These equations ignore the sector read time, which will add the equivalent of a partial disk rotational time equal to that portion of a track occupied by the n_{du} sectors.)

More sophisticated disk systems may reduce these times. For instance, all sectors may be transferred on a single spin. This may be accomplished by one of many techniques:

- A multisector transfer capability in the disk controller.
- A sufficiently fast disk driver that can issue a new disk transfer command between sectors.
- Interleaved sectors, in which logically contiguous sectors are, in fact, separated by one or more physical sectors on disk.

An intelligent disk driver may also recognize that a sector that is to be totally rewritten does not have to be read. This is especially valuable if record blocking is to be done at the application level, with disk transfer only of entire sectors.

Equations 7-7 through 7-11 can be easily modified to fit these and other examples of unstructured file manipulation.

Sequential Files

As shown in Figure 7-2b, a *sequential file* comprises a series of records that are written sequentially to the end of the file and are read sequentially. Records may vary in length but generally do not span sector boundaries (we will assume that here).

A key performance advantage of sequential files is that they make maximum use of cache. As records are written, they can be buffered in cache (or in an application-provided buffer) until a sector's worth has been accumulated, at which point the sector is written to disk. As records are being read, a physical disk read is only required once per sector into cache or into an application-provided buffer. From there, records are read at memory speeds until the sector is exhausted.

If sequential reads or writes are fairly rapid, disk cache can be counted on to do the buffering, as the sector will have a high enough activity to prevent its being flushed from cache. If file activity is going to be slow, then the use of an application program buffer guarantees memory-based operation within a sector.

One potential problem with caching sequential reads and writes is that the potentially high transfer rate can rapidly fill cache memory and can cause other data to be flushed needlessly—needlessly because caching any more than one sector is meaningless for a sequential file, since that sector will not be reused. Some systems will allow a cache block that had been used for a sequential transfer to be immediately reused; others will allow cache to be bypassed for sequential transfers. Either technique will prevent the disk cache from being needlessly flushed by a high-speed sequential file transfer.

From a performance standpoint, if there are r_s records per sector, then physical disk activity is required for only $1/r_s$ of the read or write requests. With respect to equations 7-1 and 7-2,

For sequential file reads:

$$n_{dir} = 1/r_s, \; n_{diw} = 0 \qquad\qquad (7\text{-}12)$$

For sequential file writes:

$$n_{diw} = 1/r_s, \; n_{dir} = 0 \qquad\qquad (7\text{-}13)$$

where r_s is the average number of records per sector.

Random Files

Random (or direct access) files can be written to or read from simply by specifying the record number (Figure 7-2c). Records in random files are typically fixed-length; if they vary in length, they are stored in fixed-length record slots. Records do not typically cross sector boundaries.

The file system can easily calculate the sector of the file that a record is in by knowing the number of records per sector and the sector number. For instance, if the file contains 10 records per sector, and if record 73 is desired, then it is to be found in sector 7 (assuming that the first sector is numbered 0).

Random files are very efficient for accessing data randomly. Any record in the file may be read or written with just one access. However, caching will be somewhat ineffective, since it is unlikely (in a large file, at least) that the same sector will be required soon after a previous access, except for the case of a read with intent to possibly update the record via a later operation.

For random files,

$$n_{dir} = 1, \; n_{diw} = 0 \text{ for reads} \qquad\qquad (7\text{-}14)$$

$$n_{diw} = 1, \; n_{dir} = 0 \text{ for writes} \qquad\qquad (7\text{-}15)$$

Keyed Files

We have described above the three basic file structures in predominant use today. Unstructured files are accessed by specifying a byte position within the file and a string size (b_u) to transfer. Sequential files are transferred record by record in sequence; the record size is often carried with the record to facilitate variable length records. Random (or direct) files are accessed by record number.

There are other file types in use, but for performance purposes they can usually be classified as one of these three. Though these files each have their own rudimentary file access mechanism, more complex access methods are needed for general on-line transaction processing applications.

For example, we may want to find a customer master record in the customer master file for customer HOW379A or to update an inventory record for item SCRI37. There is no way provided by these file structures to find such a record without a brute force search (reading the file sequentially or using random access to do a binary search on an ordered file).

This problem is solved via key files. A *key file* is typically a separate file that contains the values on which we would like to access another file, with pointers to the data records in that file. Each record in a key file contains the value of a key (such as customer I.D. or product code) and an address of the corresponding record in the data file. The key file is maintained in key order, and provision is made for a rapid search of the key file. For files of typical sizes, any record may be found based on its key in two to four accesses, as we will see in the following discussion. Any of the above file types can be supported with key files.

If a key is unique, there will be only one record in the key file for each key value. Customer I.D. and product code are examples of unique keys. If a key is not unique, there will be one record in the key file for every data record containing that key. A nonunique key might be customer zipcode or product availability status.

If a request is made to access a record based on a nonunique key, the data record addressed by the first key record will be returned. Subsequent data records with this same key value will then be returned on request by simply reading the key file sequentially.

Of course, there can be any number of key files supporting a particular data file. There will be one key file for every key whose value we would like to use to quickly access a data file.

From a performance viewpoint, key files are a mixed blessing. On the one hand, they provide the most rapid generalized access to the data we need to support TP applications; their efficiency is, to a great extent, the basis for the rapid response times of today's systems. On the other hand, whenever a record is created, key records must also be created. Whenever a record is updated, there is a strong likelihood that key records will have to be updated (which implies deleting old key records and inserting new key records). If we are carrying a lot of keys to facilitate rapid access, then the on-line creation and updating of records could overcome all the benefits of rapid keyed access.

Therefore, a fundamental knowledge of keyed files is paramount for TP performance analysis.

Figure 7-3 shows a data file with one of its key files. Usually, for each data record, there is a corresponding key record which contains two fields of information:

- The key value pertaining to the data record.
- A pointer to that data record.

The forms that the pointer can take will be discussed later.

Key records are typically small (say 10 bytes for the key value plus 4 bytes for a record pointer for a total of 14 bytes). One sector on disk can contain many key records; a 1K byte sector could contain 73 14-byte key records, though there is often overhead involved.

The key records are maintained in the file in key order. Thus, if the key file were read from beginning to end, one would find the key values to be in alphanumeric order.

The fast access to a particular key value is achieved through a tree structure, as shown in Figure 7-3. This structure is commonly known as a *balanced B-tree* and com-

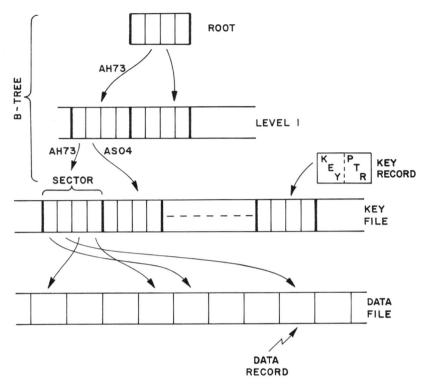

Figure 7-3 Keyed file.

prises levels of pseudo-key records pointing to sectors of key records in the next lower level.

For instance, referring to the first tree level above the key file in Figure 7-3 noted as Level 1, one record points to a key file sector and notes that the first record in that sector contains the key value AH73. The next record in the Level 1 tree points to the next sector in the key file, noting that it begins with the key value AS04. Thus, we know that the first key file sector described here contains key values from AH73 to AS04 (whether a key value of AS04 can appear in this sector or not depends upon whether or not the key is unique).

A tree level above Level 1 similarly points to the sectors in Level 1 and so on, with each tree level getting smaller and smaller (if 50 key records can fit into a sector, then each level contains 1/50 of the records in the next lower level). Ultimately, a tree level will be reached that is only one sector in length. This is the highest level and is known as the "root" of the B-tree.

Thus, a key file contains two major parts:

1. Key records, each containing a key value and a pointer to a corresponding data record.

2. A B-Tree, providing quick access to any key record containing a specified key value.

To find a data record containing a certain key value, the following sequence is followed:

1. Read the root segment.
2. Determine the sector of the next level to be searched, and read that sector.
3. Continue following the path through the levels of the tree until the last level has been read and searched. This level gives the sector containing the desired key record.
4. Read this key record sector, and find the desired key record.
5. Using the pointer in the key record, read the data record.

Thus, to find and read a data record via a key file requires $k + 2$ file reads, where k is the number of levels in the B-tree. To update a record requires $k + 1$ file reads to find the location of the data record, plus the data write.

If k_k is the number of key records that will fit in a sector, then k levels will support k_r records, where

$$k_r = k_k{}^{k+1} \qquad\qquad (7\text{-}16)$$

To get a feel for the number of levels required in a tree, let us look at the number of key records various levels will support. This is sensitive to the number of keys in a sector, and the table below shows key file size as a function of keys per sector and the number of levels. It is assumed that key records and tree records are the same size.

TABLE 7-1.   KEY FILE SIZE (k^r-RECORDS)

Levels (k)	Keys/sector (k_k) 50	100	200
1 (Root)	2,500	10,000	40,000
2	125,000	10^6	8×10^6
3	6.25×10^6	10^8	16×10^8
4	3.125×10^8	10^{10}	32×10^{10}

Thus, with only three levels, file sizes in the millions of records can be supported. Typical trees are generally two or three levels deep. Thus, a record in a keyed file can generally be accessed with a maximum of four to five accesses.

Moreover, assuming the file is accessed reasonably frequently, the root segment will almost always be found in cache; and there is a good chance that the first level below the root will also be cached. Consequently, for modest file sizes (a million records or so) with modest key sizes, the read of the key file may be a single access. This is a common assumption in performance analysis.

Thus, as a first approximation, the read of a keyed file is equivalent to two disk accesses:

$$n_{dir} = 2, \; n_{diw} = 0 \text{ for reads} \tag{7-17}$$

This value can be adjusted to reflect larger or smaller file sizes.

Adding a record to a keyed file is a different story. Not only must every add to a data file be accompanied by adds to each affected key file, but the B-tree in each key file also must be updated if the new key record has disturbed the key structure. In most cases, a free record slot will be found in the key file, and no tree update will be required.

However, if the sector into which the key record is to be inserted is full, it must be split into two sectors so that the new key record can be inserted into its proper position. Each of these sectors will now be about half full. This sector split means that a record must be added to the next higher level in the tree; doing this will occasionally also cause a sector split in that level.

The splitting of tree sectors could travel all the way up to the root and, in the worst case, cause the root to split. This will cause a new root segment to be created one level higher than the old root segment, thus adding one level to the tree.

Fortunately, sector splits do not occur all that frequently. When they do, they create room for many writes in the future. Sector splits are usually ignored for performance purposes, and a write to a keyed file is treated just as a write to any other file plus a write to all key files to be updated.

Thus, if n_k key files are to be updated on an average write to a keyed file, the number of disk accesses to write to a keyed file is (using the read assumptions for B-tree caching)

$$n_{dir} = n_k$$

$$n_{diw} = n_k + 1 \text{ for writes} \tag{7-18}$$

Though block splitting is generally ignored as a performance issue, it does impact upon the calculation of the number of tree levels. Since block splitting results in sectors being less than full, the average number of keys that will be found in a sector will be less than maximum. We will call the empty space *slack*. If the slack of a key file is 30 percent, then the maximum number of records in a sector, as used in Table 3-1 and equation 7-16, must be multiplied by .7. If 100 keys will fit into a record, and if the key file slack is .3, then two levels of B-tree will support $(70)^3 = 343,000$ records, rather than 1,000,000 records. Equation 7-16 can be rewritten to account for slack as follows, where k_s is the slack factor, or the average proportion of each sector that is unused:

$$k_r = [(1 - k_s) \, k_k]^{k+1} \tag{7-19}$$

In the absence of any other knowledge, a slack of 25% is a good assumption. This is because a block is 50% full following a block split and 100% full just before a block split, for an average of 75%.

Key files impose one significant restriction on the data file: it cannot be reorganized without totally rebuilding the key files corresponding to that data file. This is because of the nature of the pointer in the key file record. It generally will contain a byte position (for an unstructured file), a record number (for a relative file), or a sector/record identifier (for a sequential file). Whatever it is, it is "hardwired" to the current organization of the data file. Records cannot be inserted into the data file if that will displace other records, nor can the data file be compacted to recover deleted record space. In general, records once written must remain in place (except to be deleted). Any time a record is moved, the key files must be rebuilt.

For this reason, data is usually added sequentially to keyed files, i.e., written to the end of file. Any file reorganization (for instance, to recover deleted space) is done as a batch job out of hours.

This restriction is removed by the use of indexed sequential files, described next.

Indexed Sequential Files

An *indexed sequential file* is one in which the data records are maintained in key order according to a *primary key* (which is usually a unique key). It also contains its own B-tree structure to give quick access to a data record according to the primary key, as shown in Figure 7-4. In effect, the data records replace the key records in a key file.

Except for the fact that the data records are usually quite large compared to the key records, the description of a key file access given above applies directly to an indexed sequential file. However, the large data records mean that the last level of the B-tree is

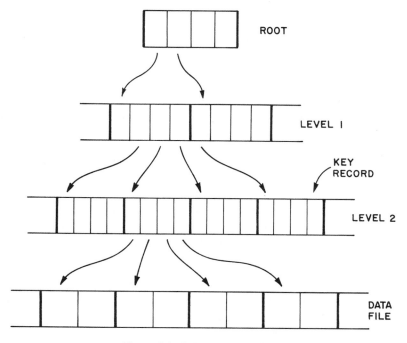

Figure 7-4 Indexed sequential file.

much larger than it would be for a key file. Consequently, an extra B-tree level is usually required. Since it is so large, it is unreasonable to assume that this level will be found in a cache. However, this extra B-tree level is often embedded with the data and typically requires an additional latency time to access. This extra time may be conveniently accounted for by simply increasing the disk access time judiciously. It can be more accurately accounted for by modifying equations 7-1 and 7-2, as follows.

A read will require reading k tree records (typically 2, as discussed above). The first will require a normal disk access of t_{da}, and the remaining $(k - 1)$ tree records will each require a latency time of $t_{dr}/2$. Finally, the data record will require a latency time of $t_{dr}/2$. Thus,

Indexed sequential read:

$$t_{fi} = a_i t_{fmi} + p_d(t_{da} + k t_{dr}/2) \tag{7-20}$$

where

$$k = \text{number of index levels not resident in cache.}$$

A cached write will require this time to read the sector to be modified plus an additional rotation time, t_{dr}, to rewrite the record.

Indexed sequential cached write:

$$t_{fi} = a_i t_{fmi} + p_d[t_{da} + (k + 2) \, t_{dr}/2] \tag{7-21A}$$

An uncached write must always perform the disk access in order to write the data, even if it does not need to access disk to read the key:

Indexed sequential uncached write:

$$t_{fi} = a_i t_{fmi} + p_d(k + 2) \, t_{dr}/2 + t_{da} \tag{7-21B}$$

Since records can now be accessed directly by their primary key, the restrictions on file reorganization no longer apply. In fact, every time a data record is inserted into its place in an indexed sequential file, potential block splits may move data records around. But just as with a key file, the primary key B-tree is immediately updated to reflect the new record structure.

Other key files may support an indexed sequential file and give access to that file via *secondary keys*. In this case, the record pointer found in a key record is the value of the primary key for the corresponding data record. Thus, to read an indexed sequential file via a secondary key, the key file is read. Then the data file is read via its primary key.

Thus, accessing an indexed sequential file by its primary key can be quite a bit faster than using a keyed file. Secondary key access will be a little slower than a keyed file access because of the extra primary key B-tree that must be searched. Often, from a performance viewpoint, so much of the access activity can be accomplished by primary keys that indexed sequential files can be a big boost to performance.

Note that secondary keys may be used to access an indexed sequential file but not to write to it. All writes must be via the primary key, which is required to be unique if record updates are to be performed.

Hashed Files

Hashing is another technique of gaining keyed access to a file. It is not as predominant in TP systems today as is keyed access but is used enough to bear mentioning.

The intent of hashing is to use the value of the primary key to calculate a sector address into which the record will be placed. Some sort of hashing algorithm is invented, one that will convert the key into a numbered value that will fall within the range of preallocated sectors for the file. That sector is then read, and the record is inserted if there is room. If there is no room for the record in that sector, then it must be written to an overflow area under some secondary algorithm.

To access a record, the key is hashed, and that sector is read. If the desired record is not found in the sector, then the overflow area must be searched.

A simple example of a hashing algorithm is to use the first three characters of a key and to treat them as a base-36 number, with 0 to 9 having values 0 to 9 and with *A* to *Z* having values 10 to 35. Then the key H7D would hash to

$$17 \times 36^2 + 7 \times 36 + 13 = 22{,}297$$

and would point to sector number 22,297. The range of this hashing algorithm is

$$36^3 = 46{,}656$$

sectors.

If the file is sparsely populated, hashing can be a very effective access method. In effect, a keyed access can be achieved with one disk access. However, if the file begins to fill up, performance can degrade rapidly. In effect, hashing trades space for time. It makes inefficient use of disk space to achieve a rapid access time.

Hashing algorithms are generally not supplied by the system vendors. Rather, they are implemented by the application programs.

DISK CACHING

Except in some very simple situations, the effectiveness of disk caching is virtually impossible to calculate because of the complexity of its use. Usually, a reasonable cache hit ratio (or cache miss ratio, p_d, as used herein) is assumed, based on experience or measurements on the actual or equivalent system. As an alternative, the cache miss ratio can be varied as a parameter, and performance calculations can be made over a range of interest. In this way, at least, one can determine the sensitivity of the system to caching.

Many systems allow the size of the disk cache to be specified as a system generation parameter. Cache size can then be adjusted during system operation to obtain the best compromise between disk caching and other memory requirements. In effect, the analyst is caught between a rock and a hard place when it comes to memory allocation. As disk cache is made larger to speed up data-base access, less memory remains for program space, resulting in a higher incidence of page faults. Reducing disk delays in one area simply increases them in another. Ultimately, if a good balance between data-base disk caching and program performance from page faulting cannot be found, the only solution may be to buy more memory—if the system will support it.

Some insight can be gained into cache effectiveness on a simple level by considering the ''longevity'' of a disk block in cache. The longevity of a disk block is the amount of time one would expect it to last unaccessed in cache before—based on the least recently used algorithm—it got flushed back to disk.

If, for instance, an application reads some data and presents it to an operator, who will later want to modify it, we are interested in knowing whether that data will still be in cache when the modifications are made. This would save the rereading of this data from disk.

Let us define the following terms:

R_d = the average transfer rate (reads and writes) of blocks from disk to cache (blocks per second).

R_a = the logical access rate of disk.

p_d = the disk cache miss ratio.

C_d = the disk cache size (blocks).

T_{cache} = the longevity of a block in cache.

If a block is read in (for either read or write purposes) and then sits in cache unused, it will be flushed from cache when it is the oldest block (assuming no distinction is made by the cache manager between clean and dirty blocks). Since blocks are being read in at a rate of R_d blocks per second, this will take a time of

$$T_{cache} = C_d/R_d \qquad (7\text{-}22)$$

where T_{cache} is the time that it will take to flush the block.

R_d is the actual transfer rate between disk and cache. In this simplified example, $R_d = p_d R_a$. That is, R_a actual block accesses per second are required of disk, and p_d of these blocks are not found in cache. Their product is the physical disk transfer rate. Thus,

$$T_{cache} = C_d/p_d R_a \qquad (7\text{-}23)$$

Let us say that our application involves highly random hits on moderately sized files. We would expect key file B-trees to be in cache, but key records and data records would not likely be cached. Let us further define

n_{dr} = the number of logical disk read requests per transaction.

n_{dw} = the number of logical disk write requests per transaction.

R_t = the transaction rate.

C_{dt} = the amount of cache used to store the B-trees.

n_k = the number of key files to be updated per transaction.

The anticipated physical disk access rate, R_d, is then $2n_{dr}R_t$ for reads (read a key file and a data file for each read request) and $(2n_{dw} + n_k)R_t$ for writes (read a key file and update a data record for each request plus update n_k key files per transaction). This can be expressed as

$$R_d = (2n_{dr} + 2n_{dw} + n_k)R_t$$

The amount of cache available for data and key record transfers is $(C_d - C_{dt})$. Using these expressions to modify equation 7-22 gives a cache longevity time of

$$T_{cache} = (C_d - C_{dt})/(2n_{dr} + 2n_{dw} + n_k)R_t \qquad (7\text{-}24)$$

Let us plug some typical numbers into this expression. Consider an inventory system dedicated to the inquiry of inventory and the placing of an order against that inventory. As a result of an operator query, a customer master file and a product file are each read according to a key. The operator returns an order, which updates an amount in the product file, updates a status key to the product file, and writes an order detail record to an order file keyed by product code and customer I.D. Thus,

n_{dr} = 2 keyed reads (customer master and product files).

n_{dw} = 2 keyed writes (product and order detail files).

n_k = 3 key file updates (product status key on the product file and customer and product keys on the order file).

Three files are involved: the customer master, product, and order files. Let us assume the following conditions:

- The customer master file contains 50,000 records of 300 bytes each.
- The customer I.D. is 10 bytes.
- The disk sector size is 2K bytes.

With this information, we can estimate the size of the customer master file B-tree, which we are assuming is cached. We do this as follows.

Each disk sector can contain $2048/14 = 146$ keys (assuming a 4-byte pointer and no overhead). Thus, there will be $50,000/146 = 343$ sectors occupied by the key records for the customer master file. Assuming a 30 percent slack, then $343/.7 = 490$ blocks is a more reasonable number. These blocks are pointed to by the first level of the B-tree (which we assume is cached). The 490 sectors of keys will require $490/(146)(.7) = 5$ sectors in the first level of the tree (with 30% slack) and a root sector. Thus, the customer I.D. B-tree for the customer master file will require 6 sectors in cache.

Let us assume that an equivalent analysis on the other key files leads to the following B-tree sizes:

TABLE 7-2. EXAMPLE B-TREE SIZES

File	Key	B-tree sectors
Customer master	Customer ID	6
Product master	Product code	4
	Product status	5
Order detail	Customer ID	4
	Product code	4
		23

Thus,

$$C_{dt} = 23 \text{ cache blocks required for B-trees (46K bytes).}$$

Finally, let us assume that we have a 1-megabyte cache memory (500 blocks). Thus,

$$C_d = 500 \text{ blocks of cache memory.}$$

Then, from equation 7-24:

$$T_{cache} = (500 - 23)/11R_t = 43.4/R_t$$

where we have assumed in our value for n_{dw} that the product file record to be updated is not found in cache, i.e., it has been read and then flushed before it could be updated. Obviously, we would like to have enough cache to ensure that, with high probability, this record is not flushed before it is updated.

Note that the longevity of a block in cache is a function of the transaction rate, R_t. As the transaction rate increases, disk activity increases, and longevity decreases. The following table gives longevity times for a range of transaction rates for this case:

TABLE 7-3. EXAMPLE LONGEVITIES

R_t (trans/sec)	T_{cache} (sec)
1	43.4
2	21.7
5	8.7
10	4.3

If it is anticipated that a user will require about 30 seconds to fill an order, then at one transaction per second, the product file record to be updated will have a good chance of remaining in cache. This would give better performance than anticipated, since it was assumed that this record would not be found in cache when it was to be updated. At transaction rates greater than 1.5 transactions per second, the probability that this record will remain in cache long enough is substantially reduced.

A feel for cache hit (or miss) ratios can be obtained from this example. The following table lists total disk requests for each operation, the number that are B-tree accesses (root and level 1) assumed to be in cache, the number that are assumed to come from disk (first-time reads or writes), and the number that are candidates for cache hits if the record has not been flushed.

TABLE 7-4.   EXAMPLE DISK ACTIVITY

Operations	Total accesses	B-tree cache	Reads/ writes	Updates
Read cust. mast.	4	2	2	
Read product	4	2	2	
Write product	4	2		2
Write status key	3	2	1	
Write order detail	4	2	2	
Write cust. ID key	3	2	1	
Write prod. code key	3	2	1	
	25	14	9	2

This table reflects the assumption that all key files are supported by a two-level B-tree. Thus, there are 25 accesses to sectors required to process this transaction. Fourteen are assumed to be in cache, and 9 are assumed to necessarily require a physical disk access. The two update accesses (one to read the product code key file and one to write to the product file) may be in cache if the update is fast enough.

Thus, the disk cache hit ratio ranges from .56 to .64 (the cache miss ratio ranges from .36 to .44), depending upon the success of finding a record that is to be updated and is still in cache. These results are typical of TP systems.

This "analysis" of disk cache has used a very simple example to illustrate the basic concepts of disk cache and to give a feel for the magnitude of parameters involved in typical TP systems. In the real world, any realistic analysis of disk caching is usually too complex to be useful (if indeed at all possible), and reasonable assumptions for cache miss ratios are usually used instead.

However, the longevity analysis that led to equation 7-24 and to the example of Table 7-3 can be useful in estimating the amount of cache memory that represents the threshold required to achieve high cache hit ratios for update activity. This can be of paramount importance in TP systems.

OTHER CONSIDERATIONS

There are several other considerations that can affect the performance of the data base in a TP environment. An understanding of these will allow the performance analyst to appropriately modify his attack on the problem of analysis.

Overlapped Seeks

A disk controller can typically drive several (say eight) disk drives. In general, however, it can be transferring data to or from only one disk drive because of hardware and I/O channel limitations. However, if there is a queue of disk requests waiting for the disk controller, many systems will allow the disk device driver (the software driver that controls the disk controller—see Figure 7-1) to "look ahead" through the queue. By doing so, the device driver can initiate seeks on other drives to get their heads properly positioned in anticipation of transferring data.

This capability is called overlapped seeking. The seeking of the read/write heads on some disks is overlapped with the seeking of other heads and also with the transfer of data from one of the disk units. Overlapped seeks can drastically reduce disk access time in busy systems (it has little effect on idle systems). Since seek time is a major component of total file management time, this can greatly improve the responsiveness of the data-base system.

There is no straightforward way to analyze the effect of overlapped seeks except to estimate the effective seek time at the anticipated load and to use that time in the analysis rather than the actual seek time. An example will illustrate the sort of estimate that can be made.

Let us assume that a preliminary analysis has shown that the average queue length of requests waiting for a controller (W in terms of chapter 4 notation) is two requests. The controller has four disks connected to it, one which, of course, is busy. This leaves three disks. The probability that the first request is for one of the free disks is 3/4. Thus, with probability .75, one overlapped seek can be started.

With probability .75, the second request can lead to an overlapped seek if the first did not. If the first request did lead to an overlapped seek, then with probability .5, the second request can lead to an overlapped seek. Thus, with probability $(.25)(.75) + (.75)(.5) = .56$, the second request will result in an overlapped seek. On the average, a request will be given an overlapped seek $(.75 + .56)/2 = .66$ of the time. If we assume, given an overlapped seek, that the seek is complete when the request is chosen for data transfer, then overlapped seeks are transparent to the requesting process, and overall seek time has been reduced by 66 percent. If seek time is 20 msec., the effective seek time is $(1-.66)(20) = 6.8$ msec. (The assumption of 100 percent seek overlap with the processing of the current request is not unreasonable, since disk processing times tend to run in the same order of magnitude as seek times.)

Alternate Servicing Order

Queues are normally serviced on a FIFO (First-In, First-Out) basis. However, there are algorithms that will look ahead through the queue and will decide which request to next service based on maximizing efficiency.

An example of this sort of servicing algorithm is the *elevator algorithm*. This algorithm searches the queue for that request which is closest to the current position of the disk head and chooses that request for service. In this way, seek time is minimized.

Algorithms such as this have a problem in that although the overall efficiency of the disk system is enhanced, some requests may get delayed an inordinate amount of time. In fact, with the elevator algorithm, it is possible to create a scenario in which a request may never be honored in a busy time. This would be a request at one edge of the disk when all activity is at the other edge. Remember our system manager who hears only from irate customers? Let's not do this to him.

Of course, the algorithm can be modified to prevent this. One form of a modified elevator algorithm always sweeps in one direction from one edge of the disk to the other, servicing all pending requests in cylinder order. It then reverses and repeats this sequence.

In this case, one can make an approximate statement concerning the enhancement provided by this modified elevator algorithm. As pointed out in chapter 4, the average distance between two cylinders chosen randomly on disk is 1/3 of the total number of cylinders. This is the average seek distance of the disk arm as it services a FIFO queue.

However, if there are n items on the average in the disk queue, and if these are serviced according to the modified elevator algorithm such that all are serviced in order as the disk arm sweeps across the disk, then the average seek distance is $1/n$ of the total number of cylinders. If n is 10, then the average access time is based on moving a total of 10 percent of the cylinders versus 33 percent, or a reduction of 3.3 in the access distance. This can be significant.

Of course, a ten-item queue is even more significant in terms of delay time. By the time the queue length is long enough to make algorithms like this meaningful, the system has long ceased performing satisfactorily.

Algorithms such as these are not typically found in today's TP systems. They are not very effective unless queue lengths are long, and good performance design dictates that queue lengths be short (70 percent resource loads yield queue lengths in the order of one or two, according to Khintchine and Pollaczek). In addition, such algorithms tend to be unpredictable and have not been found to be necessary.

However, as with overlapped seeks, one technique to handle service order algorithms is to estimate in some way an effective seek time (or access time if rotational latency enhancements are involved) and to use this modified value in the analysis.

Data Locking

A typical TP system has many users accessing the same files. As long as a file is simply being read, there is no problem. However, as soon as two users try to update the same data, a problem can arise.

Suppose user A reads an inventory record, finds 25 widgets in stock, and decides to sell 10, thereby needing to update the stock quantity to reflect the fact that 15 are left. However, before user A can return the update, user B has read the same record and decides to sell 5 widgets. User A by now has updated the file, unbeknownst to user B, to reflect a new quantity, 15. User B then returns an updated record showing a quantity of 20 widgets.

The data base now reflects 20 widgets in stock, whereas there are really only 10. The two users of the system have stepped on each other's toes.

The solution to this dilemma is *data locking*. When a piece of data is locked, no other entity (person or program) may read that data for purposes of updating (normal reading is often allowed). Depending upon the system, data locks can be applied to an entire file, a record in the file, or a data field in the record. The finer the granularity of the lock, the more efficient the system (except, of course, that the finer the lock, the more overhead is imposed on the system).

Thus, user A will read the widget record with lock (let us assume that record locking is available). User B will then try to read this record with lock. However, the attempt will fail, and user B will have to wait (either try again later or be queued by the system to the locked record). When user A updates the record to show 15 widgets left, the lock will be removed. User B's request for a read with lock will now be honored and will show 15 widgets left. Selling 5, user B will return an updated record showing 10 widgets left in stock.

Clearly, file locks can bog down a system terribly, especially if the file is kept locked while an operator takes some action on the data (what if the operator takes a coffee break while he has the file locked?). Record locks offer a much smaller chance for conflict, and data item locks are even better.

As a general design philosophy, the locking mechanism which freezes the least data should be used (record locking is quite common in contemporary systems). The lock also should be maintained for as short a time as possible (for instance, only during the updating process, after the operator has performed all other functions).

Most TP systems are designed so that the chance of data lock conflicts are negligible; lock conflicts can usually be ignored from a performance viewpoint. If lock conflicts are not negligible, delays from lock conflicts must be estimated and added to the effective file manager service time if locks are queued or to the total transaction time if the operator must wait and then resubmit the transaction. Such delays are so application-dependent that nothing more in a general sense can be said about them.

Mirrored Files

As discussed in chapter 2, critical files are often *mirrored* for reliability. When data must be written to two disk units, even though this may be done simultaneously, the average write time is longer than writing to one disk. Conceptually, one may explain this by thinking of one disk as being the "average" disk completing in an "average" time. The other disk will either complete faster, in which case the mirrored write took an "average" time, or will complete slower, in which case the mirrored write took a longer than "average" time. The net result is necessarily a mirrored write that averages longer than a single write.

An analysis of mirrored writes is given in Appendix 5. The results are quite simple. Mirroring a file adds about 40 percent to the seek time. Thus, if a disk has a 20 msec. seek time and an 8.3 msec. latency time, then single disk write time is $(20 + 8.3 + 16.7) = 45$ msec. A mirrored write will add $.4(20) = 8$ msec., yielding a write time of 53 msec.

To achieve even greater reliability, fault-tolerant systems will often write to only one disk at a time. In this case, if a failure occurs during writing, one disk is guaranteed to be readable. However, a mirrored write now requires twice the disk time of a single disk write.

One compensating advantage of mirrored drives is that both can be shared for reading. Some systems take advantage of this to some degree or another. If an application is heavily oriented to reading over writing, mirrored disk drives could prove to be a performance advantage.

Multiple File Managers

In many TP systems, the file manager can become the bottleneck for the system. This can be alleviated by partitioning the system so that it can have several file managers, each sharing a portion of the load.

Multiple file managers can alleviate another problem, in some cases. As we discussed earlier, disk processing (i.e., CPU) time and physical disk access time are substantially serial in nature. While the file manager is processing a request, the disk is idle. Then the file manager waits while the disk transfers the desired data. In typical TP systems, a disk driven by a single file manager can only be kept busy 25 to 60 percent of the time, thus sharply reducing its effective capacity. If multiple file managers could be used to drive a disk, disk utilization could be sharply improved.

There are several ways in which multiple file managers can be utilized.

File manager per disk volume.   A large TP system will typically have several disk volumes (physical disk drives) that it uses. These systems often provide the capability for (or require) separate file managers for each disk volume, as shown in Figure 7-5a. While this does not solve the problem of low disk utilization described above, it does give a mechanism for alleviating the file manager bottleneck.

To analyze the performance of this type of file manager configuration, one simply computes the total file load (file manager processing and disk access) as set forth in equations 7-1 through 7-6 and then allocates this load across the independent file managers. Often, there is not sufficient information to allocate load on any but an evenly distributed basis. In this case, if a file load of L_f is to be distributed across D file managers, each controlling their own disk system, then the load on each file manager is L_f/D.

Multiple file managers per disk volume.   Whether a TP system is large or small, it can benefit from having multiple file managers share one disk. This not only relieves the file management bottleneck to some extent but also allows disk utilization to approach 100 percent. This structure is shown in Figure 7-5b.

In order for more than one file manager to use a disk volume, requests to that disk must be appropriately partitioned between the file managers. It is not sufficient to allow them to simply work from a single queue, since the order in which certain requests are processed is critical. For instance, if a process submits two requests, one to open a file and one to read it, it is imperative that the requests be executed in that order. We would not

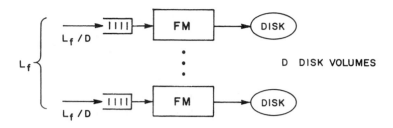

FILE MANAGER PER DISK VOLUME

(a)

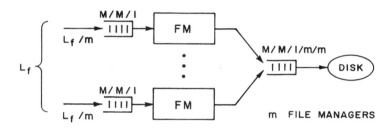

MULTIPLE FILE MANAGERS PER VOLUME

(b)

Figure 7-5 Multiple file managers.

want one file manager to start the opening of a file (a lengthy procedure) and another to immediately try to read that file before the opening procedure was complete.

One straightforward way to partition work between different file managers is to have each responsible for a defined subset of files on the disk volume. In this way, all operations on a file will be consistent.

Since requests must be partitioned, the file managers do not act as a multiserver servicing a common queue. Rather, just as in the file manager per disk volume case described above, the load is distributed to them as individual and independent servers. If there are m file managers servicing a single disk volume, and if file system load is L_f, then the load on each file manager is L_f/m.

However, the disk now sees multiple users (though nowhere near an infinite number). It will have a queue of work to do and will respond as a single server to the m file managers. The characteristics of the disk queue will be governed by the single server, finite users model M/M/1/m/m discussed in Chapter 4.

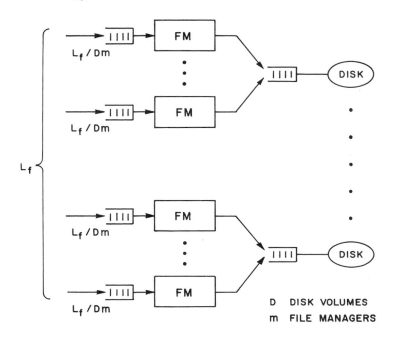

MULTIPLE FILE MANAGERS, MULTIPLE VOLUMES

(c)

Figure 7-5   *(contd.)*

Multiple file managers per multiple volumes.   The above two configurations can, of course, be combined as shown in Figure 7-5c. Multiple disk volumes are each controlled by multiple file managers. Using the above notation, the load on each file manager is L_f/Dm.

AN EXAMPLE

As an example of file management performance, let us consider the transaction discussed under cache management and apply it to various numbers of file managers in a TP system which has one file manager per disk volume.

To summarize that example, we have a standard transaction comprising:

- 2 keyed reads
- 2 keyed writes
- 3 key file updates

Let us designate these as file operation types $i = 1$, 2, and 3, respectively. As discussed earlier, the following table gives the values for n_{dir}, n_{diw}, and p_i for each file operation and also gives typical values for file management processing time, t_{fmi}:

TABLE 7-5. FILE OPERATION PARAMETERS

File operation	i	n_{dir}	n_{diw}	t_{fmi} (msec)	p_i
Keyed read	1	4		20	.29
Keyed write	2	2	2	30	.29
Key file update	3	2	1	25	.42
					1.00

We further assume the following parameters:

$$t_{da} = 28 \text{ msec.}$$
$$t_{dr} = 17 \text{ msec.}$$
$$p_d = .4$$
$$f_i = .5 \text{ for } i = 1, 2, 3$$

We further assume that writes are cached.

Based on these values, the file management times, t_{fi}, are given by equation 7-1 and are shown in Table 7-6.

TABLE 7-6. EXAMPLE FILE MANAGEMENT TIMES

Operation	i	File management time (t_{fi} – msec)
Keyed read	1	58.8
Keyed write	2	79.4
Key update	3	57.9

The average file system service time, from equation 7-4, is

$$t_f = \sum_i p_i t_{fi} = 64.4 \text{ msec.}$$

The load on the file system, given by equation 7-5 is

$$L_f = n_f t_f R_t = \frac{(7)(64.4)}{1000} R_t = .45 R_t$$

and the load on each file manager is

$$L_f/D = .45 R_t/D$$

where D is the number of disk volumes and consequently the number of file managers. From equation 7-6, the response time of a file manager is

$$t_{df} = \frac{t_f}{1 - L_f} = \frac{64.4}{1 - .45 R_t/D}$$

This response time (or file manager delay time) is plotted in Figure 7-6 for one to three file managers. It is clear from Figure 7-6 that additional file manager paths to different disks proportionately increase the capacity of the system and can have dramatic

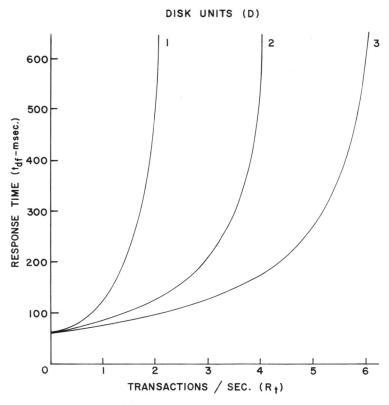

Figure 7-6   Multiple file manager response time.

effects on response time. At two transactions per second, the response time for the three cases is shown in Table 7-7.

TABLE 7-7.   EXAMPLE RESPONSE TIMES

D	t_{df} (msec)
1	644
2	117
3	92

An additional point to note is the average disk utilization. The average disk operation requires 64.4 msec. Of this,

$$\sum_i a_i p_i t_{fmi} = 17.5 \text{ msec.}$$

is processing time during which the disk is idle. Thus, during the time that the file management system is busy, the disk is only being used 73 percent of the time. In many systems this disk utilization can be less than 50 percent. It is this situation that is enhanced by utilizing multiple file managers per disk volume.

8

Application
Environment

Now that we have a vehicle, let's take a look at the passenger. Our TP vehicle includes a communication network for exchanging messages (requests and replies) with the users, a processing environment (the CPU, memory, and operating system) to act as our TP engine, and a data base that is used to maintain the status of our environment and to answer inquiries relative to that environment from our users.

It is this vehicle in which the TP application resides and by which it is hidden from the mundane problems of the real world. The communication manager worries about line protocols, data errors, network outages; it presents a clean message interface to the application. The operating system and its hardware take away the concerns of memory management, multiple processors, multiple users, interprocess communication, process scheduling, and in some cases even fault detection and recovery. The file manager or data-base manager provides a smooth path for accessing and maintaining our data.

In this environment, the application is simple, at least conceptually. It comprises one or more processes that accept messages and apply them to the data base for inquiry and update purposes. The analysis of its performance, however, still is tied to the performance issues of its vehicle and particularly its engine.

A TP application typically comprises a set of cooperating processes. The requestor-server model described in chapter 3 is a good example of this. Therefore, no matter how efficiently a process is designed, it will still be delayed by other system activities as it competes with them for resources. This chapter deals with the performance of application structures in the TP environment and describes a variety of application process structures currently in use.

PROCESS PERFORMANCE

A portion of the response time calculation is, of course, the time that is consumed by the application process in processing a transaction. However, this is not usually a major factor in response time, and it is often only a negligible factor. A transaction inquiry providing a 2-second response time might only require 50 msec. of processing time, for instance.

True, a good bit of the remaining time is used up in communications and data-base management; however, a good bit of time is also committed to process management. These are the times that we deal with here. Virtually all of the process management considerations have been touched on in previous chapters, so most of what we will discuss here will be in the nature of a review and consolidation of this knowledge.

The delay time imposed by an application process on a transaction is only partly due to its actual processing time. This delay time must also include

1. The queue delay incurred by the transaction as it waits in line for the process.
2. The dispatch time incurred while the process is waiting for the processor.
3. The processing time of the process itself.
4. The contention for the processor with application activities of higher priority.
5. The contention for the processor with the operating system as it handles interrupts and other system activities.
6. The messaging time required to communicate with other processes.

Overview

From a fundamental conceptual viewpoint, the process environment as described above is shown in Figure 8-1. We view a process here in the simplest of terms to obtain an overview tying in the above concepts as a unified whole. A message enters the process's message queue and waits in that queue for a time t_q until it reaches the head of the queue. The process receives this message, processes it, and passes it on to another process.

Figure 8-1 shows a process running in a processor. The process has an input queue that receives messages at a rate of R and processes them with an average service time of t_p. As the process completes a transaction, it passes it on to another process via an interprocessor message requiring a system time of t_{ipm}.

Once the process has processed a transaction, it relinquishes control of the processor and waits for the next transaction. It then gets back in line with other processes at its priority and waits for the processor so that it can service this next transaction. This is shown by the process being an item waiting in a greater queue—the processor queue. The amount of time that the process must wait in this queue is its dispatch time, t_d.

Note that t_q represents the time spent by a *message* in a *process* queue. t_d represents the time spent by a *process* in the *processor* queue.

As shown in Figure 8-1, the process, once running, does not have the processor all to itself. For one thing, the operating system consumes a portion of the processor capacity

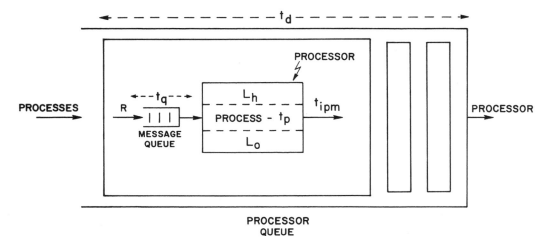

Figure 8-1 Process environment.

as it handles I/O, communication with other processes, timer-list management, and so on. The load imposed on the processor by the operating system is L_o.

Similarly, higher priority processes may be usurping the processor while the process is trying to run (this is the case of preemptive scheduling). These higher priority processes impose a CPU load of L_h.

The process requires t_p time to complete its task. But only $(1 - L_o - L_h)$ of the processor is available to the process, so that in a time $t_{s'}$ only $t_s' (1 - L_o - L_h)$ time is used on behalf of the process. Therefore, our actual processing time, $t_{s'}$ once the process is given the processor, is given by

$$t_s' (1 - L_o - L_h) = t_p$$

or

$$t_s' = \frac{t_p}{1 - L_o - L_h} \tag{8-1}$$

A message arriving at the head of the process's message queue must wait first for a time, t_d, for the process to be dispatched and then for the processing time, t_s'. Thus, the service time, t_s, so far as a message is concerned is

$$t_s = t_d + t_s' = t_d + \frac{t_p}{1 - L_o - L_h} \tag{8-2}$$

Equation 8-2 represents the effective processing time, or service time, that a message waiting in the process's message queue will experience. Before being processed, the message must wait in this queue for a time t_q. Since transactions are being received by this process at a rate of R transactions per second, then the load on the process is $L = Rt_s$. Using the M/M/1 model, the waiting time t_q is

$$t_q = \frac{L}{1 - L} t_s = \frac{Rt_s}{1 - Rt_s} t_s \tag{8-3}$$

The total delay time through the server, t_{ds}, is

$$t_{ds} = t_q + t_s = \frac{t_s}{1 - Rt_s} \tag{8-4}$$

The dispatch time, t_d, is the time the process must wait for the processor while processes of equal priority ahead of it in the processor queue are being serviced. In Appendix 6, we point out that the M/M/1 model is inappropriate for the calculation of process dispatch time if any one process accounts for a substantial portion of processor time. The M/M/1 model will lead to arbitrarily large processor queues at high loads, but we know that the processor queue length cannot exceed m-1 if there are m processes in the system. An approximation which is suggested in Appendix 6 is to simply exclude the effect of the arriving process when calculating the length of the processor queue which it will see, since it will never have to wait for itself.

Let the total arrival rate of messages to be serviced by processes at this priority be R_p, and let the average processing time of all messages at this priority be t_p'. Then the load L_p imposed upon the processor by all processes at priority p except for the process being considered is

$$L_p = R_p t_p' - Rt_p \tag{8-5}$$

We exclude the load of the process whose dispatch time we are considering, as discussed above.

From equation 6-32, the dispatch time, t_d, for our process is

$$t_d = \frac{(L_p + L_o + L_h)t'}{(1 - L_p - L_o - L_h)(1 - L_o - L_h)} \tag{8-6}$$

where

R_p = arrival rate of transactions to processes at priority p.

t_p' = average service time for all processes at priority p.

L_p = load imposed on the processor by processes at the considered priority, except for the considered process.

t' = service time averaged over all priorities, including the considered priority and higher, but exclusive of the considered process.

To complete its function, the process must send an interprocess message forwarding this transaction to another process. This requires a time t_{ipm}, which is operating system time and which typically is not affected by other loads. We assume that it does not add to process service time but rather is treated explicitly. Thus, total service time for the message is

$$t_{ds} + t_{ipm}$$

This simple model has incorporated all of our above points that affect process performance. These six points are the following:

1. Transaction (message) queue delay is t_q.
2. Dispatch time is t_d.
3. Process time is t_p.
4. Higher priority contention is L_h.
5. Operating system contention is L_o.
6. Messaging time is t_{ipm}.

As an example of the compounding effects of the process environment on process performance, assume the following parameter values (all are reasonable):

Process time (t_p, t_p', t')	10 msec.
Operating system load (L_o)	.1
Higher priority load (L_h)	.4
Interprocess message time (t_{ipm})	2 msec.
Process transaction rate (R)	15 trans./sec.
Total transaction rate at this priority (R_p)	30 trans./sec.

From equation 8-5, the load at this priority, exclusive of the process being considered, is $L_p = .15$.

From equation 8-6, the process dispatch time t_d is 37.1 msec. That is to say, once a process has work to do, it must wait an average of 37.1 msec. before it can run.

From equation 8-2, a message will require a time t_s of 57.1 msec. to be processed once it arrives at the head of the message queue. This time comprises 37.1 msec. dispatch time waiting for the processor plus 20 msec. of apparent processing time.

From equation 8-3, the time, t_q, that a message waits in the message queue is 342.9 msec. From equation 8-4, the total delay time t_{ds} for a message from the time it arrives at the process to the time that it is processed is 400 msec. Adding interprocess message time gives a total processing delay of 402 msec. All this for a processing time of only 10 msec.!

To obtain a feel for the cause of this apparent disaster, let us expand equation 8-4 for t_{ds} by substituting equation 8-2 for t_s. Using equations 8-1 and 8-6, we first write t_s as

$$t_s = \frac{Lt}{(1 - L)(1 - L_h')} + \frac{t}{(1 - L_h')} = \frac{t}{(1 - L)(1 - L_h')}$$

where we have substituted

$$t = t' = t_p \qquad\qquad = 10 \text{ msec.}$$
$$L = L_p + L_o + L_h \qquad = .65$$
$$L'_h = L_o + L_h \qquad\qquad = .5$$

Then

$$t_{ds} = \frac{t/(1-L)(1-L'_h)}{1 - Rt/(1-L)(1-L'_h)} = \frac{t/(1-L'_h)}{1 - [L + Rt/(1-L'_h)]}$$

We have in effect a server with a service time of 20 msec. (ok) which is loaded 95 percent (awful!). Note the effect of priority service. If all activities were at the same priority, then $L'_h = 0$, and t_{ds} becomes that for a server with a service time of 10 msec. which is loaded 80 percent (as we would intuitively expect). Consequently, t_{ds} would be 50 msec. instead of 400 msec. Thus, prioritized service can wreak havoc in a heavily loaded system (the results are more reasonable for lightly loaded systems). In effect, we have seen that the service time of a low priority process can be increased significantly by higher priority activity, which results in a commensurate increase in process load and in a possible dramatic increase in the delay time through the process. One should approach the design of a prioritized system with great caution.

Relative to the effect of process environment, consider the following change to our process structure. If the process were allowed to service all messages in its queue rather than just one message before relinquishing the processor, several dispatch times would be saved. A dispatch would be required only if the queue became empty, that is, for only $(1 - Rt_s)$ messages (a message will find the queue idle $1 - Rt_s$ of the time). One might expect this to significantly improve performance.

Accounting for this change, equation 8-2 is modified to give a t_s of

$$t_s = (1 - Rt_s)t_d + \frac{t_p}{1 - L_o - L_h}$$

or

$$t_s = \frac{t_d + t_p/(1 - L_o - L_h)}{1 + Rt_d}$$

This results in a t_s of 36.7 msec. for the above case and in a processing delay t_{ds} of 81.6 msec. rather than 400 msec. Quite an improvement and a further demonstration of the importance of process environment on performance.

Of course, nothing comes for free. The time that this process "owns" the processor is now significantly increased each time it is granted the processor. t' in equation 8-6 for other processes at this priority and lower is increased, and delays through these processes will necessarily increase as a result of their extended dispatch times.

This effect is elegantly stated by the M/G/I Conservation Law (see Kleinrock [15]). The weighted sum of the queue waiting times is a constant, given by

$$\sum_{p=1}^{p_{max}} L_p T_{qp} = \frac{L_t T_o}{1 - L_t}$$

where

L_p = server load at priority p.

T_{qp} = queue waiting time at priority p.

L_t = total load on the server.

T_o = time to complete the service of the current item when a new item arrives at the queue.

This is formally proved for nonpreemptive systems. Thus, if we improve the level of service for one class of items, others will surely suffer.

Process Time

There is not a great deal that can be said analytically about process time. Before a program is written, it is difficult to estimate process time except from general experience with similar systems. After a program is running, average processing time and all manner of dispersion measures can be obtained by the various performance measuring tools often provided with the system or by instrumenting the process itself.

Seldom can these values be deduced analytically. However, their accuracy has a strong impact on performance analysis. So how do we make performance predictions on a machine that hasn't been built yet, much less programmed? Or on an application that is currently being programmed? Do we pack our bags and give up? Or once again, do we invoke our cloak of devout imperfectionism and give it our best shot?

It has been the author's practice, based on experience with several systems, to use the following process times if no better information is available. They are based on a 32-bit 1 MIPS processor and should be adjusted up or down accordingly. They should also be appropriately adjusted or replaced based on the user's own knowledge and experience.

Function	Process time (msec.)
Communications (per block)	5
Application (per file call)	5
File manager (per operation)	35

To these values should be added the process context-switching time if significant (the time it takes for the operating system to switch processes). For instance, consider a process which reads a message (1 block), makes three file calls, and returns a response (1 block). Assume context-switching time is 2 msec. The process must be given control of the processor 4 times, once to read the incoming message and once at the completion of each file call. Total processing time is therefore $2 \times 5 + 3 \times 5 + 4 \times 2 = 33$ msec., or $33/4 = 8.25$ msec. per dispatch.

At least these values provide a reasonable starting point. As real values are obtained, they should replace the suggested values, and the model should then be reevaluated.

Dispatch Time

The dispatch time for a process is the time it must wait in line to obtain access to the processor, i.e., its waiting time on the ready list. Dispatch time has been thoroughly discussed in chapter 6 in the section entitled "Task Dispatching." Dispatch time expressions are given for single processor and multiprocessor environments and for preemptive as well as nonpreemptive schedulers.

As a summary of that section, dispatch time is viewed as the time a process must wait in a queue (the ready list) before it has access to the processor. The service time for items in the queue is the average time per dispatch that processes in that queue will consume, i.e., the average amount of time that these processes will be active once given the processor. This is a real time, calculated from the actual average CPU time consumed by these processes and adjusted for operating system and higher priority process activity.

The queuing models used are M/M/1 for a single processor environment and M/M/c for a multiprocessor environment. This assumes that process times are exponentially distributed and that arrivals to the ready list are random. It also assumes that the number of processes in the system is much greater than the ready list's average length.

If the number of processes is not large, then the determination of dispatch time requires an iterative calculation, as described in Appendix 6. To avoid this complex calculation, a useful approximation is to simply ignore the impact of a process on the processor's dispatch queue when calculating its dispatch time. This approximation is evaluated in Appendix 6.

In order to calculate dispatch time, the performance analyst must be able to estimate the dispatch rate and average process time per dispatch for each priority level. He must also have a feel for the overhead imposed by the operating system.

Priority

A process is affected by higher priority processes, since these steal processing capacity from all lower priorities. It is affected by processes at its own priority, since it must compete with these processes for CPU time. It may also be affected by lower priority processes if it is running with a nonpreemptive scheduler, as it may have to wait for a lower priority process to complete before it can be given the CPU.

The effects due to processes at the same priority and at lower priorities are dispatching problems and are covered in the previous section and in chapter 6 under "Task Dispatching."

Higher priority tasks not only slow down dispatching, as described previously, but also slow down the process itself if the scheduler is preemptive. This effect is taken into account in the queuing model for preemptive priority systems given in chapter 4 (the

M/M/1/∞/∞/PP model) and in the above example. In effect, the task processing time is increased by $1/(1 - L_h)$, where L_h is the load imposed by higher priority tasks.

Note that this is true only for preemptive schedulers. A nonpreemptive scheduler will cause a delay in the dispatching of a process if a lower priority process is currently running, since higher priority requests will not interrupt a process once it is scheduled. A process waiting in a processor queue must wait for the processing of all processes of equal priority that arrived earlier. It must also wait for all higher priority processes to be processed, regardless of when they come in. This latter delay takes the same amount of time regardless of whether the execution of lower priority processes is or is not interrupted by higher priority processes.

However, once given the processor, a process will not be interrupted by higher priority processes if dispatching is nonpreemptive. It will be affected only by operating system overhead.

Thus, for nonpreemptive dispatching, equations 8-6 and 8-2 become, respectively,

$$t_d = \frac{L_t}{1 - L_o - L_h - L_p} \cdot \frac{t'_p}{1 - L_o - L_h} \tag{8-7a}$$

$$t_s = t_d + \frac{t_p}{1 - L_o} \tag{8-7b}$$

L_t is the total processor load.

Operating System Load

Like process times, the operating system load is often not a subject of the performance analysis unless it is the operating system itself that is being analyzed. Rather, this load is an input parameter to the model (or in some cases is ignored as being small). Typical operating system loads are 5 to 20 percent in contemporary systems.

Note that this load does not include interprocess message time, which is handled explicitly, or process switching times, which should be bundled in with the process time (this is typically one to ten milliseconds unless powerful hardware support is provided). Operating system load does include interrupt handling, timer-list management, and fault-recovery provisions.

As TP systems get more complex, and as operating systems do more and more for us, one point to make is that the operating system overhead continues to grow with each new product. Let's keep an eye on this factor.

Messaging

In order for a TP application to be structured as a set of cooperating processes, the system must provide a mechanism for passing messages between processes. Various types of messaging mechanisms are discussed in chapter 6 in the section entitled "Interprocess Messaging."

These messaging mechanisms are generally implemented in one of three ways:

1. *Common memory,* used often for mailboxes that allow one processor to place a message in the mailbox and then to set an event that will notify the receiving process that it has a message. Common memory messaging techniques are applicable only to single computer or multiprocessor architectures in which all processes have access to a common memory.

2. *Message system,* in which a special operating system facility is provided to accept a message from a sending process and to route it to the input queue of a receiving process. This messaging mechanism is applicable not only to multicomputer systems but also to networks of multicomputer systems, since the message can be sent over the network.

3. *File system,* in which message queues are implemented as files and in which advantage is taken of disk cache to keep messages memory-resident. In this scheme, a receiving process will open a file that it designates as an input queue. Other processes open this file and insert messages for the receiving process. A special event facility is provided to alert the receiving process that a message is available. This technique is also available to networked multicomputer systems if the appropriate degree of transparency has been provided. This technique has the advantage of writing a queue to disk (via the normal disk cache flushing function) if a queue gets too long or is inactive.

All messaging systems usually provide a response facility so that a response may be made to a message. A notable exception is the UNIX pipe, which is a one-way-only message facility.

In general, common memory message systems are the fastest, and file system message systems are the slowest. Typical request/reply times for today's systems are as follows:

TABLE 8-1. TYPICAL MESSAGE TIMES

Message facility type	Request/reply CPU time (msec.)
Common memory	0.1 — 1
Message system	1 — 10
File system	10 — 100

Queuing

Given the effects of process time, dispatch time, priorities, operating system loads, and interprocess messaging, a process's service time is calculated as described in the section "Overview" and given by equation 8-2 for preemptive scheduling or by equation 8-7b for nonpreemptive scheduling. Depending on the system, interprocess message time may be includable in the process service time. This was assumed not to be the case in the example given in the Overview above.

Knowing the process service time, we can now calculate the queuing delay of messages waiting for this process and therefore the total message delay time as it passes through this process. Usually, messages can be assumed to arrive randomly from a large number of users (or at least via tandem queues that are fed by a large number of users—see chapter 4 under ''Some Properties of Infinite Populations—Tandem Queues''). It is also usually appropriate to characterize the process time, t_p, as being random. Thus, the M/M/1 queuing model is generally appropriate.

Other queuing models might be appropriate in special situations, as shown in Table 8-2. May all your models be M/M/1!

TABLE 8-2.   APPLICABLE QUEUE MODELS

Process characteristics	Queue model
Random arrivals, random service times	M/M/1
Random arrivals, constant service times	M/D/1
Random arrivals, uniformly distributed service times	M/U/1
Limited population, random service times	M/M/1/m/m
Random arrivals, process is one of many serving a common queue	M/M/c or M/G/c
Random arrivals, limited population, process is one of many serving a common queue	M/M/c/m/m

PROCESS STRUCTURES

A TP application can be implemented in a myriad of ways, from a single, large monolithic process to a complex set of independent cooperating processes. While it is not the purpose of this book to discuss issues in the design of TP systems, the structure of these systems is important for performance analysis; it helps to understand why one structure has advantages over another.

We will, in fact, be dealing primarily with the requestor-server model and its variants. This model was discussed in chapter 2 (under ''Software Architecture—Requestor-Server'') and was used as an example in chapter 3.

Monoliths

We will first dispatch *monolithic structures*. A TP application can be written as one large monolithic program. This program would handle all communications and all data-base activity required by each type of transaction submitted to the system.

Such a structure has a lot of problems—it certainly flies in the face of all we hold dear in the modern theories of software architecture—in that it is hardly modular. Some of the problems one faces with such a structure include the following:

- The application will be very difficult to maintain, whether maintenance involves bug fixing or functional enhancements.
- There is little capability to tune the system to achieve better performance.
- The monolithic structure does not lend itself to a distributed architecture. Consequently, the application cannot grow in volume by adding additional computing elements.
- It is very difficult to add new transaction types.

Requestor-Server

In contrast, a TP application built as a set of *requestors* passing transactions to a set of *servers* is a model of modularity. Since each program is small, it is easy to maintain. The system has immense tuning opportunities, especially in a distributed environment, by moving processes to less loaded computing elements, by adjusting the number of servers, and by sizing the requestors to each handle an optimum number of users.

A generalized requestor-server model is shown in Figure 8-2. Here we see that each user is served by a requestor process. A requestor process can usually service multiple users though its set of users is fixed.

Requestors pass transactions received from their users to an appropriate server for processing. There is typically one server type for each type of transaction. If a transaction represents a significant volume, there could be multiple servers of that type created that would share the transaction load. We will call this set of like servers a *server class*.

The servers send file requests to the file managers, which control disk activity.

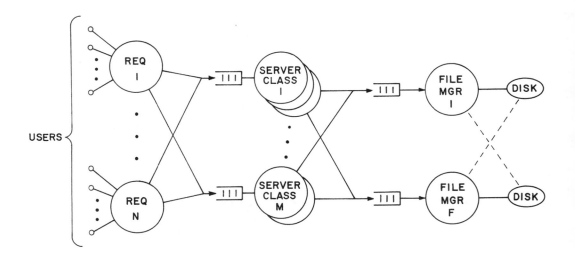

Figure 8-2   Requestor-server model.

There could be one file manager per disk volume, one per multiple disk volumes, or multiple file managers per disk volume, as discussed in chapter 7.

Each of these process types has different characteristics, as will now be described.

Requestors.   Since a *requestor* must service a set of users, each of whom may be active simultaneously with the others, it must be a multithreaded process, i.e., it must be able to handle several concurrent transactions. In effect, a requestor must have embedded in it a sort of minioperating system that will perform multitasking within the process. Every time it is given control of the processor, it should satisfy all outstanding processing for all of its users before it releases the processor. Multitasking within a process is further discussed below.

The requestors are often designed to service a particular type of user, with different requestors being provided for different classes of users. For instance, there might be a requestor type that services users directly connected by asynchronous lines, another requestor type to service users on a multidropped channel, and still another requestor type that will service users communicating over X.25 links. As many requestors of each type as necessary are provided to service the user community.

The responsibilities of the requestor include the following:

- Providing the protocol support required by the user in order to reliably transfer messages back and forth (though this is sometimes the function of the communication driver or even an intelligent communications controller or modem).

- Editing and validating messages received from the user and obtaining corrected data when necessary.

- Recognizing the type of transaction received from the user and sending it to the message queue of an appropriate server class, which will process this transaction.

- Returning replies received from the servers to the appropriate terminal.

- Saving the context of a transaction that may involve several messages and inserting contextual information when required.

The problem of context saving has been described earlier. To repeat it, consider the case of several alike servers within a class that cooperate to process one type of transaction. This transaction may be quite complex and may require several interactions with the user to complete. Each such interaction involves a message from, and a reply returned to, the user.

Now suppose that the actions to be taken on one message depend upon the contents or results of previous messages. The server that is to process this message needs to know the pertinent information that was contained in earlier messages or replies. However, it may not be the same server that processed these earlier messages, as each message is routed independently to a server based usually on some load-balancing algorithm. Therefore, the server must be given this information when it receives the new message. This information is called the *context* of the transaction; it is the context within which the message is to be evaluated.

If the server cannot hold the context of the message, something must. In some systems, the terminal is intelligent enough to save its own context. However, additional communication loading would be incurred, as this information is repetitively transmitted with each transaction. Furthermore, we must design the system to handle a broad range of terminals, many of which may not have this sort of intelligent capability.

The obvious choice, then, is the requestor. As messages carrying contextual data which must be saved pass through the requestor, the requestor is responsible for saving that data in a data area dedicated to that user. As any message subsequently passes through that requires some of this contextual data, the requestor must insert this data into that message.

One potential problem with this approach is that the context storage area is multiplied by the number of users supported by the requestor. If we are not careful, the size of the combined context area could exceed the data space limitations of the requestor, and this context area would then have to be written to a disk file. This additional disk activity could cause severe performance degradation.

Servers. Each *server* is typically designed to handle one type of transaction or perhaps a small number of alike transactions. A server is usually single-threaded; it accepts a message from its message queue, processes it—including all file accesses that are required—formulates a reply, and returns the reply to the appropriate requestor. Only then does it read the next message from its queue in order to process it.

As discussed above, a server is context-free. It must be given all the information needed to process a request in the request message. Once it returns a reply to that request, it has no further memory of that request.

Since a server is single-threaded, it has a limited capacity and could become a bottleneck. To avoid this, several alike servers can be spawned to share the load of a particular transaction type. Servers within a class could be started up at system generation time, in which case the number of servers in a class is fixed. As an alternative, servers could be spawned and killed dynamically to account for load variations. Such dynamic servers are discussed later.

When there are multiple servers in a class, different systems feed them in different ways, as shown in Figure 8-3. In some systems, each server within a class has its own queue, as shown in Figure 8-3a. A requestor sends its request to a server based on some load-balancing algorithm, typically to the server with the shortest queue, or instead on a round-robin basis. If the load on a server class of size S is L, then each server is working from an M/M/1 queue and is carrying a load of L/S.

In other systems, all servers work off of a common queue, as shown in Figure 8-3b. This is, of course, the more efficient technique. The queue in this case can be characterized by the M/M/c model, where $c = S$, the number of servers.

One problem not mentioned yet with regard to servers is data locking. In many systems, a data lock on a data base is owned by a process; only that process may remove the lock. Thus, if a server is to lock a file while an operator views some data with the

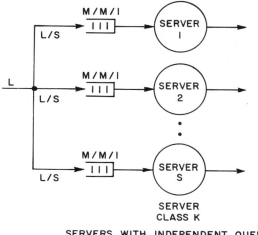

SERVERS WITH INDEPENDENT QUEUES
(**a**)

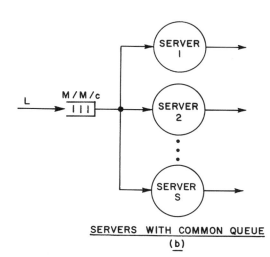

SERVERS WITH COMMON QUEUE
(**b**)

Figure 8-3 Feeding a server class.

potential to update it, that same server must do the update so that it can unlock the file. But we cannot guarantee that the same server will be the one to process that update. If another server receives the update message, it will not be able to remove the lock.

One solution to this dilemma is to design transactions so that all locks are placed and removed during the processing of a single message. This may not always be possible. Another solution is to create a separate locking process that responds to server requests to place and remove locks. Since such a process would own all locks, it could remove them. This approach is complex (and a potential bottleneck).

In other systems this is solved by vesting ownership of the lock with the transaction. Each transaction is given a unique ID, and this ID is carried with each message and with each lock. In this way, any server can unlock a data element locked by another server by simply providing the transaction ID.

File managers.   The *file manager* has been discussed in detail in chapter 7. To review its characteristics, it is responsible for receiving and executing file system requests. These typically include opening and closing of files, reading and writing of records, and maintaining data locks.

The file manager can be organized in a variety of ways (see Figure 7-5):

- There can be one file manager for the system; it handles all requests for all disk volumes. In this case, the file manager can become a significant bottleneck.
- There can be one file manager per disk volume. This relieves the file system bottleneck to the extent that there are multiple disk volumes. As with a single file manager, the disk volumes will be underutilized, since they lie idle while the file manager is processing a request. This underutilization may be in the order of 50 percent.
- There can be multiple file managers per disk volume. This can improve disk utilization significantly and therefore can further reduce the file system bottleneck.

Only in the last case will there be a queue provided for each disk volume (not shown in Figure 8-2). Since the first two architectures result in each disk volume being driven by a single file manager, no queue will build at the disk volume itself.

Multitasking

A process can be single-threaded, as are the servers in a requestor-server environment. In this case, concurrency can be achieved by creating several alike processes. If n similar processes are created, then they can process n tasks simultaneously. This is multitasking at the system level. Multiple tasks (in this case, processes) are created and managed by the operating system.

It is one thing to create 3 or 4 server tasks to provide concurrent processing for a transaction type. It is quite another thing to create 1000 processes, each to act as a requestor for a user. This is because each process imposes its own overhead, both in terms of memory space (process control blocks, file control blocks, etc.) and in terms of time for process switching. The management of a large number of processes can impose a significant overhead on a TP system. Note that code and data space requirements are basically the same whether we have many processes at one per user or one process per many users, since the code is shared and the data areas have to be separate anyway. It is the ancillary memory and time requirements that become a problem, but typically only for a large number of processes.

Therefore, it is advantageous to be able to create a process that is multitasking within itself. Such a process is multithreaded and can handle several concurrent tasks, such as the handling of multiple terminals or communication lines by the requestors in the requestor-server model. Such a process has embedded in it the elements of an operating system so that it can switch between tasks and perhaps even manage its own memory space. However, being a small version of the big guy, it imposes a comparatively smaller overhead on the system.

In a process, there are two fundamental techniques for multitasking, which are similar to the two major techniques for achieving multitasking in any operating system. One is scanning, or time sharing in the classic sense. With this technique, the tasks are serviced in round-robin fashion until the process makes a complete cycle through all the tasks and finds them idle. At this time, the process can relinquish the CPU.

The other technique is to build an event-driven process. This is, of course, equivalent to modern operating systems. With this technique, events affecting a task controlled by a process are received and queued by that process. An event might be the completion of a terminal I/O or disk I/O or the receipt of a message or a message reply. The process will work through its event queue, performing task processing as required, until it has exhausted the queue, at which point it will relinquish the CPU. It will be rescheduled by the operating system when another event is directed to that process.

Some TP systems provide one or the other of these multitasking options as part of their environment. In other systems, multitasking is a grow-your-own project. From a performance viewpoint, an event-driven multitasking process is very efficient, and its overhead often is not considered to be significant in the performance analysis. This overhead is simply taken into account in the process time (and is usually buried in the estimation error for task time anyway). If it is to be analyzed, its analysis follows the techniques already considered.

However, scanning overhead for a time-sharing multitasking process can be significant. This can be analyzed as follows.
Let

t_t = time to process an event for a task.

t_{sw} = time to switch tasks.

t_i = time to determine that an idle task needs no processing.

t_{cy} = scanner cycle time, i.e., time to cycle once through all tasks.

R_e = rate of events arriving at the process.

n_t = number of tasks serviced by this process.

Let us also assume that the event rate for a particular task is such that the arrival of more than one event per task during a cycle time t_{cy} is unlikely. Then, during a complete cycle through all tasks, which requires a time t_{cy}, there will be:

n_t task switches requiring a time of $n_t t_{sw}$.

$R_e t_{cy}$ events arriving in time to be processed, requiring a time of $R_e t_{cy} t_t$.

$(n_t - R_e t_{cy})$ tasks that are found idle, requiring a processing time of $(n_t - R_e t_{cy}) t_i$.

Thus,

$$t_{cy} = n_t t_{sw} + R_e t_{cy} t_t + (n_t - R_e t_{cy}) t_i$$

This can be solved for the cycle time t_{cy}:

$$t_{cy} = \frac{n_t(t_i + t_{sw})}{1 - R_e(t_t - t_i)}, \; t_{cy} \le n_t(t_t + t_{sw}) \tag{8-8}$$

That is, the scanner cycle time is the idle cycle time divided by 1 minus the incremental processing load per cycle. Incremental processing load is that time required to process an event over and above the idle processing time.

Note that the cycle time cannot exceed a task process plus a task switch time $(t_t + t_{sw})$ for each of the n_t tasks, since it was assumed that no more than one event per task would be processed. Thus, equation 8-5 is valid only for cycle time $t_{cy} \le n_t(t_t + t_{sw})$.

Note also that the cycle time increases as the number of tasks increases. It also increases as the transaction rate increases unless the task processing time, t_t, equals the idle processing time, t_i. In this case, it makes no difference whether an event has occurred or not for a task—the processing time is the same.

Assuming that the arrival of events to the process are random, then the probability of zero events occurring in a cycle time $P_o(t_{cy})$ is given by the Poisson distribution and is from equation 4-59:

$$P_o(t_{cy}) = e^{-R_e t_{cy}} \tag{8-9}$$

Thus, with probability 1, the process will scan through all tasks the first time. It will make a second scan if one or more events have arrived during the first scan, which will occur with probability $(1 - e^{-R_e t_{cy}})$. Likewise, the probability that it will make a third scan is the probability that it had to make a second scan and that an event arrived during that scan. Thus, the probability of a third scan is $(1 - e^{-R_e t_{cy}})^2$. And so on.

The average number of scans that the scanner must make, n_s, is

$$n_s = 1 + (1 - e^{-R_e t_{cy}}) + (1 - e^{-R_e t_{cy}})^2 + \ldots$$

or from equation 4-46

$$n_s = \frac{1}{1 - (1 - e^{-R_e t_{cy}})} = e^{R_e t_{cy}} \tag{8-10}$$

and the process will have control of the CPU for a period, t_p, of

$$t_p = n_s t_{cy} \tag{8-11}$$

Once the process releases the processor, it will be dormant until another event arrives. Since event arrivals are assumed to be random, the process will be dormant for a time $1/R_e$. Now let us define

T_{cy} = the process cycle time, i.e., the time between the invocations of the scanner process.

L_p = CPU load imposed by the scanner process.

e_p = processing efficiency of the scanner process.

The process will be invoked every

$$T_{cy} = n_s t_{cy} + 1/R_e \tag{8-12}$$

seconds. During this time, it will process $R_e T_{cy}$ events using $n_s t_{cy}$ of CPU time. Thus, the load imposed upon the processor is

$$L_p = \frac{n_s t_{cy}}{T_{cy}}$$

or, from equation 8-12,

$$L_p = \frac{R_e n_s t_{cy}}{R_e n_s t_{cy} + 1} \tag{8-13}$$

In order to process $R_e T_{cy}$ events, it will expend a useful processing time of $R_e T_{cy} t_t$ while expending an actual processing time of $n_s t_{cy}$. Thus, the efficiency, e_p, of the process, taken as the ratio of useful to actual processing time, is

$$e_p = \frac{R_e T_{cy} t_t}{n_s t_{cy}} = \frac{R_e t_t}{n_s t_{cy}} \ (n_s t_{cy} + 1/R_e)$$

or

$$e_p = R_e t_t / L_p \tag{8-14}$$

t_{cy} and n_s are given by equations 8-8 and 8-10.

An example will help to put scanner times and efficiency into perspective. Let us assume that a requestor process using scanning has the following typical parameters:

Task switching time (t_{sw}) = 1 msec.

Idle processing time (t_i) = 1 msec.

Event processing time (t_t) = 10 msec.

Number of tasks (n_t) = 32

This requestor will control 32 terminals. Let us assume that a user at a terminal is entering requests at an average of once every 10 seconds. As he enters a request, certain fields are sent on-the-fly to the requestor for verification. When the request is released, the requestor sends it, if valid, to a server and then returns a reply. Assume 4 fields are sent for validation so that the requestor must handle 6 events per transaction (4 fields, the final request, and the reply from the server). Thus, the event rate, R_e, is

$$R_e = 6 \times 32/10 = 19.2 \text{ events/sec.}$$

From equation 8-8, the cycle time, t_{cy}, for the scanner is

$$t_{cy} = 77 \text{ msec.}$$

That is, the requestor takes an average of 77 msec. to pass through all tasks that arrive during one scan cycle.

From equation 8-10, the average number of cycles that the requestor will make before finding all tasks idle is

$$n_s = e^{(19.2)(.077)} = 4.4$$

Therefore, on the average, the requestor will remain active for $n_s t_{cy} = (4.4)(77) = 339$ msec. and then will go dormant for $1/R_e = 1/19.2 = 52$ msec. During this time it will process $R_e(n_s t_{cy} + 1/R_e) = 19.2(.339 + .052) = 7.5$ messages and will do useful processing of $(7.5)(10) = 75$ msec. Thus, its efficiency, e_p, is $75/339 = .22$. This is the same result we would obtain from equation 8-14.

The load, L_p, imposed on the CPU is $339/(339 + 52) = .87$, which is the result that would be obtained from equation 8-13.

In order to be efficient, a scanner must be kept busy, which means that it must impose a heavy load on the CPU. Scanners (and event-driven requestors, too) can seize the CPU for long periods of time. For this reason, requestors are often designed to relinquish the CPU if more than a certain amount of time (or scanner cycles) has elapsed.

Dynamic Servers

We have previously discussed the concept of dynamic servers, in which the number of servers in a class is adjusted to compensate for the load being imposed on those servers. As the load increases, more servers are spawned. As the load decreases, unnecessary servers are killed. Of course, one server must always remain, even during idle times.

It is useful to be able to predict the number of servers that will exist under a given load condition. This depends upon the algorithm used to spawn and kill servers.

Suppose that we have a TP system in which each server has its own queue (as in Figure 8-3a). Requests are passed to each server on a round-robin basis. If the queue of any server exceeds a length of n, we will spawn a new server. If the length of any queue goes to zero, i.e., the server is idle, we will kill a server. Of course, there should be some time delays to ensure that we do not spawn and kill servers at a rapid rate to accommodate short term fluctuations. Assuming that queue arrivals and server service times are random, the probability that a server will find its queue exceeding n items is (from equation 4-83)

$$P(Q > n) = (L/S)^{n+1}$$

where

L = total average load on the server class.

S = number of servers.

and L/S is the average load on each server.

The probability that a server will find its queue empty is

$$P(Q = 0) = 1 - L/S$$

The steady state is achieved when these two probabilities are equal; that is, in a steady-state condition, during any reasonable observation interval we would want to spawn a process as often as we would want to kill one.

Thus, under a given transaction load, L, the number of servers that will exist is S, where S satisfies the expression

$$(L/S)^{n+1} = 1 - L/S \tag{8-15}$$

By manipulating this equation, we obtain

$$S^n(S - L) = L^{n+1} \tag{8-16}$$

This expression is evaluated in the following table for various values of L and n, giving the minumum number of servers required to satisfy equation 8-16. For good performance, we normally don't want to see queue lengths longer than 2 or 3. The table shows allowable queue lengths of 2 to 4.

TABLE 8-3a.   NUMBER OF DYNAMIC SERVERS (S)

Load (L)	Allowable queue length (n)		
	2	3	4
0	1	1	1
.5	1	1	1
1	2	2	2
2	3	3	3
3	5	5	4
4	6	6	6
5	8	7	7
10	15	14	14

Another way to consider the dynamic server case is to use the server load that will be maintained by the system on each server in order to control its queue size. From equation 8-15, the following table can be constructed:

TABLE 8-3b.   DYNAMIC SERVER LOAD

	Allowable queue length (n)			
	1	2	3	4
Server Load (L/S)	.62	.68	.73	.76

Note from Table 8-3a that over this wide range, there is never much difference in the number of servers required to maintain a queue of four or a queue of two. Therefore, there is little reason to choose higher queue lengths—at least in this example.

If the servers were fed from a common queue, the same concept would hold, except that the probability of queue lengths would be given by equations 4-93 to 4-95 for the M/M/c model. These equations, of course, would require computer-aided evaluation.

Asynchronous I/O

One other technique used in process design to speed up the system is the use of *asynchronous I/O*. Usually, when a single-threaded process makes an I/O request, it will then pause and wait for the result. Servers are generally designed that way, for instance. Since the process is synchronized with its I/O requests, we will call this synchronous I/O.

With asynchronous I/O, a process can issue an I/O request and then continue on and perhaps issue even more I/O requests. As a result, it can have several communication or disk requests pending while it continues processing. It can check periodically for the completion status of each request and carry on its processing, or it can pause if it must wait for one or more requests to complete. It will then be awakened by the operating system when a request has completed.

Asynchronous I/O can speed up the processing of a complex transaction significantly. The exact amount of performance improvement is usually difficult to evaluate, but the following heuristic argument provides a reasonable approach.

It will be argued that the total processing time of a process using asynchronous I/O for disk servicing is determined by the longest of the disk or processing times (here, disk servicing is used as just one example of I/O service). In addition, one must consider an initial disk read to "prime the pump" and a final disk write to complete processing. This is shown for two cases in Figure 8-4—when processing is the dominant time and when disk is the dominant time.

In both cases, an initial disk read time, t_r, is shown, as well as a final disk write time, t_w. In an actual case, either or both may not be required. Figure 8-4 should be considered to represent the general case.

With respect to Figure 8-4a, it is clear that the time required is the processing time, t_p, plus the initial and final disk accesses when processing time is predominant. When disk time is predominant (Figure 8-4b), then the time required is the disk time.

Thus, if t_t is the time required for the process to finish its task, and if t_p is the processing time, and if t_d is the disk time exclusive of the first read and last write, one can express this relation as

$$t_t = t_r + t_w + \max(t_d, t_p) \tag{8-17}$$

which states that the task time is the sum of the initial read and final write plus the processing or intermediate disk time, whichever is greater.

A queuing point occurs because of asynchronous I/O which has not been considered; that is, disk completions can queue for a process that has issued multiple disk requests and that is busy when these requests complete. That this does not increase the task time as a first approximation can be seen from Figure 8-4 and the following arguments:

- If processing time is predominant (Figure 8-4a), then the task time is dependent upon the processing time. The fact that disk completions are queued and waiting

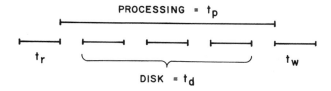

PROCESSING PREDOMINANT
(a)

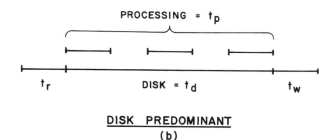

DISK   PREDOMINANT
(b)

Figure 8-4   Asynchronous I/O.

for the process will not add to the overall processing time and thus will not add to the task time.

- If disk time is predominant, it means that to a first approximation the process is available to process each disk completion as it occurs. Thus, queues of completions will not build up.

The above analysis is equally applicable to asynchronous I/O on communication lines. Simply replace disk time with communication time.

Asynchronous I/O is most effective at high loads when both disk and processor are quite busy. It can be ineffective at low loads since the system is idle and since there is insufficient activity to support overlapped disk and processor functions. In this case, the task time, t_t, would be the sum of all processing components. In actual practice, the result would lie somewhere between. Since we are more interested in loaded TP systems, we can assume that overlapped I/O is generally effective.

AN EXAMPLE

As an example of modeling an application environment, we will look at an adaptation of what is known as the ET1 benchmark. This is becoming an industry standard to measure the performance of TP systems and is described in Anon.[1].

This benchmark models a banking application. It considers a teller transaction that must update a customer account file, a teller file, and a branch file and then write an audit record to a history file. Each of the three updated files is accessed by key, but no key files need be updated.

The teller request message is a 100-byte message with a 100-byte reply. Ten thousand teller terminals are connected to the system via an X.25 network. Each teller generates one transaction every 100 seconds. To support 10,000 tellers generating 6,000 transactions per minute, the system size is significant indeed.

We define the capacity of this benchmark system as that load which will result in an average response time of two seconds.

The file characteristics and their access activity are given in Table 8-4. Note that only the history file is mirrored. All other files are protected via a transaction protection mechanism, which will not be modeled here. This will be discussed in chapter 9 as part of the discussion of fault tolerance.

TABLE 8-4.   ET1 BENCHMARK PARAMETERS

File	Record size (bytes)	File size (records)	File organization	File access
Branch	100	1,000	Keyed	Update
Teller	100	10,000	Keyed	Update
Customer	100	10,000,000	Keyed	Update
History	50	90 Days	Mirrored sequential	Write

Our system is a multicomputer system built according to the requestor-server model, as shown in Figure 8-5. Requestors are event-driven, handling up to 32 terminals each. Servers are dynamically allocated, with independent queues and a maximum queue length of 3.

The system is configured as an expandable multicomputer system of P identical modules. There are P computers and D disk units, organized so that each computer has D/P disk units. Each disk volume is driven by one file manager and has 1.5 megabytes of cache memory available to it. One disk volume is mirrored for the history file. The other files are partitioned among all disks to achieve uniform disk loading.

The purpose of this example is to illustrate the modeling of an application environment. Therefore, we will define the response time as the time from the arrival of the last byte of the request to the transmission of the first byte of the reply. In this way, we can ignore the communication network.

However, the file characteristics are important (and, in fact, dominant) in the performance of this system. We will now evaluate them in the context of chapter 7.

Let us first look at the size of the files and their key structures to obtain a feeling for disk cache effectiveness. First of all, we will assume that files are not index sequential; therefore, each is supported with a separate key file. Since key files are not to be updated in this application, we can assume that the slack factor for these files is 1. From Table 8-4

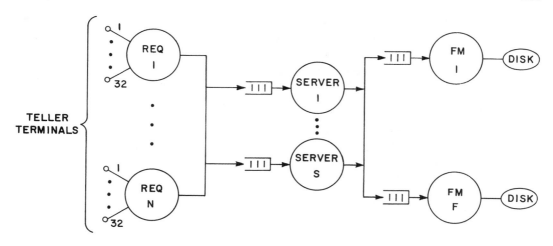

Figure 8-5   ETI requestor-server model.

and equation 7-19, we can determine the file sizes and B-tree levels for each file; these are
given in Table 8-5. To do this, we must make an assumption about key size and sector
size. For purposes of this model, we assume that a key record requires 15 bytes and that
the sector size is 1,024 bytes. Thus, a sector will hold 68 key records, 10 data records for
an update file, and 20 records for the history file.

TABLE 8-5.   ET1 BENCHMARK KEYED FILES

File	File size (bytes)	B-Tree levels	B-tree Level sizes (bytes) root	next	next	Key file size (bytes)
Branch	100K	1	1K			15K
Teller	1M	2	1K	3K		148K
Customer	1G	3	1K	32K	2,163K	147,059K

In Table 8-5, K is kilobytes (a sector size), M is megabytes, and G is gigabytes.
Since we have 1.5 megabytes of cache, we can deduce the following about cache effectiveness:

- The branch file is hit frequently, and both its key file and data file will probably
  always be in cache. This will consume 116K of cache.

- The key file for the teller file will probably always be in cache (it requires 152K), but the teller data record has a lower probability of being found in cache. We will assume that teller data records must be read from disk.
- The first two levels of the customer B-tree (33K) should always be in cache. We will assume that the lowest level of the B-tree, the key record, and the data record will be read from disk.

We will also assume that a record that has been read at the beginning of a transaction will still be in cache when we come to update it. That is, it will have a longevity rate of at least 100 seconds. This assumption will be checked later when we have determined what transaction rate each disk will support. For now, the cache usage that we have assumed is

Branch file	116K
Teller file	$(152 + 100R_{td})$K
Customer file	$(\ 33 + 300R_{td})$K
Cache usage	$(301 + 400R_{td})$K

where R_{td} is the transaction rate per disk. The R_{td} factors account for one teller sector and three customer account sectors being read from disk and surviving in cache for at least 100 seconds. Note that this condition is satisfied if

$$301 + 400R_{td} \leq 1{,}500 \ 1\text{K cache blocks}$$

or if

$$R_{td} \leq 3 \text{ transactions/second} \tag{8-18}$$

The satisfaction of this relation guarantees that a single 1.5 megabyte cache will suffice for each file manager.

Next, using the typical file management times suggested in chapter 7 (and adding one for sequential writes), we can construct the following table for file activity:

TABLE 8-6. ET1 BENCHMARK FILE ACTIVITY

File operation	B-Tree levels	Reads (n_{dir}) Cache	Disk	Writes (n_{diw}) Cache	Disk	F.M. Time (t_{fmi}) (msec.)	p_i
Read branch	1	3				20	1/7
Read teller	2	3	1			20	1/7
Read customer	3	2	3			20	1/7
Write branch	1	2		1		30	1/7
Write teller	2	3			1	30	1/7
Write customer	3	4			1	30	1/7
Write history	0			.95	.05	30	1/7
		17	4	1.95	2.05		

The history file is shown as requiring 1 disk-write to cache 95 percent of the time. This is because it is a sequential 50-byte write so that 20 records will fit in a sector. Thus, a sector need be written only once per 20 records.

Though the write to the teller and customer record will find that sector in cache according to our assumptions, the updated record must eventually be physically written to disk, as we assume that the record will not survive in cache until it is once again updated. Therefore, a disk write is shown for these two cases.

From the preceding table, we have 25 disk accesses per transaction, 18.95 of which are cached. Thus, our cache-hit ratio is .76, and the cache-miss ratio, p_d, is .24. (In this simple example we can calculate cache activity. Usually, this is not possible, and a reasonable value for p_d must be assumed.)

We can now calculate the values for file management time for each operation. These values are also based on suggested parameter values used in chapter 7, which are the following:

t_{da} = average disk access time = 28 msec.

t_{dr} = disk rotational time = 17 msec.

f_i = file manager service time ratio for cache hits = 0.5 for all i.

We must also increase t_{da} by 40 percent of the average seek time ($.4 \times 20 = 8$ msec.) to account for file mirroring when calculating history file management time (see Appendix 5). Rather than using equation 7-1, which assumes that we cannot enumerate cache hits and therefore have to assume a cache miss ratio, we can, in this simpler example, calculate file management times directly, using our knowledge from chapter 7. These results are given in Table 8-7, with the following computational notes:

- Reading a customer record involves reading a B-tree plus a key record and then a data record. The first two reads are similar to the read of a primary key and data record from an indexed sequential file; they typically require one full access plus a latency time, or $28 + 8 = 36$ msec. The data record requires another full access of 28 msec.

- Writing the customer record is a standard write access of 28 msec., since the key record and data record are assumed to still be in cache.

- By the same arguments, the read and write of the teller record are also each a single access.

- The history file requires $(28 + 8)/20 = 2$ msec. of disk time to write a block, averaged over the 20 records required to fill a sector.

- The following file manager CPU times are assumed if the data record is not in cache:

Keyed read	20 msec.
Keyed write	30 msec.
Sequential write	30 msec.

Since $f_i = 0.5$, these times will be cut in half if the data record is found in cache.

TABLE 8-7.   ET1 BENCHMARK FILE MANAGEMENT TIME

File operation	File manager CPU time $(f_i t_{fmi} -$msec.$)$	Disk time (msec.)	Total file manager time (msec.)
Read branch	10	—	10
Read teller	20	28	48
Read customer	20	64	84
Write branch	15	—	15
Write teller	30	28	58
Write customer	30	28	58
Write history	15	2	17
	140	150	290

From this analysis, each of the 7 file accesses requires an average file management time of 41.4 msec. Of this, 20 msec. is CPU time, and 21.4 msec. is disk time. Note that the physical utilization of the disk cannot exceed 52 percent (21.4/41.4). This is a clear case of the value of having a second file manager using each disk.

We can now return to our assumption concerning cache longevity, as quantified by equation 8-18. From Table 8-7, the total file management time per transaction is 290 msec. This gives a maximum transaction rate supportable by 1 disk of $1/.290 = 3.4$ transactions per second. Assuming that we will keep our disk loads less than 70 percent (which any good designer will do), the capacity per disk is $(.7)(3.4) = 2.4$ transactions per second. This is within the range specified by equation 8-18. Coupled with the facts that the transaction would probably be completed in less than 100 seconds (in fact, almost instantly in this benchmark case, since there is no intervening operator time between the read and update) and that we should have some other cache activity (especially on the teller file), our assumption of cache effectiveness appears quite secure.

Now that we have characterized the file system, let us turn our attention to the application. Figure 8-6 presents a traffic model for the ET1 benchmark. A request is received by the communication handler (1) and is passed to a requestor (2). The requestor validates the request and then sends it via an interprocess message to a server queue (3). Eventually, the server (4) will process the request; in doing so, it will issue seven file requests to the file manager (6) via its queue (5), each through an interprocess message. The file manager will access its disk (7) as required, returning each response to the server (8). Upon completion of the transaction, the server will return a reply to the requestor (9), which will pass the reply via the communication handler (10) to the terminal. The request to the server and its reply to the requestor are assumed to be carried by the same interprocess message, a WRITEREAD. Therefore, no outbound requestor queue is shown. (There will be one, but it is small and is ignored.) Communication between the communication handler and its associated requestor is assumed to be via common memory mailbox messages. This time can be ignored.

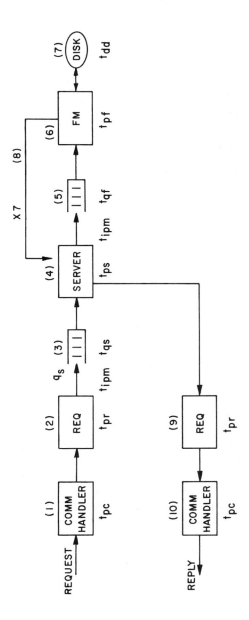

Figure 8-6   ETI traffic model.

The following times are defined in the traffic model:

q_s = maximum server queue length.
t_{ipm} = interprocess message time.
t_{pc} = communication handler time per message.
t_{pr} = requestor time per message.
t_{qs} = server queue time per transaction.
t_{ps} = server processing time per transaction.
t_{qf} = file manager queue time per file request.
t_{pf} = file manager processing time per file request.
t_{dd} = disk time per file request.

Except for the queue times that must be calculated, Table 8-8 gives assumed values for these parameters. Most of these parameter values are based on typical values suggested previously in this chapter, except that communication time has been doubled to account for X.25 complexity. File manager time and disk time per file request, t_{pf} and t_{dd}, have been shown above to be 20 msec. and 21.4 msec., respectively.

TABLE 8-8. ET1
BENCHMARK
PROCESSING TIMES

Parameter	Value (msec.)
q_s	3
t_{ipm}	10
t_{pc}	10
t_{pr}	10
t_{ps}	35
t_{pf}	20
t_{dd}	21.4

Referring again to Figure 8-6, we can also express the response time, T_r, to a transaction. It is composed of the processing times of all the processes plus queue waiting times. Queue waiting times include the file manager queue time, t_{qf}, the server queue time, t_{qs}, and the process dispatch time, t_{dj}, which is the processor queue time that must be added to the process time for each process j. For purposes of this analysis, j has the following values:

c—communication handler.

r—requestor.

s—server.

f—file manager.

Let us break this problem into simpler pieces by defining

$$T_r = \text{transaction response time.}$$

t_f = file management time per file request.

t_s = server transaction service time.

D = number of disks in the system.

S = number of servers in the system.

L_d = disk load.

L_s = server load.

t_{dj} = process dispatch time for process type j.

R_t = transaction rate.

We assume that interprocess message time is incurred by the sending process. Then, working from the top down via Figure 8-6, the response time, T_r, is

$$T_r = 2(t_{pc} + t_{dc}) + 2(t_{pr} + t_{dr}) + t_{ipm} + t_{qs} + t_s \qquad (8\text{-}19)$$

Server time, t_s, is

$$t_s = (t_{ps} + 8t_{ds}) + 7(t_{ipm} + t_{qf} + t_f) \qquad (8\text{-}20)$$

The load on the server, L_s, is

$$L_s = R_t t_s / S \qquad (8\text{-}21)$$

However, this system uses dynamic servers; the number of such servers is adjusted to maintain a maximum queue length of three. This implies that the server load will remain constant at a level given by equation 8-15. Using this relationship, we have

$$L_s^{q_s+1} = 1 - L_s \qquad (8\text{-}22)$$

which, for $q_s = 3$, results in (see Table 8-3b)

$$L_s = .73 \qquad (8\text{-}23)$$

To estimate the average server queue time, we must assume a model. Since this will be a very large system, each server will be fed by a large number of users. Therefore, we can assume an infinite population. However, the service time is made up of the sum of a large number of random service times. These include eight server dispatch times (one for the requestor message and seven for the file manager completions), eight server processing times, seven file manager queue waits, seven file manager dispatch times, seven file manager processing times, and approximately six physical disk times, or 43 service times in all. As we shall see, the resulting service time is hardly random, and the M/G/1 model is therefore applicable.

The mean and variance of the server service time are the sum of the means and variances of its components (see equations 4-32 and 4-33). Consider the simple case in which all service times are equal and random, with a mean of t. If there are n components, then the mean of the sum is nt, the variance of the sum is nt^2, and the server distribution coefficient, k_s, is, from equation 4-16,

$$k_s = \frac{1}{2}\left(1 + \frac{nt^2}{n^2t^2}\right) = \frac{1}{2}\left(1 + \frac{1}{n}\right)$$

As n becomes large, k_s approaches 0.5.

In our benchmark case, the service times are not all equal (in fact, the dispatch and queue times vary with load), but the number is large. A careful calculation will show that k_s is indeed close to 0.5, and we will take it as such. Thus, the average server queue time is

$$t_{qs} = \frac{k_s L_s}{1 - L_s}\, t_s = \frac{0.5 L_s}{1 - L_s}\, t_s \tag{8-24}$$

The file management time per request is

$$t_f = (t_{pf} + t_{df}) + t_{dd} + 6t_{df}/7$$

The final term reflects the fact that every seven file management requests result in six disk accesses (see Table 8-6), requiring an additional dispatch of the file manager. This expression can be rewritten as

$$t_f = t_{pf} + 13t_{df}/7 + t_{dd} \tag{8-25}$$

To determine the file manager queue wait time, the same argument used for the server queue model will justify the use of the M/G/1 model here. The file manager in a large system will be fed by many servers so that arrival times can be considered random from an infinite population. In this case, however, there are only $4\frac{6}{7}$ service times comprising t_f, including 13/7 dispatch times, 13/7 processing times, and 6/7 of a physical disk time. We assume the disk time is uniformly distributed, with an average time of $150/6 = 25$ msec. (see Table 8-7). Therefore, its variance is $1/3(25)^2$ (see the derivation leading to equation 4-17, and remember that the variance is the second moment less the square of the mean). As a conservative simplification, we will ignore dispatch time in the computation of the file manager distribution coefficient, k_f, as it will normally be small compared to t_{pf} and t_{dd} anyway.

Since the average file manager process time per dispatch is $20/(13/7) = 10.77$ msec. and is assumed to be random, then

$$k_f = \frac{1}{2}\left(1 + \frac{(13/7)(10.77)^2 + (6/7)(1/3)(25)^2}{[(13/7)(10.77) + (6/7)(25)]^2} = .61\right)$$

and

$$t_{qf} = \frac{k_f L_f}{1 - L_f}\, t_f = \frac{.61 L_f}{1 - L_f}\, t_f \tag{8-26}$$

Since there are seven file requests per transaction, L_f is

$$L_f = 7R_t t_f/D \tag{8-27}$$

Finally, we evaluate process dispatch times, t_{dj}. Let

$$t_t = \text{processor time per transaction.}$$

Then, from Figure 8-6 and Table 8-8:

$$t_t = 2t_{pc} + 2t_{pr} + t_{ps} + 7t_{pf} + 8t_{ipm} \tag{8-28}$$

or

$$t_t = 295 \text{ msec.} \tag{8-29}$$

The number of process dispatches per transaction can be determined by assuming that a process will be awakened whenever it receives a message or a device completion. In the case of the file manager, disk completions number approximately six according to Table 8-6. Process dispatches are enumerated in Table 8-9.

TABLE 8-9.   ET1 PROCESS DISPATCHES

	Dispatches		
Process	Messages	Completions	Total
Communication handler	2		2
Requestor	2		2
Server	1	7	8
File manager	7	6	13
			25

Thus, the number of process dispatches per transaction, n_p, is

$$n_p = 25 \tag{8-30}$$

The dispatch time for process j is approximated by calculating the processor queue wait time via the M/M/1 model but excluding the effect of the process being considered (see Appendix 6). The average processing time per dispatch for all processes except j, t_j', is

$$t_j' = \frac{t_t - t_j/x_j}{n_p - n_j/x_j} \tag{8-31}$$

where

$t_j' = $ average processing time per dispatch for all processes except process j.

$t_j = $ average processing time per transaction for all processes of type j.

$n_j = $ dispatches per transaction for all processes of type j.

$x_j = $ number of processes of type j (note that $x_s = S$).

We define

P = number of processors in the system.

L_p = total processor load.

L_{pj} = processor load imposed by all processes of type j.

L'_{pj} = processor load imposed by all processes except process j.

The load imposed on the processor by all processes except for process j, L'_{pj}, is

$$L'_{pj} = L_p - L_{pj}/x_j$$

Since

$$L_p = R_t t_t / P \tag{8-32}$$

and

$$L_{pj} = R_t t_j / P = \frac{L_p t_j}{t_t}$$

then

$$L'_{pj} = L_p \left(\frac{t_t - t_j/x_j}{t_t} \right) \tag{8-33}$$

Finally,

$$t_{dj} = \frac{L'_{pj} t'_j}{1 - L_{p_j}} \tag{8-34}$$

Because the interprocesss message time is charged to the sending process, then the t_j's have the following values:

$$t_c = 2t_{pc} = 20 \text{ msec.}$$
$$t_r = 2t_{pr} + t_{ipm} = 30 \text{ msec.}$$
$$t_s = t_{ps} + 7t_{ipm} = 105 \text{ msec.}$$
$$t_f = 7t_{pf} = 140 \text{ msec.}$$

Also, from Table 8-9, the n_j's are:

$$n_c = 2$$
$$n_r = 2$$
$$n_s = 13$$
$$n_f = 8$$

These equations represent the response time model for the ET1 benchmark, as implemented in our example distributed system. They are summarized in Table 8-11, with a definition of terms given in Table 8-10. Table 8-10 also summarizes the parameter values used (note that L_s is treated as an input parameter since its value is fixed by the dynamic server algorithm).

This model assumes a large system and is a function of the number of processors, P, and the number of disks, D. Before we launch into a major calculation ranging over all D and P, let us use a little intelligence relative to the final system. From Table 8-7, we see that the file system is utilized for 290 msec. during each transaction; equation 8-29 shows that 295 msec. of processor time is used per transaction. These are so close that it is quite reasonable to consider a processing module comprising one processor and one disk.

TABLE 8-10.   ET1 BENCHMARK PARAMETERS

Parameter	Meaning	Value
Result parameters		
T_r	Average response time (sec.)	
Input variables		
R_t	System transaction rate (transactions/second)	
Input parameters		
D	Number of disk units	1, 2
L_s	Server load per server	.73, .68
n_p	Process dispatch rate per transaction	25
P	Number of processors	1
t_{dd}	Average physical disk time per file request (msec.)	21.4
t_{ipm}	Interprocessor message time	10
t_{pc}	Communication handler time per message (msec.)	10
t_{pf}	File manager processing time per file request (msec.)	20
t_{pr}	Requestor time per message (msec.)	10
t_{ps}	Server time per message (msec.)	35
q_s	Maximum server queue length	3, 2
Intermediate parameters		
L_f	File manager load per file manager	
L_p	Processor load per processor	
L'_{pj}	Processor load per processor, exclusive of process j	
n_j	Dispatches per transaction for process type j	
t_{dj}	Process dispatch time (msec.) for process type j	
t_f	File manager service time per file request (msec.)	
t_j	Average processing time per transaction for process type j (msec.)	
t'_j	Average processing time per dispatch for all processes except process j (msec.)	
t_{qf}	File manager queue time (msec.)	
t_{qs}	Server queue time (msec.)	
t_s	Server service time (msec.)	
t_t	CPU time per transaction (msec.)	
x_j	Number of processes of type j	

This configuration can then be used as a module to build a system as big as we would like. Therefore, the ET1 benchmark will be evaluated for one processor and one disk or

$$P = 1$$

$$D = 1$$

This means there will be one file manager ($x_f = 1$). A trial calculation will show that there

TABLE 8-11. ET1 BENCHMARK MODEL

$$T_r = 2(t_{pc} + t_{dc}) + 2(t_{pr} + t_{dr}) + t_{ipm} + t_{qs} + t_s \qquad (8\text{-}19)$$

$$t_{qs} = .5L_s t_s/(1 - L_s) \qquad (8\text{-}24)$$

$$t_s = (t_{ps} + 8t_{ds}) + 7(t_{ipm} + t_{qf} + t_f) \qquad (8\text{-}20)$$

$$L_s^{qs+1} = 1 - L_s \qquad (8\text{-}22)$$

$$t_{qf} = .61L_f t_f/(1 - L_f) \qquad (8\text{-}26)$$

$$L_f = 7R_t t_f/D \qquad (8\text{-}27)$$

$$t_f = t_{pf} + 13t_{df}/7 + t_{dd} \qquad (8\text{-}25)$$

$$t_{dj} = \frac{L'_{pj} t'_j}{1 - L'_{pj}} \qquad (8\text{-}34)$$

$$L'_{pj} = L_p \left(\frac{t_t - t_j/x_j}{t_t} \right) \qquad (8\text{-}33)$$

$$t'_j = \frac{t_t - t_j/x_j}{n_p - n_j/x_j} \qquad (8\text{-}31)$$

$$L_p = R_t t_t/P \qquad (8\text{-}32)$$

$$t_t = 2t_{pc} + 2t_{pr} + t_{ps} + 7t_{pf} + 8t_{ipm} \qquad (8\text{-}28)$$

will be 6 communication processes ($x_c = 6$) and 6 requestors ($x_r = 6$). The number of servers, x_s, is that required to keep the server load below .73.

Note that at a 70 percent load, this module will carry $.7/.29 = 2.4$ transactions/second. This is a rough estimate of system capacity as the actual value will depend upon the response time characteristics.

The response time for this module is shown in Figure 8-7 as a function of transaction rate. Surprise! To achieve a response time of 2 seconds, a module can carry only a load of 1.65 transactions per second, not 2.4. In fact, it can barely approach that capacity, saturating at about 2.5 transactions per second.

This example shows one of the great benefits in performance modeling. First, it shows how educated guesses can sometimes lead us astray (though they are still useful). Secondly, the model will let us "look into" the system to see what went wrong. This can be done by perusing the calculation results summarized in Table 8-12.

TABLE 8-12. ET1 BENCHMARK FOR $P = 1$, $D = 1$, $q_s = 3$

R_t	L_p	t_d(av)	t_f	L_f	t_{qf}	L_s	x_s	t_s	t_{qs}	T_r
0.2	.06	.001	.042	.06	.002	.73	1	.42	.56	1.03
0.4	.12	.001	.043	.12	.004	.73	1	.44	.59	1.09
0.6	.18	.002	.044	.18	.006	.73	1	.47	.63	1.16
0.8	.24	.003	.045	.25	.009	.73	1	.50	.67	1.24
1.0	.30	.004	.046	.32	.013	.73	1	.54	.73	1.34
1.2	.35	.005	.047	.39	.019	.73	1	.59	.80	1.46
1.4	.41	.006	.048	.47	.026	.73	2	.67	.91	1.66
1.6	.47	.008	.049	.55	.037	.73	2	.77	1.04	1.90
1.8	.53	.010	.051	.64	.055	.73	3	.92	1.25	2.28
2.0	.59	.012	.052	.73	.086	.73	4	1.18	1.60	2.90
2.2	.65	.016	.054	.83	.159	.73	6	1.74	2.35	4.23

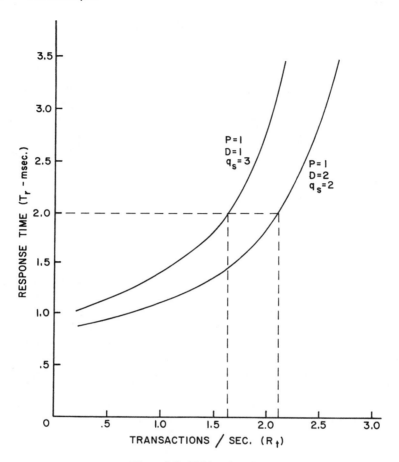

Figure 8-7   ETI benchmark.

We can deduce many things from these calculations, but one is most obvious:

The predominant factor is server queue time, t_{qs}. It accounts for over one-half of the response time.

We can reduce this a number of ways. One is to consider reducing the maximum queue size, q_s, to 2. This will be all right as long as we do not create too many servers for a module to handle. We can calculate the number of servers per module as follows. The server load, L_s, is, from equation 8-21

$$L_s = R_t t_s / S$$

Thus, the number of servers is

$$S = (R_t t_s / L_s) \qquad\qquad (8\text{-}35)$$

The server load is fixed at .68 for a queue size of 2 by the dynamic server algorithm (see Table 8-3b). Thus, at two transactions per second, the number of servers is (using $t_s = 1.18$ from Table 8-12):

$$S = \lceil (2)(1.18)/.68 \rceil = 4$$

There should therefore be no problem in reducing the maximum queue size to 2.

The server queue time t_{qs} is also a direct function of the server time t_s, which in turn is very sensitive to the file management time $t_{qf} + t_f$; in fact, it is proportional to seven times this factor. We can control t_{qf} by adding an extra disk to reduce file load, L_f. From Table 8-12 (preceding), this is not terribly important at one transaction per second but becomes significant if we approach two transactions per second (which we would like to do).

Thus, let us modify our system to contain two disks per processor, and let us reduce our maximum server queue length to 2:

$$q_s = 2$$

$$D = 2$$

Figure 8-7 shows the result. We have significantly increased the capacity of the system—up from 1.65 to 2.15 transactions per second. Not what we had hoped, but a lot closer to our original educated guess of 2.4 transactions/second.

With this configuration, each module can handle $(2.15)100 = 215$ users, since each user generates one transaction every 100 seconds. Therefore, in each module there would be 7 requestors, averaging 30.7 users each. To service 10,000 tellers simultaneously, the distributed system would comprise 47 modules (47 processors and 94 disks). A nice sale!

Let us assume a processor costs $60,000, and each disk costs $20,000. Then we can obtain a unique figure of merit for this system. Each module costs $100,000 and can support 2.15 transactions per second. Thus, this system costs $46,500 per transaction per second.

Cost per transaction per second, or $K/TPS, is becoming a common measure of transaction processing efficiency. Typical systems today range from 40 to 400 $K/TPS (Anon. [1]) so that our system is certainly competitive.

It might also be noted that the transaction processing power of today's distributed systems tends to run between 1 and 10 transactions/second per processor.

It takes a lot to handle a transaction. No wonder the world needs performance analysts.

SUMMARY

We have seen that the actual processing time consumed by an application process often represents only a minor contribution to response time. Application times may be magnified manyfold by queue delays and operating system characteristics.

One of the greatest magnifiers is the compound queue, comprising messages waiting in line for a process, which in turn must wait in line for the processor. The process time is magnified by queue delays for the processor, making its queue delays even worse.

In a multiprocessor system, compounding is even worse. Not only do messages wait in line for processes and processes wait in line for processors, but processors wait in line for common resources such as memory and locked data structures. The techniques of this chapter and those of chapter 6 can be combined to solve this problem.

9

Fault Tolerance

Transaction-processing systems have become such a part of our lives that many facets of our day-to-day existence depend upon their good health. As noted in chapter 1, we could not buy airline tickets, inquire about our bills, have our credit checked, or enjoy our current level of hospital care without these systems—at least not with the efficiency and ease that we enjoy today.

When a system goes down, we can be inconvenienced or may even suffer physically. In addition, the operator of the system will often suffer financial loss. An airline will lose customers, credit cards will be shifted with the mere flick of a new card, a hospital may lose a patient. Consequently, in many systems a substantial price tag can be placed on high availability. To meet this requirement, a variety of approaches have been taken to allow a TP system to continue operating even in the face of the failure of a significant component—a processor, a disk, a memory unit, an I/O controller, whatever.

In this chapter we analyze the impact of fault tolerance on performance. The ET1 example of chapter 8 is extended to show examples of performance degradation due to fault tolerant provisions.

The various requirements for fault-tolerant systems and contemporary approaches to fault tolerance are discussed in some detail in chapter 2 in the section entitled ''Survivability.'' There, four generic approaches to fault tolerance are discussed:

1. *Transaction protection*, in which transactions in progress at the time of failure are rolled back and must be reentered by the operator or automatically by the system.

2. *Synchronization*, in which multiple systems perform the same function and periodically check each other's results. Should there be a failure, they vote on the correct output according to some algorithm.

3. *Message queuing*, in which an active process sends every message it receives to a dormant backup process. Should the active process fail, the backup process can reconstruct the state of the active process by processing these messages before carrying on with normal activities.

4. *Checkpointing*, in which an active process updates the state of a dormant backup process at critical points so that the backup can take over immediately upon the failure of the active process.

All of these fault-tolerant systems have one thing in common—redundant hardware. This is the basic requirement for survivability, since if a component fails, the system can recover only if it has a spare component to immediately put in place.

One very important component to replicate are the disk units carrying the files required to support the TP application. This generally involves mirroring these files. Mirrored files are discussed in detail in chapter 7 under the section entitled ''Mirrored Files'' and will not be considered further here.

Beyond this, the various approaches to fault tolerance vary in terms of the amount of hardware needed, the ongoing operational load imposed upon the system by fault tolerance processing requirements, and the recovery time following a fault. These are detailed in chapter 2 but are generally summarized in the table below.

TABLE 9-1.   GENERALIZED COMPARISON OF FAULT-TOLERANT TECHNIQUES

Technique	Hardware utilization (%)	Operational load	Recovery time
Transaction protection	100	Light to heavy	Minutes
Synchronization	25–50	None to modest	Immediate
Message queuing	80–90	Modest	Seconds to minutes
Checkpointing	85–95	Light to modest	Seconds

Note that no technique is a panacea. If we want fast recovery, we have to pay for it in hardware. If we want minimum hardware, we must settle for slow recovery.

While the preceding table gives a feel for the relative characteristics of fault-tolerant approaches, it must be pointed out that there are as many approaches to survivability as there are systems. Systems developed in the future or even under development today may well improve significantly on the evaluations stated in this table. However, it is the purpose of this book to provide tools, not solutions. A familiarity with these techniques will allow the performance analyst to approach the analysis of new system architectures with confidence.

Let us now look at the operational performance issues raised with these various approaches. Note that we will not concern ourselves here with estimates of recovery time. First, this is presumed to be an infrequent activity in today's hardware art (many contemporary systems are now enjoying hardware mean time between single failures of over a year). Secondly, recovery time in many systems is a user-controlled parameter in that operating efficiency can be traded for recovery time (this is especially true for transaction-recovery and message-queuing systems, in which the volume of data that must be recovered can be reduced by more frequent cleanup procedures).

TRANSACTION PROTECTION

Even systems that are otherwise fault-tolerant often provide a transaction-protection facility. That is because one must recognize that no matter how fault-tolerant we make a system, we are protecting only against hardware faults (at least in today's art). But there is a major class of faults caused by that insidious body of black magic known as software. Though software bugs may eventually disappear in operating systems as they mature through years of use, they will always be with us in our application software. Even these will become less frequent as fourth generation application languages take hold. But software bugs, like the common roach, will live long after us.

The basic concept behind transaction protection is that we deal with a TP system in a unit called a *transaction*. A transaction can be quite complex and can involve multiple updates to our data base. If all updates cannot be made, then none should be made. For instance, if an inventory transaction is to update the quantity in stock in the inventory file and is to create a record in the order file; then both should be done; otherwise, the data base would be left in an inconsistent state. If the inventory file is updated but the order file is not, inventory would be frozen with nowhere to ship it. If the converse update occurred, the product would be shipped without reducing inventory. In either case, our system would be in trouble.

Note that a transaction can fail for several reasons:

- A hardware failure can occur that precludes the transaction from being completed, such as the failure of a common memory module in a multiprocessor system.
- A software failure can abort the transaction.
- The operator can decide to abort the transaction.

- A transaction can update files across a geographically distributed network. If a link to a remote node fails, the transaction might not be able to be completed.

All transaction protection methods provide a mechanism for marking the beginning and end of a transaction. As a transaction is started, data-base updates are made in such a way as to be only temporary. Only when the transaction has completed are the data-base updates committed. Otherwise, they are rolled back (or never applied) and never affect the data base.

A generalized transaction-protection mechanism is shown in Figure 9-1. When a transaction is received, a "start transaction" command (1) is issued. This notifies the operating system that all subsequent file activity related to this transaction is to be protected. As disk updates or writes are generated to files on behalf of this transaction, they are intercepted by the operating system. Records to be modified or written are locked (2), and the before and after images of the record to be written are captured. These images are written to an audit file (3).

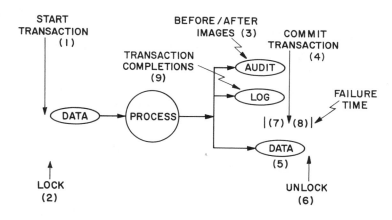

Figure 9-1 Transaction protection.

When the transaction has been completed, any remaining before/after record images pertaining to this transaction are flushed from cache to the audit file. At this time, the transaction can be considered to be safely stored, and the user is notified that the transaction is committed (4).

The actual updates to the data base also have been proceeding during this time (5). A key rule, however, is that no data-base record is modified until its before/after image has been physically written to the audit file. These data-base updates may continue while the user begins a new transaction. However, locks on all records involved in this transaction are maintained until the entire transaction has been applied to the data base. Only then will these locks be released (6).

In the event of a failure, the audit file provides two key features for recovering the data base: rollback and rollforward.

Rollback allows incomplete transactions to be backed out of the data base. Should a system failure of some sort occur before the transaction has been committed (7), then that transaction cannot be applied to the data base. However, some data-base records may already have been modified. Using the audit file before images of all records modified by the transaction, the transaction-protection facility can restore those records to their original value. Thus, an incomplete transaction will have no impact on the data base.

Rollforward allows the application of a committed transaction to be completed even if the system fails between transaction commit time and the time that the data-base update is completed (8). This is simply done by reading the after image of the modified records and by applying them to the data base.

One problem that may be apparent involves knowing which transactions are complete and which are incomplete following a failure. Many systems will provide this information by writing a log of all completed transactions (9). This log can then be read to facilitate transaction recovery following a failure.

Another solution is to establish a consistency point periodically in the system by flushing all modified data to disk. At this point, it is known that all data-base updates have been made. Recovery functions need proceed only from this consistency point.

Another type of rollforward capability must also be provided to account for media failure. If, for some reason, our disk units have crashed, or if faulty software has corrupted our data, we must be able to reconstruct it. This is done by restoring a known good copy of the data base (typically from magnetic tape) and by "playing back" all transactions that have occurred since that copy was made. These transactions will be saved in audit files, some of which may also be on tape, with the most recent ones still on disk. (It is important that they be on a physically separate disk from the one with the corrupted data so that the audit files are not also corrupted.) This form of rollforward can take hours or even days for a very large data base. It is not a very nice thing to have to do.

Data required for both rollback and rollforward must be properly recorded before the transaction is committed. Operational procedures supporting transaction protection must provide for such proper recording. The Synapse system described in chapter 2 will be used as an example for analytic purposes.

In summary, the Synapse transaction-protection technique involves the writing of two audit files. This is described in detail in chapter 2 in the section entitled "Survivability—Transaction Protection," as follows:

- A history log, which contains the before and after images of all data items updated. It must be physically written to disk before the transaction is considered complete.

- A temporary log, which contains the before images of all data items updated. It must be written before any data base update affecting these items is made.

Periodically (every couple of minutes or so), the disk cache is flushed, thus creating a *consistency point,* or CP. Following a CP, the data in the temporary log is deleted. Chapter 2 explains the recovery techniques available with this technique.

Typically, the set of data item changes will fit in one record to be written to each audit file. The audit files can be sequential files with variable record size. Each record is as long as is necessary to hold the required information for a transaction.

Under the above assumption, each transaction is burdened with an additional two sequential write operations. Note that these must be physically written to disk (cache write-through) and that the history log must be written to disk before the transaction is declared complete. (Typically, the final response to the user will be delayed until this write is ensured.)

The load on the system imposed by the consistency point is generally ignored as it seldom occurs (every few minutes or so).

Thus, transaction protection in this case is modeled from a performance viewpoint by simply adding n sequential cache write-through operations to each transaction, where n is typically equal to two.

SYNCHRONIZATION

To achieve fault tolerance via synchronization, at least two systems must be processing the same data and must be periodically comparing their results. If they must pause to do this, then a performance penalty is paid. However, this time is typically small and often zero.

The beauty of a synchronization system is that recovery time is instant (at least to the observer) should a failure occur. The failed module is simply ignored by the other modules in the system.

Basically, these are voting systems. The majority rules, and the minority is deemed to have failed. However, we have said that synchronization systems have two or more processing components. How can two take a democratic vote and have one win if they differ?

There are at least two ways this can be achieved. One way, applicable to most modern computers, is to build in enough diagnostic hardware so that any nonrecoverable error is detected and causes that system to "crash." A failed system dies and simply does not respond to the other half; it does not vote. Thus, if one system fails, the other simply carries on.

Another technique, useful in certain applications, is to implement an algorithm which can deduce the failed system. Such a mechanism was used in an early racetrack totalizator system installed by Autotote of Newark, Delaware, for the New York Racing Association. Designed by the author, each half of this system received wagering messages error-protected by encoding, processed these wagers, and compared accept/reject signals for each wager. If one system accepted the wager but the other rejected it, then the wager was rejected, keeping both systems consistent. However, the accepting system recorded a black mark for the rejecting system. If a system accumulated too many black marks, it was declared sick and taken out of service.

August Systems, as mentioned in chapter 2, offers a triplexed synchronized system. Stratus, also described in chapter 2, uses a quadraplexed synchronized system to achieve fault tolerance totally via hardware, with virtually instantaneous recovery.

Note that if p processors are used in a synchronized system, the total processor utilization is only $1/p$ of the total processing capacity. This is not necessarily an economic factor, as is shown by Stratus' strong presence in the marketplace.

A reasonably conservative approach to synchronization delay is obtained by considering the response time dispersion as discussed in chapter 4 in the section entitled "Infinite Populations—Dispersion of Response Times." The response times between systems will vary for a number of reasons, including the following:

- Scanning requestors in different systems may pick up the same transaction at different times.
- Transactions will be serviced by servers in a different order.
- Disks will receive requests in a different order, thus having different access times.

Using the tools described in the just referenced section, we can make statements concerning the distribution of this response time. Specifically, with the Gamma function, we can estimate the probability that the processing of a transaction will complete in less than a given time, given the mean time and variance of the processing time. Here a transaction is taken to mean that processing done between synchronizing points.

If we have n_e systems that will each complete a transaction in t seconds with probability $p_e = (.5)^{1/n_e}$, then the probability is $[(.5)^{1/n_e}]^{n_e} = .5$ that all will complete the transaction in t seconds. Thus, this value of t seconds is the average response time for the group of n_e systems. For instance, if three systems are involved, we will want to know that time within which the transaction will complete with probability $(.5)^{1/3} = .79$. Then we will know that all three will have completed their transaction in that time with probability $.79^3 = .5$. (This argument assumes that the response times are independent. To the extent that there is dependence among the response times, this approach is conservative.)

The Gamma function gives us these times as a function of the variance of the response time. Some typical values are given below:

TABLE 9-2. SYNCHRONIZATION OVERHEAD k_e

Processing elements (n_e)	$(.5)^{1/n_e}$ (p_e)	T^2/var (T)					
		1.0	1.2	1.4	1.6	1.8	2.0
2	.71	1.25	1.25	1.25	1.25	1.25	1.24
3	.79	1.56	1.54	1.52	1.50	1.48	1.47
4	.84	1.83	1.78	1.71	1.70	1.67	1.65

In chapter 4 it is noted that the distribution of the response time created by random arrivals at tandem queues with random service times is itself random. Therefore, its variance is equal to the square of the mean response time. Random distribution of response times is usually a conservative assumption; if all else fails, it can be used. This is the case of $T^2/\text{var}\ (T) = 1$ in the above table.

However, chapter 4 also describes a technique for estimating the variance of the response time more accurately. The example for a TP system given there yields a ratio of variance to response time-squared equal to .628. From the above table, the average response for four processing elements is 1.83 multiplied by the average response of one element, if random response times are assumed ($T^2/\text{var}\ (T) = 1$). However, if the normalized variance is .628, then $T^2/\text{var}\ (T) = 1/.628 = 1.6$; the average four element response time is 1.70 times the average response of one element, or a 7 percent performance improvement per our estimate. Thus, it can pay to go through the exercise of more accurately estimating response time variance rather than to casually assume randomness of response times.

On the other hand, the values in the table above are closely enough clustered to give us a reasonable rule of thumb for synchronized systems, as follows:

TABLE 9-3. SYNCHRONIZATION OVERHEAD

No. of processing elements (n_e)	Addition to the average response time $(k_e - 1)(\%)$
2	25
3	50
4	75

Note that these results apply to a transaction whether there is one synchronizing point or n such points per transaction. To demonstrate this, let

n_e = number of processing elements.

k_e = response time factor for n_e processing elements.

n_s = number of synchronizing points per transaction.

t_{r1} = average transaction-response time for a single element.

t_r = transaction-response time for the system.

The response time, t_r, for the system is the sum of the response times between each synchronizing point:

$$t_r = n_s(k_e t_{r1}/n_s)$$

or

$$t_r = k_e t_{r1} \tag{9-1}$$

where

$$k_e = \text{Gamma}\,[p_e,\ t_{r1}^2/\text{var}\ (t_{r1})] \tag{9-2}$$

Thus, the response time, t_r, is independent of the number of synchronizing points, n_s.

Gamma $[p_e, \, t_{r1}^2/\text{var}\,(t_{r1})]$ is the value of the Gamma function for parameters p_e and $t_{r1}^2/\text{var}\,(t_{r1})$. The parameter p_e is defined as follows. If each element completes its transaction within a time t with probability p_e, then the group of elements will complete the transaction in that time with probability 0.5:

$$p_e = (0.5)^{1/n_e} \tag{9-3}$$

Note that hardware synchronization as practiced by Stratus results in a variance of zero, since synchronization points are determined by a common clock. Thus, $k_e = 1$, and there is no performance penalty.

MESSAGE QUEUING

With message queuing (described in chapter 2 in the section entitled ''Survivability—Message Queuing''), a backup process is kept informed of the status of its primary process by queuing those messages that are also directed to its primary. In this way, if the primary process fails, the backup can process the queue of old messages to bring itself up-to-date before taking over the processing functions from the primary.

To prevent the backup from sending duplicate messages while it is processing old messages during recovery, the primary process will also send copies of its output messages to its own backup process. The backup will maintain a count of these so that it will know when to start releasing messages.

To prevent the backup queue from becoming too long, the system is ''cleaned up'' periodically. This is done by flushing all dirty memory pages to disk. (This, of course, assumes that memory paging for both the primary process and the backup process uses a common mirrored disk pair.) At this point, if the backup takes over, it will be in the same state as the primary process. Therefore, its receive queue can be deleted and its message count reset. This is the equivalent of the consistency point used with transaction protection. It is ignored for performance purposes, since it generally occurs infrequently (every several seconds to minutes, depending upon the recovery time desired and the maximum queue lengths).

The performance analysis of these systems is straightforward. For each interprocess message sent, three are actually sent:

- One to the destination primary process for normal processing.
- One to the destination backup process for replay following a failure.
- One to the sender's backup process so that it can know which messages have been sent.

In most messaging systems, this activity will incur substantially the overhead of three interprocess messages. Thus, one needs only to triple interprocess message activity to account for fault tolerance using message queuing.

CHECKPOINTING

Fault tolerance via checkpointing is described in chapter 4 in the section entitled ''Survivability—Checkpointing.'' With this technique, the status of a backup process is maintained by the primary process, which sends checkpoint messages to it at critical points. Each checkpoint message contains critical changes that have been made to the process's data space since the last checkpoint. It may also include a new starting location for the backup process to be used in the event that it has to take over processing from the primary process.

The number of checkpoints required is a function of the protection desired and the organization of the software. Checkpointing strategies are discussed in depth in chapter 2. However, a properly designed TP system can generally survive with three checkpoints per transaction.

- Once when the transaction is received (the request checkpoint).
- Once when all data records have been read and prior to any file updates (the data-base checkpoint).
- Once after the reply has been returned (the reply checkpoint).

Achieving a three-checkpoint strategy will often require that interprocess messages and records written to sequential files may have to carry sequential identification numbers and that processes use these to avoid duplication. For instance, if sequence numbering is not used, the following considerations apply:

- In a requestor-server environment, the requestor might checkpoint a message that it has received from a terminal before it sends it to a server. The requestor might also checkpoint the reply when it has been returned to the terminal. The server might checkpoint file data after reading all data records but before updating this data. If a failure occurs, the requestor might send a duplicate request to the server or the server might send a duplicate reply to the requestor, or both these actions might occur. To avoid these possibilities, two extra checkpoints will have to be added, one in the requestor following its transmission of the request to the server and one in the server following its return of the reply to the requestor.
- If writes are made to sequential files following the data-base checkpoint, then these will be repeated if the backup takes over following the data-base checkpoint. This can be avoided by checkpointing after every sequential write.

Thus, a reluctance to institute a mechanism for duplicate message or record control can lead to a significant increase in checkpointing requirements.

Whatever the strategy, it will lead to some number, n_c, of checkpoints per transaction. From a performance viewpoint, this simply adds n_c checkpoint interprocess messages to each transaction.

DATA-BASE INTEGRITY

With these fault-tolerant concepts in mind, let us take one more look at data-base integrity. In chapter 7, we discussed disk mirroring as a means for protecting the data base from a mechanical disk failure. However, mirroring plays a role in only one aspect of ensuring the integrity of the data base.

There are, in fact, three levels of integrity with which to be concerned:

1. *Data integrity*. At this level, we are concerned that each write of a data block was safely executed by the disk system and that the block can be read reliably. This is often ensured by read-after-write protection on some disk units and by error-correcting codes for reading data. It is further ensured by using mirrored disks.

2. *File integrity*. Even though we can ensure that all writes complete successfully and that all data can be reliably read block by block, this does not mean that our files are intact. An interruption of a complex file operation by a system failure can leave a B-tree garbled during a block split or can lose an end-of-file on a sequential file. Should this happen, our files are of questionable use to us. File integrity is ensured by guaranteeing process integrity via checkpointing, message queuing, or synchronization.

3. *Transaction integrity*. Even if our files are protected, the data base can still be corrupted if a transaction is interrupted. Transaction integrity is protected by transaction protection techniques, which can roll back incompleted transactions following a failure.

Transaction protection is often coupled with one of the other types of fault protection. This allows the system to continue unaffected in the presence of any single failure (and, in fact, in the presence of many multiple failures) but allows the data base to be recovered following severe failures that may have contaminated it.

AN EXAMPLE

Let us compare the performance of these various techniques by applying them to the ET1 benchmark evaluated in chapter 8. We will consider the following four techniques:

1. *Transaction protection*. If the system fails in any way, it is recovered by the transaction-protection facilities.

2. *Synchronization*. In this technique, two processors are provided to process transactions in parallel. If one fails, it is assumed that diagnostic hardware will cause it to stop so that it can cause no damage.

3. *Message queuing*. Interprocess messages are queued to a backup process for reprocessing in the event of a failure.

4. *Checkpointing*. This technique assumes three checkpoints per transaction with duplication protection.

To account for fault-tolerance overhead, the following modifications are made to the example of chapter 8:

1. *Transaction protection* is modeled by adding two write times to the transaction. Both must be cache write-through type operations. Each operation is a sequential-file write to a mirrored file. Using the values of Table 8-7, we have the results in Table 9-4.

TABLE 9-4. TRANSACTION PROTECTION FILE MANAGEMENT TIME

File operation	File manager time (msec.)	Disk time (msec.)	Total time (msec.)
ET1 processing	140	150	290
Sequential write	60	90	150
	200	240	440

Note that transaction protection significantly increases disk access time and might justify an extra disk unit per module. However, we will maintain the module configuration for consistency of results.

The server still makes only seven file requests as the audit writes are performed transparently by the operating system. Therefore, it is sufficient to simply add the audit time as overhead to the transaction's disk time. Doing this yields a file manager processing time, t_{pf}, and a physical disk time, t_{dd}, per file access of

$$t_{pf} = 200/7 = 28.6 \text{ msec.} \tag{9-4}$$

$$t_{dd} = 240/7 = 34.3 \text{ msec.} \tag{9-5}$$

or a total of 62.9 msec. per average file call.

All other equations for the model remain the same.

2. *Synchronization* is modeled by adding 25 percent to the single-system response time. Pure and simple. However, note that this requires twice the hardware.

3. *Message queuing* is modeled by tripling all interprocess messages. This is simply done by tripling the interprocess message time, t_{ipm}:

$$t_{ipm} = 30 \text{ msec.} \tag{9-6}$$

4. *Checkpointing* is modeled by adding three interprocess messages to each transaction. Two are added in the requestor following the receipt of a request and the send of a reply. The other is added to the server following the read of all data but

before any writes. Thus, equations 8-19, 8-20 and 8-28 become the following equations:

(8-19):

$$T_r = 2(t_{pc} + t_{dc}) + 2(t_{pr} + t_{dr}) + 3t_{ipm} + t_{qs} + t_s \qquad (9\text{-}7)$$

(8-21):

$$t_s = (t_{ps} + t_{ipm} + 8t_{ds}) + 7(t_{ipm} + t_{qf} + t_f) \qquad (9\text{-}8)$$

(8-28):

$$t_t = 2t_{pc} + 2t_{pr} + t_{ps} + 7t_{pf} + 11t_{ipm} \qquad (9\text{-}9)$$

The results of this exercise are shown in Figure 9-2. Based on the particular param-

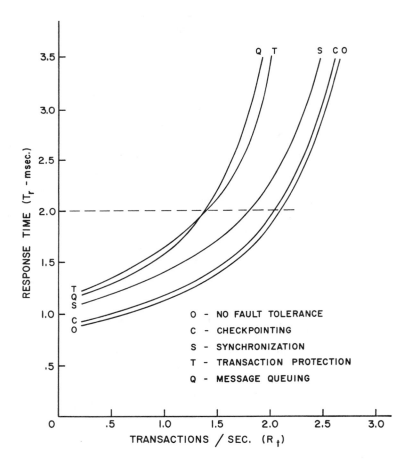

Figure 9-2 Impact of fault tolerance.

eters that we have chosen, and considering the range of interest (around a two-second average response time), checkpointing is reasonably efficient. Synchronization and transaction protection are next, but remember that the synchronization system requires twice the hardware. Message queuing imposes the heaviest load. No general conclusions can be drawn from this exercise, however, as the results of Figure 9-2 can be significantly different for different values of the system parameters. In fact, parameters can be chosen to give the advantage to any of these techniques.

Table 9-5 gives the capacity and $K\$/TPS$ for each system based on a \$100,000 module cost. This table should be considered an illustration only. It is very sensitive to system and performance parameters. For instance, if the allowable response time were 3 seconds, system costs per TPS would be much closer. If it were 1.0 second, only the checkpointing fault-tolerant system would apply (in addition to the plain vanilla system.) A message-queuing system, in particular, might well incorporate a more efficient message system (perhaps 2 msec., as is seen in some contemporary systems, rather than 10 msec.). This would make it much more competitive.

TABLE 9-5. COST OF FAULT TOLERANCE FOR THE ET1 BENCHMARK EXAMPLE

Fault-tolerant mechanism	Module cost ($K\$$)	Capacity (TPS)	Cost/performance factor ($K\$/TPS$)
None	100	2.15	46.5
Transaction protection	100	1.40	71.4
Synchronization	200	1.81	110.5
Message queuing	100	1.36	73.5
Checkpointing	100	2.09	47.8

One final comment. Any fault-tolerant system employing a backup (all but pure transaction-protected systems) will run faster if the backup is down. Synchronizing systems don't have to synchronize. Message queuing and checkpointing systems don't have to send backup messages. The author has seen at least one case (and I'm sure there are others) in which the operators actually inhibited one or more of these fault-tolerance features when the system became loaded. Bad practice! Let's design these systems correctly to start with.

10

The Performance Model Product

An in-depth performance analysis can be a very significant effort, ranging from a few days to several analyst-months. Once we have gone to all the bother of an analysis, it would certainly be nice if others could make use of it. It would be even nicer if years from now we would be remembered for our fine work.

Both these goals can be achieved through a common vehicle—*documentation*. Many of us don't like to write, but write we must if we are to complete our job as professional performance analysts. The resulting document is the tangible product of our long hours of analysis.

To take a little pain out of this chore, this chapter discusses the contents and organization of a proper performance analysis document. The next chapter then presents a sample performance analysis taken from real life.

The key to a successful performance analysis is the same as with most tasks. Work from the top down. Start by obtaining a thorough knowledge of the system and the transactions that will drive it. Then characterize the system's performance with a traffic diagram. Using this, generate the performance model as a set of equations or tables or both, as appropriate. Summarize the model so that the calculation phase can be organized, and then compute pertinent results. Finally, describe the results and the conclusions that can be derived from them.

It is always useful to begin the performance analysis document with a short executive summary of 2 or 3 pages at the most. Those readers who really count seldom read a 100-page detailed analysis. This summary should identify the system, should comment about the magnificent art of performance analysis, and should present the primary results and conclusions.

Finally, the document should have the finishing touches of a table of contents (often overlooked, but terribly important, especially for later reference) and an attractive cover sheet clearly identifying the system *and* the author.

REPORT ORGANIZATION

Executive Summary

The very first words that strike the reader who has turned past the cover sheet are those of the *executive summary*. This summary may be the only section the reader actually reads.

The executive summary contains brief statements about the following:

- The system that is analyzed and its basic functions.
- The reasons for the performance analysis.
- A word about performance analysis techniques. (Remember—this may be the first and only performance analysis the reader has come across.)
- The primary results of this performance analysis, complete with curves or tables if appropriate. However, these should be devoid of detail; instead, they should be summaries of important results.
- The conclusions to be drawn from these results and their impact on current or future activities.

The "word about performance analysis" is an advertisement for the art. In one sense it is boilerplate. In another sense it is quite useful, especially when one realizes how few people have been exposed to good performance analyses. Such people may be quite confused about how the document came to be if we don't give them a hint.

A typical short paragraph satisfying this requirement is:

The results presented in this document were obtained using a technique known as analytic performance modeling. With this technique, delays in a system which increase with the load imposed on that system can be characterized mathematically. Consequently, the response time of the system to a transaction, and thus its capacity, can be mathematically modeled and evaluated under a variety of conditions.

Table of Contents

Not much need be said about the *table of contents*, except that it should not be forgotten. It gives the serious reader a clue as to what is contained in the document and acts as a valuable quick reference tool (even for you, the author, years down the road).

System Description

In my opinion, the *system description* is the most important part of the document. If the system is imperfectly understood, the model will at best be equally imperfect.

The system description should start with an overview of the system's hardware and software architecture and the functions performed by the system. Each module that has an impact on performance is then described in detail, with all significant aspects affecting performance fully covered.

The system description performs two major functions:

1. It acts as the interface document between the performance analyst (who is presumably initially naive concerning the system) and those knowledgeable about the system. In this sense, it is an interactive document and may take several cycles of review by the system analysts and rewrites by the performance analyst before it is complete.

2. It acts as the basis for developing the transaction model and the traffic model, from which the rest of the performance analysis is derived.

For both these reasons, the system description should be completed and approved before the actual performance analysis proceeds. Otherwise, there may be a good deal of rework required.

Transaction Model

The *transaction model* characterizes the transaction load imposed upon the system. In the examples throughout this book, the transaction models were quite simple and may not have even been noticed. However, real-life systems experience a wide variety of often complex transactions.

The characterization of these transactions involves identifying them, listing their resource requirements (communications, disk accesses by type, and special processing), and their relative frequency, or probability, of occurrence.

The transaction model is often just so much bean counting and can be a tedious chore for both the system analyst and the performance analyst. But it must be done. It requires a significant contribution from those who know the system, and it can proceed in parallel with the rest of the performance-modeling activities, since its results are usually not needed until model computation time.

Traffic Model

Now the fun and excitement can finally begin. The system description, having been finally signed off by the system analysts, gives us all the information we need to model the system. The first step is to create the *traffic model*.

This is a diagram such as that given for the ETI benchmark in Figure 8-6. It shows the flow of a transaction through all pertinent processes and highlights the queuing points.

There may often have to be different traffic models for different transactions. Each should be carefully described in the text; to this end, numbering the elements in the traffic model and referring to them in the text can be a great help.

To aid in transcribing the traffic model into the performance model, it is also a help to note major parameters next to their corresponding elements on the traffic model diagram, as was done in Figure 8-6.

Performance Model

As suggested above, the *performance model,* at least at its highest level, is simply a transcription of the traffic model into a mathematical expression, such as was done with the ET1 benchmark, resulting in equations 8-19 through 8-34. In contrast, some models lend themselves to tabular descriptions instead of equations. Such an example is the file system parameter analysis tabularized in Tables 8-4 through 8-7.

Generally, the model should be generated in a top-down manner. The first step is to create the response-time relationship. Some of the parameters in this relationship will be inputs and need not be evaluated further. Others, especially queuing points, will need further evaluation.

As relationships are generated for these parameters, they will use a mix of known inputs and new parameters to be analyzed. As we work down into more and more detail, we will finally hit bottom. This occurs when all expressions are combinations of known inputs or the results of other computable expressions.

Sometimes we will come across a problem that results in a parameter that is a complex function of itself and is not directly computable. This happens, for instance, in limited population queues in which the load imposed on the server is a function of users who are not in the queue, which is a function of the load on the server. An example of this was found in the analysis of processor performance in chapter 6 (see "Physical Resources—Model Summary"). In these cases, the model must be calculated iteratively, which usually means it must be programmed and evaluated using a computer.

Model Summary

Though often included as a set of tables at the end of the performance model, the *model summary* is the final organization of the model prior to its calculation. It comprises two parts:

1. A definition of all terms with their dimensions, i.e., msec., sec., etc., to avoid scaling errors, and
2. A listing of all expressions to be used in the calculations.

It is convenient to organize the definition of the terms into four groupings:

1. *Result parameters.* Those parameters to be calculated that are the most likely candidates to be viewed as useful results.
2. *Input variables.* Those parameters that are most likely to be varied to run different tests.
3. *Input parameters.* Those parameters with known values and that need not be varied.
4. *Intermediate parameters.* Those parameters that will be calculated in order to derive the desired results.

It is important that all expressions (whether they are equations or tables) are listed in top-down order even if they were not so ordered in the text. In this way, parameters can be evaluated starting at the bottom of the table and working up. The same organization is imperative if the model is to be programmed. Table 8-11 exemplifies this organization for the ET1 benchmark example.

The expression listing should provide references to the derivation of each expression in the text by showing the equation number or table number for each.

It is useful not to consolidate equations into huge, single expressions. Rather, keep each equation simple; use a building block approach. This has several advantages:

- It makes computation and/or programming simpler.
- It makes the model more modular and therefore more maintainable in terms of making changes, fixing errors, or adding enhancements (just like programs).
- It gives us the ability to look deeper into the system to see what is going on by having a finer granularity of the intermediate parameters that we will calculate (remember our experience with the ET1 benchmark).

The last point is of paramount importance. The intermediate parameters should, at the very least, include the load on all system elements and the delay time (queue plus service times) through each element. In this way we can identify the bottlenecks by looking at the element or elements contributing most to the response time and can attempt to come up with improvements to the system to reduce bottlenecks. At least this approach will give us the tools to do that.

Scenario

The *scenario* is the last step prior to the calculation of the model. It specifies not only the particular mixes of transactions that will be imposed on the system but also other system parameters that may or may not be varied, such as the number of processors and disks, communication line speeds, and other parameters.

Model Computation

Though the details of the *model computations* need not be part of the performance analysis document (though they are often attached for posterity), the computation of results using the model is, of course, very much a part of modeling. Computation may be done either manually or by computer. Considerations for performance model programs are discussed later.

Results

Finally, *results* are available from our tedious hours of modeling and calculating. They should be presented in a clear, simple summary in tabular or chart form (see Figure 8-7 and Table 9-5, for example). Then supporting data could follow in more detailed chart or tabular form. Again, a top-down approach to results presentation is recommended.

Conclusions and Recommendations

The results will generally lead to some conclusions. One conclusion may be to praise the system and its ability to meet its requirements. Others may be recommendations for system improvement, a cost-benefit analysis of proposed performance enhancements, or the impact of a new proposed function or system change on performance. Another useful result is configuration tables to be used to size the system for different environments.

Whatever the conclusions, they should be clearly stated with adequate reference to the supporting results.

PROGRAMMING THE PERFORMANCE MODEL

Many performance models can be calculated manually with just a few hours of effort and a hand calculator. Others need to be programmed for one or more of a variety of reasons, including the following:

- They are very complex or, even worse, require iterative solutions.
- They will be used often, and it would be a convenience to have a program available.
- They will be used as a sales or management tool.

Though it is not the intent to discuss programming techniques here, there are some basic guidelines that are useful. The key term is the much used PC saw: *user friendly*.

When user friendliness is built into a program up-front, it doesn't usually cost very much. A program pieced together without thought will probably never be user friendly.

There are several areas with which to be concerned.

Input Parameter Entry and Edit

The heaviest user interface (and the one that will cause the most frustration) is entering the data. Some models can have hundreds of data entry parameters. Each should be identified on the data entry screen with its performance model symbol as well as with its full definition. Even if there are only a few data entry parameters, a screen can get heavily cluttered with parameter definitions, which must exist because even the analyst will eventually not remember what h_{sm} was.

On the other hand, we would like to arrange the parameter notation so that those knowledgeable with the model will know instantly just what the parameter is. In any event, the notation should be created as if the performance model document were nowhere to be found or, if available, were so intimidating that no one would enter it to figure out which parameter is which. The program must envelop the user with friendliness and knowledge.

A convenient way to achieve a user-friendly data entry system is to present a screen for a set of input parameters, each identified only by their parameter notation (such as h_{sm}). In this way, the screen can be uncluttered and the cursor moved easily between fields for data entry.

To give the user the definition of these terms, a *help line* is reserved at the top or bottom of the screen. When the cursor is positioned at a parameter, its definition is displayed automatically on the help line. In this way, an experienced user can move around the screen and insert data, ignoring the help line, while an inexperienced user is guided by this line. This help line must, of course, not only define the variable but also indicate its units.

To facilitate editing of data, it is important that the data-entry screens work in *page mode*. That is, the user must be able to freely move back and forth between fields until he or she releases the page, at which time the parameters are saved and the next screen full of parameters, if any, is displayed.

One subtle point remains. How do we display subscripts? Most everyday video terminals cannot display such terms as h_{sm}.

If we have adhered to the convention of single-letter parameters plus subscripts (as has been done in this book), then the display could simply show the parameters as a sequence of characters, since we know that all but the first character are subscripts. Otherwise, we can use a special character, such as the underline, to denote the following characters as subscripts, such as h_sm.

The same technique can be used in the program as symbols for the parameters. A similar method can be used for superscripts. Often, a caret is used for this purpose. Thus, h_{sm}^{c} can be symbolized on the screen and in the program as h_sm^c.

But how do we handle Greek letters? Don't know. Not my problem. As I indicated in my introduction of chapter 1, I don't use them.

Input Variable Specification

Once input parameters are entered, the range over which one or more input variables are to be varied during the calculation and the increments for these ranges must be entered. For instance, we may want to vary the transaction rate from 1 to 10 transactions per second in steps of 0.5 for a system with 1 to 5 processors.

Since we can only guess which parameters we may want to vary at the start, it is a powerful tool to allow the user to specify any set of input parameters as input variables.

To do this, the user simply enters the parameter symbol, at which point our friendly help line identifies the meaning of the symbol and its units. (If the symbol is invalid, the terminal beeps and requires a reentry.)

Once satisfied that this is the correct symbol, the user then enters the range and increment size. This process is repeated for as many input variables as the user desires and the program allows.

Report Specification

A performance model can often calculate hundreds of intermediate parameters, any one of which might be the potential cause of a system problem. But usually we are interested only in a handful. But which ones? We never know at the start.

Therefore, it is very useful to allow the user to specify which results are desired. Of course, one specification is "all," which will give the user pages of detailed results. A more specific request allows us to provide a prettier report.

The user should be able to specify not only the input variables but also the result parameters by simply typing the parameter symbol; the help line confirms the accuracy of the chosen symbol.

If a small enough number of results has been specified so that a columnar report can be generated, the report should be produced in columnar form. Otherwise, it should be a listing of results.

It is often desirable to print parameter definitions at the bottom of a report for those parameters listed on the report. This should be a user option.

It is also important to provide a facility for printing a user-specified test name on each report. Of course, all reports should carry a date and a time.

Parameter Storage

There is nothing more frustrating than typing in several dozen parameter values, a few input variable specifications, and a report format, and then having to do it all over again because you want to change the value of one variable for a subsequent calculation. There should be two facilities to help the user in this regard:

1. Whenever the user calls up screens to enter data or specifications, display what was previously entered. In this way, the user needs to change only those items that need modification.
2. Give the user a facility for saving a data set (input parameters, input variables, and report specifications) in a named file on disk and the ability to recall it for use.

Dictionary

We have hobbled the inexperienced user to some extent with the user interface described above. When entering input variables or result variables (for the report specification), one must know the symbols for the desired parameters. But we have assumed that the user does not remember these symbols.

Therefore, we should provide a dictionary of parameter symbols and their definitions. The dictionary should be organized into input symbols (variables and parameters) and output symbols (result and intermediate parameters).

The user should be able either to view these symbols on the screen or to get a hard-copy dictionary for later reference.

Help

For the really inexperienced user, a help screen should be provided. It will explain how to call up screens, manipulate the cursor controls, make corrections, and generally run the model. It is a user's manual in a disk file.

The first display of the program should inform a user how to invoke the help function (and perhaps to even print it out). In this way, the only thing the user needs to know is how to call the program (that can be written on the label of the diskette containing the program). We tacitly assume that the user knows how to boot the PC or log on to the terminal.

Model Calculation

Now that we have seen to it that the user can use the model, it is time to make a calculation once data has been entered. Usually, this has nothing to do with the user. The program will run, and the results will print.

However, there are legitimate occasions for error. A typical error is a specification of an input parameter and variable that will overload a component.

In this case, the model should continue calculating so that all requested calculations will be made rather than just aborting. However, when the results are printed for a calculation that could not be completed, inform the user what happened, i.e., disk overload.

Report

The report specification has already been described. The results can be presented in one of three ways:

- on the screen.
- in hard copy.
- graphically, if a plotter has been included in the package.

For screen or printed reports, either a columnar format or list can be used, depending upon the number of result variables specified.

The report should be titled with a user-supplied title, then should be dated and time-stamped.

As a user option, parameter definitions can be added to the report for those input variables and result variables shown on the report.

TUNING

No performance model is perfect the day it is first written. If we are lucky enough to get real values from actual measurements on the system, then we have an opportunity to "tune" our model; for we would indeed be fortunate the first time around if the model reflected the real world as accurately as it could.

Differences between model results and actual measurements can be caused by several factors:

1. The assumptions required in order to develop a model may lead to inaccuracies. These *inherent errors* in performance modeling are ones with which we live. Typically, they are not so severe as to invalidate the model. Unless we can get smarter (or work harder) and use more sophisticated techniques, there is nothing we can do about inherent modeling errors.

2. The values of the input parameters that we have been led to believe are correct may not be. These are *parametric errors*. An example of a parametric error is to estimate that a process will require 5 msec. of processing time per transaction before it is written and then find out that it actually takes 50 msec. when it is up and running. Parametric errors are corrected by simply rerunning the model with the correct parameter values.

3. Within the original system description there may have been errors that caused the modeled system to differ from the real system. These are *structural errors* and are corrected by changing the relationships in the model. For a programmed model, this requires program changes.

4. There may be problems in the real system that prevent the system from working as intended. These are *system errors* and are corrected by modifying the actual system hardware or software. This is the best kind of error for a performance analyst to find since it has proven the value of our analytic techniques.

In any event, through an iterative process of tuning, in which actual results and model results are compared, differences examined, and corrections made, a performance model can often be made increasingly accurate. When the desired accuracy is achieved, the performance model is ready for use as a management tool, a sales aid, or for whatever it is intended.

QUICK AND DIRTY

As a final point, it should be emphasized that this chapter has dealt with the formalization of the performance modeling process. A model fully developed along these guidelines could require many analyst-months and tens of thousands of dollars.

This is not to say that there is not a great need for fast answers to performance questions that can be satisfied by a quick model, minimum documentation, and a fast calculation. Or just a few minutes at a blackboard. And that is what this book has been all about: to give the performance analyst the tools and concepts needed to give educated answers to performance questions in whatever form is appropriate.

11

A Case Study

Contained in this chapter is an actual case study. The author expresses his appreciation to Syntrex Incorporated for its permission to use this material.

Syntrex is a manufacturer of word-processing systems. Its basic word processor is a stand-alone terminal called Aquarius. Gemini is a redundant data-base server that provides highly reliable access to common documents for up to 14 Aquarius terminals. Multiple Gemini systems can be networked together via SynNet.

Syntrex is extremely interested in continually improving the performance of its systems. It therefore commissioned a study to determine what could be done to improve the capacity of its Gemini data-base server.

The attached study is an ideal complement to the material in this book, as it stresses the use of concepts rather than a cookbook approach. For instance:

- The communication links connecting the Aquarius terminals to the Gemini data base use a special contention protocol designed especially for this system.
- A scanning process is used to process Aquarius messages but is continuously running in its own processor.
- Fault tolerance is achieved by synchronization at the scanner level and uses a master/slave relationship.
- Multiple file managers are used, but traffic is split based on function rather than on files.
- The Aquarius scanners interface with the file managers via a shared memory, which is a limited resource.

None of these architectures were specifically discussed in the preceding chapters. However, all are analyzed with the tools given, with a little ingenuity, and with a little devout imperfectionism.

The result is a complex model with over 50 input and 50 intermediate parameters requiring nested iterative computation. The model was programmed and run against a benchmark that had also been run on Gemini. The results are comfortably close, allowing the model to be used to peek inside Gemini to find what is bothering it. Several recommendations are consequently made for performance improvement.

The following case history document generally follows the organization suggested in chapter 10. One apology is appropriate. The transactions for this system are quite complex, and their characterization as a transaction model adds little to the performance modeling example. Therefore, they are treated as being explained in a reference document, with the results simply being presented as Tables 4-1, 4-2, and 4-3. Though the transaction model is necessary for model calculation, its development is unimportant for purposes of this example.

- A finite number of file manager processes compete for a common processor. Process dispatch time is calculated by ignoring the load of one of the file managers. This is an example of the technique suggested in Appendix 6.
- A finite number of file managers compete for a common disk. The disk queue is calculated via the M/M/l/m/m model, as an example of this technique.

Performance Evaluation of the Syntrex Gemini System

Prepared for:
Syntrex Incorporated

By:
W. H. Highleyman
December, 1983

EXECUTIVE SUMMARY

The Gemini word processing system has met with significant market success in large operations requiring fault-tolerant common access to documents by multiple terminals. However, in high-volume applications, serious response-time degradation has been noted. It is important to determine the potential for significantly expanding the capacity of Gemini in an economical way.

The stated goal is to double its capacity with a cost increase not exceeding 20 percent.

To answer this question, the performance of the Gemini system has been analyzed in some detail with a technique known as analytic performance modeling. With this technique, delays in a system that increase with the load on that system can be characterized mathematically. Consequently, the response time of the system to a transaction, and thus its capacity, can be mathematically modeled and evaluated under a variety of conditions.

The result of the following performance analysis is simply stated: Gemini is limited by the speed of its disk units. Any effort made to increase capacity must be aimed at one of two areas: speeding up the disk system or decreasing the load on the disk system.

This can be done in several ways:

1. Eliminating physical copies of documents would reduce disk activity by 50% (This approach could be applied only if we are willing to suffer the consequences of a system failure.)
2. Using only a portion of larger disks would speed up access time, with a potential reduction in disk load of up to 50%.
3. The disk process could be rewritten to reduce processing time.
4. Dual disks on each controller would reduce disk loading by 50%.
5. Aquarius terminals could be split between two Gemini systems, interconnected by SynNet.
6. A larger cache memory could be used.

Solution 2, the use of only a portion of larger disks, is recommended. It involves simply the purchase of larger disk units. Little development effort is required. This will increase the cost of a Gemini unit by about 10% but should give it twice the capacity.

TABLE OF CONTENTS

1. INTRODUCTION

This document derives analytically a performance model for the Syntrex Gemini System. Its results will serve to predict the response time of the system as a function of transaction volume, transaction mix, number of terminals, and other environmental factors.

It is well known that as a computer system becomes loaded, it "bogs down." Response times to user requests get longer and longer, leading to increased frustration and aggravation of the user population. A measure of the capacity of the system is the load (in transactions per hour, for instance) at which the response time becomes marginally acceptable.

Deterioration of response time is caused by bottlenecks within a system. These are common system resources that are required to process many simultaneous transactions; therefore, transactions must wait in line in order to get access to these resources. As the system load increases, these lines, or queues, become longer, processing delays increase, and responsiveness suffers. Examples of common resources are the processor itself, disks, communication lines, and even certain programs within the system.

One can represent the flow of each major transaction through a system by a model that identifies each processing step and that highlights the queuing points at which the processing of a transaction may be delayed. This model can then be used to create a mathematical expression for the time that it takes to process each type of transaction, as well as an average time for transactions as a function of the load imposed on the system.

This processing time is, of course, the response time that a user will see. The load at which response times become unacceptable is the capacity of the system.

Ideally, a performance model should be tuned. Its results should be compared to measured results and, if significantly different, the reasons should be understood and the model corrected. Usually, this results in the inclusion of certain processing steps initially deemed trivial or in the determination of more accurate parameter values.

A performance model, no matter how detailed it may be, is, nevertheless, a simplification of a very complex process and as such is subject to the inaccuracies of simplification. However, experience has shown that these models can be surprisingly accurate. Moreover, the trends that are predicted are even more accurate and can be used as an extremely effective decision tool in a variety of cases.

Uses of a performance model include:

Performance prediction.   The performance of a planned system can be predicted before it is built. This is a crucial tool during the design phase, as bottlenecks can be identified and corrected before implementation (often requiring significant architectural changes), and performance goals can be verified.

Performance tuning.   Once a system is built, it may not perform as expected. The performance model can be used along with actual performance measurements to "look inside" the system and to help locate the problems by comparing actual processing and delay times to those that are expected.

Cost/benefit of enhancements.   When plans call for modification or enhancement of a system, the performance model can be used to estimate the performance impact of the proposed change. This is an invaluable input to the evaluation of the proposed change. If the change is being made strictly for performance purposes, then the cost/benefit of the change can be accurately determined.

System configuration.   As a product is introduced to the marketplace, there often are several options that can be used to tailor the system's performance to the user's needs: number of disks, power of the processor, communication line speeds, and similar options. The performance model can be packaged as a sales tool to help configure new systems and to give the customer some confidence in the system's capacity and performance.

2. APPLICABLE DOCUMENTS

2.1 Edit function requirements, internal memorandum; Syntrex, Eatontown, NJ. July 17, 1983.

2.2 Martin, J. 1972. System Analysis for Data Transmission. Englewood Cliffs, NJ: Prentice-Hall.

2.3 International Business Machines (IBM). Analysis of some queuing models in real-time systems, Document no. F20-0007-1. White Plains, NY: IBM.

3. SYSTEM DESCRIPTION

3.1 General

A general view of the Gemini system is shown in Figure 3-1. It comprises a redundant file management system which can support up to 14 Aquarius terminals. Within Gemini, two identical file management systems, each with its own fixed disk, run in a master/slave relationship. Each terminal is connected to both sides of Gemini so that each Gemini side may receive all Aquarius traffic. However, only the master side will transmit to the Aquarius.

Figure 3-2 shows in more detail one side of the Gemini system. The terminal communications traffic is controlled by the Aquarius interface (AI). It is responsible for validating received messages and for storing them in a memory which is shared by the file manager. It also retrieves messages from shared memory for transmission to the terminals. The AI and file manager run in separate processors. The shared memory is a portion of the AI memory.

Another function performed by the AI is synchronization between the two halves of Gemini. The AI ensures that messages are handed to the file manager in either half in the same order; it does not return a response to an Aquarius until both sides have completed processing that request.

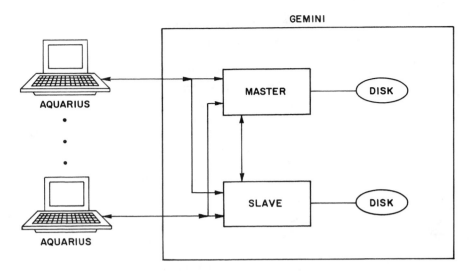

Figure 3-1 Gemini.

The file manager is responsible for executing all requests from the terminals. It runs in a multithreaded environment in which it has available several copies of itself (the subordinate file managers). As it receives terminal requests through the shared memory, it will process some itself and will pass others to its subordinates according to a routing algorithm.

Each Gemini half has a single fixed disk to store all files. Most disk transfers use a cache memory to reduce the need for physical disk accesses.

Each of these components is discussed further in the following sections.

3.2 Aquarius Communication Lines

Each Aquarius terminal is connected to the Gemini system via a high-speed, serial, synchronous, half-duplex communication line. Line speeds are

Aquarius to Gemini:	37.5 kilobytes/sec.
Gemini to Aquarius:	41.25 kilobytes/sec.

These correspond to bit rates of 300 and 330 kilobits/sec., respectively.

The protocol that is used is a contention protocol. Either side may begin transmitting without permission whenever it wishes, once it has ascertained that the other side is not already transmitting. In the event of a collision with a data packet, the sender of that packet will receive an "improper" acknowledgement and will retransmit, as described in more detail below.

A data packet may contain up to 520 bytes of data plus 27 bytes of overhead. Each data packet contains a sequence number and is acknowledged by the receiver with an

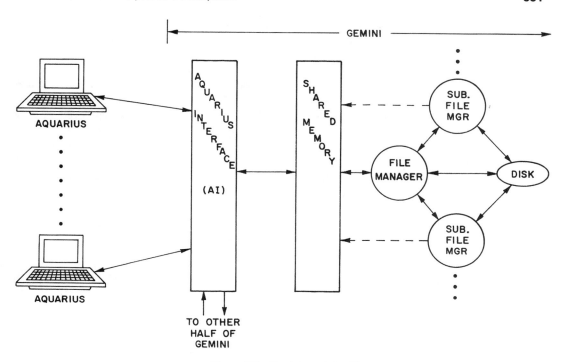

Figure 3-2 Gemini system architecture.

acknowledge packet, which is 32 bytes in length. When the line is otherwise idle, the most recent acknowledgement packets are periodically sent as an ''I'm alive'' message. Currently, this occurs about once a second, with the Gemini and Aquarius sending at slightly different rates to reduce collisions.

An acknowledgement packet may be piggybacked onto a data packet if the two are to be sent simultaneously.

If an acknowledgement packet is lost due to a collision, there is no great problem, as another will soon be transmitted anyway. However, if a data packet is lost, the sender will realize this after it receives a few (currently four) acknowledgement messages, all of which will contain the previous message sequence number. At this point, it will retransmit the message packet.

3.3 Aquarius Interface (AI)

3.3.1 Communication Control.   All communication flow between the Aquarius terminals and the Gemini system is via shared memory. Before receiving a message from a terminal, the AI allocates a block in shared memory to receive that message. The file manager places responses in shared memory for return to the terminal.

The AI controls all communication flow by scanning the terminal communication lines. As it processes each line, it provides the following functions:

Data Block Reception.   If a data block has been received from a terminal, the AI checks its completion status. If the message was received in error, it is discarded (the message will eventually be retransmitted). If the message has been received correctly, the AI checks to see if the slave side has already received it (the synchronization method between the two halves of Gemini is described in the next section). If not, no action is taken until the next scan cycle.

If the slave half has received the message properly (on the first scan cycle or on a later cycle), the master AI will queue this message to the file manager for processing and will prepare to so inform the slave, as described below. It will not return an acknowledgement at this time but will instead wait a while (currently 60 msec.) to see if a response will be available in this time. If so, the response data block will also contain the acknowledgement, thus reducing the communication load somewhat.

If the slave half receives the message in error, it is discarded by both sides. Properly received messages are synchronized with the master, as described above.

Acknowledgement messages are also synchronized as they are received, before the message sequence number is processed.

Response Block Transmission.   The AI will check to see if there is a message in shared memory for this terminal. This message may be a response message or an acknowledgement message.

If it is a response message, the AI checks to see if the slave half has responded. If not, the AI will check on the next scan cycle.

When a slave response has been received, and if it is the same response, then the AI will initiate the transmission of the block to the Aquarius. If the response is different (determined by the message size), a catastrophic error is declared, and the Aquarius is taken out of service.

If both sides have a message to send, and if one is an acknowledgement while the other is a response, the acknowledgement will be sent. The response will not be sent until the other side is ready to send it.

Acknowledgement Block Reception.   Acknowledgement block receptions require no action if they indicate the proper reception of the previous message or an appropriate idle condition. If several acknowledgements (currently four) indicate that the last block was not received, then that response block is retransmitted.

If no traffic is received for a period (typically 10 to 15 acknowledgement times) from an Aquarius terminal, then Gemini declares that Aquarius terminal to be down.

3.3.2 Synchronization.   The AI is also responsible for maintaining synchronization between the master and slave sides of the Gemini system. There are two primary goals of synchronization:

- To ensure that both sides execute file manager requests in the same order, at least insofar as critical relations are concerned. For instance, if one terminal was closing a document while another terminal was trying to open that document, success or failure of the open depends upon whether it was executed before or after the close.

- To return a response to an Aquarius only after both sides are ready with a response and only if both responses are identical.

Synchronization blocks are sent between the two Gemini halves as DMA transfers. A synchronization block, shown in Figure 3-3a, contains up to 10 message slots. Each message slot can describe an Aquarius message that has been received by that side or an Aquarius message that is ready to be transmitted by that side.

The master synchronization block' also carries a bit map showing which requests have been sent to the file manager. Each of 14 bits represent a particular Aquarius. The file manager requests are sent to the file manager in terminal number order, as will now be described.

As the AI scanner is making its rounds, it places message descriptors in the next free slot of the synchronization block each time it finds a received request or a response ready to transmit. It sends its synchronization block to the other side at the beginning of each scan cycle. It may also send one during the scan cycle if the synchronization block fills up.

The use of the synchronization blocks and the actual synchronization algorithm is shown in Figure 3-3b. In this figure, the actions of the master side are shown. The numbers in parentheses refer to processing steps to which reference will be made in the following description.

When an Aquarius request is received by the master side of the Gemini, it is stored in shared memory (1), and an entry describing this message is made in the synchronization block (2). The previously received synchronization block from the slave side is checked to see if the slave had already received the request (3). If not, the master AI proceeds with the processing of other lines and will check the slave status when this line is again serviced.

When the AI finds that the slave has also received the request (3), it queues this request to the file manager (4) and also sets the bit for this terminal in the bit map in the synchronization block (5). Note that since the synchronization block is always sent to the slave at the end of an AI scan sequence (and sometimes in between), it is guaranteed that requests are sent to the file manager in terminal sequence.

Meanwhile, the slave is processing messages in a similar manner, except that it is holding terminal requests until it receives a synchronization block from the master. At that time, it will send the requests that it is holding for terminals indicated in the master's bit map to its file manager in terminal number order. Thus, it is assured that each file manager receives requests in the same order, though the slave file manager will always get its requests later.

When the master file manager is ready to return a response, that response is stored in shared memory (6); and an entry is made in the next free slot of the synchronization block (7). A check is made to see if the slave has obtained its response by looking at the last synchronization block received from the slave (8). If not, the AI continues processing other lines and checks again when this line is serviced.

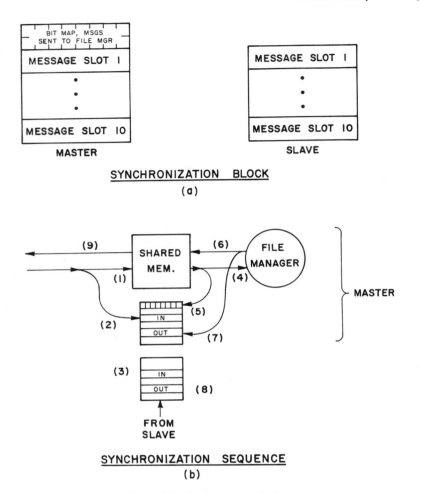

Figure 3-3 Gemini synchronization.

When the slave (which is processing responses in a similar manner) indicates that it has the response (8), and if both responses are identical (at least insofar as having equal message lengths, which would distinguish between success and failure), then the master will return the response to the Aquarius (9).

3.4 Shared Memory

All communication traffic between the Aquarius terminals and the file manager is via the shared memory, under control of the AI. Shared memory is organized into four areas:

Header section.

Disk controller buffers.

Network buffers.

AI buffers.

The header section contains shared memory control information and one 40-byte short buffer per line, which may hold an acknowledgement message to be returned to the terminal. The disk controller buffers hold responses to be returned to the terminals. As mentioned earlier, an acknowledgement is piggybacked onto a response if a response is available.

The network buffers support SynNet, the local area network which can interconnect Syntrex products. SynNet is not a subject of this study.

The AI buffers are used to receive requests from the terminals.

All buffers are 560 bytes in length (of which 520 bytes are data). The number of buffers varies with the number of terminals, but a typical configuration for a 14-terminal system would provide 20 disk controller buffers, 49 AI buffers and 30 network (NI) buffers for a SynNet system.

Three of the disk controller buffers are reserved for emergency use to break deadlocks that can occur on *long read* operations (a read of up to five contiguous disk blocks, used primarily for program download purposes). Such a deadlock can occur if multiple terminals request program downloads simultaneously, and the two sides of Gemini fill these buffers in different order so that no request is completed by both sides when the buffers become full (the order of long reads is not preserved by the file manager).

The number of AI buffers is approximately three per line. This allows some degree of look-ahead for a terminal in that one request can be acknowledged and can be queued to the file manager while the next is being received. Should a message be received when all AI buffers are full, it is discarded and must be retransmitted.

Also, should the disk controller buffers become full (not in a deadlock situation), the file managers queue up and wait for a free block.

3.5 File Manager

The file manager processes all requests from the terminals, returning the appropriate responses. As the AI detects requests in shared memory that have been completed by both sides of Gemini, those requests are queued to the file manager (as described above, the slave will queue its requests only after being notified that the master has done so).

As shown in Figure 3-2, the file manager is run in a multithreaded configuration in that there are several identical file managers running in the system (currently, five copies run simultaneously). One is designated as the main file manager; it is this process that manages the queue of requests in the shared memory. As it retrieves requests from the queue, it decides whether to process that request directly or route it to one of its subordinate file managers.

The routing algorithm is based on classifying all requests into three classes:

a. *Gets*. All Gets (requests for data) except for long reads are executed by the main file manager.

b. *Synchronized requests*. These are requests that must be executed in order, such as opens, closes, deletes. Each is handed to a free subordinate file manager, and these subordinate threads are queued (if there are more than one) so that only one executes at a time. Executions are in order.

c. *All other requests*. All other requests are handed to a free subordinate file manager.

If all subordinate file managers are busy, the main file manager is stalled. It cannot access the next request as it may not be able to deal with it. It cannot even "peek" at the next request to see if it is a Get which it could execute.

In most cases, a subordinate will return its response (usually, just a completion status) to the main file manager, who will then return it to the terminal via shared memory. However, in the case of long reads in which significant data is returned, the subordinate file manager processing that long read will return the data directly and will notify the main file manager when it has completed.

Each file manager executes its request by issuing a series of read block and write block commands to disk as necessary. These are independent commands so that no one file manager can seize the disk for more than a block read or write time. All file managers have equal priority for disk accesses.

The disk system includes an 80-block cache memory managed by an LRU (least recently used) algorithm. Certain operations effectively bypass cache, such as long reads, as it is unlikely that these operations would benefit from cache. In these cases, a cache block is marked as a candidate for immediate reuse.

3.6 File System

The Syntrex file system comprises a hierarchical structure of directories which provide unique paths to files. A document is made up of a set of files.

All files and directories (which are actually files, as will be seen later) comprise a series of 512-byte sectors (or blocks) on disk. Files are organized into a document via a directory, as shown in Figure 3-4a. The directory is a named set of sectors, each of which can contain up to 15 file names. Thus, if the directory contains 15 or less files, it is made up of one sector; for up to 30 files, the directory requires two sectors. Sectors continue to be added in this way as necessary.

A file name in a directory comprises the name of the file to which it points and a physical disk sector address (a block pointer), which points to the actual file (Figure 3-4b). If the file contains less than 512 characters, then it is contained in this single block. Otherwise, this block contains up to 64 pointers to 64 other blocks. In this case, the block is known as an indirect block.

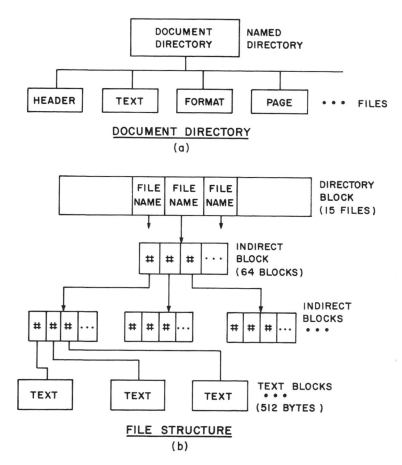

Figure 3-4   Document structure.

An indirect block may point up to 64 text blocks containing the file data or to another 64 indirect blocks. Figure 3-4b shows a directory entry pointing to an indirect block, which points to another set of indirect blocks, which point to the set of text blocks.

Thus, a file with no indirect levels can contain 512 bytes. One indirect level supports $64 \times 512 = 32K$ bytes; two indirect levels support 64×512^2, or 16 megabytes (about 5000 to 8000 pages).

The above description of the structure of a text file as a tree structure also applies to directories. A directory is just another file in which the text is a series of file names, up to 15 per block. Thus, if the directory shown in Figure 3-4 contained 100 file name entries, it would actually comprise an indirect block, which would then point to 7 text blocks, each of which could hold 15 file names. Its indirect block would be pointed to by a file name in the next higher directory and so on.

4. TRANSACTION MODEL

The transactions to be considered for this analysis of Gemini are the common set of editing functions, which include

Index Scan
Open/Close Document
Attach Copy
Physical Copy
Go To Page
Scroll
Delete/Insert
Cut
Paste
Insert Footnote
Add Text Attribute
Manual Hyphenation
Paginate
Print

The disk and processor activity for these transactions has been analyzed in reference 2.1, listed earlier in the chapter. They are summarized in Tables 4-1 through 4-3 for four classes of activity:

$$n_{tj} = \text{number of transactions for edit function } j.$$

$$n_{gj} = \text{number of Get commands for edit function } j.$$

$$n_{dj} = \text{number of disk accesses required for edit function } j.$$

$$n'_{dj} = \text{number of disk cache accesses for edit function } j.$$

These terms represent the significant results of the transaction model and are those that are required by the usage scenario developed in Section 9. The terms in Tables 4-1 through 4-3 are defined in Table 8-1.

TABLE 4-1. EDIT FUNCTION TRANSACTION ACTIVITY

j	Function	n_{tj}	n_{gj}
1	Index Scan	$4 - u + 30k_t + n_{g1}$	$\sum_{i=u}^{3} f_i/[15(1 - s_i)]$
2	Open/Close Document	$2(4 + 2f_s)$	0
3	Attach Copy	$4 + 2f_s$	0
4	Physical Copy	$8 + 8f_s + 2(p + f)d/n_{tb}$	$(p + f)d/n_{tb} + 2f_s$

TABLE 4-1. EDIT FUNCTION TRANSACTION ACTIVITY

j	Function	n_{tj}	n_{gj}
5	Go To Page	n_{g5}	$5 + b_5 + (23c_s/n_{tb})\rceil^r$
6	Scroll	n_{g6}	0 if $n_s \leq 23$
			$[(n_s - 23)c_s/n_{tb}]\rceil^r$ if $n_s > 23$
7	Delete/Insert	$1 + n_{da}/n_{tb}$	0
8	Cut	$8 + n_c/n_{tb}$	0
9	Paste	$7 + 2n_p/n_{tb}$	$1 + n_p/n_{tb}$
10	Insert Footnote	8	0
11	Add Text Attribute	2	0
12	Manual Hyphenation	2	0
13	Paginate	$13 + 12k_t + 6f_s + d/6 +$ $(p + f)d/n_{tb}$	$2 + 2f_s + (p + f)d/n_{tb}$
14	Print	$12 + 2k_t + 6f_s + d/6 +$ $(p + f)d/n_{tb}$	$2 + 2f_s + d/6 + (p + f)d/n_{tb}$

TABLE 4-2. EDIT FUNCTION DISK ACTIVITY

j	Function	n_{dj}	n'_{dj}
1	Index Scan	$\sum_{i=u}^{3} d_{oi} + 120k_t + n_{g1}$	0
2	Open/Close Document	$n_{t2}d_{o4}$	0
3	Attach Copy	$n_{t3}(3 + d_{n4})$	$2.1n_{t3}$
4	Physical Copy	$(4 + 2f_s)d_{n4} +$ $[(2b_5 + 10)p + 12f]d/n_{tb} +$ $20f_s$	$4.4 + 10.2f_s +$ $[(2b_s + 4)p + 6f]d/n_{tb} +$ $[(p + f)d/n_{tb} + 2f_s]r\{(p +$ $f)d/n_{tb} + 2f_s\}$
5	Go To Page	n_{g5}	$1 + b_5$
6	Scroll	n_{g6}	o
7	Delete/Insert	$n_{t7}d_p$	$n_{t7}d'_p$
8	Cut	$2d_{n4} + 18 + (2 + n_c/n_{tb})d_p$	$10.2 + (2 + n_c/n_{tb})d'_p$
9	Paste	$2d_{o4} + 11 +$ $(1 + n_p/n_{tb})(1 + d_p)$	$6 + (1 + n_p/n_{tb})d'_p$
10	Insert Footnote	$2d_{n4} + 33 + d_p$	$20.2 + d'_p$
11	Add Text Attribute	$11 + d_p$	$6 + d'_p$
12	Manual Hyphenation	$11 + d_p$	$6 + d'_p$
13	Paginate	$(5 + 2f_s)d_{o4} + 3 + 48k_t +$ $2f_s + 2.5d + (p + f)d/n_{tb}$	$4d/3$
14	Print	$(5 + 2f_s)d_{o4} + 2 + 16k_t +$ $2f_s + d/6 + (p + f)d/n_{tb}$	0

TABLE 4-3. EDIT FUNCTION TERM EXPRESSIONS

$d_{oi} = (1 - p_i)\, f_i/[30(1 - s_i)] + p_i(b_i + 1)$	(1-1)
$d_{ni} = 2.2 + (1 - p_i)\, f_i/[15(1 - s_i)] + p_i(b_i + 1)$	(1-2)
$p_s = pd/n_{tp} \displaystyle\sum_{j=7}^{12} n_j$	(1-3a)
$p_{\text{smax}} = 1$	(1-4)
$r\{x\} = 1 - c(x)/x$ if $c(x) \le c$	(1-8a)
$r\{x\} = 1 - \dfrac{C + (x - e)\left(1 - \dfrac{C}{R}\right)}{x}$ if $c(x) > C$	(1-8b)
$c(n) = R - (R - 1)p(n)$	(1-7)
$p(n) = 1 - \dfrac{1}{R} \displaystyle\sum_{m=1}^{n-1} p(m)$	(1-6)
$p(1) = 1$	(1-5)
$e = \min(R)$ such that $c(e) \ge C$	(1-10)
$n_{tb} = 512(1 - s_5)$	(1-3d)
$n_{tp} = 32.768(1 - s_5)$	(1-3e)
$d_{sp} = 2[65 + (b_5 - 1)(1 + pd/n_{tp})]$	(1-9b)
$d_p = 2b_5 + 9 + (12 + d_{sp})p_s$	(1-3b)
$d'_p = 2b_5 + 4 + (8 + d_{sp}r\{65\})p_s$	(1-3c)

5. TRAFFIC MODEL

A model representing the major processing steps for an Aquarius function is shown in Figure 5-1. For this discussion, the following terms are defined:

- *Transaction.* A transaction is a file manager command sent to the Gemini by an Aquarius terminal, for example, get a block, put a block, open a file, and others. Each transaction is made up of a *request* sent to Gemini and a *response* received from Gemini. An Aquarius cannot issue its next request until it has received the response to its previous request.

- *Function.* A function is an Aquarius action specified by the operator, for example, open a document, cut and paste, close, print, and others. A function comprises one or more transactions.

- *Scenario.* A scenario is a defined sequence of actions to be taken to process a document. A scenario comprises one or more functions.

Referring to Figure 5-1, when a user requests a function at the terminal (1), the Aquarius processes it (2), creates a request, and sends that request to Gemini (3). The AI processes the request, once it has been received, into shared memory (4) and then waits for the slave to indicate proper reception (5) before queuing the request to the file manager (6).

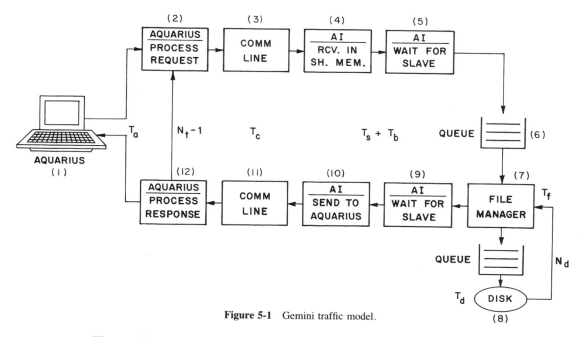

Figure 5-1 Gemini traffic model.

The multithreaded file manager will ultimately process this request (7) and may issue one or more logical disk commands (8) on its behalf. On the average, N_d disk commands (reads or writes) are issued for a request.

When the processing of the request has been completed, the file manager will store a response in shared memory. The AI will wait for the slave (9) to indicate that it has also processed the response and will then send that response to the Aquarius (10, 11).

The Aquarius will process the response (12) and may issue another request. When Aquarius has completed the function, a response is returned to the caller (a process within Aquarius). On the average, N_t Gemini transactions are created for every user-requested function.

The following performance analysis will concern itself primarily with the evaluation of transaction response time as a function of system load. Transaction response time is separated into two primitive response times:

T_r = processing request/response time, or that time required to respond to a request if there were no disk accesses required.

T_d = disk response time.

The average transaction response time, T_t, is then

$$T_t = \text{average transaction time} = T_r + N_d T_d \tag{1}$$

and the average function time, T_g, is

$$T_g = \text{average function time} = N_t(T_r + N_d T_d) \tag{2}$$

These parameters are not particularly useful for getting a feel for terminal responsiveness but form a valuable basis for determining the degradation of system performance under load and under different user scenarios and for evaluating the effect of proposed system modifications.

A more realistic feel for terminal responsiveness may be obtained by considering the total time required to execute some complex scenario of operations equivalent to actual use of the system. Let function i require N_{tij} transactions of type j and let transaction j require N_{dj} disk accesses. Then function i will require a time T_{gi}, which is expressed as:

$$T_{gi} = \sum_j N_{tij}(T_r + N_{dj}T_d) \qquad (3)$$

With this expression, the average time to perform an Open, Get, Cut and Paste, or any of the other commands can be evaluated.

The completion time for a complete scenario, T_s, requiring N_{gi} function requests for function i, is

$$T_s = \text{average scenario time} = \sum_i N_{gi}T_{gi} \qquad (4)$$

Thus, the time to complete an entire scenario can be determined as a function of load. The rate of degradation of total scenario time as a function of load, given by equation 4, can be shown to be the same as the rate of degradation of the average transaction time given by equation 1.

The simpler equation 1 can be used to evaluate average transaction time if relative performance measures are desired. The more complex scenario time can be evaluated via equation 4 to give measures more meaningful to the user.

6. PERFORMANCE MODEL

In this section, the various traffic elements described in the previous sections are characterized mathematically so that various response times can be predicted as a function of load for a variety of system conditions and scenarios.

6.1 Notation

Before proceeding with the derivation of the model, certain notational conventions will be established. They are presented as a guideline, though the limitation of the number of symbols on the author's typewriter requires occasional departures from these conventions.

A parameter in the model may be an *input variable* (one that is likely to be a candidate for variation in order to study different environmental conditions), an *input parameter* that is substantially known (such as communication line speed), a *calculated intermediate parameter*, or a *result parameter* (a calculated parameter that is likely to be of interest as an end result). Each parameter is represented by a subscripted alphabetic symbol, where typical symbols used include:

L —load carried by a server

m —message size

n,N—number of items

p,P—probability

q,Q—queue length

r,R —rate

s —communication line speed

t,T —time

The first subscript usually identifies a subsystem. Typical of these are

A—Aquarius terminal

c —communication line

d—disk

f —file manager

g—Gemini system

s —AI scanner

Thus, T_s would be the transaction delay time imposed by the AI scanner; and L_d would be the disk load.

Subsequent subscripts further qualify the parameter and are defined as necessary.

6.2 Average Transaction Time

As discussed in the previous section, the average transaction time for a transaction to flow through the Gemini system is

$$T_t = T_r + N_d T_d \qquad (2\text{-}1)$$

where T_r is the request/response time if there were no disk accesses associated with the average transaction, T_d is the time required to process a disk request, and N_d is the average number of disk accesses per transaction.

referring to Figure 5-1, T_r can be expressed as

$$T_r = T_a + T_c + T_s + T_f + T_b \qquad (2\text{-}2)$$

where

T_a = delay time imposed by the Aquarius terminal.

T_c = delay time imposed by the communication line.

T_s = delay time imposed by the AI scanner.

T_f = delay time imposed by the file manager.

T_b = delay time caused by shared memory blocking.

6.3 Aquarius Terminal

A detailed study of the Aquarius terminal is beyond the scope of this effort. However, its processing times cannot be ignored. The Aquarius is therefore characterized as a "black box" which imposes a load-independent delay time on each transaction which it generates. This delay time is the term T_a in equation 2-2 and represents the time required by the Aquarius to generate a request and then to process the response to that request.

6.4 Communication Line

Aquarius and Gemini communicate over a synchronous, half-duplex communication line via a contention protocol. When either wants to transmit, it first waits for the line to be idle. It then will transmit its data and will wait for an acknowledgement.

It is possible that the data message will collide with a data message or acknowledgement being transmitted from the other end. This can only be determined after a few acknowledgements have been received for the previous data message sent. Since acknowledgements on a presumably idle line occur only about once a second, message retransmission could induce a delay of several seconds.

Therefore, communication line time to send a message is

communication time = wait time + transmission time + retransmission time.

Let

s_a = speed of line from Aquarius to Gemini (bytes/second).

s_g = speed of line from Gemini to Aquarius (bytes/second).

m_a = average message size for a data message from Aquarius to Gemini (bytes).

m_g = average message size for a data message from Gemini to Aquarius (bytes).

m_k = acknowledge message size (bytes).

r_a = transaction rate imposed by an Aquarius terminal (transactions per second).

Let us first consider wait time for the Aquarius. Since each transaction comprises an acknowledged request and response, the probability that the Gemini will be transmitting is $r_a(m_g + m_k)/s_g$ (message rate multiplied by message time). Thus, the Aquarius will find the line busy when it wants to transmit with this probability. If it is assumed that message sizes are exponentially distributed (a conservative assumption), then the average time that the Aquarius will wait when the line is busy is an average Gemini message time (a characteristic of the exponential distribution is that the average time for an event to complete is independent of the time at which observation of the event first began).

Thus, average Aquarius wait time, t_{caw}, is (probability of wait) × (length of wait):

$$t_{caw} = r_a[(m_g + m_k)/s_g]^2 \qquad (4-1)$$

Wait time for Gemini messages is somewhat different. The probability of having to wait is similar to that for Aquarius and is $r_a(m_a + m_k)/s_a$. However, if the line is busy, the AI will continue processing other lines and will check this line on its next scan cycle. It is assumed that it will find the line idle on the next try because of the message/acknowledge protocol (a second wait could happen but with very low probability). Let

$$t_{ss} = \text{AI scanner scan time}$$

Then

Gemini wait time:

$$t_{cgw} = r_a t_{ss}(m_a + m_k)/s_a \qquad (4\text{-}2)$$

Average transmission time is that time required to send the message. Thus, Aquarius transmission time is:

$$t_{cat} = m_a/s_a \qquad (4\text{-}3)$$

Gemini transmission time is:

$$t_{cgt} = m_g/s_g \qquad (4\text{-}4)$$

There is a collision window during which one side may check the line, believe it is idle, and start transmitting when the other side is doing the same. This window starts when one side decides the line is idle and continues with the processing and communication time required to transmit the first byte and have it detected at the other side.

Let t_w = collision window for the first byte on the line, which includes:

- time to initiate transmission of the first byte once it has been decided that the line is idle.

- transmission time of the first byte.

- communication line propagation delay.

- time to indicate to the receiver that the first byte has been received.

The probability that an Aquarius message will start in this window is $r_a t_w$. The probability that a Gemini message will start in this window is $r_g t_w$, and the collision probability for a message is therefore $r_a r_g t_w^2$.

Given a collision, the message will not be retransmitted for several acknowledgement times. Let

n_k = number of acknowledgements for the previous message before a message is retransmitted.

t_k = interacknowledgement time for an idle line.

Then the average retransmission time caused by collisions is (probability of collision) $\times$ (retransmission delay), or $r_a r_g t_w^2 n_k t_k$.

The collision window time can be further expanded by assuming a propagation time on the communication line of typically half the speed of light and by assigning parameters to the processing times. Let

t_{awt}, t_{qwt} = time to initiate transmission of a byte once the line has been determined to be idle at the Aquarius/Gemini (seconds).

t_{awr}, t_{qwr} = time to detect the reception of a byte by the software once it has been received by the hardware at the Aquarius/Gemini (seconds).

b = average communication line (bus) length (meters).

c = speed of light (meters/second).

Combining all of the above with these new parameters, one obtains the following retransmission times:

Aquarius retransmission time:

$$t_{car} = r_a r_g n_k t_k (t_{awt} + 1/s_a + 2b/c + t_{awr})^2 \tag{4-5}$$

Gemini retransmission time:

$$t_{cgr} = r_a r_g n_k t_k (t_{gwt} + 1/s_g + 2b/c + t_{gwr})^2 \tag{4-6}$$

The transaction time imposed by the communication line is the sum of all these delays for the request being sent from the Aquarius and for the receipt of the response from the Gemini:

$$T_c = t_{caw} + t_{cat} + t_{car} + t_{cgw} + t_{cgt} + t_{cgr} \tag{4-7}$$

where we have ignored the probability of multiple retransmissions and where

T_c = average transaction communication time.

t_{cij} = component time, where

       $i = a$ is Aquarius.

          = g is Gemini.

       $j = w$ is wait time.

          = t is transmission time.

          = r is retransmission time.

6.5 Aquarius Interface

The AI operates by scanning the Aquarius terminals. From a performance viewpoint, the AI can be analyzed by looking at two separate issues:

- the number of scan cycles required to process a transaction.
- the average duration of a scan cycle.

6.5.1 Scan cycles.   So far as scan cycles are concerned, the transaction is delayed during the time that it is waiting for the AI to process it. When a request is first received by the master AI, the transmission must wait, on the average, one-half scan cycle for the master AI to find the received request.

This request has been received simultaneously by the slave AI, which is scanning asynchronously relative to the master AI. Thus, given any state of the two scanners, any other state is equally probable. Using this, one can determine the average synchronization delay between the two scanners for an input message.

There are four cases:

a. The slave gets to the message first. It will do so with a probability of 0.5. Given this condition,

   a1. The slave gets to its home position before the master gets to the terminal, with probability 0.5. In this case, the master will find the message and may process it immediately.

   a2. The master gets to the terminal before the slave gets to its home position, with probability 0.5. In this case, the master will not process the message until the next scan cycle, resulting in a one-cycle synchronization delay.

b. The master gets to the message first. It will do so with probability 0.5. Given this condition and after the slave has gotten the message,

   b1. The slave gets to its home position before the master gets to the terminal the second time, with probability 0.5. In this case, the synchronization delay is one scan cycle.

   b2. The master reaches the terminal a second time before the slave reaches its home position, with probability 0.5. In this case, the master must make one more scan cycle before processing the message, resulting in a synchronization delay of two scan cycles.

The above has ignored early transmissions of a synchronization block because it becomes full. This would improve performance and is, therefore, a conservative assumption.

Since each condition is equally probable, and since these conditions result in 0, 1, 1, and 2 scan cycles of synchronization delay, respectively, the average synchronization delay for input messages is $0 \times .25 + 1 \times .25 + 1 \times .25 + 2 \times .25$, or one scan cycle.

The master now queues the message to the file manager and sets a bit in the synchronization block bit map to indicate this action. An average half cycle later, the master will send this synchronization block to the slave.

It is assumed that the slave must pass through home before sending any of the messages to the file manager (a half scan cycle). The slave will then take another half scan cycle to locate this message and to send it to the slave file manager. Thus, the slave file manager is, on the average, 1.5 scan cycles behind the master.

It is further assumed that variations in processing and disk times average out and that all commands are processed in the same order by the master and slave. Thus, the slave file manager will return the response to this request 1.5 scan cycles later than the master file manager. A half cycle later, the slave will inform the master; and again, a half cycle later, the master will find that the slave has the response. This results in an output synchronization delay of one scan cycle. At this point, the response may be transmitted.

Summarizing AI scanner delays imposed on a transaction, one obtains the following:

	Scan lines
Master finds request	0.5
Input synchronization to master	1.0
Input synchronization to slave	1.5
Output synchronization	1.0
	4.0

Thus, a transaction will be delayed by four AI scan cycle times.

6.5.2 Scan time. As the AI scans the terminal lines, it basically can perform one of four functions:

1. Do nothing.
2. Process a received message.
3. Pass a request to the file manager.
4. Transmit a message.

For each transaction, the AI must receive a request, send an acknowledgement, send the request to the file manager, send a response, and receive an acknowledgement (two message receptions, two message transmissions, and one file manager hand-off).

Let

$$t_{ss} = \text{average AI scan time to service all terminals.}$$

$$N_a = \text{number of Aquarius terminals on the system.}$$

$$r_a = \text{transaction rate per Aquarius terminal.}$$

Then the number of transactions received per scan cycle is $N_a r_a t_{ss}$.

However, while the AI is scanning lines, it is also servicing interrupts, which adds to the amount of time it takes for scan processing requirements. At the interrupt level, it is processing two message receptions and two message transmissions as described above for each transaction plus the reception of a synchronization block.

Using the convention of priming to denote interrupt times, let:

$$t_{si} = \text{AI time required to process an idle line.}$$

t_{sr} = AI time required to process a received message.

t_{sf} = AI time required to send a request to the file manager.

t_{st} = AI time to process a transmitted message.

t'_{sr} = AI interrupt time to process a received message.

t'_{st} = AI interrupt time to process a transmitted message.

t'_{sb} = AI interrupt time to process a synchronization block.

t_k = interval between "I'm alive" messages (acknowledge messages on an idle line).

t_{ssi} = idle processing time.

One can then express the total average scan time as:

$$t_{ss} = N_a r_a t_{ss}[2(t_{sr} + t'_{sr} + t_{st} + t'_{st}) + t_{sf}] + t'_{sb} \\ + N_a t_{ss}(t_{sr} + t'_{sr} + t_{st} + t'_{st})/t_k + t_{ssi} \tag{5-1}$$

The first term represents the number of message receptions and transmissions and file manager hand-offs handled in an average cycle (number of transactions multiplied by processing and interrupt times per transaction). The second term is the synchronization block interrupt time, which occurs once per cycle. The third term represents the load imposed by "I'm alive" messages, which occur at a rate of $N_a t_{ss}/t_k$ messages per scan cycle.

The final term is the idle processing time required. Idle processing is required for any line which does not have an activity. Since the rate of activity is five times the transaction rate (there are five activities per transaction), then the number of active lines on a scan (assuming only one activity per line on any scan cycle) is $5N_a r_a t_{ss}$. Thus, the idle processing time during a scan cycle, t_{ssi}, is

$$t_{ssi} = N_a(1 - 5r_a t_{ss})t_{si} \quad , \quad 5r_a t_{ss} < 1 \tag{5-2}$$

$$t_{ssi} = 0 \quad\quad\quad\quad\quad\quad , \quad 5r_a t_{ss} \geq 1 \tag{5-3}$$

Finally, t'_{sb} is a function of the number of slots filled in the synchronization block. Let

t'_{sbo} = interrupt time to process an empty synchronization block.

t'_{sbb} = interrupt time to process a filled slot in the synchronization block.

Since there is a slot used for each received and transmitted message, there are four slots used per transaction. The synchronization block interrupt processing time can then be expressed as

$$t'_{sb} = t'_{sbo} + 4N_a r_a t_{ss} t'_{sbb} \tag{5-4}$$

where $4N_a r_a t_{ss}$ is the average number of slots used in the synchronization block.

Equation 5-1, which shows t_{ss} as a function of itself, could become unstable at large loads, depending upon the accuracy of the provided parameters. Therefore, a maximum value on the AI scan cycle will be imposed for the condition of one message to be transmitted, one to be received, and one to be passed to the file manager for each line:

$$t_{ss_{max}} = N_a(t_{sr} + t'_{sr} + t_{st} + t'_{st} + t_{sf})$$
(5-5)

The above analysis has evaluated the AI scan cycle as a function of load, r_a.

The AI delay, T_s, imposed on a transaction is four scan cycles, as shown in Section 6.5.1:

$$T_s = 4t_{ss}$$
(5-6)

Equations 5-1 through 5-6 represent a nonlinear set of equations for t_{ss} (due to equations 5-2 and 5-3), in which t_{ss} is expressed as a function of itself; t_{ss} can be expressed more conveniently for programming purposes as follows.

First, using equation 5-4, all terms on the right of equation 5-1 containing t_{ss}, except for t_{ssi}, are gathered and called by the parameter a:

$$a = N_a[(2r_a + 1/t_k)(t_{sr} + t'_{sr} + t_{st} + t'_{st}) + r_a t_{sf} + 4r_a t'_{sbb}]$$
(5-7)

This parameter is, in effect, the transaction load on the AI.

Then

$$t_{ss} = \frac{t'_{sbo} + k_i N_a t_{si}}{1 - (a - 5k_i N_a r_a t_{si})}$$
(5-8)*

k_i has been introduced as a switch:

$$k_i = \text{idle terminal indicator:}$$
(5-9)

1 if there are idle terminals $(5r_a t_{ss} < 1)$

0 if all terminals are busy $(5r_a t_{ss} \geq 1)$

Of course, the value of k_i is not known *a priori*. Therefore, equation 5-8 is first calculated with $k_i = 1$ to obtain a trial value of t_{ss}. If this results in $5r_a t_{ss} \geq 1$, a second calculation is made for $k_i = 0$. That value for t_{ss} is used instead.

This value is then compared to that value of t_{ss} obtained from equation 5-5, and the lesser value is used.

6.6 File Manager

The file manager comprises multiple threads that service a common queue (the linked requests in shared memory). The allocation of these requests to file manager threads is a complex process from a modeling viewpoint and cannot be represented mathematically. However, an approximation can be made which allows a reasonable characterization.

When multiple servers process the same population, there are generally two limiting

---

*Note the similarity between equation 5-8 and equation 8-8 of chapter 8. The scan cycle time is the idle time divided by one minus the incremental processing load.

cases. The best case is when all servers service a common queue. The next item in the queue is serviced by the next free server.

The "normal" worst case is when each arriving user chooses a line in which to wait and then must be serviced by that server. In this case, the multiple servers are simply a set of single servers operating in parallel. The true multiserver case described first gives significantly improved performance over parallel single servers.

There is another case in which performance is poorer than that for parallel single servers, and that is when each server services only certain classes of transactions. For instance, if a bank had a common waiting line, and if the customer at the head of the line went to the next free teller, this would be the best case. If each customer freely chose a teller waiting line when he entered a bank, this would be the next best case. If one teller serviced customers whose last name began with A–C, another D–F, and so on, this would be the worst of the above cases.

In the case of the file manager, there is a mix of these disciplines. All the Gets are handled by the main thread, an example of the worst case above. Most others are handed to the next free thread, an example of the best case above. However, synchronized requests must be executed in order and are therefore queued behind each other. This is again an example of the worst case above. Even worse, each queued, synchronized request deletes a server, since queuing is done by queuing file managers.

As long as the number of servers is small, it is assumed that this complex service algorithm is best represented by independent parallel file managers, each serving its own queue. Transactions are distributed randomly among the queues. To the extent that requests are non-Get, nonsynchronized requests, this approximation is conservative; otherwise, it is optimistic.

The file manager service time is the sum of transaction processing time and CPU waiting time required for a transaction. In addition, main thread blocking will be considered.

Let

t_f = file manager service time, exclusive of disk accesses.

t_{fp} = time required to process a transaction if no disk requests were required.

t_{fd} = delay imposed on an average transaction due to waiting for the CPU.

t_{fb} = delay imposed on an average transaction due to main thread blocking.

Then the file manager service time, t_f, is

$$t_f = t_{fp} + t_{fd} + t_{fb} \tag{6-1}$$

Since t_{fp} is an input parameter, there is no need to evaluate it further.

The amount of time that a transaction must wait in line for the CPU while it is being used by other file manager threads is t_{fd}. This will occur for each file manager dispatch required to process a transaction. There are three dispatches required to route, process, and return the transaction (between the main thread and the subordinate thread) and one required following the completion of each disk request. Thus, there are $(N_d + 3)$ dispatches per transaction, where N_d has been previously defined as the number of disk accesses required per transaction.

Let

$$t_{dp} = \text{processing time to process a disk request.}$$

Then the three required dispatches will require a processing time of t_{fp}, and subsequent dispatches to process disk requests will require a processing time of t_{dp} each. Average processing time per dispatch is $(t_{fp} + N_d t_{dp})/(N_d + 3)$. Assuming the processing times are exponentially distributed, and using the M/M/1 queue waiting time, the CPU delay, t_{fd}, for a transaction is $(N_d + 3)$ wait times:

$$t_{fd} = (N_d + 3)\, \frac{L_p}{(1 - L_p)}\, \frac{(t_{fp} + N_d t_{dp})}{(N_d + 3)}$$

or

$$t_{fd} = L_p(t_{fp} + N_d t_{dp})/(1 - L_p) \tag{6-2}$$

where L_p is the processor load. Since transactions are arriving at a rate of $N_a r_a$ transactions per second, and since each requires a processing time of $(t_{fp} + N_d t_{dp})$, then CPU load is

$$L_p = \frac{F - 1}{F} N_a r_a (t_{fp} + N_d t_{dp}) \tag{6-3}$$

for F file managers. The term $(F - 1)/F$ causes the load of a specific file manager to be ignored when calculating its dispatch time, as it will not be delayed by itself.*

Blocking occurs if all subordinate threads are busy and will continue for one file manager service time $(t_f + N_d T_d)$, assuming an exponential distribution of this time. If there are F threads in the system, then blocking occurs if at least $F - 1$ requests are in the system, none of which are Gets.

Let L_f be the load on the file management system, with each thread carrying a load (its occupancy) of L_f/F. Thus, the probability that $F - 1$ threads will be busy is $(L_f/F)^{F-1}$. If the probability that a request is a Get is p_g (derived from the scenario; see Section 9), then the probability of $F - 1$ threads servicing non-Get requests is $(1 - p_g)^{F-1}$. The probability of blocking is the product of these probabilities, and the average transaction time lost to blocking is the probability of blocking multiplied by the average blocked time, $t_f + N_d T_d$:

$$t_{fb} = [(1 - p_g)L_f/F]^{F-1}(t_f + N_d T_d) \tag{6-4}$$

where

$$F = \text{number of file manager threads.}$$

$$p_g = \text{probability that a request is a Get.}$$

---

*See Appendix 6.

$$L_f = \text{total load on the file manager.}$$

As defined above, the transaction rate is $N_a r_a$, where N_a is the number of Aquarius terminals, and r_a is the transaction rate per terminal. Since the file manager must wait for N_d disk accesses per transaction, each requiring a time of T_d (evaluated in the next section), then the total file manager load is

$$L_f = N_a r_a (t_f + N_d T_d) \tag{6-5}$$

The average delay time imposed by a file manager, T_f, including queue wait and service times, again assuming that its service time is exponential, is

$$T_f = \frac{1}{1 - L_f/F} (t_f + N_d T_d) \tag{6-6}$$

Equations 6-1 through 6-5 relate t_f as a high order function of itself and therefore must be solved iteratively.

6.7 Disk Management

All file manager threads use the disk as a common resource by placing requests in the disk queue and then awaiting their completion.

Let

t_{ds} = disk system service time to process a disk request.

t_{dp} = processing time required to process a disk request.

t_{dp1} = processing time required to process a disk request from cache.

t_{dp2} = processing time required to process a physical disk request.

t_{da} = disk access time (seek plus latency).

h = cache hit ratio.

Then

$$t_{dp} = h t_{dp1} + (1 - h) t_{dp2} \tag{7-1a}$$

$$t_{ds} = t_{dp} + (1 - h) t_{da} \tag{7-1b}$$

The time required to service a disk request is not only this service time but also the time spent waiting in the disk queue. Since the queue length cannot be greater than the number of file managers (a relatively small number), improved accuracy in the model can be obtained by not using the infinite population M/M/1 relation but rather using the relations for a finite user population (the F file managers in this case) as derived in reference 2.3.

A file manager is busy waiting for a disk response for an average time of T_d, where T_d has been defined as the total disk delay time, including waiting in the queue and then being serviced by the disk. There is then an average time of t_{fi} during which the file manager is idle relative to the disk and is a candidate for making another disk request.

The "service ratio" z is a measure of the proportion of time that the file manager is available as a candidate for issuing a disk request. It is defined as

$$z = \frac{t_{fi}}{T_d} \tag{7-2}$$

The greater z is, the more available the file manager is.

If there are F file managers, each with a service ratio z, it has been shown (see reference 2.3) that the average number of file managers that will be busy when another file manager makes its request, and thus the average number of requests in the system (including those queued to the disk plus those being serviced), is given by the following truncated Poisson distribution:

$$q_d = \sum_{k=1}^{F-1} k \, \frac{\dfrac{z^{F-k-1}}{(F-k-1)!}}{\displaystyle\sum_{j=0}^{F-1} \dfrac{z^j}{j!}} \tag{7-3}$$

This assumes an exponentially distributed disk service time and represents the number of file requests ahead of a newly arriving request.

Thus, the total disk delay time for a transaction, including queue wait and service, is

$$T_d = (q_d + 1)t_{da} \tag{7-4}$$

The set of F file managers receives transactions at a rate of $N_a r_a$ transactions per second and generates $N_d N_a r_a$ disk requests per second. Each file manager generates disk requests at a rate of $N_d N_a r_a / F$ requests per second. Thus, the interval between disk requests by a file manager is the reciprocal of this expression. This interval must also be the sum of the file manager idle time, t_{fi}, between disk services and of the disk service time, T_d. Thus,

$$\frac{F}{N_d N_a r_a} = t_{fi} + T_d \tag{7-5}$$

or

$$t_{fi} = \frac{F}{N_d N_a r_a} - T_d \tag{7-6}$$

Substituting this into equation 7-2, t_{fi} is eliminated from this set of equations:

$$z = \frac{F}{N_d N_a r_a T_d} - 1 \tag{7-7}$$

Since T_d is a function of q_d, which is a nonlinear function of z, which is a function of T_d, T_d is a function of itself; thus, these expressions must be solved iteratively.

The disk load, L_d, is

$$L_d = N_a r_a N_d t_{ds} \tag{7-8}$$

6.8 Buffer Overflow

Input requests and output responses are buffered in shared memory. If the input buffers become full, incoming messages are discarded and must be retransmitted. If output buffers become full, the file managers are stalled. Either represents a delay in the processing of a transaction.

The transaction delay due to full input buffers can be determined as follows. A request is allocated to a buffer when it is received and remains there until the file manager begins to process it. Its occupancy of the buffer occurs in two phases:

- Waiting for AI synchronization before it can be queued to the file manager.
- Waiting in the queue for the file manager.

As described in section 6.5.1, a message waits in the slave buffer for 1.5 AI scanner cycles longer than in the master. Thus, the slave input buffer occupancy represents the critical case and requires three scan cycles of a time t_{ss} for AI synchronization (see section 6.5.1) before placing the request in the file manager queue.

Assuming an exponential distribution of file manager service time, the average time a request will wait in the queue for the file manager, t_{fq}, is

$$t_{fq} = \frac{(L_f/F)}{1 - L_f/F} \, t_f \qquad (8\text{-}1)$$

where t_f, L_f, and F have been previously defined as the file manager service time, file manager load, and number of file managers, respectively.

Input blocks are also used by acknowledge messages. As described in section 6.5.1, an acknowledge message (on either side) will require an average of 1.5 AI scan cycles to be detected by both sides. Acknowledge messages are received once for each transaction plus approximately once per second (actually every t_k seconds as previously defined) for "I'm alive" messages. (The reduction in these later messages as system activity increases is ignored as a simplifying and conservative assumption.)

Thus, the total occupancy time of an input buffer is $(4.5t_{ss} + t_{fq})$ for each transaction since a transaction requires both a request and a response. In addition, an input buffer is required for $1.5t_{ss}$ for each "I'm alive" message. Since transactions arrive at a rate of $N_a r_a$ transactions per second, since "I'm alive" messages are generated at a rate of N_a/t_k, and since this traffic is spread over B_i buffers, the proportion of time an input buffer will be occupied (that is, its occupancy, L_i) is

$$L_i = N_a[r_a(4.5t_{ss} + t_{fq}) + 1.5t_{ss}/t_k]/B_i \qquad (8\text{-}2)$$

where

$$B_i = \text{number of input blocks.}$$

Input blocking will occur if $B_i + 1$ or more input blocks are required. This occurs with a probability of $L_i^{B_i+1}$. Should there be an input buffer blockage, an incoming request will be discarded and will have to be retransmitted. This requires a time equal to n_k times the interacknowledge time of t_k, terms previously defined in section 6.4.

Thus, the average transaction delay due to input buffer blocking, t_{bi}, is the probability of this occurrence multiplied by the time delay:

$$t_{bi} = n_k t_k L_i^{B_i+1} \qquad (8\text{-}3)$$

So far as output buffers are concerned, there are two possibilities for blocking. One is that long reads may cause a deadlock, which is broken by use of the emergency buffers. It is assumed that this happens seldom enough not to be a performance issue.

The other concern is buffer exhaustion. If all output buffers are full, the file managers will stall.

The average life of a response in an output buffer can be deduced from the AI scanner activity described in section 6.5.1. As noted in that section, the slave is about 1.5 AI scan cycles behind the master in terms of completing its file management services, so the slave buffers will have a lower occupancy than those of the master. Therefore, the following analysis will deal with the master only.

From Section 6.5.1, a response will sit in a buffer an average time of 2.5 AI scan times plus an acknowledge time. These AI scan times include 1.5 scan cycles for input synchronization for the slave (the reason the slave is behind) and one for output synchronization.

It is assumed that the Aquarius terminal responds with an acknowledgement within one AI scan cycle. Thus, the master will see it on the next scan cycle. As argued in Section 6.5.1, the average additional time for the master to be notified that the slave has seen this message is one scan cycle.

Thus, a response message will occupy an output block for 4.5 scan cycles as follows:

	Scan cycles
Input synchronization lag	1.5
Output synchronization	1
Receive acknowledge	1
Acknowledgement synchronization	$\dfrac{1}{4.5}$

Responses are arriving into output memory at the transaction rate, $N_a r_a$, and are distributed among B_o buffers. Thus, the average occupancy of an output block, L_o, is

$$L_o = 4.5 N_a r_a t_{ss}/B_o \qquad (8\text{-}4)$$

where

B_o = number of output (Disk Controller) blocks, excluding emergency blocks.

t_{ss} = the previously derived AI scan cycle.

If there are B_o output blocks, blocking of the file managers occurs if $B_o + 1$ or more blocks are needed. This condition will occur with a probability of $L_o^{B_o+1}$ and will last $4.5/2 = 2.25$ scan cycles on the average (since the time of block occupancy is fairly constant).

Thus, the average time that transactions are delayed by output blocking is

$$t_{bo} = 2.25 t_{ss} L_o^{B_o+1} \tag{8-5}$$

The total blocking delay time, T_b, is

$$T_b = t_{bi} + t_{bo} \tag{8-6}$$

7. SCENARIO

In order to make a statement about Gemini performance, a specific scenario of the system's use must be specified. This scenario may be tailored to approximate various user environments but will be constrained by the following assumptions:

    a. One to 14 Aquarius terminals may be specified, each performing similar tasks.

    b. The Aquarius terminals may be either token or nontoken. For token systems, no programs are downloaded from Gemini; they are all resident on the terminal diskette, i.e., programs that are downloaded are assumed to be infrequently used.

    c. All tasks are editing tasks. Document creation is via OCR, and its load is ignored.

    d. The profile of a typical document will be specified, including the following:
- its average length, in pages,
- average number of characters per page,
- number and length of supporting files (headers, footers, footnotes, saves),
- average size of directories.

    e. The profile of a typical editing session will be specified, including the following:
- procedure used to search for and specify document to be edited,
- the selection of how the copy will be made, either via an attach (edit copy) or a physical copy (index copy),
- average number of opens of other text/format file pairs,
- a repetitive sequence of editing functions, including a page Go To, scrolling for a designated number of lines, and execution of edit commands from a specified mix of commands,
- average number of repetitions before the document is closed,
- average number of prints during edit session,
- proportion of edits that are paginated before close.

    f. The proportion of documents that are printed after editing.

    g. The specification of background tasks such as pagination and spelling check.

This scenario can be characterized as follows via input variables. Let

d = average document length, in pages.

p = average page length, in characters.

f_i = average directory length at level i, in number of entries, where:

   $i = 0$ is file room.
   $= 1$ is cabinet.
   $= 2$ is drawer.
   $= 3$ is folder.
   $= 4$ is document.

n_j = average number of edit functions of type j to be performed on each document, where:

   $j = 1$ is Index Scan.
   $= 2$ is Open/Close Document.
   $= 3$ is Attach Copy.
   $= 4$ is Physical Copy.
   $= 5$ is Go To Page.
   $= 6$ is Scroll Line.
   $= 7$ is Delete/Insert Text.
   $= 8$ is Cut.
   $= 9$ is Paste.
   $= 10$ is Insert Footnote.
   $= 11$ is Add Text Attribute.
   $= 12$ is Manual Hyphenation.
   $= 13$ is Paginate.
   $= 14$ is Print.

Section 4 puts in tabular form the number of transactions and disk accesses required to perform each of the above functions in terms of the parameters d, p, f_i, and other parameters.
   Let

   n_{tj} = number of transactions required to execute the edit function j.

   n_{dj} = number of disk accesses required to execute the edit function j.

   N_{ts} = total number of transactions required by the scenario.

   N_{ds} = total number of disk accesses required by the scenario.

   N_{fs} = total number of edit functions required by the scenario.

Then

$$N_{ts} = \sum_j n_j n_{tj} \qquad\qquad (9\text{-}1)$$

$$N_{ds} = \sum_{j} n_j n_{dj} \qquad (9\text{-}2)$$

$$N_{fs} = \sum_{j} n_j \qquad (9\text{-}3)$$

The average number of transactions, N_t, per edit function is

$$N_t = N_{ts}/N_{fs} \qquad (9\text{-}4)$$

The average number of disk accesses per transaction, N_d, is

$$N_d = N_{ds}/N_{ts} \qquad (9\text{-}5)$$

If the scenario is to be accomplished in T_u seconds, then the transaction rate per Aquarius terminal, r_a, in transactions per second, is

$$r_a = N_{ts}/T_u \qquad (9\text{-}6)$$

Also, let

N_{gs} = number of Get transactions in the scenario.

n_{gj} = number of Get transactions for the appropriate jth edit function.

Then

$$N_{gs} = \sum_{j} n_j n_{gj} \qquad (9\text{-}7)$$

and the probability that a transaction will be a Get is

$$p_g = N_{gs}/N_{ts} \qquad (9\text{-}8)$$

This is a parameter needed by the model, along with N_d, N_t, and r_a.

The model will calculate an average transaction response, T_t, to an average transaction, as well as the transaction response time component without disk accesses, T_r, and the disk access component, T_d. These are related by

$$T_t = T_r + N_d T_d \qquad (9\text{-}9)$$

The response time to the edit function of type j, T_j, is:

$$T_j = n_{tj} T_r + n_{dj} T_d \qquad (9\text{-}10)$$

Reference 2.1 gives a means by which to estimate the cache hit ratio, h, via the parameter n'_{dj}, which is the estimated cache hits for each edit function. This estimate is

$$h = \frac{\sum_{j} n_j n'_{dj}}{N_{ds}} \qquad (9\text{-}11)$$

8. SCENARIO TIME

The *scenario time*, i.e., the time it takes for an operator to complete the specified sequence of operations, is a function of the response time of the system, which in turn is a function of the load imposed upon the system, which loops back to being a function of the scenario time.

The preceding sections have predicted system response time for a preset scenario time, T_u. A more useful number might be the actual scenario time that would result when a number of Aquarius terminals are given a scenario and left to do it in all possible haste. This would involve guessing at a scenario time T_u, using that to calculate a transaction rate r_a (equation 9-6), and then calculating a scenario time T_u that will be different from the guess. The guess for T_u is then adjusted until the calculated value for T_u is sufficiently close to the actual value for T_u.

In order to be reasonably accurate, the operator time must be included in the scenario time. Let

T_{oj} = operator time required to initiate the edit function of type j.

Then the scenario time, T_u, is

$$T_i = \sum_j n_j (T_{oj} + T_j) \tag{10-1}$$

where n_j and T_j have been previously defined as:

n_j = average number of the edit functions of type j to be performed on each document.

T_j = average time for the edit function of type j.

A reasonable initial guess would be to set transaction rate r_a to zero and to calculate T_u. This would give the minimum possible value of T_u, which could then be incremented until the solution was found.

9. MODEL SUMMARY

The Gemini performance model is summarized in Tables 9-1 and 9-2. Table 9-1 defines the parameters, organizing them into four sections:

  a. *Result parameters,* which are those calculated parameters that are likely to be of interest for results.
  b. *Input variables,* which are likely to be varied to determine performance under varying environments.
  c. *Input parameters,* which are inputs to the model that are fairly stable.
  d. *Intermediate parameters,* which are all calculated parameters, except for result parameters.

Table 9-2 summarizes the model equations into several groups:

  a. results,

b. communication response-time component,

c. AI response-time component,

d. file manager response-time component,

e. disk system response-time component,

f. shared buffer overflow response-time component,

g. scenario,

h. edit functions.

TABLE 9-1. GEMINI PERFORMANCE MODEL PARAMETERS

a. *Results*

T_t	Average transaction time (seconds)
T_j	Average time for edit function of type j (seconds)

b. *Input Variables*

b_i	Number of indirect levels at directory level i
c_s	Average line length (characters)
C	Cache size (blocks)
d	Average document length (pages)
f	Average number of format characters per page
f_i	Average number of files at directory level i
f_s	Average number of support objects (text and format file) used in edit session per document (footnotes, headers, footers)
i	Directory level:
	$i = 0$ is room
	$= 1$ is cabinet
	$= 2$ is drawer
	$= 3$ is folder
	$= 4$ is document
	$= 5$ is text
j	edit function type:
	$j = 1$ is Index Scan
	$= 2$ is Open/Close Document
	$= 3$ is Attach Copy
	$= 4$ is Physical Copy
	$= 5$ is Go To Page
	$= 6$ is Scroll Line
	$= 7$ is Delete/Insert Text
	$= 8$ is Cut
	$= 9$ is Paste
	$= 10$ is Insert Footnote
	$= 11$ is Add Text Attribute
	$= 12$ is Manual Hyphenation
	$= 13$ is Paginate
	$= 14$ is Print
k_t	token switch ($0 =$ if token, $= 1$ if not token)
n_c	average number of characters in a cut
n_{da}	average number of characters affected in a delete/insert sequence (the greater of the number of characters inserted or deleted)
n_j	average number of edit functions of type j to be performed on each document

TABLE 9-1.   GEMINI PERFORMANCE MODEL PARAMETERS—Continued

n_p	average number of characters in a paste
n_s	average number of lines scrolled between edit actions
N_a	number of Aquarius terminals
p	average page length (characters)
p_i	probability that directory level i is hashed
R	number of reference blocks on disk
s_i	the proportion of unused space in a block at directory level i (slack).
T_u	average scenario (user) time (seconds)
u	user level in directory from which index scans are made ($u = 0, 1, 2, 3$)

c. *Input Parameters*

b	average communication line (bus) length to Aquarius (meters)
B_i	number of AI blocks in shared memory
B_o	number of disk controller blocks in shared memory, exclusive of emergency blocks
c	speed of light (3×10^8 meters per second)
F	number of file manager threads
h	average cache hit ratio (may also be calculated)
m_a	request-message length (bytes)
m_g	response-message length (bytes)
m_k	acknowledge-message length (bytes)
n_k	number of acknowledgements for the previous message before the current message is retransmitted
s_a	Aquarius communication line speed (bytes/sec.)
s_g	Gemini communication line speed (bytes/sec.)
t_{awr}	time to detect the reception of a byte by the software once it has been received by the hardware at the Aquarius (sec.)
t_{awt}	time to initiate the transmission of the first byte of a message once the line has been determined to be idle by the Aquarius (sec.)
t_{da}	disk average access time (seek plus latency) (sec.)
t_{dp1}	CPU processing time required to process a disk access from cache (sec.)
t_{dp2}	CPU processing time required to process a physical disk access (sec.)
t_{fp}	file manager CPU processing time required to process a transaction exclusive of disk accesses (sec.)
t_{gwr}	time to detect the reception of a byte by the software once it has been received by the hardware at the Gemini (sec.)
t_{gwt}	time to initiate the transmission of the first byte of a message once the line has been determined to be idle by the Gemini (sec.)
t_k	interacknowledge message time on an idle line (sec.)
t_{sf}	AI processing time required to queue a request to the file manager (sec.)
t_{si}	AI processing time required to process an idle line (sec.)
t_{sr}	AI processing time required to process a received message (sec.)
t_{st}	AI processing time required to process a transmitted message (sec.)
t'_{sbb}	AI interrupt time required to process a message indicator in a synchronization block slot (sec.)
t'_{sbo}	AI interrupt time required to process an empty synchronization block (sec.)
t'_{sr}	AI interrupt time to process a received message (sec.)
t'_{st}	AI interrupt time to process a transmitted message (sec.)
T_a	Aquarius time required to process a transaction (sec.)

d. *Intermediate Parameters*

a	AI load attributable to activities whose frequency is a function of AI scan time, exclusive of idle processing

TABLE 9-1.   GEMINI PERFORMANCE MODEL PARAMETERS—Continued

$c(n)$	number of physical disk accesses required to update n reference counts
d_p	number of virtual disk accesses to Put a text block
d_p'	number of cache accesses to Put a text block
d_{ni}	number of disk accesses required to open a new file (create a file) at directory level i
d_{oi}	number of disk accesses required to open an existing (old) file at directory level i
d_{sp}	number of disk accesses required to copy a pointer block
e	number of reference count updates required to completely fill cache
f	average number of format characters per page
k_i	AI idle line switch:
	$= 1$ if $5r_a t_{ss} < 1$ when $k_i = 1$
	$= 0$ otherwise
L_d	disk load
L_f	file manager total load
L_i	occupancy of an AI buffer
L_o	occupancy of a disk controller buffer
L_p	file manager processor load
n_{dj}	number of disk accesses required for the edit function of type j
n_{dj}'	number of disk cache accesses required for the edit function of type j
n_{gj}	number of Get commands required for the edit function of type j
n_{tb}	number of text characters in a disk block (512 less slack positions)
n_{tj}	number of transactions required for the edit function of type j
n_{tp}	number of text characters pointed to by a pointer block (32,768 characters minus slack positions)
N_d	average number of disk accesses per transaction
N_{ds}	total number of disk accesses in a scenario
N_{fs}	total number of edit functions in a scenario
N_{gs}	total number of Get transactions in a scenario
N_t	average number of transactions per edit function
N_{ts}	total number of transactions in a scenario
p_g	probability that a transaction is a Get
$p(n)$	probability of a physical disk access while updating the nth reference count
p_s	probability of a pointer block split during a block Put
q_d	average length of disk queue
$r\{x\}$	cache hit ratio for x reference count blocks
r_a	transaction rate per Aquarius (transactions per second)
t_{bi}	average transaction time because of AI buffer blocking (sec.)
t_{dp}	average CPU processing required to process a disk access (sec.)
t_{bo}	average transaction time because of disk controller blocking (sec.)
t_{car}	average retransmission time for an Aquarius request (sec.)
t_{cat}	average transmission time for an Aquarius request (sec.)
t_{caw}	average wait time before an Aquarius can begin transmitting a request because of Gemini traffic (sec.)
t_{cgr}	average retransmission time for a Gemini response (sec.)
t_{cgt}	average transmission time for a Gemini response (sec.)
t_{cgw}	average wait time before a Gemini can begin transmitting a response because of Aquarius traffic (sec.)
t_{ds}	average time required to process a disk access, including queue delay and processing (sec.)
t_f	average time for the file manager to process a transaction, excluding disk processing but including file manager blocking, CPU queuing, and file manager queuing (sec.)
t_{fb}	average transaction time because of file manager blocking (sec.)

TABLE 9-1.   GEMINI PERFORMANCE MODEL PARAMETERS—Continued

t_{fd}	average transaction time because of queue delays for the file manager CPU (sec.)
t_{fq}	average transaction time because of waiting in the file manager queue (sec.)
t_{ss}	average AI scan cycle time (sec.)
T_b	average delay time because of shared memory blocking (sec.)
T_c	average delay time because of the communication line (sec.)
T_d	average delay time because of processing a disk access (sec.)
T_f	average delay time because of file manager activity (sec.)
T_{oj}	operator time required to initiate the edit function of type j (sec.)
T_r	average delay time excluding disk activity (sec.)
T_s	average transaction time due to AI activity (sec.)
z	file manager service ratio

TABLE 9-2.   GEMINI PERFORMANCE MODEL SUMMARY

a. *Response time*

$$T_t = T_r + N_d T_d \tag{2-1}$$
$$T_r = T_a + T_c + T_s + T_f + T_b \tag{2-2}$$
$$T_j = n_{tj} T_r + n_{dj} T_d \tag{9-10}$$
$$T_u = \sum_j n_j (T_{oj} + T_j) \tag{10-1}$$

b. *Communication time*

$$T_c = t_{caw} + t_{cat} + t_{car} + t_{cgw} + t_{cgt} + t_{cgr} \tag{4-7}$$
$$t_{caw} = r_a [(m_g + m_k)/s_g]^2 \tag{4-1}$$
$$t_{cat} = m_a/s_a \tag{4-3}$$
$$t_{car} = r_a r_g n_k t_k (t_{awt} + 1/s_a + 2b/c + t_{awr})^2 \tag{4-5}$$
$$t_{cgw} = r_a t_{ss} (m_a + m_k)/s_a \tag{4-2}$$
$$t_{cgt} = m_g/s_g \tag{4-4}$$
$$t_{cgr} = r_a r_g n_k t_k (t_{gwt} + 1/s_g + 2b/c + t_{gwr})^2 \tag{4-6}$$

c. *AI time*

$$T_s = 4t_{ss} \tag{5-6}$$
$$t_{ss} = \frac{t'_{sbo} + k_i N_a t_{si}}{1 - (a - 5k_i N_a r_a t_{si})} \tag{5-8}$$
$$k_i = 1 \text{ if } 5\, r_a t_{ss} < 1 \tag{5-9}$$
$$\quad = 0 \text{ otherwise}$$
$$t_{ss_{max}} = N_a (t_{sr} + t'_{sr} + t_{st} + t'_{st} + t_{sf}) \tag{5-5}$$
$$a = N_a [(2r_a + 1/t_k)(t_{sr} + t'_{sr} + t_{st} + t'_{st}) + r_a t_{sf} + 4r_a t'_{sbb}] \tag{5-7}$$

d. *File manager time*

$$T_f = (t_f + N_d T_d)/(1 - L_f/F) \tag{6-6}$$
$$t_f = t_{fp} + t_{fd} + t_{fb} \tag{6-1}$$
$$t_{fd} = L_p (t_{fp} + N_d t_{dp})/(1 - L_p) \tag{6-2}$$
$$L_p = \left(\frac{F - 1}{F}\right) N_a r_a (t_{fp} + N_d t_{dp}) \tag{6-3}$$
$$t_{fb} = [(1 - p_g) L_f/F]^{F-1} (t_f + N_d + N_d T_d) \tag{6-4}$$
$$L_f = N_a r_a (t_f + N_d T_d) \tag{6-5}$$

e. *Disk time*

$$T_d = (q_d + 1) t_{da} \tag{7-4}$$
$$t_{ds} = t_{dp} + (1 - h) t_{da} \tag{7-1b}$$
$$t_{dp} = h t_{dp1} + (1 - h) t_{dp2} \tag{7-1a}$$
$$L_d = N_a r_a N_d t_{ds} \tag{7-8}$$

TABLE 9-2. GEMINI PERFORMANCE MODEL SUMMARY—Continued

$$q_d = \sum_{k=1}^{F-1} k \, \frac{\dfrac{z^{F-k-1}}{(F-k-1)!}}{\displaystyle\sum_{j=0}^{F-1} \frac{z^j}{j!}} \tag{7-3}$$

$$z = \frac{F}{N_d N_a r_a T_d} - 1 \tag{7-7}$$

f. *Buffer Overflow time*

$$T_b = t_{bi} + t_{bo} \tag{8-6}$$

$$t_{bi} = n_k t_k L_i^{B_i+1} \tag{8-3}$$

$$t_{bo} = 2.25 t_{ss} L_o^{B_o+1} \tag{8-5}$$

$$L_i = N_a [r_a (4.5 t_{ss} + t_{fq}) + 1.5 t_{ss}/t_k]/B_i \tag{8-2}$$

$$t_{fq} = \frac{(L_f/F)}{1 - L_f/F} \, t_f \tag{8-1}$$

$$L_o = 4.5 N_a r_a t_{ss}/B_o \tag{8-4}$$

g. *Scenario*

$$N_t = N_{ts}/N_{fs} \tag{9-4}$$

$$N_d = N_{ds}/N_{ts} \tag{9-5}$$

$$r_a = N_{ts}/T_u \tag{9-6}$$

$$p_g = N_{gs}/N_{ts} \tag{9-8}$$

$$N_{ts} = \sum_j n_j n_{tj} \tag{9-1}$$

$$N_{ds} = \sum_j n_j n_{dj} \tag{9-2}$$

$$N_{fs} = \sum_j n_j \tag{9-3}$$

$$N_{gs} = \sum_j n_j n_{gj} \tag{9-7}$$

$$h = \frac{\displaystyle\sum_j n_j n'_{dj}}{N_{ds}} \quad \text{(optional, if not given as input)} \tag{9-11}$$

Note: n_{tj}, n_{gj}, n_{dj}, and n'_{dj} are given in Tables 4-1 through 4-3.

10. RESULTS

10.1 Benchmark Comparison

The performance model was evaluated for the scenario shown in Table 10-1. This same scenario was used to run a benchmark test on the system. Table 10-1 lists the operator activities required to process a document under this benchmark and also shows those activities used by the model to approximate this benchmark.

The model was evaluated for the nontoken case, with reference counts in memory. The number of Aquarius terminals was varied from 1 to 14. The time that was measured experimentally for this case is shown as the dashed line in Figure 10-1. This is a curve of the time required for an operator to complete the benchmark as a function of the number of terminals on the system and ranges from 840 seconds for one terminal to 3960 seconds for 12 terminals (Figure 10-1 has extrapolated the curve to 14 terminals).

TABLE 10-1. GEMINI BENCHMARK

Function	Benchmark	Model
1. Index Scan	4	4
2. Open/Close Document[1]	4	5
Delete Document	1	
3. Attach Copy	0	0
4. Physical Copy	1	1
5. Go To Page	4	4
6. Scroll	24	24
7. Delete/Insert[2]	20	20
8. Cut	3	3
9. Paste	4	4
10. Insert Footnote	1	1
11. Add Text Attribute	3	3
12. Manual Hyphenation	0	0
13. Paginate	4	4
14. Print	1	3
Spell Check[3]		

Notes:

[1]Delete Document is taken as equivalent to an Open/Close Document.

[2]Gemini Benchmark included 20 Search/Replace, which are taken as equivalent to 20 Scroll and Delete/Insert.

[3]Spell Check is taken as equivalent of 2 Print.

The model calculations are shown as the family of solid lines in Figure 10-1. Each is for a different cache hit ratio. As opposed to the intuitively expected curve of the experimental results, the predicted curves are surprisingly linear; this effect is discussed later and is shown to be caused by disk saturation.

Furthermore, the worse-than-linear performance that was actually measured is because of reduced cache effectiveness as load increases. If the model is taken as giving representative results, then one would conclude that the Gemini cache effectiveness was greater at low loads (around .7) and decreased to about .45 as load increased. This is to be expected, since the greater disk activity at higher loads will flush out data that would otherwise be available at lower loads.

The model makes its own conservative estimate of cache effectiveness, assuming that only frequently accessed blocks are in cache. These include:

- Free list.
- Directory block for current directory.
- Indirect blocks for current text block.

It would be expected that the model's prediction would be close to that measured for high

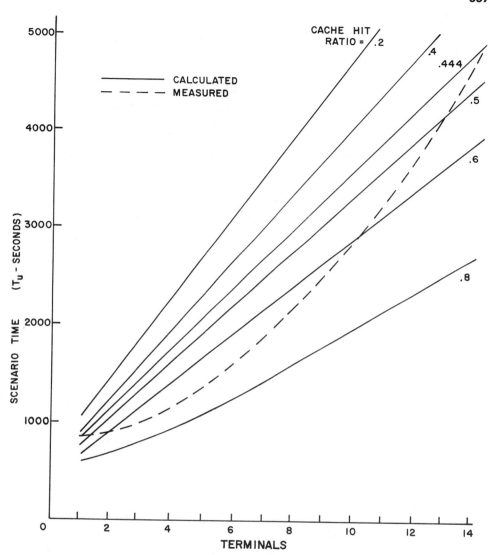

Figure 10-1 Scenario time.

loads. In fact, the model predicts a cache hit ratio of .444, very close to that measured for high loads (.45).

Thus, it can be concluded that the model gives reasonable results compared to those actually measured. Using the cache hit ratio estimated by the model gives conservative results at moderate loads and fairly accurate results at high loads.

10.2 Component Analysis

Using terms from the model, we define the following terms:

> *Transaction* is a request submitted by an Aquarius terminal to the Gemini.
> *Function* is an edit action, such as an open, scroll, paste, etc.
> *Scenario* is the set of edit functions required to process a document.

Thus, a scenario comprises a set of functions, each of which comprises a set of transactions. Let

$$T_u = \text{time required to complete the scenario.}$$

$$T_t = \text{time to complete a transaction.}$$

$$N_{ts} = \text{number of transactions in the scenario.}$$

Then

$$T_u = N_{ts}T_t$$

The benchmark test required 75 functions totaling 3046 transactions ($N_{ts} = 3046$).

Transaction time, T_t, comprises a processing component and a disk system component. Let

$$T_r = \text{processing time per transaction (exclusive of disk processing time).}$$

$$N_d = \text{number of disk accesses per transaction.}$$

$$T_d = \text{disk time (processing, seek and rotational time) per disk access.}$$

Then

$$T_t = T_r + N_dT_d$$

In the benchmark scenario, there are 2.92 disk accesses per transaction (8887 disk accesses per scenario).

Figure 10-2 shows T_t and its components for a cache hit ratio of .444, as calculated by the model. At high loads, T_r is clearly the predominant factor. Though it curves slightly at low loads (as would be intuitively expected), this curvature is offset by a flattening of the disk time, T_d, resulting in a linear T_t.

Disk time "saturates" because the disk system is fed by a finite number of sources (four file managers), thus limiting the size of the disk queue. At higher loads, the disk queue approaches a constant value (3.6 accesses waiting or being serviced), resulting in constant disk service times.

Loading for the disk system, file managers, and processor are shown in Figure 10-3, as calculated by the model. Note that the processor load is quite small (15-20 percent at high loads). However, the disk system and file manager quickly saturate, the disk system at about 4 terminals and the file manager at about 8 terminals.

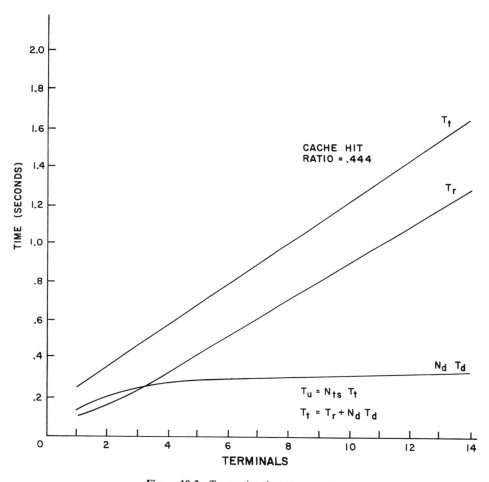

Figure 10-2   Transaction time components.

As mentioned above, the predominant component in the transaction time, T_t, is the processing time, T_r, not the disk time, T_d. But we just said that the disk system was heavily loaded and the processor lightly loaded. The answer to this apparent anomaly is given in Figure 10-4, where the culprit is shown to be the file manager.

Here, the components of T_r are shown as:

$$T_a = \text{Aquarius time.}$$

$$T_c = \text{communication time.}$$

$$T_s = \text{AI scanner time.}$$

$$T_f = \text{file manager time.}$$

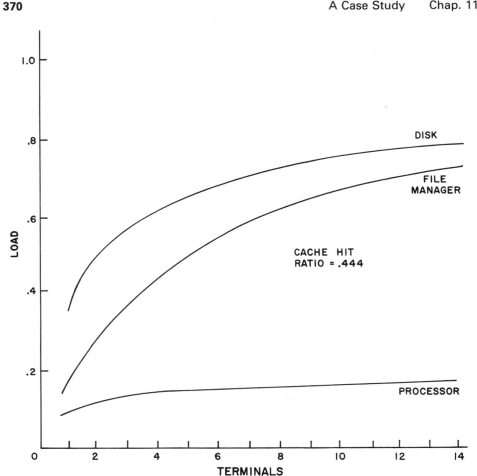

Figure 10-3 Component loads.

Note that communication time, T_c, decreases as load increases. This is due to reduced collisions because of the lighter terminal traffic at higher system loads, i.e., Aquarius is running slower.

Because the file manager must wait for multiple (2.9) accesses to a saturated disk system, its growth is substantially linear. That is, since the saturated disk system is giving fixed response times above four terminals (see Figure 10-2), then doubling the load will approximately double the file manager time.

As seen from Figure 10-4, the file manager time, T_f, is the predominant factor in T_r, which is the predominant factor in T_t, to which scenario time, T_u, is proportional. Since T_f is now explained to be linear (at least at higher loads), the scenario time, T_u, will be linear also.

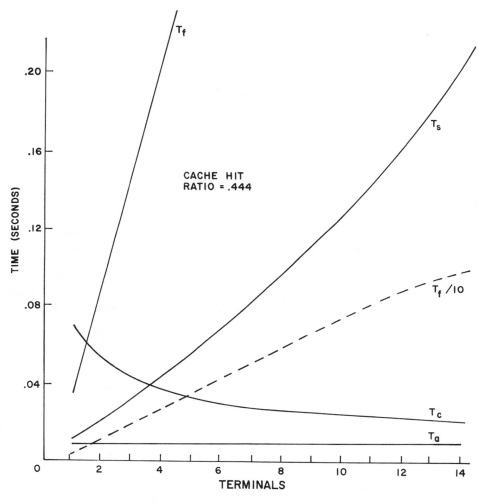

Figure 10-4 Processing time components.

11. RECOMMENDATIONS

A calculation has been made of Gemini performance using the performance model. This model appears to agree well with benchmark results. The message is clear:

> **The only way to significantly improve Gemini performance is to reduce disk system load.**

Disk system includes the physical disk as well as the disk process.

Running at loads equivalent to the Gemini benchmarks, one finds the following:

- Average response time is 4 times longer than in an unloaded system.
- A 20% peak increase (which will easily happen) causes the response time to further degrade to 10 times that of an unloaded system.
- Ninety percent of the response time is related to disk activity.

Reducing disk system load by 50% accomplishes the following:

- Average loaded response time will be about 30% longer than unloaded response time (rather than 400%).
- A 20% peak increase in load will cause a 25% increase in response time (rather than 250%).

Thus, *nearly an order of magnitude decrease can be made in the load characteristics of Gemini by cutting the disk system load in half.*

There is no easy way to achieve this reduction. The token configuration and the movement of reference counts to memory will buy a 10–15% reduction in disk system load (which translates to a 40% reduction in response time under load conditions.) Other options available (with no comment on their associated agony) include the following:

a. Eliminate physical copies of documents. This accounts for about 50% of disk activity.

b. Use faster and larger disks (use only a subset of tracks to reduce seek time) to achieve nearly a 50% reduction in disk access time.

c. Decrease the disk process processing time.

d. Use dual disks on each controller, with overlapped seeks, to achieve nearly a 2:1 increase in allowable access rates.

e. Split the Aquarius terminals between two Gemini systems interconnected with SynNet.

f. Use a bigger cache. One significant observation is the fact that the disk system saturates at about 4 terminals in this benchmark. At this point, the cache hit ratio is about 0.7. If cache size were tripled, this same cache hit ratio (or better) ought to be achieved for 12 terminals (this amount of cache would now be available for each group of 4 terminals). The additional effectiveness of all terminals sharing a larger cache would add even more to the attractiveness of this solution. Scenario time would be reduced from about 5000 seconds to 3200 seconds, about a 50% improvement (taken as 5000/3200). The flattening of the experimental scenario time for less than 4 terminals suggests that a larger cache than this might not add much.

Solution a. may be unacceptable from a reliability viewpoint. Solution c. requires a large software effort with questionable results. Solution e. will cause perhaps an equal performance degradation because of the speed and imposed load of SynNet. Solution f. requires major hardware modifications to increase cache addressability.

Solutions b. and d. require simple purchased hardware changes, with b. being the far more economical. Since both solutions result in a substantial and almost equal performance improvement, solution b., using a portion of larger disks, is recommended. A capacity improvement of 2:1 can be expected.

APPENDIX 1

General Queuing Parameters (as used in Appendix 2)

Parameter	Meaning
c	number of servers
$E(T^2)$	second moment of T
k	Khintchine-Pollaczek distribution coefficient
L	load (occupancy) of a server (at the considered priority and higher priorities, if priorities are involved)
L_h	total load imposed on a server by all users at a higher priority than that being considered
L_t	total load imposed on a server by all users at all priorities
m	number of users in a finite population
n	number of items (users) in a queue
p_o	probability that the length of a queue is zero (probability that the queuing system is idle)
p_n	probability that the length of a queue is n items (or users)
Q	average queue length, including the item (user) being serviced
R	average arrival rate of items (users) to a queue
T	average service time of a server (at the considered priority and higher priorities, if priorities are involved)
T_a	average availability of a user in a finite population
T_d	average delay time for an item (user) being serviced by a queuing system, including waiting and being serviced
T_{dp}	average delay time for an item (user) at priority p, including waiting and being serviced
T_p	average service time for an item (user) at its priority
T_q	average queuing (waiting) time for an item (user) in a queue, excluding its service time
T_{qp}	average queuing (waiting) time for an item (user) at priority p, excluding its service time
T_t	service time of an item (user) averaged over all priorities
$\overline{T^2}$	second moment of T

$\overline{T^3}$	third moment of T
W	average number of items (users) waiting in line for service, excluding the item being serviced
z	service ratio for an item (user) in a finite population

APPENDIX 2

Queuing Models

The following tables summarize the results of chapter 4 for each of the queuing models. Note that the full set of parameters is not available for all models. The set of parameters that are available is given. Definitions of parameters are given in Appendix 1.

The Kendall classification for queuing models is summarized below for reference. Each table is titled by its Kendall classification. A queuing model is classified as

$$A/B/c/K/m/Z$$

where

- A is the arrival distribution of items into the queue:
  - M—random.
  - D —constant.
  - U —uniform.
  - G —general.
- B is the service time distribution of the servers and can have the same values as A.
- c is the number of servers.
- K is the maximum queue length.
- m is the size of the population.
- Z is the queue discipline.
  - A —Any.

FIFO—First-In, First-Out
PP   —Preemptive Priority.
NP   —Nonpreemptive Priority.

If any of the last three characteristics are left out, the defaults are infinite queue length, infinite population, and FIFO queue discipline ($/\infty/\infty/$FIFO).

General

$$Q = W + L \tag{4-20}$$

$$T_q = \frac{WT}{L} \tag{4-21}$$

$$T_d = \frac{QT}{L} = T_q + T \tag{4-22}$$

M/G/1/∞/∞/A

$$W = \frac{kL^2}{1-L} \tag{4-4}$$

$$Q = \frac{L}{1-L}[1 - (1-k)L] \tag{4-6}$$

$$T_q = \frac{kL}{1-L} T \tag{4-9}$$

$$T_d = \frac{1}{1-L}[1 - (1-k)L]T \tag{4-8}$$

$$\text{var}(T_d) = \frac{R\overline{T^3}}{3(1-L)} + \frac{R^2\overline{T^2}^2}{4(1-L)^2} + \overline{T^2} - \overline{T}^2 \tag{4-71}$$

$$k = \frac{1}{2}\frac{E(T^2)}{T^2} \tag{4-16}$$

M/M/1/∞/∞/A

$$W = \frac{L^2}{1-L} \tag{4-88}$$

$$Q = \frac{L}{1-L} \tag{4-10}$$

$$T_q = \frac{LT}{1-L} \tag{4-12}$$

$$T_d = \frac{T}{(1-L)} \tag{4-11}$$

$$\text{var}(Q) = \frac{L}{(1-L)^2} \tag{4-82}$$

$$\text{var}(T_d) = \frac{T^2}{(1-L)^2} \tag{4-72}$$

$$p_o = (1-L) \qquad (4\text{-}79)$$
$$p_n = L^n(1-L) \qquad (4\text{-}80)$$
$$P(Q > n) = L^{n+1} \qquad (4\text{-}83)$$

Note: M/G/1 model with $k = 1$

M/U/1/∞/∞/A

$$W = \frac{2}{3}\frac{L^2}{1-L} \qquad (4\text{-}4)$$

$$Q = \frac{L}{1-L}\left(1 - \frac{L}{3}\right) \qquad (4\text{-}6)$$

$$T_q = \frac{2}{3}\frac{L}{1-L}\,T \qquad (4\text{-}9)$$

$$T_d = \frac{1}{1-L}\left(1 - \frac{L}{3}\right)T \qquad (4\text{-}8)$$

$$\mathrm{var}(T_d) = \frac{T^2}{(1-L)^2}\left(\frac{1}{3} + \frac{L^2}{9}\right) \qquad (4\text{-}73)$$

Note: M/G/1 model with $k = \frac{2}{3}$

M/D/1/∞/∞/A

$$W = \frac{1}{2}\frac{L^2}{1-L} \qquad (4\text{-}4)$$

$$Q = \frac{L}{1-L}\left(1 - \frac{L}{2}\right) \qquad (4\text{-}13)$$

$$T_q = \frac{L/2}{1-L}\,T \qquad (4\text{-}15)$$

$$T_d = \frac{1}{1-L}\left(1 - \frac{L}{2}\right)T \qquad (4\text{-}14)$$

$$\mathrm{var}(T_d) = \frac{T^2}{(1-L)^2}\left(\frac{1}{3} - \frac{L^2}{12}\right) \qquad (4\text{-}74)$$

Note: M/G/1 model with $k = \frac{1}{2}$

M/G/1/∞/∞/PP

$$T_{qp} = \frac{kLT}{(1-L)(1-L_h)} \qquad (4\text{-}92a)$$

$$T_{dp} = \frac{kLT}{(1-L)(1-L_h)} + \frac{T_p}{(1-L_h)} \qquad (4\text{-}92b)$$

M/G/1/∞/∞/NP

$$T_{qp} = \frac{kL_tT_t}{(1-L)(1-L_h)}$$ (4-91a)

$$T_{dp} = \frac{kL_tT_t}{(1-L)(1-L_h)} + T_p$$ (4-91b)

M/M/c/∞/∞/FIFO

$$W = \frac{L(cL)^c}{c!(1-L)^2} p_o$$ (4-97)

$$Q = W + cL$$ (4-98)

$$T_q = \frac{(cL)^c}{c(c!)(1-L)^2} p_oT$$ (4-99)

$$T_d = T_q + T$$ (4-100)

$$p_o^{-1} = \sum_{n=0}^{c-1} (cL)^n/n! + (cL)^c/c!(1-L)$$ (4-95)

$$p_n = p_o(cL)^n/n!, \ 1 \le n \le c$$ (4-93)

$$p_n = p_oL^nc^c/c!, \ n \ge c$$ (4-94)

M/G/c/∞/∞/FIFO

$$W \approx \frac{kL(cL)^c}{c!(1-L)^2} p_o$$ (4-101)

$$Q \approx W + cL$$ (4-102)

$$T_q \approx \frac{k(cL)^c}{c(c!)(1-L)^2} p_oT$$ (4-103)

$$T_d \approx T_q + T$$ (4-104)

$$p_o^{-1} = \sum_{n=0}^{c-1} (cL)^n/n! + (cL)^c/c!(1-L)$$ (4-95)

$$p_n = p_o(cL)^n/n!, \ 1 \le n \le c$$ (4-93)

$$p_n = p_oL^nc^c/c!, \ n \ge c$$ (4-94)

M/M/c/∞/∞/PP

$$T_{qp} = \frac{(cL)^c}{c(c!)(1-L)^2(1-L_h)} p_oT$$ (4-107a)

$$T_{dp} = T_{qp} + \frac{T_p}{1-L_h}$$ (4-107b)

$$p_o^{-1} = \sum_{n=0}^{c-1} (cL)^n/n! + (cL)^c/c!(1-L)$$ (4-107c)

M/M/c/∞/∞/NP

$$T_{qp} = \frac{(cL_t)^c}{c(c!)(1-L_t)(1-L)(1-L_h)}\, p_o T \tag{4-106a}$$

$$T_{dp} = T_{qp} + T_p \tag{4-106b}$$

$$p_o^{-1} = \sum_{n=0}^{c-1} (cL_t)^n/n! + (cL_t)^c/c!(1-L_t) \tag{4-106c}$$

M/M/1/m/m/FIFO

$$W = m - (z+1)L \tag{4-114}$$

$$Q = m - zL \tag{4-115}$$

$$T_q = \frac{W(z+1)}{m-W}\, T \tag{4-112}$$

$$T_d = T_q + T \tag{4-116}$$

$$L = \frac{m-W}{z+1} = \sum_{n=1}^{m} \frac{\dfrac{z^{m-n}}{(m-n)!}}{\displaystyle\sum_{j=0}^{m} \frac{z^j}{j!}} \tag{4-113, 119}$$

$$p_n = \frac{\dfrac{z^{m-n}}{(m-n)!}}{\displaystyle\sum_{j=0}^{m} \frac{z^j}{j!}} \tag{4-118}$$

$$z = T_d/T \tag{4-108}$$

$$R = L/T \tag{4-110}$$

$$P(\text{user busy}) = 1 - \frac{zL}{m} \tag{4-117}$$

M/M/c/m/m/FIFO

$$W = m-(z+1)L = \sum_{n=c+1}^{m} (n-c)p_n \tag{4-114, 124}$$

$$Q = m - zL \tag{4-115}$$

$$T_q = \frac{W(z+1)}{m-W}T \tag{4-112}$$

$$T_d = T_q + T \tag{4-116}$$

$$L = \frac{m-W}{z+1} \tag{4-113}$$

$$p_n = \binom{m}{n}\frac{1}{z^n}\, p_o, \; 1 \le n \le c \tag{4-120}$$

$$p_n = \frac{n!}{c!c^{n-c}} \binom{m}{n} \frac{1}{z^n} p_o, \; c \leq n \leq m \tag{4-121}$$

$$p_o = 1 - \sum_{n=1}^{m} p_n \tag{4-123}$$

$$z = T_a/T \tag{4-108}$$

$$R = L/T \tag{4-110}$$

$$P(\text{user busy}) = 1 - \frac{zL}{m} \tag{4-117}$$

APPENDIX 3

Khintchine-Pollaczek Equation for M/G/1 Queuing Systems

The following derivation of the Khintchine-Pollaczek equations for the M/G/1 queuing system is a summary of one given by Saaty [24]. It follows the simplified analysis introduced in chapter 4, and reference to Figure 4-1 is suggested.

We assume that a queue is observed in its steady state. This implies that over any two given time periods with lengths that allow statistically significant averages to be observed, the mean and variance of the queue length will be the same.

Should we observe the queue length at the instant after an item leaves the server, we observe q items waiting in line, including the next one to be serviced. The service time for this next item is t. We then observe the queue t seconds later and find the queue length to be q'.

During this time interval t, r items arrive. Thus, q' and q can be related as follows:

$$q' = q - 1 + r \text{ if } q > 0 \tag{A3-1}$$

$$q' = r \qquad \text{if } q = 0 \tag{A3-2}$$

That is, if the first item left q items behind, then q' is q reduced by the leaving of the next item and increased by the arrival of r items. If the first item left no items behind ($q = 0$), then q' is equal to the number of newly arrived items, r.

Note intuitively that r is indicative of the load on the server. If $r = 1$ item arrives during each service time t, the load on the server will be 1.

Equations A3-1 and A3-2 can be combined as follows:

$$q' = q - 1 + r + j \tag{A3-3}$$

where

$$j = 0 \text{ if } q > 0 \tag{A3-4}$$
$$j = 1 \text{ if } q = 0 \tag{A3-5}$$

Taking the expected values of the variables in equation A3-3, we have

$$E(q') = E(q) - 1 + E(r) + E(j) \tag{A3-6}$$

Since the system is in equilibrium, $E(q') = E(q)$; and therefore, from equation (A3-6)

$$E(j) = 1 - E(r) \tag{A3-7}$$

Let us now assume that arrivals to the queue are random, that is, they are generated by a Poisson process and arrive at an average rate of R items per second. From chapter 4, equations 4-60 and 4-61, we know that the mean $\bar{r}$ and second moment $\overline{r^2}$ of r items arriving randomly in a period of t seconds are

$$\bar{r} = Rt \tag{A3-8}$$

$$\overline{r^2} = (Rt)^2 + Rt \tag{A3-9}$$

Averaging $\bar{r}$ over time t, we have

$$E(\bar{r}) = \bar{r} = E(Rt) = R\bar{t} = RT = L \tag{A3-10}$$

where we use T to denote the expected value of t and L to represent the server load, RT. T is the average service time of the server.

Using equation 4-31, we also can average $\overline{r^2}$ over time:

$$E(\overline{r^2}) = \overline{r^2} = E(Rt)^2 + E(Rt)$$
$$= E[R^2 \text{var}(t) + E^2(Rt)] + E(Rt)$$

or

$$\overline{r^2} = R^2 \text{var}(t) + L^2 + L \tag{A3-11}$$

Let us now square equation A3-3. This gives

$$q'^2 = q^2 - 2q + 2qr + 2qj + 1 \\ - 2r - 2j + r^2 + 2rj + j^2 \tag{A3-12}$$

We note the following concerning j:

$$j^2 = j \qquad \text{from equations A3-4 and A3-5}$$
$$q(1-j) = q \qquad \text{from equations A3-4 and A3-5}$$
$$E(j) = 1 - L \qquad \text{from equations A3-7 and A3-10}$$

We also note that r is independent of q. Also, r is independent of j, since j is a function only of q. Therefore, whenever we take the expected value of rq or rj, the expected value of the product is the product of the expected values.

Taking the expected values of the terms in equation A3-12 and applying the above observations, one obtains

$$E(q'^2) = E(q^2) - 2E(q) + 2E(q)E(r) + 1 - 2E(r)$$
$$- 2(1-L) + E(r^2) + 2(1-L)E(r) + (1-L)$$

Since the queue is in equilibrium, $E(q'^2) = E(q^2)$. Eliminating these terms and substituting the values for $E(r)$ and $E(r^2)$ from equations A3-10 and A3-11 gives

$$0 = -2E(q)(1 - L) + 2L - L^2 + R^2\text{var}(t)$$

Solving for $E(q)$,

$$E(q) = \frac{2L - L^2 + R^2\text{var}(t)}{2(1 - L)}$$

Denoting the expected value of $E(q)$ by Q, and noting that $R = L/T$, this can be rewritten as

$$Q = \frac{L}{1-L}\left[1 - L + \frac{L}{2}\left(1 + \frac{\text{var}(t)}{T^2}\right)\right] \tag{A3-13}$$

We now define the distribution coefficient, k, as

$$k = \frac{1}{2}\left(1 + \frac{\text{var}(t)}{T^2}\right) \tag{A3-14}$$

Equation A3-13 then can be expressed as

$$Q = \frac{L}{1-L}[1 - (1-k)L] \tag{A3-15}$$

Equation A3-15 is the same as the expression for Q given by equation 4-6, which was derived by a less rigorous but more intuitive approach. Equation A3-14 is that reported as equation 4-16.

The relations for W, T_q, and T_d now can be determined from the general expressions given by equations 4-5, 4-3, and 4-7, respectively.

Note that these equations were derived only under the following assumptions:

- Arrivals to the queue are Poisson-distributed.
- The queue is in equilibrium.
- Service time is independent of arrival time or any other characteristic of the times being serviced.

Therefore, these equations apply for any distribution of service times and for any servicing order of the queue (so long as an item is not selected for service based on one of its characteristics, such as its service time). Thus, the solution is general for the M/G/1/∞/∞/A case of queuing systems.

APPENDIX 4

The Poisson Distribution

In chapter 4 we began the derivation of the Poisson distribution. It was determined that the probability of n items arriving in a time t, $p_n(t)$, was given by the following system of differential-difference equations:

$$p_0'(t) = -rp_0(t) \tag{4-57}$$

$$p_n'(t) = -rp_n(t) + rp_{n-1}(t) \tag{4-58}$$

The following solution to this set of equations is a summary of that solution found in Saaty [24].

Let us define a generating function $P(z,t)$ such that

$$P(z,t) = \sum_{n=0}^{\infty} z^n p_n(t) \tag{A4-1}$$

If we should differentiate this equation n times with respect to z, we have

$$\frac{\partial^n P(z,t)}{\partial z^n} = n! p_n(t) + \frac{(n+1)!}{1!} z p_{n+1}(t) + \frac{(n+2)!}{2!} z^2 p_{n+2}(t) + \ldots$$

Setting z to zero, we obtain

$$\frac{\partial^n P(z,t)}{\partial z^n} = n! p_n(t), \ z = 0 \tag{A4-2}$$

Thus, by differentiating the generating function $P(z,t)$ n times with respect to z, dividing the result by $n!$, and setting $z=0$, we obtain $p_n(t)$.

Let us now consider a time t as discussed in chapter 4 and assume that i items have arrived in the queue up to time t. That is, by the definition of $p_n(t)$,

$$p_i(0) = 1$$
$$p_n(0) = 0 \text{ for } n \neq i$$

Thus, from equation A4-1, for $t=0$,

$$P(z,0) = z^i p_i(0) = z^i \tag{A4-3}$$

Also, if z is set to 1, from equation A4-1,

$$P(1,t) = \sum_{n=0}^{\infty} p_n(t) = 1 \tag{A4-4}$$

Now let us multiply the differential-difference equations 4-57 and 4-58 by z^n, obtaining

$$z^0 p_0'(t) = -rz^0 p_0(t)$$
$$z^n p_n'(t) = -rz^n p_n(t) + rz^n p_{n-1}(t)$$

If we sum these over all n, we obtain

$$\sum_{n=0}^{\infty} z^n p_n'(t) = -r \sum_{n=0}^{\infty} z^n p_n(t) + r \sum_{n=1}^{\infty} z^n p_{n-1}(t) \tag{A4-5}$$

The left-hand term of this expression is simply $\frac{\partial P(z,t)}{\partial t}$. The first term on the right is $-rP(z,t)$. The second term on the right is

$$rz p_0(t) + rz^2 p_1(t) + rz^3 p_2(t) + \ldots$$
$$= rz[p_0(t) + zp_1(t) + z^2 p_2(t) + \ldots]$$
$$= rzP(z,t).$$

Thus, equation A4-5 can be written as the linear differential equation

$$\frac{\partial P(z,t)}{\partial t} = r(z-1)P(z,t) \tag{A4-6}$$

The solution to this is

$$P(z,t) = Ce^{r(z-1)t} \tag{A4-7}$$

which can be verified by substituting $P(z,t)$ from equation A4-7 into both sides of equation A4-6.

The value of C is dependent upon how many items, i, are received by time $t=0$. Let us assume that at $t=0$, zero items have been received in the queue ($i=0$). In this way, $p_n(t)$ will truly be the probability of receiving n items in the subsequent interval t. From equation A4-3, setting $i=0$,

$$P(z,0) = z^i = 1$$

Thus, $C=1$ in equation A4-7 and

$$P(z,t) = e^{r(z-1)t} \tag{A4-8}$$

As we pointed out earlier with reference to equation A4-2, $p_n(t)$ is derived from $P(z,t)$ by differentiating $P(z,t)$ n times with respect to z, dividing by $n!$, and setting z to zero. Performing these operations on equation A4-8 yields

$$p_n(t) = \frac{(rt)^n}{n!}e^{-rt} \tag{A4-9}$$

This is the solution for the Poisson distribution referenced as equation 4-59.

APPENDIX 5

Mirrored Writes

A. DUAL LATENCY TIMES

Consider a disk transfer request arriving at two independent disks simultaneously. Assume that both disks initiate the processing of this transaction simultaneously, that both heads are initially at the same track, and that both heads arrive simultaneously at the new track.

At this point, the rotational position of the two disks is random. What is the average time that it will take for the first disk to make the transfer? What is the average time for both disks to wait their rotational latency time in order to complete the disk transfer? (A single disk, of course, requires a half rotation on the average.)

Let the disk which has the smallest distance to go be designated disk B, and it must await a fractional rotation of B, where $0<B<1$. Let the other disk be disk A; it must await a fractional rotation of A, where $B<A<1$.

The following notation is used:

$p(y)$ is the probability of y.
$p(x|y)$ is the probability of x given y.
$p(x) = p(x|y)p(y)$
$E(x)$ is the expected (average) value of x.

For the case of the leading disk:

$$p(A) = dA$$

$$p(B|A) = \frac{1}{A}dB$$

$$p(B) = \frac{1}{A}dBdA$$

$$E(B) = \int Bp(B) = \int_{A=0}^{1}\int_{B=0}^{A}\frac{B}{A}dBdA$$

$$= \int_{A=0}^{1}\left[\frac{B^2}{2A}\right]_{B=0}^{A}dA$$

$$= \int_{A=0}^{1}\frac{A}{2}dA$$

$$= \left[\frac{A^2}{4}\right]_{A=0}^{1}$$

$$E(B) = \frac{1}{4}$$

For the case of the lagging disk:

$$p(B) = dB$$

$$p(A|B) = \frac{1}{(1-B)}dA$$

$$p(A) = \frac{1}{(1-B)}dAdB$$

$$E(A) = \int Ap(A) = \int_{B=0}^{1}\int_{A=B}^{1}\frac{A}{(1-B)}dAdB$$

$$= \int_{B=0}^{1}\frac{1}{(1-B)}\left[\frac{A^2}{2}\right]_{A=B}^{1}dB$$

$$= \frac{1}{2}\int_{B=0}^{1}(1+B)dB$$

$$= \frac{1}{2}\left[B + \frac{B^2}{2}\right]_{B=0}^{1}$$

$$E(A) = \frac{3}{4}$$

Thus, on the average, dual disks that seek in synchronism will require 3/4 of a rotation for each to find the sector.

B. SINGLE DISK SEEK TIME

Consider a disk transfer request arriving at a disk for a sector whose track is randomly positioned relative to the track at which the head is currently positioned. What is the average distance the head must move?

Let the total seek distance be normalized to 1 and the total seek path be measured from 0 to 1. The current head position is at C, where $0<C<1$. The head must move a distance of S. There are two cases to consider: the final position is either prior to C or beyond C.

The following notation is used:

$p(y)$ is the probability of y.

$p(x|y)$ is the probability of x given y.

$p(x) = p(x|y)p(y)$.

$E(x)$ is the expected (average) value of x.

Case 1: Final Position Prior to C

$$p(\text{case } 1) = C$$

$$p(C) = dC$$

$$p(S|C) = \frac{1}{C}dS$$

$$p(S) = \frac{1}{C}dSdC$$

Case 2: Final Position Beyond C

$$p(\text{case } 2) = 1 - C$$

$$p(C) = dC$$

$$p(S|C) = \frac{1}{1-C}dS$$

$$p(S) = \frac{1}{1-C}dSdC$$

The average value of S is

$$E(S) = \sum_{n=1}^{2} p(\text{Case } n)Sp(S)$$

$$E(S) = \int_{C=0}^{1}\int_{S=0}^{C} \frac{SC}{C}dSdC + \int_{C=0}^{1}\int_{S=0}^{1-C} \frac{S(1-C)}{(1-C)}dSdC$$

$$= \int_{C=0}^{1} \left[\frac{S^2}{2} \right]_{S=0}^{C} dC + \int_{C=0}^{1} \left[\frac{S^2}{2} \right]_{S=0}^{1-C} dC$$

$$= \int_{C=0}^{1} \left[C^2 - C + \frac{1}{2} \right] dC = \left[\frac{C^3}{3} - \frac{C^2}{2} + \frac{C}{2} \right]_{C=0}^{1} = \frac{1}{3}$$

Thus, on the average, the disk head must seek a distance of 1/3 of the total head span.

C. DUAL DISK SEEK TIME

Consider a disk request arriving at two independent disks simultaneously. Each disk immediately executes a seek to the appropriate sector. However, we assume that the current position of the head on one disk is random compared to the head's position on the other disk. This is caused, for instance, by one disk performing a read that the other disk did not perform. In Appendix 5B, it was shown that the average seek for a single disk accessing data randomly was 1/3 of the tracks. In this appendix we consider the average seek time of the two disks together.

Let the disk which has the farthest seek distance be designated disk A and the other disk disk B. The maximum seek distance is normalized to 1. Disk B must seek a distance of B, where $0<B<1$. Disk A must seek a distance of A, where $B<A<1$.

The sector to be transferred is at a distance of X from the origin, where $0<X<1$. There are four cases of interest, which are analyzed below. As before,

$p(y)$ is the probability of y.
$p(x|y)$ is the probability of x given y.
$p(x) = p(x|y)p(y)$.
$E(x) =$ expected (average) value of x.

Case 1: Disks A and B Positioned Prior to X

$$p(\text{case } 1) = X^2$$

$$p(X) = dX$$

$$p(B|X) = \frac{1}{X} dB$$

$$p(B) = \frac{1}{X} dB dX$$

$$p(A|B) = \frac{1}{X-B} dA$$

$$p(A) = \frac{1}{X(X-B)} dA dB dX$$

Case 2: *Disks A and B Positioned After X*

$$p(\text{case } 2) = (1-X)^2$$

$$p(X) = dX$$

$$p(B|X) = \frac{1}{1-X} \, dB$$

$$p(B) = \frac{1}{1-X} \, dBdX$$

$$p(A|B) = \frac{1}{1-X-B} dA$$

$$p(A) = \frac{1}{(1-X)(1-X-B)} dAdBdX$$

Case 3: *Disk A Prior to X, Disk B After X*

$$p(\text{case } 3) = X(1-X)$$

$$p(X) = dX$$

$$p(B|X) = \frac{1}{1-X} \, dB \qquad\qquad \text{for } B < X, \text{ 0 otherwise}$$

$$p(B) = \frac{1}{1-X} \, dBdX \qquad\qquad \text{for } B < X, \text{ 0 otherwise}$$

$$p(A|B) = \frac{1}{X-B} \, dA \qquad\qquad \text{for } B < X, \text{ 0 otherwise}$$

$$p(A) = \frac{1}{(1-X)(X-B)} \, dAdBdX \qquad \text{for } B < X, \text{ 0 otherwise}$$

Case 4: *Disk A After X, Disk B Prior To X*

$$p(\text{case } 4) = X(1-X)$$

$$p(X) = dX$$

$$p(B|X) = \frac{1}{X} \, dB \qquad\qquad \text{for } B < 1-X, \text{ 0 otherwise}$$

$$p(B) = \frac{1}{X} \, dBdX \qquad\qquad \text{for } B < 1-X, \text{ 0 otherwise}$$

$$p(A|B) = \frac{1}{(1-X-B)} \, dA \qquad\qquad \text{for } B < 1-X, \text{ 0 otherwise}$$

$$p(A) = \frac{1}{X(1-X-B)} \, dAdBdX \qquad \text{for } B < 1-X, \, 0 \text{ otherwise}$$

The conditions on B for cases 3 and 4 result from the facts that B must be less than A and that A is limited to X for case 3 and to $1-X$ for case 4.

It is useful to note that

$$\sum_{n=1}^{4} p(\text{case } n) = X^2 + (1-X)^2 + 2X(1-X) = 1$$

The average value of A is the average dual disk access time and is

$$E(A) = \sum_{n=1}^{4} Ap(A \text{ for case } n)p(\text{case } n)$$

where an integration is taken over all possible values of A, B, and X. Note that cases 3 and 4 react differently depending upon whether $X < 1/2$ or $X > 1/2$. In these cases:

$$\text{if } X < 1/2, \text{ then } 0 < B < X$$
$$\text{if } X > 1/2, \text{ then } 0 < B < 1-X$$

The resulting expression for $E(A)$ is then

$$E(A) = \int_{X=0}^{1} \left[\int_{B=0}^{X} \int_{A=B}^{X} \frac{AX^2}{X(X-B)} \, dAdB \right. \qquad \text{(case 1)}$$

$$+ \int_{B=0}^{1-X} \int_{A=B}^{1-X} \frac{A(1-X^2)}{(1-X)(1-X-B)} \, dAdB \left. \right] dX \qquad \text{(case 2)}$$

$$+ \int_{X=0}^{1/2} \left[\int_{B=0}^{X} \int_{A=B}^{X} \frac{AX(1-X)}{(1-X)(X-B)} \, dAdB \right. \qquad \text{(case 3A)}$$

$$+ \int_{B=0}^{X} \int_{A=B}^{1-X} \frac{AX(1-X)}{X(1-X-B)} \, dAdB \left. \right] dX \qquad \text{(case 4A)}$$

$$+ \int_{X=1/2}^{1} \left[\int_{B=0}^{1-X} \int_{A=B}^{X} \frac{AX(1-X)}{(1-X)(X-B)} \, dAdB \right. \qquad \text{(case 3B)}$$

$$+ \int_{B=0}^{1-X} \int_{A=B}^{1-X} \frac{AX(1-X)}{X(1-X-B)} \, dAdB \left. \right] dX \qquad \text{(case 4B)}$$

Cases 1, 3A, and 3B reduce to the form

$$\int_{X} \int_{B} \int_{A=B}^{X} \frac{AX}{X-3} \, dAdBdX$$

$$= \int_{X} \int_{B} \frac{X}{X-B} \left[\frac{A^2}{2} \right]_{A=B}^{X} \, dBdX$$

$$= \frac{1}{2} \int_{X} \int_{B} X(X+B) \, dBdX$$

$$= \frac{1}{2}\int_X \left[X^2B + \frac{XB^2}{2} \right]_B dX$$

For cases 1 and 3A, B ranges from 0 to X:

$$= \frac{1}{2}\int_X \left(X^3 + \frac{X^3}{2} \right) dX = \frac{3}{4}\int_X X^3 dX = \left[\frac{3}{16}X^4 \right]_X$$

For case 1, X ranges from 0 to 1

$$= \frac{3}{16} \qquad \qquad \text{(case 1)}$$

For case 3A, X ranges from 0 to 1/2

$$= \frac{3}{256} \qquad \qquad \text{(case 3A)}$$

For case 3B, B ranges from 0 to $1-X$ and X ranges from 1/2 to 1:

$$\frac{1}{2}\int_{X=1/2}^{1} \left[X^2B + \frac{XB^2}{2} \right]_{B=0}^{1-X} dX = \frac{1}{4}\int_{X=1/2}^{1} (X-X^3)dX$$

$$= \frac{1}{4}\left[\frac{X^2}{2} - \frac{X^4}{4} \right]_{X=1/2}^{1} \qquad \qquad \text{(case 3B)}$$

$$= 9/256$$

Cases 2, 4A, and 4B reduce to the form

$$\int_X \int_B \int_{A=B}^{1-X} \frac{A(1-X)}{(1-X-B)} \, dAdBdX$$

$$= \int_X \int_B \frac{(1-X)}{(1-X-B)}\left[\frac{A^2}{2} \right]_{A=B}^{1-X} dBdX$$

$$= \frac{1}{2}\int_X \int_B (1-X)(1-X+B) \, dBdX$$

$$= \frac{1}{2}\int_X \int_B [(1-X)^2 + (1-X)B] \, dBdX$$

$$= \frac{1}{2}\int_X \left[(1-X)^2B + (1-X)\frac{B^2}{2} \right]_B dX$$

For cases 2 and 4B, B ranges from 0 to $1-X$:

$$= \frac{3}{4}\int_X (1-X)^3 dX = \frac{3}{4}\left[X - \frac{3X^2}{2} + X^3 - \frac{X^4}{4} \right]_X$$

For case 2, X ranges from 0 to 1:

$$= \frac{3}{16} \qquad \qquad \text{(case 2)}$$

For case 4B, X ranges from 1/2 to 1:

$$= 3/256 \qquad \text{(case 4B)}$$

For case 4A, B ranges from 0 to X; and X ranges from 0 to 1/2:

$$\frac{1}{2}\int_{X=0}^{1/2}\left[(1-X)^2B + (1-X)\frac{B^2}{2}\right]_{B=0}^{X} dX$$

$$= \frac{1}{2}\int_{X=0}^{1/2}\left[X(1-X)^2 + (1-X)\frac{X^2}{2}\right] dX$$

$$= \frac{1}{2}\int_{X=0}^{1/2}\left[X - \frac{3}{2}X^2 + \frac{1}{2}X^3\right] dX \qquad \text{(case 4A)}$$

$$= \frac{1}{2}\left[\frac{X^2}{2} - \frac{1}{2}X^3 + \frac{1}{8}X^4\right]_{X=0}^{1/2}$$

$$= 9/256$$

Thus, average disk access time for dual disks is

$$E(A) = \frac{3}{16} + \frac{3}{16} + \frac{3}{256} + \frac{9}{256} + \frac{9}{256} + \frac{3}{256} = \frac{15}{32}$$

$E(A) = .469$ of a unit seek (versus .333 for a single disk—see Appendix 5B).

Thus, on the average, the seek time of dual disks is .469/.333 = 1.4 that of a single disk. For disks with an average access time of 35 msec. and with an average latency time of 8 msec., the average seek time is 27 msec. From Appendix 5A, it is seen that the effective latency time of such a dual disk is increased by 4 msec., whereas from the above it is seen that the effective seek time of a dual disk is increased by about 11 msec. over that of a single disk.

Thus, by the time the last disk has finished its seek, the first most probably has finished its latency (to a first degree of approximation). Therefore, the last disk need only wait a single disk latency time, on the average.

As a result, 40% of the average seek time for a single disk should be added to the average access time for a single disk to obtain the average access time for a mirrored disk.

This discussion has considered the case in which writes to both disks of a mirrored pair are executed simultaneously. In many fault-tolerant systems, these writes are done one at a time to ensure that at least one disk always has a good copy of the file (i.e., a power spike could cause write errors on both disks if both were active simultaneously). In this case, the time to write to both sides of the mirrored pair is simply twice a single write time.

APPENDIX 6

Process Dispatch Time

Process *dispatch time* is defined as the time a process must wait in the scheduling queue, or "ready list," for the processor. The effective service time for a process is the sum of its dispatch time plus its processing time. Thus, a transaction selected for service by a process will experience an effective service time that increases with processor load.

Dispatch time throughout the text of this book has been approximated by using the M/M/1 model for a single processor system and the M/M/c model for a multiprocessor system. This is a reasonable approach if the number of processes making demands on the processor system is much greater than the expected length of the scheduling queue and if no process represents a significant portion of the processor load. If the number of processes is small, but all processes are nearly identical in terms of processing activity, then the M/M/c/m/m model can be used. However, this model can be shown to produce optimistic results (as will be argued later).

In this appendix, it is shown that the use of the infinite population models is conservative in that the processor load of the process being considered is counted twice. More accurate models for dispatch time are derived, but these require iterative calculation. It is concluded that a reasonable approximation giving increased dispatch time accuracy is simply not to include the processor load of the process for which dispatch time is being calculated in the calculation of the scheduling queue length.

A. INFINITE POPULATION APPROXIMATION ERROR

Let us consider a single processor system serving m identical processes, and let us further use the simple M/M/1 model to represent the processor scheduling queue. We assume that there are many more processes than the anticipated length of the scheduling queue, so the assumption of an infinite population feeding the scheduling queue is reasonable.

We consider the case of a very simple process that services a transaction by using T seconds of processor time. When one or more transactions are in a process's queue, that process enters the scheduling queue, waits its dispatch time (its waiting time in the scheduling queue), and then processes the transaction at the head of its queue. It then exits the processor and reenters the scheduling queue if there is another transaction in its queue.

In this case, the processor is busy if at least one transaction exists in any one or more of the process queues. The only effect of the process structure from a performance viewpoint is to reorder the transactions. They will not be served strictly in the order in which they enter the process/processor system but instead in some order determined by what is effectively the round-robin servicing of busy processes. Since servicing order is not important in queues of this sort, a transaction should see a delay (response) time of $T_r = T/(1-L)$, where L is the load on the processor.

Let us derive the process's response time by using the simple view that the scheduling queue and the process queues are all M/M/1 queues. Let

R = average arrival rate of transactions to the system.

m = number of processes.

T = average processor service time.

L = processor load = RT.

t_d = process dispatch time.

T_d = processor delay time = process service time.

T_r = transaction response time.

Then the time which a process must wait in the scheduling queue (its dispatch time) is $LT/(1-L)$. The service time for a process is its dispatch time plus its processing time, or $LT/(1-L)+T = T/(1-L)$.

Since each process is handling a transaction rate of R/m, it is busy $(R/m)T/(1-L)$ of the time (its load). Therefore, its response time to a transaction entering its queue is

$$T_r = \frac{T/(1-L)}{1 - (R/m)\ T/(1-L)} = \frac{T}{1 - (L + L/m)} \tag{A6-1}$$

Since T_r should be $T/(1-L)$ as argued above, it is seen that the approximate response time is in error due to the effective load in the denominator of equation A6-1 being increased by L/m, the load of one process. In effect, the load imposed on the processor by the process under consideration has been counted twice, once in the term L and once by the term L/m.

Let us redo this calculation by not including the load of the process under consideration when calculating dispatch time. Then the effective load on the processor is

$(1-L/m)$, and the process dispatch time, t_d, is

$$t_d = \frac{(L-L/m)T}{1-(L-L/m)} \qquad \text{(A6-2)}$$

The process service time, T_d, is

$$T_d = t_d + T = \frac{T}{1-(L-L/m)} \qquad \text{(A6-3)}$$

The transaction response time is

$$T_r = \frac{T_d}{1 - (R/m)\ T_d} \qquad \text{(A6-4)}$$

Substituting equation A6-3 into A6-4 and simplifying gives

$$T_r = \frac{T}{1-L} \qquad \text{(A6-5)}$$

as expected.

In effect, we have considered the scheduling queue from the viewpoint of a particular process. That process sees the queue occupied by other processes, which are imposing a load $(L-L/m)$ on the processor. The average delay (t_d+T) experienced by the process in passing through the processor is less than that predicted by our simple M/M/1 approximation, as the load on the processor is taken as less than the full load so far as scheduling queue length is concerned (see equation A6-3). The extra delay is made up by the transaction's delay in the process's queue.

The insight from this example is carried through in the next sections to calculate more accurately the process dispatch times when the number of processes may be small and their processing asymmetric. Both single processor and multiprocessor systems are considered.

B. DISPATCHING MODEL

In many cases, a system is comprised of a finite number of single-threaded processes competing for common processing resources (one or more processors). Each process receives transactions from what is effectively an infinite population. This situation is depicted in Figure A6-1.

As shown in this figure, there are m processes, labeled P_1 through P_m, being served by c processors. Each receives transactions from an infinite population of users. The ith process, P_i, receives transactions at a rate of R_i transactions per second.

Whenever a process has one or more transactions in its queue, it enters the scheduling queue to await the availability of a processor for purposes of working on the transaction at the head of its queue. Upon reaching the head of the scheduling queue, the

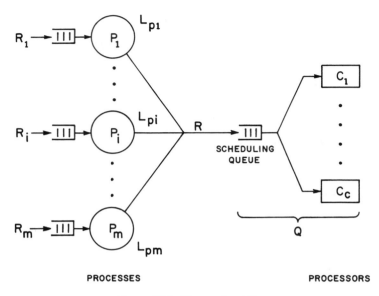

Figure A6-1 Process dispatching.

process will be assigned to the next processor that becomes available. When the process has finished with the processor, it waits for its next transaction and then reenters the scheduling queue for further processing.

The amount of time that a process must wait in the scheduling queue is called its dispatch time. In the text of this book, dispatch time has been calculated by assuming that there are a large number of processes and that the scheduling queue, therefore, has the properties of an M/M/c queue.

A more accurate solution to this problem can be attained by considering the plight of a single process P_i competing with the other processes for processor time. Let us define the average dispatch time for process P_i as t_{di} and the average delay time through the processor system for process P_i as T_{di}. T_{di} is the time that process P_i must wait in the scheduling queue plus its processor service time T_i:

$$T_{di} = t_{di} + T_i \tag{A6-6}$$

where:

T_{di} = average time spent by process P_i in the processor system on each entry.

t_{di} = average process dispatch time for process P_i.

T_i = average service time for process P_i.

The load L_{pi} on process P_i (that portion of time that it is busy awaiting service or is being serviced by the processor) is

$$L_{pi} = R_i T_{di} \tag{A6-7}$$

L_{pi} also can be interpreted as the probability that process i will be in the system. The average number of processes in the processor system (scheduling queue plus processors) when process P_i enters the scheduling queue is the sum of the process loads of all the other processes. This excludes its own load since it cannot already be in the processor system. The average number of items in a system generally has been designated by Q:

$$Q = \sum_{j=1}^{m} L_{pj} \qquad (A6\text{-}8)$$

The number of processes Q_i seen by process P_i when it enters the system is then

$$Q_i = Q - L_{pi} \qquad (A6\text{-}9)$$

where:

Q = average number of processes in the system.

Q_i = average number of processes in the system when process P_i arrives.

L_{pj} = portion of time process P_j is in the system.

R_j = arrival rate of transactions to process P_j.

Let us also define:

T_i' = average processor service time for all processes except process P_i.

$$T_i' = \frac{\sum\limits_{j \neq i} R_j T_j}{\sum\limits_{j \neq i} R_j} \qquad (A6\text{-}10)$$

We also define L_i as the processor load imposed by process P_i and L_i' as the processor load imposed by all processes except for process P_i:

$$L_i' = \sum_{j=1}^{m} L_j - L_i \qquad (A6\text{-}11)$$

The waiting line length is the number of processes in the system, excluding those being served. From equation 4-20, the average waiting line length, W_i, seen by process P_i is

$$W_i = Q_i - L_i' \qquad (A6\text{-}12)$$

From equation 4-21, the average waiting time for a process entering the system before it is assigned to a processor is

$$t_{di} = \frac{W_i}{L_i'} T_i' = \left(\frac{Q_i}{L_i'} - 1 \right) T_i' \qquad (A6\text{-}13)$$

where:

t_{di} = dispatch time for process P_i (i.e., the amount of time it must wait before it gets a processor).

W_i = waiting line length seen by process P_i.

L_i = processor load imposed by process P_i.

L_i' = processor load imposed by all processes except for process P_i.

Note that the dispatch time for each process is different. It is affected by the load (the percent of the time busy) of all other processes but not by its own load. A seldomly used process will be more affected by busy processes than a busy process will be affected by seldomly used processes.

Equation A6-13 represents the general solution for process dispatch time. Note that it must be solved interatively, since the dispatch time for process P_i (equation A6-13) depends on the dispatch times of all other processes P_j (see equations A6-9, A6-8, A6-7, A6-6), which in turn depend upon the dispatch time for process P_j. It will be shown later, however, that equation A6-13 reduces to a closed form if all processes are identical.

The preceding model is a general model for the case of an open system with a finite population of heterogeneous users. As such, it has application to many other cases which must often be modeled. Examples include:

- terminals waiting for a common communications line and
- disk units waiting for a common disk controller.

Before proceeding, we clarify a point made earlier. In the introduction to this appendix, it was stated that the use of the finite population closed system model (the M/M/c/m/m model) provided optimistic results if the system were, in fact, an open system. The reason for this can be understood as follows. In the M/M/c/m/m model, a randomly distributed think time is assumed. Therefore, the probability of a think time of zero seconds is exactly zero.

However, in an open finite system, queues build at the users (see Figure A6-1). If the length of a user queue is nonzero, then the user will immediately reenter the system, giving an effective think time of zero. The probability of a think time of zero seconds is nonzero in an open system.

The result of this is that the arrival of users from a finite population to an open system will tend to occur in batches. During instances of system activity, users will tend to reenter the system immediately. This distorts the probability distribution of queue sizes towards larger queues, thus resulting in larger average queue sizes and larger average delays for an open system than those for a closed system.

As pointed out in chapter 4, a closed finite population system experiences graceful degradation as busy users are removed from the population of users eligible to enter the queue. There is no such effect in an open system.

C. SINGLE PROCESSOR SYSTEM

We now constrain the model to a set of processes with identical service time distributions represented by a common distribution coefficient, k. For the single processor case, the probability that a process is being serviced when process P_i arrives in the system is L_i'. Thus, the dispatch time for process P_i is the time remaining for the process currently being serviced, $kL_i'T_i'$, plus the wait time for the processes awaiting service, W_iT_i':

$$t_{di} = W_iT_i' + kL_i'T_i'$$

Using equation A6-12,

$$t_{di} = Q_iT_i' - (1-k)L_i'T_i' \qquad (A6\text{-}14)$$

where k = Khintchine-Pollaczek distribution coefficient. Process delay time is

$$T_{di} = t_{di} + T_i \qquad (A6\text{-}15)$$

A very important case is the simplest case of homogeneous processes with random service times using a single CPU. Each process entering the scheduling queue requires an average of T seconds of processing time. If there are m processes, and if the total system transaction rate is R transactions per second, then

$$k = 1$$
$$R_i = R/m$$
$$T_i = T_i' = T$$
$$L_i = L/m$$

We also define for convenience

$$T_{di} = T_d$$
$$Q_i = Q'$$
$$W_i = W'$$
$$L_i = L'$$
$$t_{di} = t_d$$
$$L_{pi} = L_p$$

The prime (') is used to denote the system as seen by an arriving process. From equations (A6-8) and (A6-9),

$$Q' = (m-1)\frac{R}{m}T_d \qquad (A6\text{-}16)$$

where we have used (A6-7):

$$L_p = \frac{R}{m}T_d \qquad (A6\text{-}17)$$

Noting that

$$L = RT \qquad (A6\text{-}18)$$

and

$$L' = L - \frac{L}{m} = \frac{m-1}{m} L \tag{A6-19}$$

where L is the total processor load on the system, the dispatch time is, from equations (A6-14) and (A6-16),

$$t_d = Q'T = L'T_d \tag{A6-20}$$

From equations (A6-15),

$$t_d = L'(t_d + T)$$

or

$$t_d = \frac{L'}{1-L'} T \tag{A6-21}$$

Note that equation (A6-21) is identical to equation (A6-2). The argument following equation (A6-2) holds here as well, i.e., the transaction response time will be $T/(1-L)$.

From equations (A6-15), (A6-20), (A6-8), and (A6-13), other relationships include

$$T_d = t_d + T = \frac{1}{1-L'} T \tag{A6-22}$$

$$Q' = t_d/T = \frac{L'}{1-L'} \tag{A6-23}$$

$$Q = RT_d = \frac{L}{1-L'} \tag{A6-24}$$

$$W' = \frac{L't_d}{T} = \frac{L'^2}{1-L'} \tag{A6-25}$$

Also, the probability that a specific process will be found in the system, L_p, is [from equations (A6-17) and (A6-22)]

$$L_p = \frac{L/m}{1-L'} \tag{A6-26}$$

The maximum queue length that can be seen by an arriving process occurs when $L=1$. From equations (A6-23) and (A6-19), the queue length for $L=1$ is $m-1$, as would be expected.

Note that this system of equations for an open system with a finite, homogeneous population of users is equivalent to the M/M/1 model for an infinite population, except that the processor load is taken as that load exclusive of the process being considered.

The distribution of queue lengths seen by an arriving process is discussed in the next section for the case of multiple servers. These reduce to the single server case by letting the number of servers, c, be one.

D. MULTIPROCESSOR SYSTEM

The parameter Q_i given by equation (A6-9) represents the total number of transactions in the processor system (the scheduling queue plus the one or more processors) when process P_i arrives. If there is more than one processor, it is the length W_i of the scheduling queue that is important. Given c processors, a process will experience no process dispatch delay if there are less than c processes in the processor system.

If there are c or more processes, the newly arrived process will have to wait for a processor. The number of processes already in the processor system exceeding c is called W_i. W_i is the average length of the waiting line for processors seen by process P_i, exclusive of those processes currently being serviced.

When process P_i arrives at the processor system, it will find n processes already in the system with probability $p_i(n)$. W_i is the sum of these probabilities for $n>c$, weighted by the length of the waiting line $(n-c)$:

$$W_i = \sum_{n=c+1}^{m-1} (n-c)p_i(n) \tag{A6-27}$$

Note that the maximum length of the waiting line seen by process P_i is $(m-1)-c$. The dispatch time for process P_i is, from equation (A6-13),

$$t_{di} = \frac{W_i}{L_i'} T_i' = \left(\frac{Q_i}{L_i'} - 1 \right) T_i' \tag{A6-28}$$

Process delay time T_{di} is given by equation (A6-6) as $t_{di} + T_i$.

We proceed by determining the probabilities $p(n)$ that there are n processes in the system. From this distribution, we calculate Q and then Q_i, which leads to the dispatch time t_{di}.

We first introduce the following notation:

$$y(n) = C_n^m\{x_j(1-x_k)\}, \; j \neq k \tag{A6-29}$$

This notation is used in the following expressions to imply the sum of the products of all combinations of m diverse items x_j taken n at a time, with the remaining x_k items formed as $(1-x_k)$. If the x_i are homogeneous with all $x_i = x$, then this expression becomes

$$y(n) = \frac{m!}{(m-n)!(n)!} x^n(1-x)^{m-n} \tag{A6-30}$$

In the following analysis, we assume that service times are random. For $n<c$, all n processes in the system will be assigned to a processor. Let

$$L = \sum_j R_j T_j \tag{A6-31}$$

be the total load on the processors imposed by all processes. Then the average load imposed on each processor is L/c. For n processes in the system and $n<c$, n processors will be busy with probability $(L/c)^n$, and $n-c$ processors will be idle with probability $(1-L/c)^{n-c}$. Since there are C_n^c possible combinations of n out of c processors being busy,

then

$$p(n) = C_n^c \left(\frac{L}{c}\right)^n \left(1 - \frac{L}{c}\right)^{c-n}, \, n<c \qquad (A6\text{-}32)$$

where

$p(n)$ = probability that n processes are in the system, and

$$C_n^c = \frac{c!}{(n-c)!n!} \qquad (A6\text{-}33)$$

The probability that all c processors will be busy is

$$\sum_{n=c}^{m} p(n) = p_c = \left(\frac{L}{c}\right)^c \qquad (A6\text{-}34)$$

where

p_c = probability that all processors are busy.

There are C_c^m combinations of c processes in the processors when all processors are busy. The probability of any particular set of processes being processed is, on the average, p_c/C_c^m.

When $n \geq c$, an arriving process j will have to enter the processor queue and wait for a time t_{dj}. The probability that process j is in the system is L_{pj}, where

$$L_{pj} = R_j(T_j + t_{dj}) \qquad (A6\text{-}35)$$

Thus, for $n \geq c$, the number of processes in the system will include c processes being serviced, $n-c$ processes waiting for service, and $m-n$ processes idle. The number of different combinations of $n-c$ processes waiting in line, taken from the total population of $m-c$ processes which are not being serviced, is C_{n-c}^{m-c}. Since the probability that process j is in the system is L_{pj}, then the probability that $n-c$ processes will be waiting is

$$C_c^m\{C_{n-c}^{m-c}\{L_{pj}(1-L_{pk})\}\}$$

From equation (A6-34), then,

$$p(n) = \frac{p_c}{C_c^m} C_c^m\{C_{n-c}^{m-c}\{L_{pj}(1-L_{pk})\}\}, n \geq c \qquad (A6\text{-}36)$$

This distribution of queue lengths can be averaged to determine the average number of items, Q, in the system:

$$Q = \sum_{n=1}^{m} np(n)$$

Noting that

$$Q_i = Q - L_{pi} = Q - R_i(t_{di} + T_i),$$

equation (A6-28) can be used to solve for the dispatch time for each process. L_{pi} depends on the probabilities L_{pj} that each of the other processes is in the system. Likewise, the L_{pj} depends on L_{pi}. Therefore, these equations must be solved iteratively.

However, $p(n)$ can be evaluated specifically for the homogeneous case. We first note that

$$\sum_{n=0}^{m} C_n^m x^n (1-x)^{m-n} = 1 \qquad (A6\text{-}37)$$

by exhaustive enumeration as follows. Since

$$(1-x)^a = \sum_{k=0}^{a} \frac{a!}{(a-k)!k!}(-1)^k x^k \qquad (A6\text{-}38)$$

then

$$C_n^m x^n (1-x)^{m-n} = \sum_{k=0}^{m-n} \frac{m!}{(m-n)!n!} \frac{(m-n)!}{(m-n-k)!k!}(-1)^k x^{n+k}$$

$$= \sum_{k=0}^{m-n} \frac{m!}{(m-n-k)!n!k!}(-1)^k x^{n+k}$$

enumerating for a few n, we have:

$$n = 0 \quad \frac{m!}{m!} - \frac{m!}{(m-1)!}x + \frac{1}{2}\frac{m!}{(m-2)!}x^2 - \frac{1}{6}\frac{m!}{(m-3)!}x^3 + \dots$$

$$n = 1 \quad \frac{m!}{(m-1)!}x - \frac{m!}{(m-2)!}x^2 + \frac{1}{2}\frac{m!}{(m-3)!}x^3 - \dots$$

$$n = 2 \quad \frac{1}{2}\frac{m!}{(m-2)}x^2 - \frac{1}{2}\frac{m!}{(m-2)!}x^3 + \dots$$

$$n = 3 \quad \frac{1}{6}\frac{m!}{(m-3)!}x^3 - \dots$$

All terms but the first cancel, satisfying equation (A6-27).
Also,

$$\sum_{n=0}^{m} n C_n^m x^n (1-x)^{m-n} = mx \qquad (A6\text{-}39)$$

as can be seen by a similar exercise (simply multiply each row in the above enumeration by n).

Returning to the homogeneous solution, equation (A6-36) becomes

$$p(n) = p_c C_{n-c}^{m-c} L_p^{n-c} (1-L_p)^{m-n}, \ n \geq c \qquad (A6\text{-}40)$$

where we have used $L_p = L_{pj}$ for the probability that a process will be in the system (as defined earlier).

From equations (A6-32), (A6-34), and (A6-37), we see that

$$\sum_{n=0}^{m} p(n) = \sum_{n=0}^{c-1} p(n) + \sum_{n=c}^{m} p(n) = \sum_{n=0}^{c-1} p(n) + p_c$$

$$= \sum_{n=0}^{c} C_n^c \left(\frac{L}{c}\right)^n \left(1 - \frac{L}{c}\right)^{c-n} = 1$$

as must be the case.

Also, from equations (A6-32) and (A6-39), the average number of processors that are busy is

$$\sum_{n=0}^{c-1} np(n) + cp_c = \sum_{n=0}^{c} n C_n^c \left(\frac{L}{c}\right)^n \left(1 - \frac{L}{c}\right)^{c-n} = L$$

as would be expected.

According to equation (A6-34), the sum of the $p(n)$ given by equation (A6-40) over the range c to m should yield p_c. That this is true is demonstrated as follows:

$$\sum_{n=c}^{m} p(n) = p_c \sum_{n=c}^{m} C_{n-c}^{m-c} L_p^{n-c} (1-L_p)^{m-n}$$

Letting $q = n - c$, this is rewritten as

$$\sum_{n=c}^{m} p(n) = p_c \sum_{q=0}^{m-c} C_q^{m-c} L_p^q (1-L_p)^{m-c-q}$$

From equation (A6-37), this becomes

$$\sum_{n=c}^{m} p(n) = p_c$$

The average waiting line length W is

$$W = \sum_{n=c}^{m} (n-c)p(n)$$

$$W = p_c \sum_{n=c}^{m} (n-c)C_{n-c}^{m-c} L_p^{n-c} (1-L_p)^{m-n} \tag{A6-41}$$

Substituting $q = n - c$ in a manner similar to the argument given above, and using equations (A6-34) and (A6-39), we have

$$W = \left(\frac{L}{c}\right)^c (m-c)L_p \tag{A6-42}$$

The average number of processes in the system is the number of processes waiting for service, W, plus the number of processes currently being serviced. On the average, the processors will be busy L of the time, which is the average number of processes being serviced. Thus [see also equation (4-20)],

$$Q = W+L = \left(\frac{L}{c}\right)^c (m-c)L_p+L \qquad (A6\text{-}43)$$

From equation (A6-9), the queue length that an arriving process i sees is

$$Q' = Q-L_p \qquad (A6\text{-}44)$$

and its dispatch time t_d, is, from equation (A6-13),

$$t_d = \left(\frac{Q'}{L'}-1\right)T.$$

For the homogeneous case,

$$Q = mL_p$$

$$Q' = (m-1)L_p = \frac{m-1}{m}Q$$

Thus,

$$Q' = \frac{m-1}{m}\left[\left(\frac{L}{c}\right)^c (m-c)L_p+L\right] \qquad (A6\text{-}45)$$

For the single processor case ($c=1$),

$$Q' = \frac{m-1}{m}L[(m-1)L_p + 1] \qquad (A6\text{-}46)$$

The probability that a process will be in the system in the single server homogeneous case is, from equation (A6-26),

$$L_p = \frac{L/m}{1-L'}$$

Remembering that $L' = \frac{m-1}{m}L$, equation (A6-46) then reduces to

$$Q' = \frac{L'}{1-L'}$$

which agrees with equation (A6-23) for the single processor case.

E. AN APPROXIMATE SOLUTION

The exact solutions to the dispatch time for process P_i have been derived by calculating the number of transactions Q_i and/or the length of the scheduling queue W_i, exclusive of the load imposed on the processor by the ith process P_i. This gives rise to a simple approximate technique, which is to use the M/M/1 or M/M/c queuing model as appropriate but to base the calculation of processor load (and therefore Q or W length) on all processes except that one for which dispatch time is being considered.

Different dispatch times will be calculated for different processes. This approximation approaches the simpler technique of calculating a common dispatch time based on total processor load if each process represents only a small portion of the total processor load.

This dispatch time approximation has been shown to be exact for the important case of a single server with random service time and with a finite, homogeneous population.

The analysis presented above represents an intuitive approach to the general problem of a finite-population open system. A more rigorous approach would view this problem in terms of a Markovian system as described by Kobayshi (see Appendix 10, Bibliography).

APPENDIX 7

Priority Queues

The following analysis of priority queues is based on Kleinrock [15], chapter 3, and Saaty [24], chapter 11. Let items queued for a server be ranked by priority, with priorities being numbered from 1 to p_{max}. Items with higher priority numbers are chosen for service before items with lower priority numbers.

Without regard for any priority queuing discipline whatsoever, we observe that an item entering the queue at priority p suffers three types of delay before being chosen for service:

1. The item must wait for the item currently being serviced, if any, to complete its service. We denote this time as T_o.

2. The item must wait for the servicing of all items that are in the queue prior to its arrival and that will be served prior to it. There are N_{ip} such items from priority i.

3. The item must wait for the servicing of all items that arrive subsequent to its arrival and that will be served prior to it. There are M_{ip} such items from priority i.

Let T_i be the average service time for an item at priority i. The average time that an item at priority p will have to wait in the queue before being chosen for service, T_{qp}, is

$$T_{qp} = T_o + \sum_{i=1}^{p_{max}} N_{ip}T_i + \sum_{i=1}^{p_{max}} M_{ip}T_i \qquad \text{(A7-1)}$$

We are interested in the case in which items with higher priorities are chosen for service before items with lower priorities and in which items within a priority class are served on a first-come, first-served basis. Then

$$N_{ip} = 0, \qquad i < p \tag{A7-2}$$

$$N_{ip} = R_i T_{qi} \qquad i \geq p \tag{A7-3}$$

$$M_{ip} = 0, \qquad i \leq p \tag{A7-4}$$

$$M_{ip} = R_i T_{qp} \qquad i > p \tag{A7-5}$$

That is, items already in the queue at priorities less than p will not be serviced so long as an item of priority p is in the queue. Items of priority p or greater already in the queue will be serviced before the newly arrived item. If T_{qi} is the average time an item of priority i remains in the queue, and if R_i is the arrival rate of priority i items, then there will be an average of $R_i T_{qi}$ items of priority i in the queue at any given time.

Similarly, items that arrive after our item has entered the queue and that are of the same priority or less will not be serviced until after our item has been serviced. However, during the time, T_{qp}, that our item waits in the queue, $R_i T_{qp}$ items will arrive for each priority i. Those of higher priority will be serviced first.

Using equations A7-2 through A7-5, equation A7-1 can be rewritten as

$$T_{qp} = T_o + \sum_{i=p}^{p_{max}} R_i T_{qi} T_i + \sum_{i=p+1}^{p_{max}} R_i T_{qp} T_i \tag{A7-6}$$

Noting that the load imposed by priority i items on the server is $L_i = R_i T_i$, we have

$$T_{qp} = T_o + \sum_{i=p}^{p_{max}} L_i T_{qi} + \sum_{i=p+1}^{p_{max}} L_i T_{qp} \tag{A7-7}$$

We wish to prove that the solution to this equation is

$$T_{qp} = \frac{T_o}{(1 - L)(1 - L_h)} \tag{A7-8}$$

where

$$L = \sum_{i=p}^{p_{max}} R_i T_i \tag{A7-9}$$

$$L_h = \sum_{i=p+1}^{p_{max}} R_i T_i \tag{A7-10}$$

We do so by induction. Given equation A7-8 for the queue delay at priority p, let us evaluate the queue delay for the next lower priority, T_{qp-1}. From equation A7-7,

$$T_{qp-1} = T_o + \sum_{i=p-1}^{p_{max}} L_i T_{qi} + \sum_{i=p}^{p_{max}} L_i T_{qp-1} \tag{A7-11}$$

This can be rewritten as

$$T_{qp-1} = T_o + \sum_{i=p}^{p_{max}} L_i T_{qi} + L_{p-1} T_{qp-1}$$

$$+ \sum_{i=p+1}^{p_{max}} L_i T_{qp} - \sum_{i=p+1}^{p_{max}} L_i T_{qp} + \sum_{i=p}^{p_{max}} L_i T_{qp-1} \qquad \text{(A7-12)}$$

But the first, second, and fourth terms are T_{qp}, from equation A7-7. Thus, using equations A7-9 and A7-10,

$$T_{qp-1} = T_{qp} + L_{p-1} T_{qp-1} - T_{qp} L_h + T_{qp-1} L \qquad \text{(A7-13)}$$

or

$$T_{qp-1} = \frac{T_{qp}(1 - L_h)}{1 - (L + L_{p-1})} \qquad \text{(A7-13)}$$

Using equation A7-8,

$$T_{qp-1} = \frac{T_o}{[1 - (L + L_{p-1})](1 - L)} \qquad \text{(A7-14)}$$

This is what we would expect from equation A7-8.

Finally, in the limiting case for the highest priority, equation A7-7 yields

$$T_{qp_{max}} = T_o + L_{p_{max}} T_{qp_{max}} \qquad \text{(A7-15)}$$

or

$$T_{qp_{max}} = \frac{T_o}{1 - L_{p_{max}}} \qquad \text{(A7-16)}$$

This is exactly what equation A7-8 yields. Thus, equation A7-8 is proved for all p.

APPENDIX 10

References and Bibliography

REFERENCES

1. Anon., et al. 1985. A measure of transaction processing power, *Datamation* 31:112-118.

2. American National Standards Institute (ANSI). 1971. *Procedures for the use of the communication control characters of American national standard code for information interchange in specified data communication links.* New York.

3. Borg, A., J. Baumbach, and S. Glaser. 1983. A message system supporting fault tolerance. *Ninth Symposium on Operating System Principles,* Association for Computing Machinery.

4. Chou, W., et al. 1983. *Computer communications,* Vol. 1. Englewood Cliffs, N.J.: Prentice-Hall.

5. Date, C. J. 1982. *An introduction to database systems.* Vol. 1. Reading, Mass.: Addison-Wesley.

6. Gallagher, R. 1968. *Information theory and reliable communications.* New York: John Wiley and Sons.

7. Gorney, Leonard. *Queuing theory: A problem solving approach.* New York: Petrocelli.

8. Hamming, R. W. 1980. *Coding and information theory.* Englewood Cliffs, N. J.: Prentice-Hall.

9. Hammond, J. L., and P. J. P. O'Reilly. 1986. *Performance analysis of local computer networks.* Reading, Massachusetts: Addison-Wesley.

10. Highleyman, W. H. 1982. Survivable systems. *Computerworld.* Four part series. 14(5):19-22; 14(6):1-12; 14(7):9-18; 14(8):1-10.

11. International Business Machines (IBM). 1971. *Analysis of some queuing models in real-time systems.* Document number F20-0007-1. White Plains, N.Y.: IBM.

12. International Standard Organization (ISO). 1982. *International processing systems* — Open systems interconnection — Basic reference model. Geneva, Switzerland: ISO.

13. Kendall, D. G. 1951. Some problems in the theory of queues. *Journal of the Royal Statistical Society,* Series B13, pp. 151-185.

14. Kleinrock, L. 1975. *Queuing systems*. Vol.1, *Theory*. New York: John Wiley and Sons.

15. ———. 1976. *Queuing systems*. Vol. 2, *Computer applications*. New York: John Wiley and Sons.

16. Lazowska, Edward D., et al. 1984. *Quantitative system performance*. Englewood Cliffs, N.J.: Prentice-Hall.

17. Liebowitz, B. H., and J. H. Carson. 1985. *Multiple processor systems for real-time applications*. Englewood Cliffs, N. J.: Prentice-Hall.

18. Little, J.D.C. 1961. A proof of the queuing formula $L = \lambda W$. *Operations Research* 9:383-387.

19. Martin, J. 1967. *Design of real time systems*. Englewood Cliffs, N. J.: Prentice-Hall.

20. ———. 1972. *Systems analysis for data transmission*. Englewood Cliffs, N. J.: Prentice-Hall.

21. Meijer, A., and P. Peeters. 1982. *Computer network architectures*. Rockville, Md.: Computer Science Press.

22. Nyquist, H. 1928. *Certain topics in telegraph transmission theory*. AIEE Transactions. 47(April).

23. Peck, L. G., and R. N. Hazelwood. 1958. *Finite queuing tables*. New York: John Wiley & Sons.

24. Saaty, T. L. 1961. *Elements of queuing theory*. New York: McGraw-Hill.

25. Stallings, W. 1985. *Data and computer communication*. New York: Macmillan.

BIBLIOGRAPHY

Mathematical Foundations

ALLEN, A. O. 1978. Probability, statistics and queuing theory with computer science applications. Academic Press, New York.

FELLER, W. 1950. An introduction to probability theory and its applications. John Wiley, New York.

KNUTH, D. E. 1968. The art of computer programming. Vol. 1: Fundamental algorithms. Addison-Wesley, Reading, MA.

KNUTH, D. E. 1969. The art of computer programming. Vol. 2: Semi-numerical algorithms. Addison-Wesley, Reading, MA.

KNUTH, D. E. 1973. The art of computer programming. Vol. 3: Sorting and searching. Addison-Wesley, Reading, MA.

TRIVEDI, K. S. 1982. Probability and statistics with reliability, queuing, and computer science applications. Prentice-Hall, Englewood Cliffs, NJ.

Analytic Modeling

BEIZER, B. 1978. Micro-analysis of computer system performance. Van Nostrand Reinhold, New York.

DENNING, P. J., and J. P. BUZEN. 1978. The operational analysis of queuing network models. Computing Surveys 10(3): 225-261.

FERRARI, D. 1978. Computer systems evaluation performance. Prentice-Hall, Englewood Cliffs, NJ.

FREIBERGER, W. 1972. Statistical computer performance evaluation. Academic Press, New York.

GELENBE, E., and I. MITRANI. 1980. Analysis and synthesis of computer systems. Academic Press, New York.

HELLERMAN, H., and T. F. CONROY. 1975. Computer system performance. McGraw-Hill, New York.

KOBAYASHI, H. 1978. Modeling and analysis. Addison-Wesley, Reading, MA.

LAVENBERG, S. S., ed. 1983. Computer performance modeling handbook. Academic Press, New York.

MacNAIR, E. A., and C. H. SAUER. 1985. Elements of practical performance modeling. Prentice-Hall, Englewood Cliffs, NJ.

SAUER, C. H., and K. M. CHANDY. 1981. Computer systems performance modeling. Prentice-Hall, Englewood Cliffs, NJ.

Modeling Tools

BEILNER, H., and J. MATER. 1984. COPE: Past, present and future. Proceedings of the International Conference on Modelling Techniques and Tools for Performance Analysis, Paris.

BHARATH-KUMAR, K., and P. KERMANI. 1984. Performance evaluation tool (PET): An analysis tool for computer communication networks. IEEE Journal on Selected Areas in Communications SAC-2. 1 (January):220-225.

BOOYENS, M., et al. 1984. SNAP: An analytic multiclass queuing network analyzer. Proceedings of the International Conference on Modelling Techniques and Tools for Performance Analysis, Paris.

INFORMATION RESEARCH ASSOCIATES. 1983. PAWS/A User Guide, Austin, TX.

MERLE, D., D. POTIER, and M. VERAN. 1978. A tool for computer system performance analysis *in* Performance of Computer Installations. Ferrari, North Holland, Amsterdam.

QUANTITATIVE SYSTEM PERFORMANCE, INC. 1982. MAP reference guide. Seattle, WA.

QUANTITATIVE SYSTEM PERFORMANCE, INC. 1982. MAP user guide. Seattle, WA.

REISER, M., and C. H. SAUER. 1978. Queuing network models: Methods of solution and their program implementation. Pp. 115-167 in Current trends in programming methodology, Vol. III: Software modeling and its impact on performance. K. M. CHANDY, and R. T. YEH (eds.) Prentice-Hall, Englewood Cliffs, NJ.

SAUER, C. H., M. REISER, and E. A. MacNAIR. 1977. RESQ — A package for solution of generalized queuing networks. Proceedings 1977 National Computer Conference. Dallas, TX. Pp. 977-986.

SAUER, C. H., E. A. MacNAIR, and J. F. KUROSE. 1982. The research queuing package version 2: Introduction and examples. IBM Research Report RA-138. Yorktown Heights, NY.

VERAN, M., and D. POTIER. 1984. A portable environment queuing systems modelling. Proceedings of the International Conference on Modelling Techniques and Tools for Performance Analysis. Paris.

WHITT, W. 1983. The queuing network analyzer. The Bell Technical Journal 62 (9):2779-2815.

Index